THE NEW BOOK OF KNOWLEDGE ANNUAL

1981

HIGHLIGHTING EVENTS OF 1980

THE NEW BOOK OF KNOWLEDGE ANNUAL

THE YOUNG PEOPLE'S BOOK OF THE YEAR

GROLIER
INCORPORATED
DANBURY, CONN.

ISBN 0-7172-0612-2
ISSN 0196-0148
The Library of Congress Catalog Card Number: 79-26807

EXECUTIVE EDITOR   FERN L. MAMBERG

ART DIRECTOR   MICHÈLE A. McLEAN

ASSISTANT EDITOR   PAMELA CARLEY PETERSEN

STAFF

EDITORS   ELAINE P. SEDITO
DANIEL DOMOFF
CLAUDIA TINNIN
LEO SCHNEIDER
PATRICIA ELLSWORTH WILSON
WAYNE JONES

INDEXERS   JILL SCHULER
SUSAN DEROMEDI

PRODUCTION EDITOR   MARILYN BULLOCK

PICTURE RESEARCHERS   DIANE T. GRACE
BARBARA LATZ COHEN

PROOFREADER   ALEXIS KASDEN

STAFF ASSISTANT   SHIRLEY HOLLISTER

· · · · ·

MANUFACTURING DEPARTMENT

DIRECTOR   HARRIET RIPINSKY

GENERAL MANAGER   WESLEY J. WARREN

PRODUCTION   JOSEPH J. CORLETT, Manager
ALAN PHELPS

· · · · ·

YOUNG PEOPLE'S PUBLICATIONS DEPARTMENT

EDITOR IN CHIEF   WILLIAM E. SHAPIRO

· · · · ·

GROLIER INCORPORATED

SENIOR VICE-PRESIDENT, PUBLISHING   HOWARD B. GRAHAM

VICE-PRESIDENT AND EDITORIAL DIRECTOR   BERNARD S. CAYNE

5

CONTENTS

CONTRIBUTORS

BELL, James O.
Assistant National Editor, The *Los Angeles Times*
RONALD WILSON REAGAN

BLANCHARD, Wendie R.
Managing Editor, *Creative Crafts* magazine
POPULAR CRAFTS

BLOCK, J. R.
Executive Director of Research and Resource Development, Hofstra University
SUIT YOURSELF

CAPEN, Peter D.
Author and Photographer, Terra Mar Productions; Fellow, the Explorers Club
THE UNDERWATER WORLD OF A CORAL REEF

CRONKITE, Walter
CBS News Correspondent
THE YEAR IN REVIEW

FREEDMAN, Russell
Author, *Animal Architects; How Animals Learn; The Brains of Animals and Man; How Birds Fly*
ANIMAL HOME-BUILDERS

FRENCH, Bevan M.
Discipline Scientist, Planetary Materials, National Aeronautics and Space Administration; author, *The Moon Book; Mars: The Viking Discoveries; What's New on the Moon?*
ENCOUNTER WITH SATURN
SPACE BRIEFS

GENNARO, Joseph F., Jr.
GRILLONE, Lisa
Authors, *Small Worlds Close Up*
SEEING THINGS IN A NEW WAY

GOLDBERG, Hy
Co-ordinator of sports information, NBC Sports
SPORTS, 1980
THE 1980 OLYMPIC GAMES

HAHN, Charless
Stamp Editor, *Chicago Sun-Times*
STAMP COLLECTING

JOHNSON, Lorna
Education Services, National Gallery of Canada
NATIONAL GALLERY OF CANADA

KULL, David J.
Senior Associate Editor, *Medical Laboratory Observer* magazine
HEARING-EAR DOGS

KURTZ, Henry I.
Author, *Captain John Smith; John and Sebastian Cabot*
BOSTON—THE CRADLE OF LIBERTY
THE OLD RHINEBECK AERODROME
A SPY FOR THE UNION

LAND-WEBER, Ellen
Author, *The Passionate Collector*
START A COLLECTION

THE WORLD IN 1980

On November 4, 1980, Ronald Wilson Reagan was elected the 40th president of the United States.

THE YEAR IN REVIEW

by WALTER CRONKITE

A mood of reassessment colored many of the events of 1980. In the United States, it was reflected in the election of a new president. And in countries around the world, people seemed to question past policies and to consider new directions for the decade that was beginning.

Strain between Western nations and the Soviet Union appeared to threaten détente, the policy of easing tensions that had been followed in the 1970's. The year began with sharp criticism of the Soviets, who in the closing days of 1979 had sent thousands of troops into Afghanistan. The troops stayed, supporting a new government and attempting to crush a Muslim rebellion. By the end of 1980, it appeared that the Soviets had settled in for a long fight.

The Soviet action was condemned by the United Nations and by individual countries as well. The United States called for a ban on grain sales to the Soviets and led a boycott of the Summer Olympic Games, which were held in Moscow. The U.S. Senate put off consideration of a new U.S.–Soviet arms treaty. And because the Soviets' action seemed to show that they were ready to use force to accomplish their aims, it prompted debate about the strength and readiness of U.S. armed forces. In July, the United States began registering 19- and 20-year-old men for a possible military draft.

The threat of Soviet intervention was faced later in the year by one of the Soviet Union's European allies, Poland. In August, massive strikes crippled Poland's already weak economy and shook its Communist system to the roots. For the first time, workers in a Communist country won the right to form independent unions and to strike. Poland's top leaders were replaced. But disagreements continued between the new unions and the government. In December the Soviet Union, apparently concerned that unrest might spread to its own workers or to workers in other Communist countries, massed troops along its border with Poland. The United States and its European allies agreed on economic and political moves to be taken if the Soviet troops should cross the border.

The presence of Soviet troops in Afghanistan raised questions about the balance of power in the Middle East, a region that is vital because it supplies much of the world's oil. During 1980, the Middle East continued to be troubled by conflicts. Israel and Egypt, who had ended 30 years of war with a peace treaty signed in 1979, exchanged ambassadors and opened their common border for trade and travel. But other Arab countries remained opposed to the treaty. And Egyptian-Israeli talks on the question of a homeland for the Arabs of Palestine—a key issue between Israel and the Arab countries—seemed stalled. In the Persian Gulf region, war broke out between Iraq and Iran. Within Iran, deep divisions among various groups helped delay the release of 52 American hostages. Iran set terms for the hostages' release in November, after economic and diplomatic pressures and an unsuccessful U.S. military raid had failed to free them.

Events in the Middle East were a factor in the price of oil, which continued to rise in 1980. High energy costs in turn contributed to the inflation and other economic woes that plagued many countries, the United States among them. And economic problems and relations with other countries both were important issues in the U.S. election.

On these and many other issues, the presidential candidates appeared to offer voters a clear choice. President Jimmy Carter stressed his support of the traditional goals of the Democratic Party. Ronald Reagan, ex-governor of California, had long been known as a spokesman for conservatives in the Republican Party. An unusual element was added to the race by the presence of a strong independent candidate, Representative John Anderson of Illinois.

The outcome was a resounding victory for Reagan. Republicans won not only the presidency but also, for the first time since the 1950's, a majority in the Senate. Whether the Republican victory stemmed from dissatisfaction with Carter's administration, a growth of conservative feeling, or both, some changes in U.S. policy seemed assured.

The year brought important elections in other countries as well. In Canada, where a Progressive Conservative government had been elected in 1979, voters returned the Liberals, headed by Pierre Elliott Trudeau, to power. In Africa, elections and official independence ended a long and bitter civil war in Zimbabwe, the former British colony of Southern Rhodesia. Voters in India brought back Indira Gandhi, who had been defeated in 1977.

Several important leaders died during the year—among them Mohammed Reza Pahlavi, the deposed Shah of Iran; Yugoslavia's Marshal Tito; and Aleksei N. Kosygin, ex-premier of the Soviet Union. And the world was saddened by the loss of some well-known entertainers—comedian Jimmy Durante; film director Alfred Hitchcock; film stars Peter Sellers, Steve McQueen, and Mae West; and singer John Lennon.

In 1980, too, people were sharply reminded of the power of nature. Mount St. Helens, a long-dormant volcano in the state of Washington, erupted in May, killing a number of people and causing serious damage. Severe drought afflicted many parts of the world. And earthquakes in Algeria and Italy took thousands of lives.

But 1980 also brought a measure of hope for the future. Breakthroughs in science and technology—in fields as far apart as genetics and electric cars—seemed to hold promise. And the reassessment that was reflected in many of the events of 1980 was itself a hopeful sign—it seemed to indicate that people were seeking new solutions to the tensions and problems that continued to trouble the world.

4 Mohammed Mahmoud Ould Luly, president of Mauritania since June, 1979, was overthrown in a coup. Premier Mohammed Khouna Ould Haidalla became the new president.

10 George Meany, a pioneer leader of the U.S. labor-union movement, died at the age of 85. Meany was the first president of the American Federation of Labor–Congress of Industrial Organizations (AFL-CIO). He held this position for 25 years, until 1979.

14 Indira Gandhi was elected prime minister of India. Gandhi had previously held this position from 1966 to 1977. Her return to leadership followed her party's overwhelming victory in parliamentary elections held earlier in the month.

Indira Gandhi again became prime minister of India, after January elections.

Americans living near the Canadian border expressed their
thanks to Canada for helping six Americans escape from Iran.

14 The U.N. General Assembly voted 104–18 to "strongly deplore"
the Soviet Union's intervention in Afghanistan. Thousands of
Soviet troops had entered Afghanistan in December, 1979, causing concern in many countries around the world. (On January 29,
the Soviet invasion was also condemned by 36 Muslim nations,
during a three-day meeting of their international Islamic organization. These nations suspended Afghanistan's membership in
the organization, and urged members to boycott the Summer
Olympics in Moscow if the Soviet troops were not withdrawn.)

19 William O. Douglas died at the age of 81. Douglas had been a
U.S. Supreme Court justice for 36 years, from 1939 to 1975,
longer than any other justice. He was a strong defender of individual liberties.

25 Abolhassan Bani-Sadr was elected president of Iran. The former
finance minister became the first president of the country since
Iran declared itself an "Islamic republic" in April, 1979.

28 Six employees of the U.S. embassy in Teheran escaped from Iran
with the help of Canadian diplomats. The six had eluded the
Iranian militants who seized the embassy on November 4, 1979.
They eventually made their way to the Canadian embassy. The
Canadians hid the Americans for almost three months, then got
them out of Iran with forged Canadian passports. Meanwhile, 53
Americans continued to be held hostage in the U.S. embassy.

29 Jimmy Durante died at the age of 86. Nicknamed "Schnozzola"
because of his prominent nose, the American comedian entertained audiences for more than 60 years.

4 The U.S. Government issued dietary guidelines aimed at improving American eating habits and promoting better health. The guidelines recommend that Americans avoid eating excessive amounts of sugar, fat, cholesterol, salt, and alcohol. School lunch programs were adjusted to follow the recommendations. Schools decreased the amount of fat and salt in their foods.

18 In parliamentary elections in Canada, the Liberal Party, headed by Pierre Elliott Trudeau, won the most seats. Trudeau thus became prime minister. He replaced Joe Clark, leader of the Progressive Conservative Party. Trudeau had previously been prime minister for eleven years, until Clark's party won the May, 1979, elections.

18 Edward Babiuch was named premier of Poland. He succeeded Piotr Jaroszewicz, who had held the position for nine years.

In Los Angeles, roads washed out by heavy rains caused serious accidents. Arizona and northern Mexico were also hard hit by the storm.

22 Nine days of heavy rains caused at least 36 deaths in California, Arizona, and northern Mexico. Damage to property was estimated at more than $500,000,000. Many homes had to be evacuated because of flooding. Particularly hard hit were hillside areas around Los Angeles, where mud slides destroyed buildings, cars, and vegetation.

25 Army sergeants staged a coup in Surinam. They overthrew the government of Prime Minister Henck A. E. Arron. Arron had been in power since late 1975, when Surinam became an independent nation.

27 In Bogotá, Colombia, leftist guerrillas seized the embassy of the Dominican Republic. The guerrillas took about 60 people hostage, including 15 ambassadors. The guerrillas demanded a ransom of $50,000,000 and the release of Colombian leftists jailed for terrorist activities. (During negotiations between the guerrillas and the Colombian Government, many of the hostages were released, and one hostage, the ambassador from Uruguay, escaped. On April 27, the remaining hostages were safely released.)

The Red Cross delivered food to the hostages during the two-month siege of the Dominican Republic embassy in Colombia.

3 Prem Tinsulanonda became premier of Thailand. He succeeded Kriangsak Chamanand, who had held the position since late 1977.

4 It was announced that in elections held February 27-29, Robert Mugabe's party had won a majority of seats in Rhodesia's new parliament. Mugabe, leader of one of the guerrilla groups that had long fought for black majority rule, thus became prime minister. He replaced Bishop Abel T. Muzorewa, who had come to power in 1979 in an election that Mugabe and other guerrillas refused to recognize. (On April 18, Rhodesia became the independent nation of Zimbabwe.)

11 Julius Chan became prime minister of Papua New Guinea. He succeeded Michael Somare, who had been prime minister since the country became independent in 1975.

24 Engineers finally succeeded in capping Ixtoc 1, an oil well in the Gulf of Mexico that had exploded June 3, 1979. The well had spilled more than 3,000,000 barrels of crude oil into the Gulf. This was the largest oil spill in history.

A Norwegian platform, used as a floating dormitory for oil workers, capsized in the North Sea, killing 123 people.

Jesse Owens, one of the greatest track stars in history, died.

27 A Norwegian platform in the North Sea capsized in a gale. The platform had been used as a floating dormitory for people who worked on nearby oil rigs. Of the 212 people who were on the platform at the time of the accident, 89 were saved. The other 123 workers died in the stormy waters.

31 Jesse Owens, the black American athlete, died at the age of 66. Owens was one of the greatest and most famous track stars in history. He won four gold medals in the 1936 Olympic Games held in Berlin. Adolf Hitler, Germany's leader, had said that the Games would prove that "Aryans" (Germans and some other white peoples of northern Europe) were a superior race. Thus, the victories by Owens and other black athletes were important politically as well as athletically.

12 William R. Tolbert, president of Liberia since 1971, was killed during a coup staged by Liberian soldiers. Samuel K. Doe, a 28-year-old sergeant, became the new president. Martial law was declared, and a number of high-ranking officials in the former government were executed for "high treason, rampant corruption, and gross violation of human rights."

15 Jean-Paul Sartre, the French philosopher, died at the age of 74. Sartre expressed his ideas in many writings, including novels and plays. He was an existentialist—he believed that people have the freedom to choose their own situations and are solely responsible for what they do. His existentialist philosophy and leftist political views greatly influenced writers and thinkers around the world.

21 Abdul Fatah Ismail, president of Yemen (Aden) since late 1978, resigned. He was succeeded by premier Ali Nasser Mohammed.

24 A U.S. airborne mission to rescue the American hostages in Iran ended in failure. The operation involved the use of six planes and eight helicopters. All six planes but only six of the helicopters succeeded in landing in the Iranian desert, 200 miles (320 kilometers) from Teheran, the city where the hostages were being held. When one of these helicopters developed mechanical problems, the mission was called off. During the withdrawal of the rescue team from the desert, a helicopter collided with a plane, killing eight men.

Edmund S. Muskie was named U.S. secretary of state.

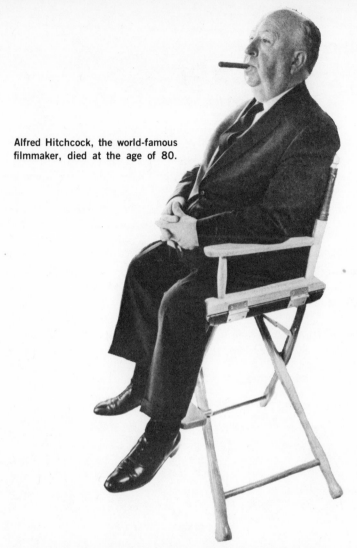

Alfred Hitchcock, the world-famous filmmaker, died at the age of 80.

28 Cyrus R. Vance resigned as U.S. secretary of state because he could not support President Jimmy Carter's decision to try to rescue the hostages in Iran. Carter named Edmund S. Muskie, a senator from Maine, to succeed Vance.

29 Alfred Hitchcock, the American filmmaker, died at the age of 80. Hitchcock was a master of suspense. Among his best-known movies were *Psycho*, *The Birds*, *The 39 Steps*, and *North by Northwest*.

30 Queen Juliana of the Netherlands abdicated after a 32-year reign. Her daughter Princess Beatrix succeeded to the throne, becoming the nation's sixth monarch.

30 Luis Muñoz Marin, the first elected governor of Puerto Rico, died at the age of 82. His well-known economic program, Operation Bootstrap, greatly improved the island's economy and brought roads and schools to rural areas.

MAY

4 Josip Broz Tito, president of Yugoslavia, died at the age of 87. He had been the leader of Yugoslavia since the end of World War II. Tito had followed a foreign policy of nonalignment. During his rule, Yugoslavia had tried to remain independent of the Soviet bloc and the West. Following his death, the presidency of Yugoslavia became a collective position, shared by eight people who represent the country's six republics and two provinces.

5 Constantine Caramanlis, premier of Greece, was elected president by parliament, effective June 19. (On May 8, George John Rallis was chosen to succeed Caramanlis as premier.)

11 Godfrey Binaisa, president of Uganda since June, 1979, was overthrown in a military coup. Members of the army will rule until the next election.

A young clean-up squad helps clear the streets of volcanic ash after Mount St. Helens erupted.

Youngsters express their concern about living in the dangerously polluted Love Canal area.

18 Mount St. Helens, a volcano in southwest Washington, erupted. Tons of hot ash were expelled. At least 32 people died as they tried to escape the ash and the fires, mudslides, and floods caused by the eruption.

18 The South Korean Government put the entire country under martial law. Universities were closed. Political gatherings and labor strikes were prohibited. The move followed two months of widespread protests by workers and students who want a democratic government.

20 In a special referendum, Quebec voters rejected a proposal to move toward independence. They chose, by a margin of 59 percent to 41 percent, to remain part of Canada.

21 President Carter declared a federal emergency at Love Canal in Niagara Falls, New York. Plans were made to relocate more than 700 families from the area. Love Canal had been used as an industrial dump site for poisonous chemical wastes from 1947 to 1952. By 1952, close to 22,000 tons of chemical wastes had been deposited there. The dump was then covered with landfill, and a school and houses were built on the site. But by the 1970's some 82 different chemicals—a number of which are suspected of causing cancer—began bubbling to the surface and seeping into basements. Studies showed an unusually high number of cases of cancer and other disorders among people who lived in the area. In 1978, 239 families were evacuated.

JUNE

12 Masayoshi Ohira, premier of Japan, died at the age of 70. Ohira had been in office since December, 1978. Ohira's death left Japan leaderless just ten days before national elections were to be held. (In the June 22 elections, Ohira's Liberal Democratic Party won majorities in both houses of the parliament. The parliament would elect a new premier.)

23 The leaders of the seven major industrial democracies ended a two-day meeting in Venice, Italy. The countries represented were Britain, Canada, France, Germany, Italy, Japan, and the United States. The seven nations pledged to conserve oil. And they vowed to develop and use other energy sources so that oil consumption could be substantially cut by 1990. The industrial nations agreed that energy problems must be solved in order to fight inflation. The leaders also condemned the Soviet invasion of Afghanistan and discussed the problems of the world's refugees.

The leaders of the seven major democracies met in Venice, Italy, for a two-day economic meeting.

26 President Valéry Giscard d'Estaing announced that France had developed and tested a neutron bomb. A neutron bomb is a modified hydrogen bomb. Unlike a hydrogen bomb explosion, a neutron bomb explosion does not cause extensive damage to buildings and other property. But it releases more deadly, concentrated radiation.

27 Canada's Parliament declared *O Canada* the official national anthem. The 100-year-old song has both English and French lyrics. (At noon on July 1, Dominion Day, Canadians all over the country stopped whatever they were doing to sing the song.)

27 President Carter signed a controversial draft registration bill. Under the bill, young men aged 19 and 20 must register with the Selective Service System. (Registration began on July 21. But there were no immediate plans for actually drafting the men into the armed services.)

28 José Iturbi, the Spanish-born pianist, conductor, and actor, died at the age of 84. Iturbi starred in several 1940's film musicals, including *A Song to Remember* and *Anchors Away*.

English- and French-speaking Canadian youngsters gather to sing
O Canada, which Parliament declared the official national anthem.

JULY

11 Richard I. Queen, one of the 53 American hostages held in Iran since the U.S. embassy was seized in November, 1979, was released. The release was ordered by Ayatollah Ruhollah Khomeini because of Queen's need for medical treatment.

13 Sir Seretse Khama, president of Botswana since it became independent in 1966, died at the age of 59. (On July 18, Quett Masire, vice-president under Khama, was named the new president.)

17 Bolivia's armed forces seized control of the country. The object of the coup was to prevent Hernán Siles Zuazo from becoming president. Siles had won the most votes in elections held in June. General Luis García Meza, the commander of the army, was sworn in as president.

17 Zenko Suzuki was elected premier of Japan by the parliament. He succeeded Masayoshi Ohira, who died in June.

Peter Sellers (*right*) who died in July, was known for his zany film roles. Here he is shown as Inspector Clouseau.

24 Peter Sellers, the British comedian, died at the age of 54. He was known for his masterful impersonations and zany film roles. One of his best-loved movie roles was that of the bumbling Inspector Clouseau, in *The Pink Panther* series.

27 The deposed Shah of Iran, Mohammed Reza Pahlavi, died at the age of 60. The Shah had left Iran in January, 1979. He was given temporary asylum in several countries before going to Egypt in March, 1980.

28 Fernando Belaúnde Terry, winner of elections held in May, became president of Peru. His inauguration ended twelve years of military rule in the country.

29 Scientists at Stanford University, in California, reported that they had developed cells that produce human antibodies. Antibodies are a person's first line of defense against disease. They are special proteins that attack bacteria and other foreign materials that enter the body. Laboratory-produced antibodies may eventually be used to treat various diseases, including cancer.

30 New Hebrides, a group of South Pacific islands, became the independent nation of Vanuatu. The islands had been ruled jointly by Britain and France for 74 years. Walter Lini, an Anglican minister, became the first prime minister.

Vanuatu, a group of South Pacific islands formerly known as New Hebrides, celebrates becoming an independent nation.

11 Hurricane Allen ended a week-long rampage, during which it tore across the Caribbean, Mexico's Yucatan Peninsula, and the Texas Gulf Coast. It was one of the strongest and most damaging storms of the 20th century. Particularly hard hit were St. Lucia, Haiti, and Jamaica. More than 270 people died as a result of the storm. Thousands of homes and millions of dollars worth of crops were destroyed.

14 Some 17,000 Polish workers at the Lenin Shipyard in Gdansk went on strike. The strike spread throughout much of Poland, causing a national crisis. (By the end of August, an estimated 500,000 workers were on strike. The workers began returning to their jobs in early September, after having been promised wage increases and important political gains. As a result of the strike, the country's leader, Edward Gierek, was forced to resign on September 6. He was replaced by Stanislaw Kania.)

15 A U.S. expedition announced that it had located the *Titanic*. The famous luxury liner sank in 1912 in the mid-Atlantic. It was on its first voyage when it hit an iceberg. More than 1,500 people died.

This marina in Corpus Christi, Texas, was particularly hard hit by Hurricane Allen.

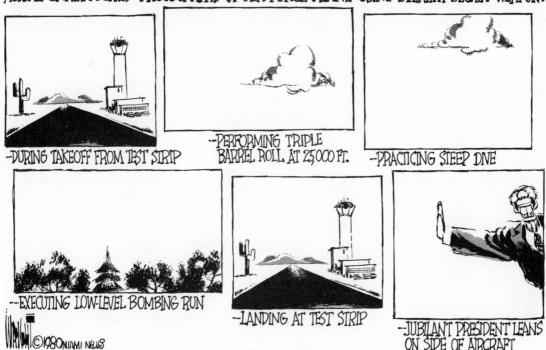

ACTUAL UNRETOUCHED PHOTOGRAPHS OF AIR FORCE PLANE USING "STEALTH" SECRET WEAPON!

—DURING TAKEOFF FROM TEST STRIP

—PERFORMING TRIPLE BARREL ROLL AT 25,000 FT.

—PRACTICING STEEP DIVE

—EXECUTING LOW-LEVEL BOMBING RUN

—LANDING AT TEST STRIP

—JUBILANT PRESIDENT LEANS ON SIDE OF AIRCRAFT

©1980 MIAMI NEWS

The 1980 expedition used sonar signals in its search for the ship. Deep in a submarine canyon in the area where the *Titanic* went down, sonar signals indicated an object the same length, width, and height as the ship. Additional surveying was halted because of stormy seas. A second expedition was planned for 1981.

16 Choi Kyu Hah, president of South Korea since December, 1979, resigned. (On August 27, he was replaced by retired general Chun Doo Hwan.)

20 The United States revealed that it had developed an "invisible" airplane. The plane, called the stealth aircraft, can avoid detection by radar. It was built in a shape designed to eliminate sharp angles, which are good reflectors of radar waves. The plane was also coated with a special material that helps to weaken radar waves. The disclosure of the project became a political issue in the presidential election campaign. Republican candidate Ronald Reagan charged that the disclosure would threaten U.S. national defense. President Jimmy Carter responded that thousands of people already knew of the project and said, "You cannot keep something like this secret."

25 The newly independent nation of Zimbabwe was admitted to the United Nations. It became the 153rd member of the world body.

SEPTEMBER

5 The world's longest road tunnel opened in Switzerland. The tunnel is 10 miles (16 kilometers) long. It runs through the Alps underneath the St. Gotthard Pass, which has been a major route between northern and southern Europe for over 900 years. Using the tunnel would make the trip about four hours shorter than using the pass.

12 A military junta took power in Turkey. Suleyman Demirel, prime minister since October, 1979, was ousted and parliament was dissolved. (On September 20, retired Admiral Bulent Ulusu was appointed prime minister.)

16 The 35th regular session of the United Nations General Assembly opened at U.N. headquarters in New York City. Baron Rüdiger von Wechmar of West Germany was elected to serve as assembly president for one year.

Terry Fox is awarded the Order of Canada by Governor General Edward R. Schreyer. The Order of Canada is the highest medal a Canadian civilian can receive.

Iraqi troops in Iran. War between the two countries broke out in September.

16 Jean Piaget, the Swiss psychologist, died at the age of 84. Piaget was famous for his pioneering work on child development. His theories of learning greatly influenced child psychology and education systems.

17 Anastasio Somoza Debayle was assassinated in Paraguay. Somoza had been president of Nicaragua until July, 1979, when he resigned under pressure and went into exile.

19 Terry Fox was awarded the Order of Canada, the highest medal a Canadian civilian can receive. The 22-year-old from British Columbia was the youngest person to receive the medal, which was awarded for his courage and perseverance. Fox had lost part of his right leg in 1977 because of bone cancer. After he was outfitted with an artificial leg, he began training to become a long-distance runner. On April 12, 1980, he left St. John's, Newfoundland, on a 5,300-mile (8,530-kilometer) cross-Canada run, to raise money for medical research. He had completed more than half the distance before illness forced him to stop. His efforts raised millions of dollars for the Canadian Cancer Society.

22 Iraqi airplanes bombed airfields in Iran, marking the beginning of open warfare between the two countries. (On September 23, Iraqi troops crossed into Iran. Control of Iran's oil-producing Khuzistan Province seemed to be their objective. Initial efforts by the United Nations to stop the fighting were unsuccessful. The fighting resulted in extensive damage to both countries' oil-producing facilities and threatened to affect world oil supplies.)

2 The U.S. House of Representatives ousted Michael Myers, a Democrat from Pennsylvania, following his conviction in August of bribery. This was the first time a member of the House had been expelled since 1861. Myers' conviction was a result of an FBI investigation called Abscam. FBI agents pretended to represent wealthy Arabs who wanted Myers to help them immigrate to the United States. Video tapes showed Myers accepting a $50,000 bribe from the agents.

10 Two earthquakes struck northwestern Algeria. Al Asnam, a city with a population of 125,000, was almost completely destroyed. About 20,000 people were believed to have been killed.

11 Two Soviet cosmonauts returned to Earth after setting a new record for time spent in space. Leonid Popov and Valery Ryumin spent 185 days aboard the Salyut 6 space station.

Lawrence R. Klein, winner of the Nobel prize for economics, reads a congratulatory note attached to a bunch of balloons. He joked by saying that balloons were a "real example of inflation."

18 Arnaldo Forlani became premier of Italy. He replaced Francesco Cossiga, who had held the position since August, 1979.

23 Aleksei N. Kosygin resigned as premier of the Soviet Union. He had held the position for 16 years. He was succeeded by Nikolai A. Tikhonov.

30 In national elections in Jamaica, the Jamaica Labor Party won the most seats in Parliament. The party's head, Edward P. G. Seaga, thus became prime minister. He replaced Michael N. Manley, who had been prime minister since 1972.

THE 1980 NOBEL PRIZES

Chemistry: Paul Berg and Walter Gilbert of the United States and Frederick Sanger of Britain, for their independent research that helps explain how DNA "governs the chemical machinery of the cell." Sanger was the first person ever to receive two Nobel prizes in chemistry. He had been awarded the prize in 1958 for his research on the chemistry of insulin.

Economics: Lawrence R. Klein of the United States, for the development of mathematical models that can be used to forecast economic trends. The models can also be used to predict the effect on the economy of such policies as tax cuts and increased government spending.

Literature: Czeslaw Milosz, who emigrated from Poland and became a U.S. citizen, for his poetry, novels, and essays, written in Polish. His writings depict "the world in which man lives after having been driven out of paradise."

Peace: Adolfo Pérez Esquivel of Argentina, for his human rights activities. Pérez Esquivel worked to establish community groups in Latin America. These groups helped poor people improve their human, social, and economic conditions.

Physics: Val L. Fitch and James W. Cronin of the United States, who showed that subatomic particles do not always behave according to a principle of physics called the law of symmetry. The kind of imbalance demonstrated by their work would explain how the universe could form containing more matter than antimatter. (Particles of antimatter are like particles of matter but have opposite electrical charges. The two destroy each other.)

Physiology or Medicine: Baruj Benacerraf, a Venezuelan-born American; George D. Snell of the United States, and Jean Dausset of France, for their independent discoveries of how the body fights diseases and other "foreign" cells. Their work helps explain why some people are better able than others to defend themselves against disease. The work also led to the successful transplanting of organs from one person to another.

NOVEMBER

4 In U.S. elections, Republicans Ronald W. Reagan and George H. Bush were elected president and vice-president. They defeated the incumbent Democratic candidates, Jimmy Carter and Walter F. Mondale. The Republicans also gained 12 seats in the Senate, to obtain a majority. They gained 33 seats in the House of Representatives, where the Democrats kept their majority.

7 Steve McQueen, the American actor, died at the age of 50. Among his best-known movies were *The Great Escape, The Thomas Crown Affair,* and *Papillon.*

14 Luiz de Almeida Cabral, president of Guinea-Bissau since the country became independent in 1974, was overthrown in a coup. Prime Minister Joâo Bernardo Vieira, who led the coup, became head of government.

21 A fire in the MGM Grand Hotel in Las Vegas, Nevada, killed at least 84 people. It was the most deadly hotel fire in the United States since 1946. The cause of the fire was not immediately known.

Steve McQueen, shown here in *The Thomas Crown Affair,* died.

Italy was hit by a major earthquake, in which about 3,000 people died.

22 Jules Léger, governor-general of Canada from 1974 to 1979, died at the age of 67. During his term in office, some important powers of government held by Britain were transferred to Canada. These included the power to declare war and sign peace treaties.

22 John W. McCormack, the U.S. politician, died at the age of 88. McCormack was a member of the House of Representatives for 42 years. He was Speaker of the House for eight years, until his retirement in 1970.

22 Mae West, the American actress, died at the age of 87. Her best-known movies included *She Done Him Wrong, I'm No Angel,* and *My Little Chickadee.*

23 The worst earthquake to hit Italy in 65 years caused extensive damage in more than 170 communities in southern Italy. More than 3,000 people were killed, and hundreds of thousands were made homeless. The ancient remains of Pompeii suffered much damage.

24 George Raft, the American actor, died at the age of 85. He was best known for gangster roles in such movies as *Scarface* and *Invisible Stripes.*

25 Sangoulé Lamizana, leader of Upper Volta since 1966, was ousted in a military coup. He was succeeded by a military junta, headed by Colonel Saye Zerbo.

DECEMBER

1 A report issued by the U.S. Surgeon General indicated that all cigarettes, including those with low nicotine and tar contents, are harmful to one's health. Smoking, said the report, is "the single most important preventable cause of death and disease . . . even the lowest-yield cigarettes present health hazards much greater than those encountered by nonsmokers."

3 The *Solar Challenger,* an airplane powered by the rays of the sun, made a 22-minute flight over the Arizona desert. It was the longest solar flight on record. The *Solar Challenger* and an earlier test plane, the *Gossamer Penguin,* were the first to take off and fly using energy converted directly from the sun. The energy was gathered by solar cells on the wing and tail of the plane. The cells converted the solar energy to electricity, which ran the plane's motor.

5 Francisco Sá Carneiro, premier of Portugal since January, was killed in a plane crash. He was 46 years old. He was succeeded by Francisco Pinto Balsemão.

8 John Lennon, the British singer and songwriter, was shot and killed in New York City. He was 40 years old. Lennon gained fame as one of the four members of the Beatles, the British rock group that shaped the course of popular music in the 1960's. Many fans considered Lennon the most talented of all the Beatles. In November, 1980, Lennon and his wife, Yoko Ono, released *Double Fantasy,* his first album in five years. (On December 14, in response to a request by Ono, millions of people around the world observed 10 minutes of silence in memory of Lennon. Concerts and other memorial events were also held.)

13 José Napoleón Duarte was named president of El Salvador. He was the first civilian president in 49 years.

13 In elections in Uganda, the Uganda People's Congress, headed by Milton Obote, won a majority of the seats in parliament. Obote thus became president and began his second term in office. His earlier term ended in 1971, when he was overthrown by Idi Amin.

18 Aleksei N. Kosygin, the Soviet political leader, died at the age of 76. Kosygin was premier of the Soviet Union from 1964 to October, 1980, when he resigned because of poor health.

Right: John Lennon and his wife, Yoko Ono, in 1980. Bottom: Lennon (*far right*) and the other members of the Beatles rock group, in 1966. Lennon was shot and killed in New York City on December 8.

On January 20, 1981, Ronald Reagan was to be inaugurated the 40th president of the United States.

THE U.S. PRESIDENTIAL ELECTION

In the 1980 presidential election, the people of the United States voted for change. By a solid margin, they chose Ronald Reagan, a Republican, over Democratic President Jimmy Carter. Reagan, a former movie star and ex-governor of California, had sought the presidency twice before. At 69, he was the oldest person ever elected to the office. And when he and his running mate, George Bush, defeated Carter and Vice-President Walter Mondale, the longest presidential campaign in U.S. history came to an end.

Reagan and Carter had received their parties' nominations only after long struggles against other contenders. The race started in August, 1978, when Republican Philip Crane announced that he was running for president. Other Republicans began tossing their hats into the ring, too—Reagan; Bush, a former congressman from Texas and, later, U.S. delegate to the United Nations; Howard Baker, senator from Tennessee; Robert Dole, senator from Kansas; John Connally, former governor of Texas; John Anderson, congressman from Illinois.

In other years, a president in office could often be assured of being automatically renominated by his party. But in 1980, two prominent Democrats rose to challenge Carter for the nomination—Jerry Brown, governor of California, and Ted Kennedy, senator from Massachusetts.

▶ PRIMARIES AND CAUCUSES

Between February and June, 1980, 37 states held primary elections. A primary gives people a chance to vote for the candidate they think their party should nominate. Delegates representing the primary winners go to the national party convention, where the candidate is actually chosen. In the states that did not have primaries, the parties held caucuses (meetings) in each of their districts. At these meetings, local party members voted for candidates or delegates.

Gradually, some of the presidential hopefuls withdrew because they did not have enough support. In the Republican race, the choice narrowed down to Reagan, Bush, and Anderson. By May, Reagan had enough delegates to win the nomination, and Bush abandoned his campaign.

Anderson hadn't won any primaries. But a good many Democrats, as well as liberal Republicans, supported him. He decided to run as an independent. He was the most important candidate to challenge the two big parties. Other candidates, such as Barry Commoner of the Citizens' Party and Ed Clark of the Libertarian Party, were not expected to draw many votes.

The Democratic fight was affected when, late in 1979, Iranians seized the U.S. embassy in Teheran and held some 50 Americans there hostage. Carter said the crisis would prevent him from traveling around the country, and he limited his campaign efforts to press conferences. Kennedy charged that Carter was using the crisis to avoid discussing important issues.

In April, the United States made an unsuccessful attempt to rescue the hostages. After that, Carter began to campaign more actively. In primaries and caucuses, he won 60 percent of the delegates to the Democratic convention. Brown withdrew. But Kennedy said that people who had voted for Carter in the early primaries no longer favored him. Kennedy wanted to change a convention rule that required delegates to vote for their candidates. Carter said that if the rules were changed, people who had voted for him in the primaries would be cheated.

The Republicans held their convention in Detroit from July 14 to 17. They adopted a conservative platform. (A platform is a statement of the party's positions on various issues.) Then they overwhelmingly endorsed Reagan as their candidate. In his acceptance speech, Reagan called for a renewal of the American spirit.

Even before the convention began, the biggest question had been who would be Reagan's running mate. Many Republicans felt that former president Gerald Ford would be the best choice. But Reagan and Ford failed to agree on the amount of authority that Ford would have as vice-president. And so, at the last moment, Reagan turned to the person who had been his most serious challenger for the presidential nomination—George Bush.

The Democratic National Convention was held in New York City from August 11 to 14. Early on the first day, Kennedy lost his fight to change the convention rules, and he withdrew from the race. But several of his programs became part of the party platform at the convention.

Carter, in accepting his party's nomination, said: "This election is a stark choice between . . . two sharply different pictures of what America is and what the world is. But it's more than that. It's a choice between two futures."

▶ A CLEAR CHOICE

The presidential candidates and their parties had significantly different positions on a number of important issues.

The Economy. Reagan called for a large income tax cut—30 percent over three years. He also said that the federal budget could be greatly cut and could be balanced by 1983. He favored the growth of private business to create jobs and improve the economy.

Carter favored a relatively small tax cut, saying a large cut would add to inflation. He said the budget couldn't be balanced (a promise he had made during his 1976 campaign) without losing important programs. The Democratic platform proposed government action to create jobs.

Energy. Reagan emphasized energy production. He said that the energy crisis had been caused primarily by federal regulations that discouraged production of oil and gas in the United States. He placed more stress on ending such controls than on conserving energy resources.

Carter stressed conservation. He felt that the government should play a major role in financing the development of synthetic fuels and other new energy sources.

Environment. Reagan said that many environmental regulations were unnecessary and had resulted in the loss of jobs. He favored

John Anderson, who ran as an independent, was the most important candidate to challenge both major parties.

President Jimmy Carter and Reagan greet each other before their October 28 debate.

giving states control over large tracts of undeveloped land now owned by the federal government.

Carter supported existing laws that protect the environment. He said he would not sacrifice environmental protection for industry. He favored legislation that would protect federal wilderness lands in Alaska.

Foreign Policy. The Republicans called for a strong stand against the spread of Communism. Reagan said that the United States should have a "hands-off" attitude toward the domestic policies, including human rights policies, of friendly countries. And he was cautious about developing closer ties with China.

Carter had established full diplomatic relations with China, and his concern about human rights had influenced U.S. policy toward other countries. The Democratic platform condemned aggressive Soviet acts but called for the easing of tensions between East and West.

Defense and Military Issues. Reagan said he would scrap the SALT II arms control treaty and negotiate a new agreement. He said the United States must maintain military superi-

ority, and he called for a buildup of military equipment. Reagan opposed registration for the draft.

Carter supported SALT II. He had ordered registration of 19- and 20-year-olds for the draft, but he said he was against a peacetime draft. He also called for increased military spending.

Social Issues. Reagan opposed the Equal Rights Amendment (ERA), although he said he favored equal rights for women. The Republican platform called for a constitutional amendment that would ban abortions. It opposed the use of quotas for minority groups in school admissions and employment.

Carter supported the ERA. He said he opposed abortion, but he was against a constitutional amendment banning it. The Democratic platform was in favor of programs for minority groups.

▶ THE FINAL CAMPAIGN

As September approached, Anderson remained an important factor in the race. He had chosen Patrick Lucey, a former Democratic governor of Wisconsin, as his running mate. Their platform was generally conservative on economic issues and liberal on social issues. Carter forces were particularly worried about Anderson. They feared he would attract voters who would normally choose the Democratic candidate.

The League of Women Voters organized televised debates between the main presidential candidates, inviting Anderson to participate in the first debate. But Carter refused to participate if Anderson were included. He said the first debate should be a two-man encounter between the major party candidates. Carter's argument was rejected. On September 21, Reagan and Anderson debated. Both men picked up support as a result of the debate. But as the election drew nearer, Anderson's support seemed to gradually decrease.

A two-man debate between Carter and Reagan was finally held on October 28. Carter focused on the issues of war and peace. Reagan focused on the economy. The debate was one of many events in the two men's hectic schedules. At stop after stop during the final days of the campaign, Reagan and Carter repeated their messages to the voters.

▶ HOW THE COUNTRY VOTED

In the November 4 election, only 52.4 percent of the Americans eligible to vote actually did so. It was the lowest turnout in a presidential election since 1948. Reagan received 51 percent of the vote; Carter received 41 percent; Anderson received 7 percent. Reagan led in 44 states and thus received those states' 489 electoral votes (a majority of electoral votes—270 votes—is needed to become president). Carter carried only the District of Columbia and six states, for 49 electoral votes. Anderson and the other candidates did not win any states.

The Republican victory spread far beyond the White House. The Republicans picked up twelve seats in the Senate, to obtain a majority for the first time since the 1950's. In the House of Representatives, they gained 33 seats, but the Democrats still retained a majority. The Republicans also gained four governorships.

Why did voters turn to Reagan and the rest of the Republican ticket? Many people said they were unhappy with Carter's performance. Some election analysts said that people's unhappiness with the economy probably hurt Carter more than any other issue.

Will Reagan be able to get the economy moving again? Will he be able to improve America's position in the world? Will he be able to cut federal spending and decrease U.S. reliance on imported fuels? These are just a few of the challenges that faced Reagan as he prepared to take office.

HOW THE COUNTRY VOTED
(The numbers are each state's electoral college votes—270 were needed to win.)

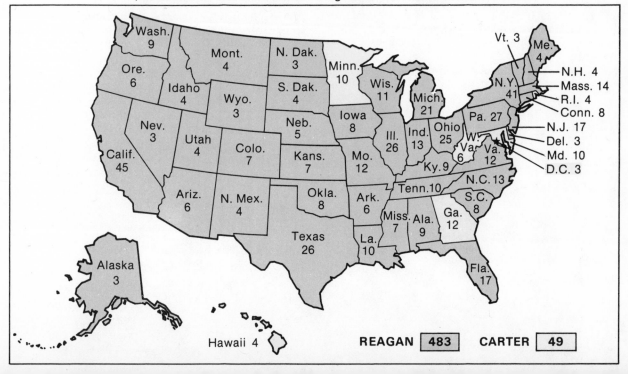

Wash. 9 | Ore. 6 | Idaho 4 | Mont. 4 | N. Dak. 3 | S. Dak. 4 | Minn. 10 | Wis. 11 | Mich. 21 | Vt. 3 | Me. 4 | N.H. 4 | N.Y. 41 | Mass. 14 | R.I. 4 | Conn. 8 | Pa. 27 | N.J. 17 | Del. 3 | Md. 10 | D.C. 3 | Nev. 3 | Utah 4 | Wyo. 3 | Colo. 7 | Neb. 5 | Iowa 8 | Ill. 26 | Ind. 13 | Ohio 25 | W. Va. 6 | Va. 12 | Ky. 9 | N.C. 13 | Calif. 45 | Ariz. 6 | N. Mex. 4 | Kans. 7 | Okla. 8 | Mo. 12 | Ark. 6 | Tenn. 10 | S.C. 8 | Ga. 12 | Miss. 7 | Ala. 9 | La. 10 | Texas 26 | Fla. 17 | Alaska 3 | Hawaii 4

REAGAN 483   CARTER 49

SOVIET TROOPS IN AFGHANISTAN

It's a rugged, mountainous country. Much of the land is barren. It's not a wealthy country, but for centuries it was overrun and ruled by foreign armies. What is it about Afghanistan that has caused it to have such a turbulent history? The answer is its location—this Central Asian country has been called the "crossroads of Asia." Through the centuries, powerful nations have sought to control Afghanistan as a way of protecting their own interests.

The pattern repeated itself in 1980. At the end of December, 1979, Soviet troops had entered Afghanistan. By February, 1980, about 90,000 of them were in the country. And by the end of 1980, the Soviets had become an occupation army. They controlled the large cities and towns but not the rest of the country, where anti-Soviet Afghan guerrillas were resisting.

▶ **WHY THE SOVIET UNION WENT IN**

The Soviet Union has thousands of miles of borders with other countries. The Soviets have always been concerned that the countries along the borders be friendly to them. In Europe, for example, pro-Soviet Communist nations form a "buffer" between the Soviet Union and the non-Communist nations of Western Europe. The border between Afghanistan and the Soviet Union is over 1,000 miles (1,610 kilometers) long. The Soviets feel that it is vital that Afghanistan have a pro-Soviet government.

In September, 1979, Hafizullah Amin took power and became president of Afghanistan. Amin's government was pro-Soviet, but it was beleaguered by anti-Communist Muslim rebels. These rebels were opposed to the Communist ideas of the Afghan Government, and they were fighting a guerrilla war against the Afghan army. The Soviets suggested to Amin that Soviet troops be brought in to put down the rebellion. Amin said no. But the Soviet troops entered Afghanistan anyway, aided in the overthrow of Amin, who was killed, and supported a new regime by Babrak Karmal. The Soviets claimed that a friendship treaty with Afghanistan had given them the right to enter the country.

The Soviets remained in Afghanistan, fighting the guerrillas and establishing control over the large cities, the roads, and the airports. But the guerrillas, often poorly equipped and poorly fed, continued to fight. They held parts of the countryside and mountain regions.

For these Muslim rebels, the fight against the Soviets had become a holy war. In the Middle East and elsewhere, recent years have seen an upsurge in political action among Muslims who want to preserve the traditional values of their religion. The 1979 revolution in Iran was an example of this upsurge. More than 20,000,000 Soviet citizens are Muslims. Many of them live near the Afghanistan border. So, fearing the spread of guerrilla warfare into its Muslim

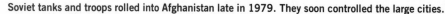

Soviet tanks and troops rolled into Afghanistan late in 1979. They soon controlled the large cities.

Muslim guerrillas fought the Soviets throughout 1980. They held parts of the countryside.

areas, the Soviet Union felt even more the need to crush the Afghan rebellion.

Afghanistan is a landlocked country. But control of Afghanistan would bring Soviet forces much closer to the Persian Gulf. A good portion of the world's oil is transported through that waterway from the oil-producing countries of the Middle East. Some people thought that this, too, was a reason for the Soviet action.

▶ PROTESTS AGAINST THE SOVIET UNION

The response around the world was one of outrage and protest. U.S. President Jimmy Carter called the Soviet incursion into Afghanistan "a serious threat to peace." He added that any attempt "to gain control of the Persian Gulf region will be regarded as an assault on the vital interests of the United States of America, and such an assault will be repelled by any means necessary, including military force."

In January, 1980, U.S. and British navy ships moved closer to the Persian Gulf area. In that same month, the United Nations passed a resolution deploring the incursion and calling for the immediate withdrawal of "foreign troops" from Afghanistan. The United States called for a grain embargo, and the grain-producing nations, with the exception of Argentina, declared that they would

cut their shipments to the Soviet Union. The most publicized action against the Soviets was the boycott of the Moscow Olympic Games by the United States and many other countries of the world. But all these actions did not force a Soviet withdrawal.

Within Afghanistan itself, the Muslim rebels kept up their guerrilla war. Many soldiers in the Afghan Army, which was supporting the Soviets, went over to the guerrilla side. Even in the Soviet-controlled cities and towns, there were protests against the Soviets. In February, Afghans in the capital, Kabul, and six other cities took part in a mass strike. This strike showed that the Soviet incursion was not supported by the Afghan people, as the Soviets were claiming. The Soviets responded harshly to these demonstrations. Using tanks, helicopters, and Soviet-directed Afghan troops, they killed hundreds of Afghan protesters.

In November, the U.N. General Assembly passed a second resolution against the Soviet incursion, but this resolution was weaker in tone than the January one. The Soviets maintained that their action was justified and, further, was nobody else's business. And so Soviet troops remained in Afghanistan at the end of 1980, and the world wondered if they would become a permanent occupation army.

THE MIDDLE EAST

Geography and history have worked together to make the Middle East one of the world's most fought-over areas. It lies at the junction of Africa, Asia, and Europe, and it is surrounded by important waterways. In ancient times, countless peoples migrated across the area. Great empires—Egypt, Babylonia, Persia, and others—rose and fell. The religions of Judaism, Christianity, and Islam all began in the Middle East.

The rich but often violent history of the region was reflected in the events of 1980. It could be seen in conflicts between Arabs and Jews, for example, and between Arabs and Iranians (who are descended from the Persians of old). Even the religion of Islam, long considered a unifying force in the Middle East, was troubled by divisions.

On the surface, the conflicts involved the individual interests of the region's separate countries and cultures. But because the Middle East is the source of much of the world's oil, its troubles are also the world's. Oil has made the region so important that any crisis there has the potential to expand into a full-scale war between major powers.

▶ EGYPT AND ISRAEL

Israel has been at odds with the Arab countries of the Middle East since its creation, in 1948, as a homeland for the Jews. In that year, under a U.N. plan, the British territory of Palestine was to be divided into two states—one Jewish, the other Arab. The Arabs of Palestine felt that this plan deprived them of their land, and they went to war against Israel. Arab-Israeli wars broke out repeatedly—in 1956, 1967, and 1973. In the years of fighting, Israel gained control of the Golan Heights (from Syria), the West Bank of the Jordan River and the eastern, Arab section of Jerusalem (from Jordan), and the

Arabs in the West Bank area. The question of a Palestinian Arab homeland remained unsolved in 1980.

Gaza Strip and nearly all of the vast Sinai Peninsula (from Egypt).

By 1980, there were about 4,000,000 Palestinian Arabs. Many of them lived in the West Bank and the Gaza Strip, which Israel has held since 1967, or were refugees in nearby countries. Most of the Palestinian Arabs felt that they should have an independent country of their own. And the question of a Palestinian Arab homeland remained one of the biggest roadblocks to peace in the Middle East in 1980.

Just two years earlier, the outlook had been bright. In 1978, Egyptian President Anwar el-Sadat and Israeli Prime Minister Menahem Begin, with the help of U.S. President Jimmy Carter, reached a two-part agreement for peace. One part resulted in a peace treaty between Israel and Egypt, signed in March, 1979. It was the first peace treaty between Israel and any Arab country. The treaty called for Israel to withdraw from the Sinai Peninsula within three years and for normal relations to begin between the two countries. The other part of the agreement was a commitment to work out a formula for a self-governing homeland for the Arabs of the West Bank and the Gaza Strip. Details of how the homeland would be set up and governed were to be decided in the following year, with Jordan and representatives of the Palestinian Arabs taking part.

But Jordan and the other Arab countries rejected the Israeli-Egyptian agreement, as did the leading Palestinian Arab group, the Palestine Liberation Organization (PLO). And within days of the treaty's signing, most Arab countries ended economic and diplomatic relations with Egypt.

Throughout the rest of 1979 and 1980, the terms set forth in the peace treaty were met. By late January, 1980, most of the Sinai Peninsula had been returned to Egypt, and the border between the two countries was officially opened. In February, Egypt and Israel exchanged ambassadors and opened embassies in each other's capitals.

But talks on the issue of a Palestinian Arab homeland did not go as smoothly. Israel was reluctant to turn over control of land and water resources in the West Bank or to give up certain powers. Many Israelis feared that if an independent Palestinian state were set

The Israeli embassy in Cairo. Israel and Egypt opened embassies in each other's capitals in February.

up, their own country would be in greater danger of war with Arab countries.

Even while talks with Egypt continued, new Israeli settlements were set up in the West Bank, and existing settlements were strengthened. Egypt broke off talks because of this in May. The talks resumed but stopped again after July 30, when Israel passed a law making all of Jerusalem, including the eastern sector, its capital. The law infuriated Arabs because Jerusalem is sacred to Muslims, as well as to Jews.

Meanwhile, each country faced internal problems. Peace and U.S. aid failed to boost Egypt's lagging economy, and the shunning of Egypt by the other Arab countries was a blow to Sadat's prestige. In Israel, Begin also lost support over economic issues. And many Israelis opposed his stand on Jerusalem and the West Bank settlements. Among the Palestinian Arabs, there were demonstrations, protest strikes, and a number of terrorist attacks in which Israelis were killed. Israel answered the attacks with military force and by deporting Arab leaders.

In the fall, Israel and Egypt agreed to resume talks. But serious disagreements remained on important issues.

▶ IRAN

More than 50 Americans continued to be held hostage in Iran in 1980. And struggles for power marked that country's second year of rule by Islamic religious leaders.

Iran had been a leading oil producer and a rapidly modernizing country until early 1979. In that year a Muslim cleric, Ayatollah Ruhollah Khomeini, came to power in a revolution that overthrew Shah Mohammed Reza Pahlavi. Khomeini's goal was to establish a government that would restore the Islamic traditions of ancient times.

Khomeini continued as Iran's top leader in 1980. But under him, several factions formed. One was made up of Muslim funda-

mentalists, who wanted the government to strictly follow ancient religious codes. Moderates were more flexible in applying the codes. There were also leftist and Communist groups.

A moderate, Abolhassan Bani-Sadr, was elected president in January. But in parliamentary elections in March, fundamentalists won more than half the seats. Throughout the year, disagreements between the president and parliament held up government appointments and other business. And there was street fighting between the leftists and the Revolutionary Guards, who were controlled by the fundamentalists.

There was also conflict between the government and Iran's minorities. The Kurds, a people who live in the area where Iran, Iraq, and Turkey meet, have long sought an independent homeland of their own. They were in open rebellion against the Iranian Government. There was unrest among other groups as well, including the Arabs of Khuzistan

People in the United States cheered Canada for arranging the escape of six Americans from Iran in January.

In April, a raid aimed at freeing the U.S. hostages in Teheran ended in failure in the Iranian desert.

province in southwestern Iran. Most of Iran's oil is found in this area.

Meanwhile, freedom seemed no closer for the American hostages. At the start of the year, 50 Americans were being held by militant students at the U.S. embassy in Teheran, and three others were in government custody. The militants had seized the embassy on November 4, 1979, after the Shah entered a U.S. hospital. Although the Shah left the United States a few weeks later, the militants continued to insist that the hostages would not be released unless he were returned to Iran to stand trial. There was strong feeling in Iran against the United States, which had supported the Shah, and the new rulers backed the demand.

In January, six Americans who had managed to avoid the militants escaped from Iran with a daring assist from Canada. Five of the six had been inside the embassy when it was seized. They had left by a rear door and made their way to the Canadian embassy, where they had been joined by the sixth American.

For more than two months, the six stayed hidden in the homes of Canadian diplomats. Meanwhile, Canadian ambassador Kenneth Taylor gradually reduced his embassy staff in Iran and obtained false passports and exit visas for the Americans. On January 28, the Americans used their false papers to board a plane for Frankfurt, West Germany. Later that day, the last Canadian diplomats also left Iran.

While people in the United States cheered the Canadians for arranging the escape, efforts to free the hostages in the U.S. embassy continued. Early in the year, Iran said that its yet-to-be-elected parliament would decide the hostages' fate. In April, the United States banned trade with Iran and asked its allies to do the same. (Some European countries imposed a partial ban in May.) Then, on April 25, the United States tried to rescue the hostages with a military raid.

The U.S. plan called for at least six Navy helicopters to fly at night to a remote spot in the desert southeast of Teheran. There they

Hostage Richard Queen (*left*) is greeted by President Carter. Queen was released in July, when he became ill.

would meet transport planes carrying Army commandos, fuel, and supplies. The helicopters would ferry the commandos to a mountain hideout near Teheran. Then, under cover of darkness, the commandos would storm the embassy and free the hostages, and the helicopters would carry them out.

But the raid did not turn out as planned. Eight helicopters set out on the mission from an aircraft carrier near the Strait of Hormuz. One helicopter was abandoned when a cracked rotor blade was discovered. Another turned back when its gyrocompass, a key piece of navigational equipment, failed in the midst of a dust storm over the Iranian desert. The remaining six arrived at the rendezvous, where the transport planes were waiting. But one helicopter was unable to take off again because a hydraulic pump had failed.

Five helicopters were too few to complete the mission, and the raid was called off. The helicopters moved up to the transport planes to refuel for the return flight, but in the darkness one helicopter collided with a plane. Both craft burst into flames, killing eight men. The rest of the helicopters were abandoned, and the force withdrew.

In the aftermath of the raid, the militants said they would move the hostages to various locations around the country. It was not known how many hostages remained in the embassy or where the others were. In July one hostage, Richard I. Queen, was released when he became seriously ill. Later that month the Shah, who had taken refuge in Egypt, died. But Iran said that the fate of the hostages would still be decided by the new parliament.

Two days before the anniversary of the embassy takeover, the Iranian parliament set four conditions for the hostages' release. The conditions were that the United States would 1) promise not to intervene in Iran's affairs; 2) return the Iranian assets that had been held in U.S. banks since the seizure of the embassy; 3) drop the legal claims of Americans whose property had been taken over by Iran's new government; and 4) return the Shah's personal wealth to Iran.

U.S. officials said that the first two demands could be met easily, but that legal questions and the problem of identifying the Shah's wealth would make the other conditions difficult. The two governments exchanged a series of messages, attempting to clarify their positions. Meanwhile, the hostages spent their second Christmas in captivity.

▶ IRAN AND IRAQ

War broke out between Iran and Iraq in 1980. The immediate cause was a complex dispute over the Shatt al Arab, a waterway between the countries that leads into the Persian Gulf. Tankers used this waterway to carry oil from both countries to the rest of the world. Iraq had taken control of the Shatt al Arab in 1937, but during the Shah's rule the border had been moved to the middle of the waterway.

After the Shah was overthrown, Iraq reasserted its claim, and there were border clashes. In September, 1980, Iraqi planes bombed airfields, cities, and oil installations in Iran, and Iraqi troops crossed into Iran. Iranian bombers struck back at targets in Iraq.

Iraqi officials said that their goals included control of Iran's oil-rich province of Khuzistan. Iraq seemed to be making a bid to become the most powerful country in the Persian Gulf region. But Iran's army was stronger than Iraq had expected, and fighting continued in the province through December. Meanwhile, oil exports from both countries dropped dramatically.

Although a border dispute had sparked the war, hostility between the two countries went back to the 7th century. At that time, Arab rule spread to Mesopotamia (the area between the Tigris and Euphrates rivers that is now Iraq), and Persia (now Iran) blocked further Arab expansion. At that time, too, the religion of Islam split into two branches, Sunni and Shi'ite. Today most of Iran's people—and its leaders—are Shi'ites. But while most Iraqis are also Shi'ites, Iraq is ruled by Sunnis. Iraq's rulers were uneasy about the Shi'ite unrest that had toppled the Shah—the more so because there was similar unrest in their own country and elsewhere in the Middle East.

The war pointed up a split in the Arab world. Jordan, Saudi Arabia, and some other countries ruled by Sunnis supported Iraq as a fellow Arab state and because they, too, were concerned about Shi'ite unrest. Supporting Iran were Libya and Syria, who were among the most hostile opponents of Israel. They seemed concerned that the more moderate Arab countries, especially Jordan, might join in the West Bank negotiations. In late November, Syria moved troops up to its border with Jordan.

The United States and the Soviet Union said they would remain neutral in the war between Iraq and Iran. But with vital oil at stake, concern remained that the war would spread to involve other countries in the Middle East and beyond.

An Iranian oil refinery burns after being struck by Iraqi bombers.

ZIMBABWE—A NEW NATION

Shouts of jubilation rang out as the red, green, gold, and black flag of Zimbabwe was raised for the first time in Salisbury, the new nation's capital, on April 18, 1980. The flag signaled independence—in the words of Robert Mugabe, Zimbabwe's newly elected leader, the "final, priceless reward" for years of suffering and racial discrimination.

Zimbabwe, which was long the British colony of Southern Rhodesia, had been torn by civil war for many years. The roots of the trouble went back to 1965. In that year the colony's white government, representing about 4 percent of the population, declared independence. But Britain and other nations refused to recognize an independent Rhodesia unless the black majority were properly represented. And black groups within the country began fighting a guerrilla war.

In 1979, after years of fighting and pressure from other countries, the whites allowed an elected black government to take office. It was led by Bishop Abel T. Muzo-rewa. But the guerrilla groups said that Muzorewa's government did not truly represent the blacks, and fighting continued. Late in the year, an agreement was hammered out between British officials, representatives of Muzorewa's government, and guerrilla leaders. The plan called for a cease-fire and a brief return to British colonial rule until new elections could be held.

The elections were held in February, 1980. Leading the three strongest parties were Muzorewa and two guerrilla leaders, Robert Mugabe and Joshua Nkomo. Nkomo drew most of his support from the southwest, where many members of his tribe lived. Mugabe and Muzorewa were stronger among the people who lived in the more populated eastern region. The campaign was marked by charges that voters were being intimidated, and there were incidents of violence. In the election, Mugabe's party won a majority of the seats in the new parliament, and he became prime minister.

In the February elections, some voters cast their ballots at floating polling stations.

As a result of the elections, Robert Mugabe (*second from right*) became prime minister of Zimbabwe.

At independence, the new government took office in an atmosphere of hope. The economy was strong, and Mugabe assured the whites that their property would not be seized. Although Mugabe described himself as a Marxist, it did not appear that he would set up a rigid socialist (government-run) system. He called for unity, saying, "The wrongs of the past must now stand forgiven and forgotten." Change, he indicated, would be gradual.

The long conflict had left deep scars, however, and it soon became apparent that the transition to majority rule would not be completely smooth. An estimated 850,000 people, mostly rural blacks, had lost their homes during the course of the civil war, and 20,000 had been killed. Many fields had not been planted. The new government said it would need $4,500,000,000 (billion) in aid to get the country back on its feet. It appealed to foreign countries, including the United States. But it got far less aid than it asked for.

There were also problems between blacks and whites and between various black groups. Mugabe was pressured by radical members of his party to bring about change more quickly. And whites began to leave in increasing numbers, feeling that even gradual change would mean they would have a poor future in the new country.

There were incidents of violence, too. The two main guerrilla factions, led by Mugabe and Nkomo, had been ordered to turn in their weapons and be integrated into a national army. But few did, and armed bands roamed the countryside, terrorizing both blacks and whites. In one incident, a white farmer was killed, and a member of Mugabe's cabinet was arrested and charged with taking part in the crime. And because the guerrillas represented different tribal groups, there were clashes even between guerrillas. Heavy fighting broke out in November, after the guerrillas had been moved into large camps near cities.

People in other countries as well as in Zimbabwe watched anxiously to see how the new government would meet these challenges. They hoped that, after so many years of war, the new nation would at last find peace.

CANADA—A YEAR OF DEBATE

During 1980 there were three major developments in Canadian politics. In a national election on February 18, the Liberal Party, led by Pierre Elliott Trudeau, defeated the Progressive Conservative (PC) Party, led by Joe Clark. On May 20, the government of Quebec asked its people in a referendum whether the province should become an independent state. And later in the year, proposals for important changes in Canada's constitutional system caused fierce national debate.

▶ THE LIBERALS RETURN TO POWER

The PC Party had been in power only seven months, since the election of May, 1979. In that election, the PC's had won 136 of the 282 seats in the House of Commons. But because they did not hold 50 percent of the seats, they depended on the support of the Social Credit Party, which held six seats, in any close votes. In December, the Social Credit Party withdrew its support during a debate on the budget, and the PC's were outvoted. The PC government was defeated, and Clark was forced to call a new election.

The election of February 18 was fought mainly between the Liberals and the PC's. The New Democratic Party (NDP) was an important third party in Ontario and the western provinces. The efforts of the Social Credit Party were mostly confined to Quebec. Trudeau had announced the previous fall that he would retire from politics. This left the Liberals without a strong leader for the 1980 election. But Trudeau was persuaded to reverse his decision, and he once more led the Liberal Party in a national election campaign.

The Liberals waged a low-key campaign,

In a national election on February 18, the Liberal Party defeated the Progressive Conservative Party. Pierre Elliott Trudeau thus once again became the prime minister of Canada.

In Montreal, supporters of a "no" vote in the Quebec referendum carry Canadian and Quebec flags.

saying little about their own program. Instead, they concentrated their attack on the PC's economic and fiscal policies, as set forth in their December budget. That budget had been highly unpopular with the voters— it had proposed some drastic increases in taxes and a sharp rise in Canadian oil prices. (Government controls were keeping oil prices well below the world level.) The Liberal campaign strategy was successful. The party won 146 seats, to 103 for the PC's and 32 for the NDP. The Social Credit Party failed to win a single seat.

Although the Liberals had won an overall majority in Parliament, there was one major concern for the party. Liberal strength was heavily based in the east. West of Ontario, the Liberal Party had won only two seats of a possible 77. Because of this, some critics argued that the Liberals did not have national support.

▶ THE QUEBEC REFERENDUM

The referendum held in the province of Quebec on May 20 arose from a commitment made by the Parti Québecois (PQ) when it came to power in the province in 1976. The PQ had promised that sometime during its term of office, the people of Quebec would be asked if they wanted the government of Quebec to negotiate a new relationship with the rest of Canada. The details of the government's proposal were outlined in an official "white paper" issued in November, 1979. The white paper called for a new partnership between Canada and Quebec. This partnership was called sovereignty-association. In it Quebec would become a sovereign state, a separate country with control over all its own affairs. Quebec would make its own laws, levy its own taxes, and establish relations abroad. But it would continue to be associated with Canada in some form of economic and monetary union. The referendum question asked the voters whether they would allow the provincial government to negotiate sovereignty-association with the federal government.

According to the rules governing the referendum, all political parties or organizations participating in the campaign had to belong to one of two committees: a committee that favored a "yes" vote to the question or a committee that favored a "no" vote. The "yes" committee consisted mainly of the Parti Québecois and a few Quebec nationalist organizations. René Lévesque, the PQ leader, was the president of the committee. The "no" committee was headed by Claude Ryan, leader of the provincial Liberal Party. This group included not only the provincial Liberals but also the Quebec wing of the federal Liberal Party and a number of minor parties, such as the Union Nationale and Social Credit parties and a small group of federal PC's.

During the referendum campaign, the supporters of sovereignty-association emphasized what they saw as the disadvantages to the province of the existing federal system. They stressed the economic and cultural benefits they felt Quebec would enjoy as a sovereign, independent country in an economic union with Canada.

Those opposed emphasized that rejection of sovereignty-association did not mean support for the existing constitutional system. Instead, they favored a "revised federalism." This new federalism, as outlined by Ryan, proposed a number of constitutional reforms. It was hoped that these would eliminate most of Quebec's grievances against the federal system.

The arguments of Ryan and his followers carried the day. Lévesque's proposal for sovereignty-association was defeated by a popular vote of approximately 60 percent to 40 percent, with 88 percent of the eligible voters casting their ballots.

▶ A NEW CANADIAN CONSTITUTION?

A new constitution for Canada has been the subject of discussions between the federal and provincial governments for a number of years. In 1980, the Quebec referendum sharply intensified this constitutional debate. Both the federal and the provincial Liberal parties pledged to work toward a revised federal system after the referendum.

The main problem with Canada's constitutional system is that most of its basic principles are to be found in the British North America (BNA) Act, passed by the British Parliament in 1867. The act not only is out of date but, in certain areas, such as those that touch on provincial rights, it can only be amended by the British legislature.

In such cases, the procedure for amending the BNA Act has been for both houses of the Canadian Parliament to pass a resolution requesting Britain to make the desired amendment. This presents no practical problem because Britain has traditionally complied with any Canadian request. It does, however, put Canada in the embarrassing position of having to ask the parliament of another country to amend its most basic constitutional document. As a result, there is widespread interest in "patriating the constitution" and making it possible to amend the act wholly within Canada. The debate on a new amending procedure has been closely linked to other proposals for changes in the BNA Act. Minority language rights, control over natural resources, the role and composition of the Senate and Supreme Court, native rights, and other such matters have all been debated.

Shortly after the Quebec referendum, Prime Minister Trudeau met with the premiers of all ten provinces. They set up a constitutional committee of key ministers from both the federal and the provincial governments. These ministers studied the various areas where constitutional revisions were needed. The committee spent several months drawing up a report, which was submitted to a summit meeting of federal and provincial heads of government in Ottawa in early September.

From the beginning of the summit meeting, it was apparent that agreement on most subjects would be difficult. Although there were differences between provinces, the really important split was between the federal government and the provinces. On the federal side, Trudeau's main concerns were patriation of the constitution, a new all-Canadian amending formula, and enshrining in a new constitution a charter of rights. The main concerns of the provinces, on the other hand, were to keep the powers they had from being taken over by the federal government and, in some fields, to expand their legislative and financial powers at the expense of the central government.

The demands of the provinces varied depending on the particular interests and priorities of each. Quebec, the only province with a French-speaking majority, was opposed to any restrictions on its control over educational and language rights. It also wanted

In the discussions on a new Canadian constitution, there was a major split between the federal government and the provinces. Alberta, a major oil producer *(above)*, wanted complete control over its resources.

increased powers over such matters as communications and immigration. The western provinces and Newfoundland were mostly concerned with exclusive control over natural resources, such as oil and gas. Most provinces wanted more control over their trade with the other provinces. They all wanted more powers of taxation. While all provinces were agreed in principle to patriation of the constitution and a new amending procedure, they felt these issues should be settled after all other differences with the central government had been ironed out.

The summit meeting ended without agreement. Trudeau decided to carry out an action he had suggested earlier—to patriate the constitution unilaterally (that is, without the consent of the provinces). He introduced a resolution into the Canadian Parliament, asking the British Parliament to pass legislation that would transfer to Canada the full power of amendment of the Canadian constitution. The legislation would also provide for a number of other changes, including a "charter of rights and freedoms." The charter's most important feature would be a guarantee of educational and language rights for French- and English-speaking minorities.

The Liberal government's resolution met with strong opposition from the federal PC Party. The NDP initially opposed the resolution but supported it after certain concessions had been made. The strongest objections, however, came from the provincial governments. Six provinces announced that they would challenge the constitutionality of Trudeau's action before the Supreme Court of Canada. Some provinces and political groups planned to send protests directly to the British Parliament.

Trudeau had taken decisive action. But debate on the resolution continued, and there were still uncertainties in the situation. Would the pressures on Trudeau force him to make further concessions to the opposition? Would the British Parliament agree to put through this controversial legislation as automatically as it had other proposals in the past?

Whatever happens to the legislation, it is well to remember that its passage would be only a first step in a long process—the creation of a new and comprehensive constitution for Canada.

HERBERT F. QUINN
Concordia University

FLIGHT FROM CUBA

On the night of April 22, 1980, the U.S. fishing boat *El Mer* chugged across the dark waters of the Straits of Florida toward the harbor at Key West. Crowded on board were 33 Cuban refugees, their faces tense from the rough sea voyage and their eyes straining toward the shore. As the *El Mer* eased up to the wharf at Key West, cheers broke out from an anxious group of people that had gathered there.

The refugees on the *El Mer* were among more than 125,000 Cubans who reached the shores of the United States in 1980. Most arrived during April and May, when Cuba's Communist government, headed by Fidel Castro, suddenly lifted emigration restrictions. And many of the people who met the refugees were friends and relatives—some of the 800,000 Cubans who had fled the island since Castro came to power in 1959.

The 1980 emigration began with a small incident. Early in April, about 25 Cubans forced their way into the Peruvian embassy in Havana, Cuba's capital, seeking political asylum. A Cuban soldier guarding the embassy was killed in the incident. Cuba, in protest, withdrew the rest of its guards. Within days, 10,000 people had crowded into the embassy grounds in the hope of leaving the country. And the Cuban Government announced that they would be granted exit permits if they could find new homes.

Several countries—including Costa Rica, Peru, Spain, and the United States—offered to admit the Cubans. An airlift to Costa Rica was begun, but Cuba halted it in mid-April. In response, hundreds of small boats set out from U.S. ports, bound for Cuba to pick up the refugees. And soon, Cuba was granting exit permits to thousands of other people who also wanted to leave.

By May, small boats with Cuban-American crews were bringing Cubans to southern Florida at the rate of 3,000 a day. The trip was dangerous, and Florida was finding it difficult to find food and shelter for all the newcomers. Adding to the problem were refugees from other parts of the Caribbean, particularly Haiti. A steady flow of Haitians had been emigrating to the United States for several years, and by mid-1980 some 30,000 lived throughout the country.

In May, U.S. President Jimmy Carter ordered a halt to the dangerous and disorganized small-boat rescue missions. The Coast Guard refused to allow boats to leave for

American boats filled with Cuban refugees wait for permission to leave Cuba. By the end of the year, more than 125,000 Cubans had reached the shores of southern Florida.

Thousands of Haitians were also emigrating to the United States, and Florida was finding it difficult to house and feed all the refugees.

Cuba, and it seized those that returned with refugees. But many boats evaded the Coast Guard patrols. And refugees continued to trickle into southern Florida until the Cuban Government cut off the exodus at the end of September.

Why did so many people want to leave Cuba? Lack of freedom was one reason the refugees gave. Economic factors were also important—housing was crowded, food was scarce, and clothing and other necessities were expensive. Many of those who left saw little chance for a better life on their island.

Once in the United States, the refugees were screened to see if they could be admitted under the Refugee Act of 1980. This act, which had been signed into law in March, eased entry restrictions for people who might be persecuted if they were sent back to their home countries. Most of the Cubans qualified and were quickly relocated to new homes.

But some of the refugees faced long delays at processing centers in Arkansas, Florida, Pennsylvania, and Wisconsin. They were for the most part single men. Some spoke no English or had no friends or relatives in the United States. Others had been jailed for serious crimes or had been placed in institu-

tions for psychological problems while in Cuba. Cuba refused to take these people back. And as the delays in resettlement continued, there were riots at several of the refugee centers. Meanwhile, outside the centers, some Cubans were disappointed with life in the United States. A few even hijacked airplanes to return to their home island.

Haitians also faced some difficulties. Because Haiti's government is not Communist, the Haitians at first were not considered qualified for admission under the Refugee Act. But the Haitians argued that their government was a repressive dictatorship and that their reasons for leaving were no different from those of the Cubans. They were finally allowed to stay under a six-month "parole."

The number of refugees from Cuba and Haiti quickly exceeded the limits set by the U.S. Government at the start of the year. The last big wave of emigration from Cuba had started in 1965 and ended in 1973. It had brought more than 250,000 Cubans to the United States. In 1980, half that number arrived in just a few months. Many of the problems created by this new wave of emigration were unsolved at the end of the year.

The purpose of the registration was to compile names. An actual draft would have to be approved by Congress. And there has been no military draft in the United States since 1973. In that year, U.S. military involvement in the Vietnam War ended. The law that had ordered the draft was allowed to expire, and service in the United States military forces became completely voluntary. The Selective Service System, the federal agency that had overseen the draft, continued to register young men until 1975, when registration also stopped.

But in January, 1980, President Jimmy Carter proposed that registration begin again. Soviet troops had entered Afghanistan and it was in response to this Soviet move that President Carter called for the sign-up. Registration, he said, would show the Soviets that the United States was ready and willing to resist military aggression.

In July, when President Carter signed the proclamation requiring young men to register, he said, "We are deeply concerned about the unwarranted and vicious invasion of Afghanistan by the Soviet Union." He also said, "I would like to emphasize that the registration act is not a draft. I am not in favor of a peacetime draft."

▶ THE CONTROVERSY

The great majority of the 4,000,000 eligible young men did register. But a number of them questioned the registration. Many people wondered if an actual draft would soon follow. The controversy swirled around some basic questions about drafting people in times of peace.

• Do the armed forces need a draft now?

President Carter said that he was opposed to a peacetime draft. But many who support a draft say that the U.S. armed forces have become weaker, and that a draft would strengthen them. They say that a strong U.S. military might prevent other nations from starting war. A draft, they believe, would send a message to the world that the United States means business.

Opponents of a draft say that the United States could not fight a long land war in such current "hot spots" as the Persian Gulf. They say that wars of the future will be

Many people were against the draft registration because they were afraid an actual draft might follow.

A PEACETIME DRAFT?

On July 21, 1980, American men born in 1960 began registering for a possible military draft. A week later, those born in 1961 followed suit. No one was called to serve in the armed forces. No one was even given a physical fitness exam. To sign up, a 19- or 20-year-old had only to go to a post office and give his name, address, phone number, Social Security number, and date of birth. But this seemingly simple act was the subject of a large controversy.

fought more with technology—missiles, for example—than with troops. Thus there is no need, the opponents say, for drafting thousands of people.

• Can the United States rely completely on the volunteer army?

It hasn't worked, say those in favor of a draft. Not enough people are volunteering. And a large number of the volunteers are from low-income groups. The pro-draft people say that the draft will bring more middle-class people into the service. They say a "citizen army," built on the draft and representing all groups, is necessary for a democracy's well-being.

Opponents of the draft say that people who are forced to serve do not make good soldiers in peacetime. And they say that the draft is unfair unless everybody serves (except for the obviously unfit). If the armed forces cannot draft everyone who is eligible —rather than selecting a few—then no one should be drafted, opponents say.

• Should both women and men be drafted into the armed forces?

Three days before registration was to begin, a federal court in Philadelphia ruled that the registration act was unconstitutional because it excluded women. The next day, a Supreme Court justice stayed that ruling, allowing registration to proceed as planned. But the question of constitutionality was not decided. It was to be brought before the Supreme Court in 1981.

▶ UNANSWERED QUESTIONS

It was not known how many young men did not register. Pro-draft people said that only 2 percent did not, but some antidraft people put the figure at 20 percent. The truth probably lay somewhere in between.

The law states that a young man who does not register could face a fine of up to $10,000 or a jail sentence of up to five years, or both. But some people thought it unlikely that those who did not register would be prosecuted before the question of constitutionality had been decided.

While campaigning for the presidency, Ronald Reagan said that he was against the draft. The next registration, for men born in 1962, was scheduled for January, 1981. Whether the registration would continue— and whether the United States would once again have a draft—were questions facing the new president.

Despite the protests, the draft registration began on July 21.

CHANGES IN EASTERN EUROPE

Important events took place in two Eastern European countries during 1980. In Yugoslavia, Marshal Tito, the leader of the country for nearly 35 years, died in May. His death seemed to signal the end of an era for the country. And in Poland, hundreds of thousands of workers walked off their jobs in August. By the time the strikes had ended, the workers had brought about a historic change in their country's Communist system.

▶ END OF AN ERA IN YUGOSLAVIA

During World War II, Tito (who was born Josip Broz) led a strong resistance movement against the German forces that occupied Yugoslavia. After the war, he brought the Communist Party to power, and he remained its head until his death. But Tito may be best remembered for his part in the first major split among Communist countries.

After the war, Tito turned to the Soviet Union for economic help. But he refused to let Yugoslavia become a Soviet satellite and developed a Communist system along his own lines. As in most Communist countries, the government owned industry, but Tito allowed some free enterprise. Yugoslavs also

Marshal Tito led Yugoslavia for nearly 35 years.

had more personal freedom than was common in Communist countries. And Yugoslavia became a leader of the nonaligned nations—those that try to remain independent of the major world powers.

Tito's strong leadership succeeded in holding together the patchwork of ethnic groups and languages that make up Yugoslavia. There were fears that after his death conflicts might break out. To prevent this, power passed to a Communist Party Presidium and a presidential council. The country's ruling positions were to rotate among the members, who represented Yugoslavia's republics and provinces.

In 1980, it was too soon to tell what Yugoslavia would be like under its new collective leadership. Some people wondered if personal freedom would be curtailed. There was also concern that the Soviet Union might try to assert more control over Yugoslavia. The new leaders seemed likely to continue Tito's policy of independence. But without his strong leadership, the country seemed certain to take a less prominent role among the nonaligned nations.

▶ THE LABOR STRIKES IN POLAND

The Polish labor strikes were remarkable because in Communist countries, strikes are illegal. A Communist government claims to be the true representative of the workers. It controls the economy and runs the factories, mines, and businesses, supposedly for the workers' benefit. So, the reasoning goes, a strike would be against the interests of the workers themselves.

The Polish Government had kept down the prices of basic items such as meat by paying part of the cost itself. But in 1980, Poland was deeply in debt, and the government could no longer afford these subsidies. Some factories stood idle for want of parts, and people lined up for short supplies of everything from bread to newspapers. When the government increased the price of meat in July, some workers in Warsaw walked off their jobs. The unrest spread and, by mid-August, reached the industrial region along the Baltic coast.

In Poland, hundreds of thousands of workers went on strike and won new rights.

In Gdansk, on the Baltic, workers took over the huge Lenin Shipyard. These strikers captured the world's attention because their demands went beyond wages—they seemed aimed at the Communist system itself. The workers demanded the right to form independent labor unions and the right to strike. They also demanded an end to censorship and political repression.

For ten tense days, the government refused to meet with the Gdansk workers. Adding to the strain was the question of how the Soviet Union would react. In the past, when Communism seemed threatened in one of its satellite states, the Soviet Union had sent in troops. This happened in Hungary in 1956 and in Czechoslovakia in 1968.

Then, on August 24, the Polish premier and several other top officials were dismissed. Talks with the strikers began. Meanwhile, miners in Silesia joined the strike, echoing the Gdansk demands. They brought the total number of strikers to over 500,000.

The government signed agreements with the Gdansk workers on August 31 and with the miners a few days later. The workers won the right to independent unions, the right to strike, and "respect of the freedom of expression," along with economic benefits. In exchange, they agreed not to challenge the rule of the Communist Party.

In the wake of the Gdansk strike, the head of Poland's Communist Party, Edward Gierek, resigned. And while small strikes continued to break out, the benefits of the Gdansk agreement were extended to workers in other parts of the country. In September, many local workers' groups joined together to form a federation of independent labor unions called Solidarity.

But it was not clear if the workers would benefit by their new charters. In October, Solidarity called an hour-long, nationwide strike. The workers were protesting what they said was the government's failure to live up to the agreements that had ended the summer strikes. Later in the fall, a dispute arose over Solidarity's official charter. But the Polish Government averted another strike by dropping its demand that the charter grant a "leading role" to the Communist Party.

Unrest had brought promises of reform in Poland before. In 1956 and 1970, as in 1980, it had led to changes in leadership. But for the most part, the promised benefits had failed to materialize. And in 1980, Poland's economic troubles and its close links with the Soviet system seemed to speak against a quick solution. The Gdansk charter marked the first time a Communist Party had recognized a workers' organization separate from itself. But by mid-December, Soviet troops were poised at Poland's border.

MEXICO'S OIL BOOM

What is the number-one oil country in the world? Saudi Arabia, you might answer. Speaking today, you would be right. Saudi Arabia has about 150,000,000,000 (billion) barrels of proven reserves—enough to last 30 years at the current rate of production. (Proven reserves are deposits of petroleum that drilling tests have shown are definitely in the ground.)

But there could be a new number-one country in a few years. In September, 1980, Mexico announced that it had found 60,000,000,000 (billion) barrels of proven oil reserves. These proven reserves rank Mexico fifth among the oil-rich countries. But Mexico has another 200,000,000,000 (billion) barrels of possible reserves. If the possible reserves become proven reserves, Mexico could very well become the richest oil country in the world.

▶ OIL AND MEXICO'S FUTURE

Mexico has been producing oil since the late 1800's. But it has been just in the past five years that Mexico has gone from oil rags to riches.

When José López Portillo became president in 1976, Mexico was suffering from severe economic and social problems. To solve some of these problems, López Portillo decided that Mexico should double its efforts to find new oil fields. He called on Pemex, the government-owned oil company, to drill intensively in the states of Tabasco and Chiapas, where oil fields had already been found. Pemex searched and found vast new oil deposits, in those areas and elsewhere. Said the head of Pemex, ''We're sitting on a sea of oil.'' And Mexico found itself in an important position in the world oil market.

But will Mexico's oil improve the quality of life of its people? Many of the people do not have enough to eat, and they live in poor rural areas or city slums. About 20 percent of the workers have no jobs, and millions of others do not have full-time employment. Mexico's population is increasing by more than 2,000,000 people a year—creating an even more overwhelming need for jobs. Illiteracy is widespread throughout the country, and the population is growing faster than schools can be built and teachers trained.

Mexico's new oil riches can help solve some of these problems. But money alone is not the answer. The government is afraid that if it pours too much money too quickly into the economy, inflation, already a problem, could rise still further. And while the oil industry has greatly expanded, it has not created enough jobs to relieve the unemployment problem. Once the wells are dug and are producing, most of the operations are automatic.

President López Portillo has warned against developing the new-found oil too quickly and has stressed conservation. "This opportunity will come only once in history," he has said. "We have to transform a nonrenewable resource into a permanent source of wealth." Thus, the amount of oil pumped per day is being limited, to make the wealth last. And oil earnings are being used to expand old industries and create new ones. In these ways, Mexico is trying to build a more secure future for its people.

Mexico is trying hard to make its new-found oil wealth last in an effort to improve the quality of life of its people.

▶ THE OIL-THIRSTY NATIONS

In early 1980, the United States was getting about three fourths of Mexico's crude oil exports, and Spain and Israel were getting most of the rest. Since then, several other oil-thirsty countries have been courting Mexico. Canada and Japan obtained agreements for oil purchases. But they did not succeed in contracting for as much oil as they wanted. Both were told that if they wanted more oil, they would have to increase their investments in Mexico's development.

While Mexico would like to have many customers for its new oil, the U.S. market is probably the most natural one. But a long-standing history of strained relations between the two countries has made Mexico reluctant to sell more oil to the United States.

The problems go back to the Mexican War of the 1840's, when Mexico lost vast territory to the United States. In addition, Mexicans feel that the United States exploited Mexican oil in the past. Until 1938—when oil production was taken over by the Mexican government—U.S. companies controlled most of Mexico's oil fields.

In recent years, relations between the two countries have been strained over several issues. One is the price to be paid for oil. Tension has also been caused by the flow of illegal aliens across the U.S. border and by smuggling—of drugs into the United States and of American goods into Mexico. And Mexicans have felt that the United States has not shown a great enough interest in their problems.

But attitudes are shifting, and relations between the two countries are improving. The United States has agreed to pay prevailing world prices for Mexico's oil. And American firms have been investing more heavily in Mexican industry. In return, Mexico is cooperating in efforts to stop the flow of drugs across the border. Hopefully, if the bonds of friendship grow stronger, Mexico will help the United States solve some of its energy problems. But it is Mexico's decision. As President Jimmy Carter said, "The Mexican oil belongs to the Mexican people, to be sold as Mexico sees fit."

JOHN TEDFORD
Consultant, Editorial Cumbre, Mexico

NEWSMAKERS

"You can never forget about it, not for one moment," **Queen Beatrix** of the Netherlands has said of her position. Beatrix came to the throne in April, 1980, when her mother, Queen Juliana, abdicated. Born in 1938, Beatrix spent her early years in exile in Britain and Canada during World War II. After the war, in Amsterdam, her childhood was much like anyone's—she attended grammar school and rode her bicycle on city streets. Beatrix earned a doctorate in law at the University of Leyden and, in 1966, married Claus von Amsberg, a German. The Dutch throne has been held by women since 1890. But this seems sure to change—Queen Beatrix and Prince Claus have three sons.

George Herbert Walker Bush was elected vice-president of the United States in 1980, after a long career in business and government. Born in Milton, Massachusetts, on June 12, 1924, Bush served as a Navy carrier pilot during World War II. In 1945 he married Barbara Pierce and entered Yale University, where he earned a degree in economics. After Yale, the family left the Northeast for Texas. There, Bush became a partner in several oilfield equipment companies and, in 1946, was elected to the U.S. House of Representatives. He later served in turn as U.S. delegate to the United Nations, Republican Party national chairman, head of the U.S. liaison office in Peking, and director of the Central Intelligence Agency. In 1980 he sought the Republican presidential nomination but fell short of gaining the support won by Ronald Reagan, who chose Bush as his running mate.

Abolhassan Bani-Sadr (center, with glasses) became the first president of Iran's Islamic republic in a landslide victory in January. Born in 1933 in Hamadan, in western Iran, he is a longtime supporter of Iran's religious leader, Ayatollah Ruhollah Khomeini. Bani-Sadr joined the anti-Shah movement while a student at Teheran University, was arrested several times, and went into exile in Paris in 1965. After the Shah was deposed in 1979, he became Iran's foreign minister. He was removed from office when he spoke out against the militants who seized the U.S. embassy later that year. As president, Bani-Sadr has opposed the more militant supporters of Khomeini, who are strongly represented in Iran's parliament.

Seventy-five-year-old **Nikolai A. Tikhonov** (TEE-khun-uhf) became premier of the Soviet Union in October, 1980, replacing Aleksei Kosygin. Until then, Tikhonov had been little known, even in his own country. He was born in Kharkov, in the Ukraine, and worked his way up to become a plant manager in heavy industry. As an industrial manager in the 1940's, he met Leonid Brezhnev, now head of the Communist Party, and his career advanced as Brezhnev came to power. Tikhonov became First Deputy Premier in 1976 and gradually took over many duties from Kosygin, who suffered from heart trouble. His speeches and writings indicate that he favors easing tension abroad and, at home, boosting industrial production through hard work.

65

Owls are mysterious animals that few people ever see. Yet they are found almost everywhere in the world. If you're lucky, you may just see a group, like these baby screech owls, perched on the limb of a tree.

ANIMALS

WHOOOOO'S THAT HUNTER?

Darkness blankets the land. All is quiet. A hunter sits on a tree branch—watching, listening, waiting.

A mouse scurries along the ground. The patter of its tiny feet is heard by the hunter. In less than a second the hunter's eyes focus on the mouse. It swoops down, grabs the mouse with its sharp claws, and returns to the branch. It swallows the mouse whole.

The hunter is a barn owl. Within minutes of swallowing the mouse it is on the lookout for another victim. If the owl is fortunate, it will feed again and again during the night. It's a fact that one barn owl actually caught sixteen mice, three gophers, a rat, and a squirrel in only 25 minutes. He did not, however, eat all these animals himself. He shared them with his mate and their nestful of hungry youngsters.

The largest owl is the eagle owl (*above*), and the smallest is the least pygmy owl (*below*).

▶ MANY KINDS IN MANY PLACES

There are more than 130 kinds of owls. The smallest are the least pygmy owl of Central and South America and the elf owl of southern North America. They are about 5 inches (12 centimeters) long—about the size of a sparrow. The largest owl is the eagle owl that lives in Europe, Asia, and northern Africa. It may reach 30 inches (75 centimeters) in length.

Owls are found everywhere on the earth except Antarctica. They live in almost every kind of climate and habitat. Snowy owls prowl the snow-covered fields and tundra of the Arctic. Hawk owls, which have long tails and fly like falcons, inhabit woodlands. Elf

owls live in deserts. The Madagascar grass owl lives in tropical rain forests. Screech owls live in towns and cities.

▶ DISTINCTIVE FEATURES

Owls are easily recognized, for they share certain distinctive features. They have large heads and no obvious necks. Their eyes are large and are surrounded by feathers that radiate outward. The eyes are very sensitive, and owls can see in the dimmest light. In fact, some can see as well by starlight as people can see by moonlight.

An owl cannot move its eyes from side to side. If it wants to change its field of vision, it turns its head. Some types of owls can turn their heads more than 270 degrees to one side or the other. An owl can even turn its head upside down!

Owls are the only birds that blink like humans, by dropping their upper eyelids. (Other birds raise the lower lids.) When owls

Owls are found almost everywhere. Snowy owls live in the snow-covered Arctic . . .

sleep, however, they close their eyes by raising the lower lids.

The plumage of owls is very soft. Owls can puff up their feathers, and this helps keep them warm. It also makes them look bigger, which helps frighten enemies. Owls are never brightly colored. The plumage is a pattern of browns, grays, black, and white. This helps the owl blend into its surroundings so that it is nearly invisible to both prey and enemies. A snowy owl, which lives in snowy areas, is white or white and black. Owls that live in tropical rain forests are dark brown. Desert owls are generally pale and yellowish.

The owl's large, sensitive ears are hidden by feathers on the sides of its head. Some types of owls, like the long-eared owl and the great horned owl, have feathery ''ears'' or ''horns'' on their heads. These are not really ears or horns but simply tufts of long feathers that are a kind of decoration.

. . . screech owls may live in towns and cities . . .

. . . and hawk owls inhabit woodlands.

71

The long-eared owl has feathery "ears" on the top of its head. They are not really ears but a kind of decoration.

An owl has short, powerful feet and very sharp claws. These are efficient weapons, both for catching prey and for fighting enemies. The outer toe can be moved forward, outward, and even backward. This makes it easier for the owl to grasp and hold a victim.

▶ A DIET OF MEAT

Owls are meat eaters. They do not eat plant matter. In general, rodents form the basis of their diets. But owls also eat other small mammals, reptiles, amphibians, insects, and earthworms. The oriental hawk owl is known to eat crabs. Some eagle owls dine almost exclusively on frogs. In Africa and Asia, there are species of owls that are fishers. They use their very sharp claws to scoop fish out of the water.

The larger the owl, the more it must eat and the larger the animals on which it can prey. The great hawk owls of Australia can tackle prey as large as rabbits and possums. Snowy owls eat primarily small rodents called lemmings. But they also eat larger animals such as hares and muskrats. They even catch ducks and other birds.

Most owls swallow small prey whole. Digestive juices secreted by the stomach break down the soft parts of the food. The parts that cannot be digested are regurgitated in neat little packages that are called pellets, or boluses.

By studying the contents of pellets, it is possible to learn about the diets of owls. Many interesting and important discoveries have been made in this manner. For example, giant barn owls once lived in the Caribbean. Their fossilized pellets are the only clue we have to the diet of these extinct birds.

Thanks to pellet analysis, the little owl of Europe was proved innocent of very serious charges. In the early 1900's, English farmers and gamekeepers accused the little owl of being a terrible poultry thief and a killer of game and song birds. Many English people wanted to kill the little owl, even though people in other parts of Europe were praising these birds for their ability to keep down rodent and insect populations.

An inquiry was made by a British scientific

A CLOSER LOOK AT OWL PELLETS

On the average, an owl forms two pellets each day. These can be found near the place where the owl roosts. If the owl changes its roosting spot often, its pellets will be scattered over a wide area. But if the owl always roosts in the same place, as barn owls do, then a pile of pellets will accumulate in one place.

If you find some owl pellets, try to identify the contents. First soak the pellets in warm water. When they are soft, use needles and tweezers to gently pull apart each pellet. Look at the contents of what you see.

Some of the things you will probably find are skulls, beaks, teeth, jaws, bones, fur, feathers, insect exoskeletons, and the tiny bristles from earthworm bodies. Mammal guidebooks are useful in identifying teeth. Bird guidebooks can be used to identify beaks and feathers from the pellets.

Most owls do not build their own nests. The tiny elf owl, for example, nests in holes in the giant saguaro cactus—holes made by other birds.

group. Nearly 2,500 food pellets from little owls were analyzed. Only two pellets contained the remains of young game birds. Only seven contained remains of poultry chicks. Most of the pellets contained the remains of rodent and insect pests. One pellet, for example, contained the remains of 343 earwigs! Since the results of the study were published, few English people have complained about the little owl.

▶ NESTS AND SONGS

Most owls do not build nests. Some use nests abandoned by eagles, crows, and other birds. Some lay their eggs in holes in trees. The tiny elf owl, for example, nests in holes in the giant saguaro cactus—holes made by woodpeckers and flickers.

The burrowing owl nests underground, usually in a prairie-dog community. It uses tunnels built by ground squirrels, armadillos, and other animals.

A female owl lays from one to twelve eggs. She sits on the eggs until they hatch. Meanwhile, her mate shares the food he catches with her. Depending on the species, it takes 27 to 36 days for the eggs to hatch. The baby birds, which are called nestlings or owlets, are born with their eyes and ears closed. The eyes and ears open when the birds are about a week old.

Owls generally do not live very long in the wild. A study of barn owls in Switzerland indicated that some reached the age of 9 years. But the average age of the barn owls was 16 months. In captivity, owls live longer. One tawny owl lived for 22 years in captivity, and an eagle owl reached the grand age of 68.

Not all owls call "whoo, whoo." The screech owl, the most common owl in North America, whistles. The barking owl of Australia can sound like a growling dog. Other owl calls include snores, coughs, and even pretty chirps.

An owl's calls serve the same functions as do the calls of other birds. Some calls are territorial: "This is my land, keep out." Other calls are made to attract mates. There are also calls that indicate fear, anger, and hunger. Most of the calls are not very loud. But some calls will carry over surprisingly great distances. The deep booming call of a snowy owl can be heard up to 7 miles (11 kilometers) away.

If you go for a walk tonight, watch and listen. Perhaps you will see or hear an owl. If you see one, stand quietly and watch it hunt. If you hear one, try to imitate its call. If you are successful, the owl may fly toward you, perch overhead, and call back to you.

JENNY TESAR
Series Consultant
Wonders of Wildlife

HEARING-EAR DOGS

For many years, seeing-eye dogs have used their vision to help people who are blind. Now dogs are being trained for a new task—to lend their ears to people who are deaf. The hearing dogs are taught to recognize important sounds and to alert their human masters to them.

If you can hear, you probably don't think twice about all the important messages you get from sounds. The ring of an alarm clock tells you when to wake up. A knock on the door lets you know a visitor has arrived. The blare of a smoke detector can warn you of a dangerous fire. Imagine how difficult life is for people who can't hear these sounds. Now, hearing dogs can relay these messages to those who live in a silent world.

The Hearing Dog Program is run by the San Francisco Society for the Prevention of Cruelty to Animals (SPCA). It was started in 1978 by Ralph Dennard, and it is the first of its kind in the United States.

The dogs in the program are carefully selected from hundreds of homeless, abandoned dogs at the SPCA animal shelter. Dogs of any breed can learn the tasks, and most of the ones chosen are mixed breeds. The trainers look for dogs that seem intelligent, alert, healthy, and, of course, friendly to people. Dogs selected are between 6 and 18 months old. It costs about $2,500 to train and place a dog, but the dogs' new masters receive them free of charge.

The trainer first works with a dog for about an hour to see how well it hears and learns. If it passes this test, it is assigned to the hearing dog school. Only about one in every 200 dogs at the shelter qualifies.

The hearing dog course lasts about four months. First the dog receives obedience training and learns to respond to voice and hand signals. Most of the later training takes place in a center that is set up like a real home. In this home setting, the dog is taught to recognize important sounds—such as alarm clocks, doorbells, smoke alarms, and unusual noises that may mean a prowler is nearby. The dog also learns to give specific

John and Janet Henry were especially proud of their hearing-ear dog, Cookie. One night, when their baby, Elizabeth, had trouble breathing, Cookie quickly rushed to wake up the Henrys.

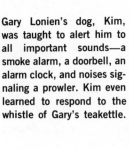
Gary Lonien's dog, Kim, was taught to alert him to all important sounds—a smoke alarm, a doorbell, an alarm clock, and noises signaling a prowler. Kim even learned to respond to the whistle of Gary's teakettle.

responses to alert a person to these sounds. For example, if the doorbell rings, the hearing dog is trained to brush up against its master to get attention. Then it runs back and forth to the door to show that someone is there. If the alarm clock rings, the dog wakes its master by jumping on the bed and licking the person's face. Each dog also learns to respond to particular sounds that its new master asks for, such as oven timers and teakettle whistles.

After the four-month intensive training period, the dog goes to its new home. One of the trainers works with the dog there for about a week, to make sure that dog and master are getting along well together. If the dog performs well in the home for three months, it earns an orange collar that is its "graduation diploma" and the mark of an official hearing dog.

John and Janet Henry of Pacifica, California, had a special request for their hearing dog, Cookie. They were new parents. Because they were both deaf, they wanted a dog that would let them know when their baby, Elizabeth, needed them. The SPCA trainers taught Cookie to do just that.

Cookie learned to alert her masters whenever Elizabeth cried to be fed or changed. But one night when the baby had a bad cold, Cookie became a hero. In the middle of the night, Elizabeth began coughing and had trouble breathing. Cookie realized that something was wrong and ran to wake the Henrys. When they reached Elizabeth, she was blue from lack of air. Because of Cookie's fast action, the Henrys were able to save Elizabeth's life.

It's likely that other hearing dogs will perform life-saving acts like Cookie's. But it's certain that all of them will provide help to their hearing-impaired masters in many little ways every day. Just by being around in case of an emergency, they'll give their masters a feeling of security. And the hearing dogs will provide company, play, and love—just as best-friend dogs should.

DAVID J. KULL
Senior Associate Editor
Medical Laboratory Observer magazine

In spring, many squirrels build airy leaf nests high in the treetops.

ANIMAL HOME-BUILDERS

At this moment, animals are building homes. These animal architects are hard at work digging, cutting, carrying, spinning, weaving, chiseling, cementing, gluing, and plastering. They build for the same reasons humans do: to provide shelter and protection for themselves and their young.

An animal is guided by instinct when it builds. It inherits its construction skills from its parents, just as it inherits the shape of its body. Any animal can build the right kind of nest the first time it tries.

The underground burrow is the most popular type of home used by small mammals, such as these prairie dogs.

▶ WHERE MAMMALS LIVE

During the winter, a gray squirrel lives in a snug tree hole. It sleeps on a mattress of shredded bark and leaves. In spring, it moves outside and builds an airy leaf nest high above the ground.

It may steal a bird's nest and put a roof of twigs and leaves over the top. Or the squirrel may lay its own foundation by wedging sticks and twigs into the crotch of a tree. It builds a roof by lacing smaller twigs and leaves into the foundation, and it shingles the roof with large leaves to keep out rain. When the nest is finished, it looks like a ragged cluster of leaves the size of a basketball. A small hole on one side serves as a doorway. Inside the nest, the hollowed-out living chamber is lined with soft grass and moss.

Anyone can see squirrels' leaf nests perched in the treetops of woods or city parks. The nests of mice and other small rodents are just as common, yet few people notice them because they are carefully hidden. A white-footed mouse builds a typical nest. Working with tooth and paw, it fluffs out strands of shredded grass and weaves them into a hollow ball the size of an apple. The inside of the nest is padded with the softest bedding available, such as milkweed floss or cattail down. The nest may be hidden anywhere—between rocks, in a hollow log, beneath a pile of brush, in a knothole. White-footed mice often move into cabins in the wilderness, where they build nests of shredded rags, cotton, or newspaper among the rafters or in empty boxes or drawers.

Many other kinds of mice live in underground burrows. In fact, the burrow is the most popular type of home used by mammals. Wolves, foxes, and coyotes dig burrows as temporary nursery dens. Their pups are born in a dark chamber at the end of a long tunnel. When the pups are big enough to keep up with the adults, the den is then abandoned.

Ground squirrels, chipmunks, gophers, woodchucks, and many other mammals live in underground burrows all year long. A woodchuck (or groundhog) may occupy the same burrow for several years. It constantly enlarges and remodels its underground home, digging through soil with its heavy claws, cutting away roots with its sharp teeth. The burrow has an entrance hole surrounded by a mound of excavated soil and two or more emergency exits. Underground, a network of tunnels connecting several rooms may extend for 50 feet (15 meters) or more. During the winter, the woodchuck hibernates in a grass-lined sleeping chamber several feet underground.

The most accomplished mammal architect is the beaver. Beavers use their sharp orange teeth to cut down trees and trim off branches and twigs. They build dams across marshes and streams by piling up this timber and cementing it together with mud and stones. A well-constructed beaver dam will last for many years and may be used as a bridge by other animals.

As water backs up behind a beaver dam, a pond is formed. In the middle of this pond, safely away from shore, the beavers construct a sturdy timber and mud lodge. Its walls are plastered with plenty of mud to make them waterproof. The top of the roof is not plastered, leaving ventilation holes that allow air to circulate.

The only entrance to a beaver lodge is a narrow underwater tunnel. It leads to a circular room. The floor of this room stands a few inches above water level. Raised above the floor is a sleeping shelf lined with shredded wood.

During the winter, snow covers the lodge and locks in the heat given off by the beavers' bodies. Warm air rises to the ceiling, escapes through the ventilation holes in the roof, and forms vapors of steam that look like smoke rising from a chimney.

▶ BIRDS AND THEIR NESTS

Some people think that birds fly home at night to sleep in their nests, or that they use their nests as hiding places. A few birds, such as owls and woodpeckers, actually do live in their nests. But most birds live in the open. They build nests only during the breeding season and use them for one special purpose—as a sheltered cradle for their eggs and young.

The location of a nest reveals a great deal about a bird's young. Ground-nesting birds, like ducks and geese, usually have chicks that run about soon after they hatch. If danger threatens, the chicks can tumble out of the nest and race for safety. Birds whose young are born blind and helpless usually avoid the open ground. They try to build their nests out of sight or out of reach.

Cliff swallows build nests of mud mixed with their own sticky saliva. They smear the mud against the face of a cliff or the wall of a building and shape it into a neat little pottery jug with a round opening at the top. The inside is filled with grass, moss, and feathers to cushion the eggs. These nests are always placed beneath overhanging ledges, so that

Cliff swallows build their nests—which look like neat little pottery jugs—beneath ledges to keep out the rain.

An African weaverbird builds a grass nest that hangs from the branch of a tree. And sometimes, you will find that birds build their nests in very surprising places.

rain will not soften the mud and wash the nest away.

A hole in a tree provides an ideal nesting site. Woodpeckers have an advantage because they can drill their own nesting holes. Abandoned woodpecker holes are in great demand. Birds like wrens, swallows, bluebirds, and starlings will sometimes fight noisily over the possession of an empty woodpecker hole.

Crows, hawks, and eagles carry branches and sticks to the tops of trees and cliffs, where they build large platform nests. Eagles can airlift branches as big around as a person's arm. They sometimes line their nests with pieces of trash, such as old brooms and tablecloths. Eagles return to the same nests year after year, adding more branches and twigs. As the nest grows older, it also grows bigger. A famous nest in a tree near Vermilion, Ohio, was used continuously for 36 years before the tree collapsed in a storm. It weighed more than two tons.

A hummingbird's nest, made from moss and plant floss bound together with cobwebs, measures barely an inch (2.5 centimeters) across the top. It is small enough to fit into a teaspoon, yet big enough for the hummingbird's two pea-sized eggs.

Many common songbirds build cup-shaped nests. A goldfinch weaves its cup-shaped nest from strands of grass, strips of moss, and bits of plant fiber. The nest is lined with thistledown and feathers. Goldfinch nests are so tightly woven that at times they hold rainwater and drown the young.

In the tropics, small perching birds often build hanging nests that are completely covered to keep out tree-dwelling enemies. The nest of an African weaverbird hangs by a loop from the branch of a tree. It may contain more than 300 strands of grass woven tightly into a ball. Inside the nest, the weaverbird hollows out a nesting chamber. The entrance is a long, narrow tube that is big enough for a weaverbird to squeeze through, yet small enough to keep out tree snakes.

If a bird can't find the building materials it usually uses, it will seek the best substitutes it can find. In New York City, a street-wise pigeon fashioned a nest from wires, nails, and paper clips. In Switzerland, a sparrow built its nest entirely of small watchsprings. And in Bombay, India, a pair of crows constructed their nest with gold spectacle frames that they stole from an open shop window.

▶ BUILDING UNDERWATER

A surprising number of fish build simple nests at the bottoms of lakes and streams.

The nest is often constructed by the male, who may also watch over the eggs and newly hatched fry. A smallmouth bass is typical. He uses his mouth to loosen gravel and debris at the bottom of a lake and to carry off larger stones. Then he turns around and uses his tail to scoop out a nesting hollow.

The most skillful nestbuilders among fish are sticklebacks, found in ponds and streams throughout North America. A three-spined stickleback is about the size of your little finger. The male collects bits and pieces of water plants, squirts them with a sticky fluid released by his kidneys, and glues the pieces together. Pressing against the pile with his body and snout, he forms a neat, tunnel-shaped nest with a front entrance, a rear exit, and a stream of water flowing through it.

When the nest is ready, the stickleback leads several females into the tunnel. After they deposit their eggs, he chases them away. The male stays behind to guard the eggs. He fans fresh water through the tunnel so the eggs will get plenty of oxygen.

Some of the most interesting underwater structures are built by newly hatched insect larvae called caddis worms, which look like small caterpillars. They hatch from eggs laid in cool mountain ponds and streams. As soon as they wriggle out of their eggs, they begin to build sturdy, case-like dwellings where they can live until they leave the water as adult caddis flies.

There are many kinds of caddis insects, and each kind prefers certain building mate-

Caddis worms build underwater case-like dwellings, where they can live until they become adult caddis flies.

rials. Caddises that hatch in quiet ponds and lakes usually build cases of wood, bark, pine needles, and other lightweight materials. In swift mountain streams, they construct heavy stone cases that won't be tossed about by the currents. A stone case may be shaped like a tube, a trumpet, a coiled snail's shell, or a domed turtle's shell. The caddis worm picks up tiny pebbles and grains of sand in its mouth. It cements these building stones together with a sticky silk that pours out of its mouth and hardens in water. The caddis starts by building a ring of stones around its body. It adds more and more stones, gradu-

Insects construct some of the architectural wonders of the animal world. This flourishing beehive in the wild hangs from a limb high in a tree. And this air-conditioned "skyscraper" built by African termites towers above the ground.

ally forming a hollow tube. The rear of the tube is sealed with silk, but the front is left open so the caddis can climb part way out. As it crawls along the stream bed looking for food, it drags its stone case behind it. If danger threatens, it retreats inside.

▶ INSECT CITIES

Only a small percentage of the earth's insects build nests, yet they construct some of the architectural wonders of the animal world. The nests of bees, ants, and termites are populous insect cities that may last for many generations.

Honeybees usually build their hives in hollow trees or in wooden boxes provided by beekeepers. The interior of the hive contains row after row of neat, six-sided cells, made of wax that oozes from the abdomens of worker bees. The cells at the center of the hive are nurseries for the developing eggs and young. Surrounding these brood cells are storage cells for honey and pollen.

A flourishing beehive has a population of perhaps 50,000 bees. Guards stationed at the entrance to the hive will attack and sting any outsider. Inside the hive, worker bees constantly build new wax cells, repair old ones, and carry away refuse.

The brood cells must be kept at a very high temperature, or the eggs and larvae cannot develop successfully. In cool weather, the bees cluster by the thousands on top of the brood cells, keeping them warm with the heat of their bodies. In hot weather, the bees cool the hive by fanning their wings. If fanning isn't enough, the bees carry drops of water into the hive and spread a thin film of moisture over the brood cells. They continue to fan their wings, and the nest is cooled as the moisture evaporates.

Most ants live underground. An ant hill is made of soil that the insects have excavated and is actually an extension of the nest. Beneath an ant hill, the ground is riddled with tunnels and nursery chambers. A large nest may penetrate 15 feet (4.5 meters) into the earth, cover an area larger than a football field, and contain several million ants. Worker ants shuttle back and forth from one nursery chamber to another, carrying eggs and larvae in their jaws. During the day, workers carry the brood to sun-warmed nurseries in the upper parts of the nest. In the evening, they carry the brood back down to deep underground nurseries, where heat has accumulated during the day. The entrances to these nurseries are sealed to keep out the cool night air.

Some of the strangest insect nests are the towering, air-conditioned mounds built by African termites. Constructed of soil that the termites chew and mix with their own saliva, these insect skyscrapers may rise 20 feet (6 meters) into the air. Their thick, sun-baked walls are as hard as concrete.

Termites must avoid the sun. Their soft, pale bodies dry out quickly in open air, causing them to shrivel and die. If temperatures drop too low, they become paralyzed. They need darkness, moisture, and warmth to survive. In Africa, they create the special conditions they need by building climate-controlled mounds.

At the base of a termite mound is a "cellar," a large hollow space below ground level. Tunnels branch out from the cellar to underground sources of food and water. At the top of the mound is another large hollow space, the "attic." Between the cellar and the attic stands the nest itself, where the termites live in perpetual darkness.

A network of air channels is built into the walls of the mound. These channels absorb fresh air from outside the mound. As air seeps into the channels, it rises up to the attic and flows down to the cellar. The nest in the center of the mound is surrounded on all sides by endlessly moving streams of air.

Termites are constantly at work inside the air channels, opening and closing them to regulate the flow of air. When the nest is too warm, new channels are opened to bring in fresh, cool air from the outside. When the nest is not warm enough, some of the channels are closed.

Some of the African termite mounds look like giant mushrooms or miniature pyramids. Others resemble towers, steeples, or craggy mountain peaks. Each species of termite follows its own architectural blueprint—the blueprint of its ancestors. Guided by their instincts, termites have been building climate-controlled nests for millions of years.

RUSSELL FREEDMAN
Author, *Animal Architects*

THE UNDERWATER WORLD OF A CORAL REEF

Hugging the low shoreline of jagged coral rock, a boat chugs through the transparent, turquoise waters of the Caribbean. The boat, with a small group of divers aboard, is headed toward the Mexican island of Cozumel. As it travels southward, small greenish brown patches of coral growth become visible beneath the water. A school of dolphins mysteriously appears off the bow. Diving over and under one another, the dolphins playfully try to get the best position to ride the wave of water pushed forward by the boat's prow. A sea turtle lazily basking on the surface is startled by the engines. It swims off with great flapping thrusts of its powerful front legs. Several flying fish suddenly pop out of the water and go skimming off across the surface. They glide for some distance until they lose speed and plop back into the sea.

Nearing the southern end of the island, the boat angles away from shore and moves out into deeper water. The boat soon comes to a stop, and the anchor is dropped over the side. The divers have arrived at their destination. Beneath the ocean's surface, but visible through the clear water, is Palancar Reef—one of the most spectacular coral reefs in the Caribbean. The divers will now enter a fantastic underwater world, a world that is at the same time both beautiful and eerie.

But what are corals, and how do they help make a coral reef?

Brain coral

Star coral

Staghorn coral

THE REEF BUILDERS

Although corals may appear to be exotic plant life, they are actually the skeletons of tiny sea animals called coral polyps. The skeletons of billions of certain kinds of corals make up a coral reef.

Corals belong to the same family as sea anemones and jellyfish. The body of a coral polyp is tubular, and it has a mouth surrounded by tiny tentacles. Its limestone skeleton grows outside its body and usually takes the shape of a cup. The cup protects the coral just as a shell protects a crab. During the day, the tentacles rest in the cup. At night, they reach out to search for small prey and push the food into the polyp's mouth.

Each kind of coral takes a form that is different in size and shape. Some shapes resemble tree branches, flowers, or mushrooms. Many corals have been named for the fascinating patterns they form—such as brain coral, star coral, hat coral, and staghorn coral. It is the colors of the living coral polyps that give color to the skeletons—red, green, orange, blue, yellow.

Most corals live together in colonies. When the polyp dies, its skeleton remains part of the colony. And as more and more coral skeletons pile up, they may form the base of a coral reef. The reef will continue to grow upward and out, very slowly, only a few inches a year at the most. But over centuries, a reef can grow to tremendous proportions. A reef may be made up of many thousands of coral colonies, created by billions of individual polyps. The only living part of the reef is the top layer of coral polyps.

KINDS OF CORAL REEFS

Corals are found in all the oceans of the world. But the true reef-forming corals live in the warm, clear waters of the tropics. They cannot live in waters that are colder than 65°F (18°C).

There are three types of coral reefs—fringing reefs, barrier reefs, and atolls.

A fringing reef is found in shallow water and closely borders the shore.

A barrier reef is much farther out from the shore and is separated from the shore by wide channels of water. It forms a barrier between the water near the shore and the

Not all corals are reef builders. But many, like these golden corals, live in coral-reef communities. And like all corals, they use their tiny tentacles to capture and eat food.

open sea. The most famous such reef is the Great Barrier Reef, off the northeastern coast of Australia. It is about 1,250 miles (2,000 kilometers) long. Palancar, also a barrier reef, is only 6 miles (10 kilometers) in length.

An atoll is found in the open sea and is unconnected with any land mass. It forms a ring of low coral islands and encircles a body of water called a lagoon. There are hundreds of atolls scattered across the South Pacific.

A coral reef creates a special kind of underwater community. The coral skeletons form the reef structure. Ocean waves carry tiny plants toward the reef. The plants root and thrive on the reef, forming a cover of vegetation. This plant life provides food for fish and other creatures. And the complicated architecture of the reef offers all these creatures shelter. The reef becomes a bustling community where plants and animals depend on one another. It resembles an incredibly beautiful underwater garden, filled with oddly shaped formations and blooming with the color of the living corals and of the strange creatures that dwell there.

(A)

(B)

▶ LIFE AT PALANCAR REEF

The towering formations of Palancar Reef reach up like underwater skyscrapers from the ocean floor. Narrow, sandy canyons knife their way through the towering structures. Within the reef are the entrances of grottos, leading back into the dark recesses of the coral. Strange and colorful creatures swim through this silent, underwater world.

At Palancar, as on other coral reefs, competition for space is fierce, and many animals dwell closely together. Living with the coral polyps are such creatures as sea anemones (**A**), sponges (**B**), tube worms (**C**), and sea whips and sea fans. Sea whips and sea fans are related to corals. But rather than having hard skeletons, they have soft, horny ones.

The long, delicate arms of an orange feather star reach out from a narrow crevice (**D**). A basket star lies curled up in a tight ball far down among a sea whip's branches. In a niche of the coral is a large speckled coral crab (**E**). Peeking out from another crevice is a small goldentail moray eel. One of the reef's most familiar residents is the little arrow crab. While larger crabs hide during the day, the tiny arrow crab fearlessly clambers out in the open over the coral or pauses to rest on a convenient sponge.

The reef is teeming with brilliantly colored tropical fish. Schools of tiny blue chromis hover about the branches of the coral (**F**). Some French grunts mingle in a group near

(C)

(D)

the shallow edge of the reef. A zebra-striped banded butterfly fish swims leisurely past, followed by a stunning queen angelfish. Nearby, an equally striking male princess parrotfish pauses briefly at a coral head, takes a bite out of it with its beaklike front teeth, and then hurries on its way. Lurking back in the shadows of the crevices are squirrelfish and blackbar soldierfish. Quiet during the day, they will come out at night to hunt. Swimming back and forth in one small crevice is a tiny black-and-white striped spotted drum. Perfectly concealed among the branches of a sea whip, an elongated trumpetfish suddenly darts out and seizes an unsuspecting shrimp.

With the setting of the sun, the reef community undergoes a transformation. The fish and other creatures that were active during the day find a sheltered spot in the coral and settle down for the night. In turn, the squirrelfish and blackbar soldierfish move out into the open to begin their evening search for food. So do the moray eels, crabs, and octopuses. Basket stars emerge from among the branches of the sea whips and unfurl their long, netlike arms. They rotate their arms to capture microscopic animals that go drifting past in an endless stream. And all over the reef, billions of coral tentacles are extended, also gathering food. The corals will probably not live long. But their skeletons will remain, adding to the formation of the coral reef.

PETER D. CAPEN
Author and Photographer
Terra Mar Productions

(E)

(F)

ANIMALS IN THE NEWS

Question: What does this mouse have in common with a bee? Answer: Both carry pollen from flower to flower, making plant reproduction possible. The plants in question are air plants that grow on trees in some forests of Costa Rica. Their flowers open only at night. The mice scramble up the trees and push their noses into the flowers to drink the nectar. And their noses get dusted with pollen, which is carried to the next flower they visit. The U.S. botanist who made this discovery in 1980 said it was the first time anyone had seen a rodent pollinating plants.

Dima, a baby woolly mammoth found perfectly preserved in Siberia in 1977, is giving scientists answers to some puzzling questions. U.S. and Soviet researchers think the mammoth probably died of starvation about 40,000 years ago. The body froze and then was covered with earth in a landslide. In 1980, scientists tested some protein from the mammoth's tissues. They found that it was closely related to proteins from modern elephants, supporting the belief that elephants descended from the long-extinct mammoths.

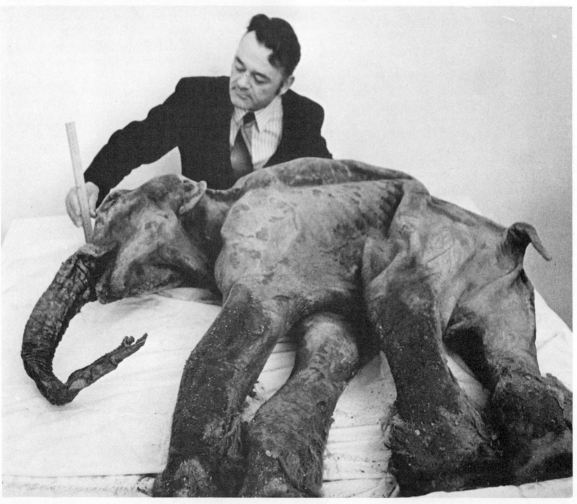

BALD EAGLE

GIANT TERATORN

Siberian huskies are famous for pulling sleds across frozen Arctic lands. In recent years, they've become popular as pets. And in 1980, a Siberian husky from Maryland, Champion Innisfree's Sierra Cinnar, took the best-in-show award at the famous Westminster Kennel Club show, in New York City. Rust-colored Cinnar thus became the first of his breed to win the top honor on the dog-show circuit.

Scientists in Argentina uncovered fossils of what may be the biggest bird ever to have flown. The bird is called the teratorn, from Greek words meaning "wonder bird." (Remains of larger flying creatures, the pterosaurs, have been found. But these were reptiles, not birds.) The teratorn's wingspan reached 25 feet (7.6 meters)—more than three times that of the bald eagle, and two and a half times that of the largest flying bird alive today, the Andean condor. On the ground, the teratorn could have looked an adult man straight in the eye and might well have matched his weight, too. That's an alarming prospect because teratorns were birds of prey. They once hunted over South America and southern North America. But the last of them died out about 10,000 years ago, and the fossils found in 1980 are thought to be 5,000,000 years old.

ANIMALS IN DANGER

Pandas, sea turtles, condors, manatees—four very different kinds of animals. But they share a common problem. All of them are threatened with extinction. Their populations are getting smaller and smaller. Unless something is done to help these animals, they may soon cease to exist.

The animals' problems have been caused mainly by people. People have destroyed the forests where pandas lived. They have killed condors for their feathers, sea turtles for their meat and shells, and manatees for their meat, blubber, and hides. Poisons put out to kill predators have instead been eaten by condors. Motorboat propellers have injured and killed manatees. Shrimping nets have caught sea turtles, causing them to drown.

Biologists and other people are trying to save these four animals. It is too soon to know if their efforts will be successful. It would be a tragedy if even one of the four became extinct. Here is what the world would lose:

▶ **THE GIANT PANDA**

Everyone knows the giant panda. This black and white creature is one of the world's most loved animals. It looks like a bear, but it is believed to be more closely related to the raccoon family. Of course, it is much bigger than a raccoon. A full-grown giant panda can weigh up to 300 pounds (135 kilograms). When it stretches up on its hind legs it reaches a height of about 5 feet (1.5 meters).

The giant panda is a shy animal. It lives alone except during the mating season. Its home is in China, in dense mountain forests. Its main food is bamboo. It may eat 20 pounds (9 kilograms) of bamboo a day. It also eats fruits, berries, bulbs, and even small animals.

The panda is a night creature. During the day it sleeps in a tree hollow or on a shady branch. It uses its tail as a pillow—or to cover its face.

A panda is very tiny at birth. It weighs only about 5 ounces (140 grams) and looks like a hairless mouse. It spends much of its time eating, and within ten weeks weighs 25 to 30 times as much.

Mother pandas take very good care of their babies. When the baby is 2 months old, the mother begins to play with it—tossing it

These pandas are dining on bamboo, the most important food of their diet. Many pandas have starved to death because some species of bamboo are scarce.

from one arm to another, tickling it, perhaps playing a game of peekaboo. If the baby is unhappy, she will caress it with her paw, much as a human mother caresses her baby.

The giant panda is the national symbol of China. No one knows how many giant pandas exist, but scientists believe there are fewer than 1,000. Recently, China established a special nature preserve in the western part of the country to protect the pandas that live there. The Chinese have also had some success in breeding pandas in zoos. In 1980, a panda was born in a zoo in Mexico City—the first born in captivity outside China. But it lived barely more than a week. Zookeepers are hopeful that in the next few years they will have greater success in breeding pandas.

▶ SEA TURTLES

When Spanish explorers first traveled to the Americas, they had a unique way of navigating through the fog off Grand Cayman Island. They would follow the sounds made by huge herds of sea turtles.

There are seven species of sea turtles. Six of them are endangered. The Atlantic ridley is closest to extinction. As recently as 40 years ago, they were still plentiful. People could watch 40,000 ridleys nesting on a beach in Mexico. Today, there are probably only 500 to 1,000 nesting females left on earth.

Sea turtles are big. Some weigh 500 pounds (225 kilograms) or more. Unlike land turtles, a sea turtle cannot pull its head or legs into its shell. The front legs are broad and flat. They are used to propel the animal through the water. The back legs are short and serve as rudders for steering.

International efforts to protect sea turtles are under way. Many countries have passed laws that make it illegal to capture turtles. But these laws are hard to enforce. One reason for the difficulty is that many sea turtles travel great distances. When it is time to nest, sea turtles return to the beach where they were born. How they find the beach is still a mystery to scientists. So is the reason for the migration. Why do they travel as much as 2,000 miles (3,200 kilometers) to reach the beach where they were born when other beaches—used by other turtles of the same species—are nearer?

Generally, the males stay in the shallow coastal waters while the females go onto the beach. The females go to sand dunes high on the beach, well above the high tide mark. They dig holes in the sand, lay their eggs, and then cover the eggs with sand.

A sea turtle's broad front legs are used to propel the animal through water. Sea turtles have been hunted for their meat and shells.

The California condor is the largest bird in North America. Only 30 of these birds remain on earth.

When the young turtles hatch, they immediately head for the water. This is the most dangerous moment in their lives. Many are caught and eaten by predators such as gulls and wild dogs before they can reach the water.

Scientists are experimenting with raising baby turtles in laboratories. The turtles are kept in the lab until they are a year old. Then, when they are old enough to fend for themselves, they are released into the sea.

Some people are trying to raise sea turtles on "farms." Not everyone agrees with this. Supporters say farming is a way to save sea turtles and at the same time meet people's demands for turtle soup and turtle steaks. Critics say farming will only increase the demand for turtle products, thereby increasing the illegal hunting of these scarce animals.

▶ THE CALIFORNIA CONDOR

The California condor is the biggest bird in North America. Large specimens weigh about 30 pounds (14 kilograms) and have wingspans of about 9 feet (3 meters).

On the ground the condor seems awkward. But few birds are as beautiful in the air. Once it is high in the sky, it moves on rising currents of warm air. It can soar for an hour or longer without once flapping its wings. If it spots food, it will quickly return to earth. The condor is a scavenger. It eats only the flesh of dead animals—mainly cattle, sheep, and deer but also small mammals such as rodents and rabbits.

The condor lives in rocky, mountainous areas around the southern end of California's San Joaquin Valley. It roosts in a tree or on a cliff. Its favorite roost is a tall dead conifer. These trees have no leaves to block the condor's view or to obstruct its flight. And such trees do not sway much in the wind. This is important because the condor's toes cannot grasp strongly.

The bird likes to sun itself in the early morning. It extends its wings to the sides to catch the sun. Every so often it turns around, to sun its other side. After a day of sunning, soaring, and eating, the bird tucks its head under the feathers on its back and goes to sleep.

At one time, condors could be found throughout California and in Oregon, Nevada, Utah, and Arizona. But as people cultivated more land and turned ranchlands into housing developments, the large grazing animals on which condors feed became scarce. People also shot many condors. And in recent years the birds have been killed by eating poisoned meat meant for coyotes. Only about 30 California condors remain on earth. Even optimists place their chance of survival at no more than 50–50.

▶ MANATEES

When Christopher Columbus sailed to the New World, he wrote in his log: "I saw three mermaids, but they were not as beautiful as they were painted." What Columbus actually saw were manatees—large gray mammals with whiskers and wrinkled skin. Not very beautiful, perhaps. But manatees are among the gentlest and most trusting animals on earth.

There are three species of manatees. One is found in the coastal waters of the Caribbean. The second lives in the Amazon basin. And the third species lives in the rivers of western Africa.

Manatees are plant eaters. They feed on water hyacinths and other water plants. A manatee eats at least 60 pounds (27 kilograms) of food a day. When eating, manatees use their flippers much as you use your hands, to guide the plants to their mouths. Their huge appetites can be very helpful to people—manatees can be used to keep waterways free of weeds.

When not eating, manatees like to rest just beneath the water's surface. Every few minutes they will stick their nostrils above the water's surface to breathe.

Adult manatees can weigh up to 1,200 pounds (550 kilograms). Like whales, they have been hunted for their meat, blubber, and hides. Many have been killed by sport hunters, and some countries have now set up special manatee refuges.

No one knows how many manatees are alive today. About 1,000 are thought to live in Florida, where there are a number of refuges. Boaters are warned to reduce their speed in these areas, so that they can see and avoid hitting the manatees. And there are fines and jail sentences for people who bother these gentle creatures.

Manatees are among the gentlest of animals. They have been injured and killed by motorboat propellers.

ANIMAL PARTNERSHIPS

Life can be very dangerous for a little fish in a big ocean. Lots of big fish are always eager to eat little fish. One little fish has a good solution to this problem. The fish is the pilotfish. Its solution: it lives with sharks. It is not uncommon to see a shark accompanied by six or more pilotfish. Any big fish foolish enough to chase one of these pilotfish risks the chance of being eaten by the shark.

Don't the sharks eat the pilotfish? No. The sharks also benefit from the relationship. Pilotfish eat some of the harmful parasites that live on the sharks' bodies.

Sharks have a similar relationship with remoras. Remoras are warm-water fish that have powerful suckers on the tops of their heads. They use these suckers to attach themselves to sharks, swordfish, porpoises, and other large sea animals. One kind of remora, the whalesucker, attaches itself to whales.

The remora benefits in several ways. It is protected from enemies. It gets some food. And it gets a free ride to new fishing grounds. The larger animal benefits from the remora's parasite-cleaning activities.

Partnerships between two different kinds of animals are common in nature. The best partnerships are those from which both animals benefit. But there are also partnerships from which only one of the animals appears to benefit. Butterfish often spend the first year of their lives under the umbrella of jellyfish. They gain protection and can feed on the tiny animals that get trapped by the tentacles of the jellyfish. The jellyfish do not seem to get any benefit from the relationship. A jellyfish may occasionally eat one of the butterfish. In general, however, the thick mucus that covers the butterfish seems to protect them from a jellyfish's hunger.

Many crabs form partnerships with other animals. One partnership involves crabs and sponges. The crab—called, appropriately enough, the sponge crab—looks around until it finds the right kind of sponge. The crab detaches the sponge from its resting place and puts it on top of its shell. Small hairlike structures on the crab's shell help hold the sponge. The crab may also use its hind legs to hold the sponge.

As the crab grows bigger, so does the sponge. Eventually, the sponge completely covers the crab's shell, thus hiding the crab

Remoras are small fish that attach themselves to sharks. They are thus protected from enemies, and they get a free ride. The shark benefits from the remora's parasite-cleaning activities.

A sponge crab carries a sponge on the top of its shell. The sponge hides the crab from its enemies. And as the crab moves along the ocean floor, water currents carry food to the sponge.

from enemies (almost no one likes to eat sponges). As the crab moves along the ocean floor, water currents pass around and through the sponge, carrying food particles that the sponge can eat.

Grenadier crabs carry sea anemones in their claws. If an enemy approaches, a grenadier crab stretches out its claws, right into the face of the attacker. Instead of an easy dinner, the attacker must deal with the poisonous tentacles of the anemones.

In addition to providing protection, the anemones sometimes provide the crab with food. But they do not do this willingly. If an anemone catches a small fish with its tentacles, it must quickly push the fish into its mouth. Otherwise, the grenadier crab may steal the fish.

The grenadier crab isn't faithful to its helpful anemones. If it sees an anemone larger than one of those it is carrying, it will drop the anemone in its claw and pick up the larger one.

▶ SMALL FEATHERED FRIENDS

Several large mammals have bird partners. Rhinoceroses, water buffalo, and other African land mammals are frequently followed by cattle egrets. These are white-feathered birds with long necks and long legs. As the mammals walk across a plain, they disturb insects in the grass. The insects fly up—right into the mouths of the watchful egrets. When the rhinos and water buffalo rest, the egrets hop onto their backs, where they feed on flies and other pests that are irritating to the mammals. The small brown-feathered tick-bird also helps mammals in this way.

The egrets also help the mammals by acting as sentinels. If they see enemies approaching, the egrets fly into the air. This warns the mammals of the danger.

Cattle egrets are natives of Africa. But early in the 20th century, some crossed the Atlantic Ocean to South America. Today they are found throughout the Americas. Instead of living with rhinos and water buffalo, they live with cattle.

Zebras and ostriches often live together. Each helps alert the other to the approach of enemies. The ostrich has excellent eyesight. This, together with its long neck, enables it to see enemies before the zebra can. The zebra has an excellent sense of smell. It may smell enemies before the ostrich can see them.

Another animal with a bird partner is the crocodile that lives in the Nile River. Its partner is the Egyptian plover. The crocodile is often bothered by leeches. Leeches are blood-sucking worms, and they attach themselves to the gums of the crocodile's mouth. When the crocodile spots a plover, it opens its mouth wide. The plover hops in and eats the leeches.

▶ LIVING WITH PLANTS

Some partnerships involve plants. Among the best known is that between bees and certain flowering plants. The bees visit the flowers to gather nectar and pollen. In return, they pollinate the flowers, thereby ensuring the formation of seeds. Without the flowering plants, the bees would starve to death. Without the bees, the plants would not be able to produce seeds. They would disappear from the earth.

Some species of hydra (tiny relatives of

Grenadier crabs carry sea anemones in their claws. If an enemy approaches, the crab thrusts the anemone into the face of the attacker, who must deal with the poisonous anemone tentacles.

Water buffalo have partnerships with cattle egrets and tickbirds. The birds hop onto the water buffalo's back and eat flies and other insects that irritate the mammal.

"What do you do with your bird when you go in the water?"

S. GROSS

jellyfish) have algae living in their cells. The algae are protected from animals that might eat them. The benefit to the hydra is not known. But scientists have found that hydras with algae function better than hydras that do not contain algae. Perhaps the hydra needs the oxygen produced when the algae make food.

Sometimes an "outsider" benefits from a partnership. Certain ants in South America have a partnership with cecropia trees. The stalks of a cecropia tree contain many small chambers. Colonies of ants live in these chambers, and ants can always be found swarming over the leaves and other parts of the tree. One animal that loves to eat cecropia leaves is the three-toed sloth. As it feeds on the leaves, the sloth cannot help but eat some of the ants. These ants supply certain nutrients that the sloth needs. Without the partnership between the cecropia tree and the ants, the sloth might not survive.

The sloth is involved in some interesting relationships of its own. Green algae live in the sloth's fur, giving the animal a greenish color. This helps the sloth blend into its surroundings. Enemies are less likely to see a greenish sloth among the tree leaves than a brown sloth. However, too much algae can be harmful to the sloth. The algae population is kept under control by a small insect called the sloth moth. This moth only lives in the fur of three-toed sloths. It is provided with a good supply of food. And the sloth is provided with an efficient fur cleaner.

As you can see, animal partnerships involve all kinds of animals—and plants. They provide a variety of benefits: food, protection, camouflage, removal of parasites, and transportation.

Do people have partnerships with animals? What about the relationship between a person and a pet dog? Between a gardener and songbirds? Between a farm family and their egg-laying hens? Do you think both the people and the animals benefit from these relationships?

JENNY TESAR
Series Consultant
Wonders of Wildlife

SCIENCE

Mount St. Helens, a volcano in southwestern Washington, blew its top on May 18, 1980. The eruption was the first in a series that continued throughout the year.

Early on that Sunday morning, Mount St. Helens blew its top. It was a volcanic eruption with a force equal to 500 atomic bombs. Hot ash, gases, and rocks were hurled as high as 12 miles (19 kilometers) into the sky. The ash, rocks, and melting snow formed mudslides that clogged rivers. And a shockwave caused by the explosion leveled thousands of acres of Douglas fir trees—trees that had been the basis of the area's important lumber industry.

At least 34 people died as a result of the eruption. Another 28 were missing and presumed dead. The death toll of wildlife was almost impossible to imagine. Scientists believe that at least 1,500,000 game birds and mammals were killed. Nearly 11,000,000 fish died. And unknown millions of reptiles, amphibians, and insects also lost their lives.

The enormous mushroom-shaped cloud of particles thrown into the sky was carried eastward by air currents. It dropped huge amounts of ash and dust on the ground. This created major problems as far as 500 miles (800 kilometers) east of the volcano. The farmlands of eastern Washington were coated with the fine particles, and many crops were killed. In Idaho and Montana, the falling ash was so dense that days seemed to turn to dusk. In less than a week, the massive cloud of particles had passed over the eastern United States and Canada. It moved across the Atlantic and around the world. Fallout from the cloud will probably continue, at an ever decreasing rate, for years.

▶ A VOLCANIC MOUNTAIN CHAIN

Mount St. Helens is located in southwestern Washington, about 50 miles (80 kilometers) northeast of Portland, Oregon. It is part of the Cascades, a range of volcanic mountains that run from northern California into British Columbia. There are fifteen major volcanic mountains in the range. Among the best known are Lassen Peak, Mount Hood, Mount Rainier, Glacier Peak, and Mount Garibaldi. All these mountains have been active at some time during their lives. The last to erupt was Lassen Peak, in northern California. It erupted over a period of three years, from 1914 to 1917.

The last time Mount St. Helens erupted was in 1857. But scientists were expecting

MOUNT ST. HELENS AWAKENS

For 123 years, Mount St. Helens slept. It was a beautiful, peaceful sight. But in March, 1980, the mountain began to awaken. Earthquakes were the first signs of life. Then for more than six weeks the mountain hurled steam and ash into the sky.

Still, few people were prepared for the events of May 18.

another eruption. In 1975 the United States Geological Survey said that Mount St. Helens was the Cascade volcano most likely to reawaken from dormancy (sleep), "perhaps before the end of this century."

The May 18 eruption was just the first of many for Mount St. Helens. A May 25 eruption dumped ash on cities in coastal Oregon and Washington. Portland International Airport had to be closed temporarily, and telephone and electric transmission lines failed. In June, July, August, and October it erupted again. How many more times it will erupt is unknown. It may return to a dormant state, or it may continue to spew material into the air for years and years.

▶ SOME GAINS FROM THE DESTRUCTION

Scientists immediately showed a great interest in Mount St. Helens' activity. They conducted research at the mountain in the hope of learning what causes volcanoes to explode. They also searched for signs that would indicate an eruption was about to occur. Such signs would enable scientists to predict eruptions.

Other scientists tried to determine the long-term effects of Mount St. Helens' eruptions on people and their activities. The ash and other material expelled by the eruptions were not expected to affect human health. Whether they would affect the weather was debated. Some scientists believed that the particles remaining in the atmosphere would have a slight cooling effect on the earth's temperature.

The ash that fell on farmlands may improve the soil because it contains minerals needed for plant growth. As a matter of fact, volcanic regions often make good farmlands for this reason.

Some of the millions of trees laying like matchsticks on the mountain's slopes were salvaged. They will provide lumber for housing and other construction. When all the logs are removed, the area can be reseeded.

But it will be years before forests again cover the slopes of Mount St. Helens— assuming of course, that the slopes will remain. Whole sections of the mountaintop have been blown away. It's possible that future eruptions will destroy even more of the mountain. Perhaps Mount St. Helens will disappear, as did another volcanic mountain in the Cascades. About 6,600 years ago, a mountain called Mazama exploded. It no longer exists. Its location is marked by a beautiful lake named, appropriately enough, Crater Lake. Will Mount St. Helens suffer the same fate as Mazama?

Below: The particles thrown into the sky from the volcano dropped huge amounts of ash on the ground. Right: The explosion also leveled thousands of fir trees —the basis of the area's important lumber industry.

SAVING ENERGY ON THE ROAD

Ten years ago, gasoline sold for 35 cents a gallon in the United States. Today it sells for about $1.35 a gallon. And no one expects the price to go down. In fact, the experts tell us that prices will go up . . . and up.

The rising cost of gasoline has had a big impact on Americans. It has affected driving habits and auto sales. The auto industry is working hard to develop cars that will use less gas. And scientists and engineers are trying to develop alternatives to gasoline and gasoline engines.

▶ **THE SHRINKING AUTOMOBILE**

Until the mid-1970's, America's favorite cars were big cars. Many people didn't care if they got only a few miles to a gallon of gasoline. Gas was plentiful and cheap. Car buyers wanted power, speed, and roominess. Manufacturers encouraged this attitude because they could make bigger profits on bigger cars.

Of course, there were some people who didn't want big cars. They preferred the smaller cars, which cost less money to buy and got better gas mileage. These people often bought foreign cars. In 1970, about 15 percent of the cars sold in the United States were foreign-made.

Then several developments occurred that caused many Americans to rethink their car-buying habits. The first development was the 1973 oil embargo by oil-producing countries in the Middle East. This temporarily cut off a major supply of crude oil to the United States. Because gasoline is made from crude oil, the result was a widespread shortage of gasoline.

The second development was a law passed by the federal government that lowered highway speed limits to 55 miles (88.5 kilometers) per hour. This made the powerful engines of big cars less important.

The third development was inflation. Prices of everything kept going up. Small cars began costing as much as big cars had cost a few years before. And big cars began to seem like unaffordable luxury items to many people.

The fourth development was another gasoline shortage, in 1979. Gas prices jumped during the shortage, and they continued to climb after supplies had returned to normal.

More and more people began to buy smaller cars. U.S. manufacturers were not making enough small cars, so people turned to European and Japanese manufacturers. In 1980, more than 25 percent of the cars sold in the United States were foreign-made.

Because U.S. manufacturers were selling

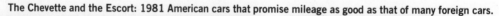

The Chevette and the Escort: 1981 American cars that promise mileage as good as that of many foreign cars.

UNIVERSAL PRESS SYNDICATE
©1980 WASHINGTON STAR

FIRING

HIRING

BETTER IDEAS

REPLACES THE PINTO, I BELIEVE

'LIGHTER, SMALLER, COMPETITIVE, FUEL-EFFICIENT... I THINK RESEARCH AND DEVELOPMENT MAY HAVE DONE IT AGAIN!'

fewer cars, they lost money. They had to lay off workers and even close some of their manufacturing plants.

Today, U.S. manufacturers have realized that the era of big cars is over. They are spending billions of dollars to develop cars that are more fuel-efficient. By 1985, American-made cars are expected to average 28 miles per gallon (12 kilometers per liter). This is twice as much as the 1975 average.

Some of the new, smaller American cars came on the market in the fall of 1980. They give gas mileage that is comparable to that of the small imported cars.

▶ ELECTRONIC FUEL SAVERS

Smallness is not the only gas-saving improvement planned by auto makers. Better functioning engines are another. One way to accomplish this is by putting a minicomputer in a car. Some researchers believe that such a computer can cut a car's use of fuel by as much as 25 percent.

By the late 1980's almost every car is expected to contain a computer. The computer will control various engine functions.

• It will adjust the intake of fuel and air, so that the engine receives the most efficient burning mixture.

• It will control the recirculation of gases given off by the engine. This will save gas and decrease pollution.

• It will check the performance of engine parts and diagnose problems.

A computer terminal will be located on the dashboard of the car. The terminal will tell the driver if there is an engine problem. It will indicate how well the antipollution exhaust system is working, and it will indicate the tire pressure.

Computers in automobiles will have other uses, too. They might even be used by passengers to play games—such as computer chess, baseball, or space wars.

In West Germany, engineers have developed a computer system that gives a driver information about road and weather conditions. When a driver begins a trip, he or she enters the destination in the car's computer. The computer sends this information to computers installed along the roads. The roadside computers tell the car computer which is the best route to take. This information is flashed on a screen on the dashboard. As the car travels along, the roadside computers will keep it informed of any sudden changes in travel conditions, such as an accident or unexpected flooding. When this happens, the roadside computers will tell the car computer what other routes can be used.

▶ PUT SOME CORN IN THE TANK

Because gasoline is becoming more and more expensive to use as a fuel, scientists are studying substitute fuels. At the present time, gasohol is receiving the most attention.

Gasohol is 90 percent gasoline and 10 percent alcohol. The alcohol is made from various crops, such as corn, sugarcane, and sorghum. Gasohol is being sold by more than 1,000 stations across the United States. It is particularly popular in the corn-growing areas of the Midwest.

Gasohol costs more than gasoline. But users say they get better mileage with gasohol than with gasoline. Other people disagree. They say that gasohol mileage is less. This is to be expected, they say, because alcohol does not contain as much energy as gasoline. Thus it should not provide as good mileage.

The mileage controversy has not yet been solved. In addition, the use of gasohol can cause pollution problems. Burning gasohol produces more hydrocarbon emissions than does burning gasoline. There are also maintenance problems. Researchers report that gasohol can damage rubber and plastic parts, such as tubing.

Still another problem occurs at the production end. The amount of energy used to grow corn and make gasohol is greater than the amount of energy in the gasohol. This is because energy is needed to produce fertilizers and to power tractors and harvesters. The process of converting the corn into alcohol also uses energy.

Some of these problems can probably be solved. Energy costs would decrease if garbage instead of crops were used as the alcohol source, and if the manufacturing process were improved. The U.S. Government is spending millions of dollars to support gasohol research. The hope is that gasohol will be one more way that the country can cut its dependence on imported fuel.

▶ DON'T FILL IT, CHARGE IT

Gasoline engines aren't the only way to power an automobile. The most realistic alternative is electricity. Instead of an engine, the car has a large battery. The battery changes chemical energy into electrical energy. Eventually all the chemical energy is changed to electrical energy. When the battery needs more chemical energy, the battery can be recharged. This is simple. Just plug the battery into an electric outlet. During recharging, electricity is changed into chemical energy in the battery. In this way the battery can be used again and again.

Electric vehicles are not a new idea. In fact, at the beginning of the 20th century there were more electric cars on American roads than gasoline cars. But gasoline became plentiful, and gasoline engines were greatly improved. By the 1920's, electric cars had almost disappeared from the roads.

In the 1960's, concern over air pollution caused by gasoline engines led to renewed interest in electric cars. Several companies began to sell electric vehicles. But the range of these cars was limited. They couldn't go very far before they had to be recharged, and they couldn't go very fast.

Scientists and engineers are working on developing better batteries. In 1980, Gulf and Western Industries (G&W) announced the development of a new battery. It installed the battery in a Volkswagen. The Volkswagen was able to travel a distance of 150 miles (241 kilometers) without a recharge. G&W said that the battery could be on the market by 1984.

Filling up with gasohol, a substitute fuel from crops.

Another way to save energy is to use electricity instead of gasoline to power a car. This G&W van is powered by a new kind of electric battery, which could be on the market by 1984.

The G&W battery contains zinc. The battery is connected to a tank containing chlorine hydrate. When the chlorine hydrate is pumped into the battery, it reacts with the zinc to form zinc chloride. In the process, an electric current is produced. When the battery is recharged, the process is reversed. Chlorine hydrate and zinc are formed. It takes six to eight hours to recharge the G&W battery, using a regular electric outlet. This can be done at night, while the car's owner is asleep.

According to G&W, recharging the electric Volkswagen was a lot cheaper than buying gasoline. It cost about one third as much as the gas needed to drive the same distance.

Electric vehicles have other advantages in addition to saving money. They don't produce wastes that pollute the air. And they aren't as noisy as gasoline-powered cars.

Most trips that people take are relatively short. They go shopping, to work, or to school. Electric vehicles with a 150-mile range would be ideal for this kind of trip. Some analysts believe that by the end of the 20th century, 40 percent of all new cars in the United States will be battery-powered.

SMART DRIVING SAVES ENERGY

Here are six tips that will help drivers save gasoline:

1. To get the best mileage, drive at or below 55 miles (88.5 kilometers) per hour. Most cars use 20 percent less gas when driven at lower speeds than when they are driven at 70 miles (113 kilometers) per hour. That's like saving 25 cents or more on a gallon of gas.

2. Avoid quick, jackrabbit starts. They use more gas than brisk but smooth starts.

3. Avoid idling. A minute of idling uses twice as much gas as restarting the engine.

4. Keep the car tuned and in top operating condition. To get good mileage, it is important that carburetors, valves, and other engine parts be clean.

5. Keep tires properly inflated. Every two pounds (0.9 kilograms) of pressure added to non-radial tires (up to the maximum stated on the tire) increases gas mileage about 1 percent.

6. Remove unnecessary weight from the car. The lighter the car, the less fuel is needed to "push" it a certain distance.

NEW HELP FOR THE BLIND

Helen Keller would have enjoyed the meeting that was held in her honor in June, 1980. Keller, who overcame being blind and deaf and inspired millions with her work, would have been 100 years old on June 27. The Helen Keller Centennial Congress, in Boston, marked the event.

Keller died in 1968. But had she lived to attend the congress, she surely would have been amazed by the new electronic devices demonstrated there. The devices use scientific discoveries to help solve some of the special problems of the blind. They can make it easier for blind people to live on their own and to work in many jobs that usually require sight. Helen Keller devoted her life to seeking that kind of independence for the blind.

Helen Keller and Anne Sullivan. The 100th anniversary of Keller's birth was celebrated in 1980.

▶ HELEN KELLER—BLIND AND DEAF

Helen Keller was born on a farm in Alabama in 1880. She was a normal infant for the first 18 months of her life. Then an illness erased her sight and hearing. And because she couldn't hear, she couldn't learn to talk. Keller might never have learned much of anything if it hadn't been for her teacher, Anne Sullivan. Using a system of touch signaling on Helen's hand, Sullivan taught her words. With this touch code, Keller learned a great deal. In fact, she graduated from Radcliff College with honors in 1904.

For the rest of her life, Keller worked to prevent blindness and to help those who were blind. She made many friends and became famous around the world. In 1980, many of those who admired her celebrated the 100th anniversary of her birth by studying the problems of the blind and by searching for solutions. The centennial congress in Boston was part of that celebration.

▶ ELECTRONIC AIDS

According to the World Health Organization, there are about 42,000,000 blind people today. The organization warns that unless something is done about the causes of blindness, that number will double by the year 2000. Poor nutrition causes most blindness in children. And nearly 80 percent of all blindness can be prevented by improved diet and the use of modern medicines.

Not all blindness is preventable, of course. For those who are blind, the problem is much like Keller's. They must find other ways to learn the things most people learn by seeing. The electronic devices shown at the centennial congress will help.

Just to get through the day, people must continually be aware of their surroundings and their situations. A worker may have to know when it's time to catch the bus, for example. That's not easy when you can't see the numbers on a watch. A new pocket-sized clock for the blind solves this problem. At the touch of a button, the clock tells the time in words, using an electronic voice.

Most people can use their sight to avoid bumping into things. A laser cane can help the blind do that. The cane sends out beams of laser light. When the light bounces off an object, sensors on the cane pick up the reflection and a warning is sounded. The cane sends out beams in three directions—up, down, and straight ahead. It sounds three different warnings to tell the user where the obstacle is.

Most of our day-to-day activities involve finding small bits of information—telephone numbers, addresses, recipes. If you can't see to look these things up, you have a problem. New electronic information storage systems can help. The systems look and work much like tape recorders. They record and play back spoken words. But they also store and play back messages in braille—the alphabet system that uses raised dots to stand for letters and numerals. As a tape plays, a line of braille rises on a panel that the user reads by touch. After the line is read, those dots go down and the next line of braille comes up. The blind can use these systems to store notes from business meetings or classes, to record bills and bank statements, and to save any other kind of information they'd like to have at their fingertips. Later, when the person wants a bit of information, the instrument will scan rapidly through its files to find it.

Perhaps the most important way people learn is by reading. Helen Keller was lucky in having Anne Sullivan to read to her. Few of the books she needed for her college studies were available in braille. The situation is not much better today. But braille books are no longer the only way for blind people to read. One other way is by using a device that works much like the touch panels on the braille information systems. Dots on a page-sized board go up and down to make braille letters. A small tape recording directs the dots into patterns just like those on a page in a braille book. One tape can hold hundreds of pages and costs much less than a braille book. These tapes, however, have to be specially made.

There are many other things to read besides books. There are typed reports, letters, and magazines, for example. Other inventions can help the blind read these things, as well as any printed book. With one device, the user puts the written material face down

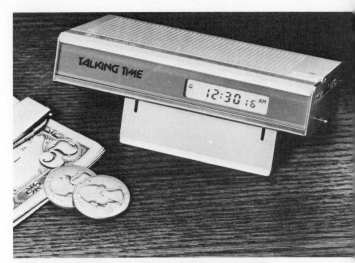
Using an electronic voice, this new pocket-sized clock will tell the time in words to people who are blind.

on a glass plate. A scanner passing under the plate detects the letters as patterns of black dots on a white background. A computer in the device recognizes the patterns as letters. Then it recognizes groups of letters as words, and an electronic voice speaks them. The machine reads to the user!

All these new machines will help blind people to learn, work, and live on their own. Helen Keller would have liked that.

This device uses tapes to direct dots into braille patterns. One tape can actually hold hundreds of book pages.

YOUNG SCIENTISTS AT WORK

What the world needs now is some good ideas about the energy problem. And we need them badly. Oil and coal, the fossil fuels that provide most of our usable energy, won't last forever. Many other energy sources are currently too expensive or don't provide enough fuel. Unless we do something soon, our homes might be cold in winter, electric lights might go out, and cars and trucks might roll to a stop.

There is no simple solution to the problem. Scientists do not expect to come up with one big discovery, such as a miraculous new energy source. Instead, they are looking for many little discoveries to make better use of the energy we already know about. And a group of young people in the United States is helping. They, too, are trying to find ways in which little improvements can make a big difference.

These young people, thousands of junior and senior high school students, are participating in a program called the Student Exposition on Energy Resources (SEER). The National Energy Foundation sponsors SEER to encourage students to develop their energy ideas. It also gives them a chance to display their projects in local expositions around the country. Prizes go to the outstanding exhibits, and some companies invite exhibitors to visit energy projects already being tried around the world. SEER students have toured a recycling plant in Virginia, solar power stations in Israel, a paper mill in Canada, and an oil rig in the Gulf of Mexico.

In 1980, SEER held its first national exposition, at the American Museum of Natural History in New York City. More than 15,000 students had entered the competition. About 750 of them had been chosen for regional expositions. Judges then had selected 26 finalists for the national exhibit, from which the two grand prizewinners were chosen.

Paul Oei, a high school junior from New York, won the senior division prize. Paul used special mirrors and lenses to catch and focus the sun's rays. His system would direct the intense light beam onto a glass box, raising the temperature inside by thousands

Paul Oei won the senior division prize at SEER's first national exposition.

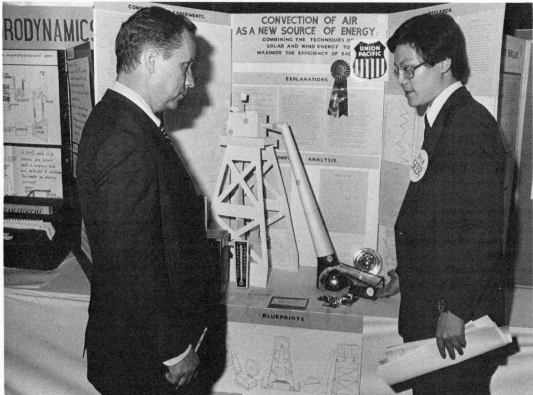

of degrees. The heated air would expand and escape through a tunnel, with enough speed and pressure to propel a turbine and generate electricity.

The winner in the junior division was Gretchen Alspach, a 14-year-old from New Jersey. Her project also used the sun's energy. In this case, the sun's rays were captured in a solar panel made up of cells that give off electricity when hit by sunlight. Gretchen attached the panel to a rotary motor from a TV antenna. The motor rotated the panel, so that the panel would always face the sun as it moved across the sky. That would allow the panel to catch more rays than it would if it were not following the sun.

Although Kenneth Jacobsen didn't make the finals, he came up with a new way to produce gasohol, which some people use instead of gasoline as an auto fuel. Gasohol is a mixture of gasoline and alcohol, and the alcohol generally comes from plants. People have long known how to distill (boil out) alcohol from plants. But the distillation process itself uses up a lot of energy. Kenneth's idea would use sunlight to power a still, the device that makes the alcohol. The best place for such a still would be the desert, where there is plenty of sunlight. But the desert would not have enough plants to feed the still. Kenneth's plan, therefore, also called for a desert-based hydroponic farm, where plants would grow in specially fertilized liquid. Since there is little moisture in the desert, his system would rely on continually recycled water.

One of the most interesting, although very costly, projects was exhibited by Frank Donato. He suggested a way of squeezing the most out of piezoelectric substances. These are crystalline cells that produce small amounts of electricity when they are put under pressure. Frank's idea was to build future highways over a layer of piezoelectric cells. The pressure of traffic rolling along the highway would produce enough electricity to power streetlights.

The SEER students did not solve the world's energy problems. But they made a good start by contributing lots of their own energy to the task. Not all their plans will work, of course. That's the way it is with difficult problems. But we have to keep searching for solutions—by looking at old ideas in new ways and by coming up with as many new ideas as we can.

Gretchen Alspach won the junior division prize. Both winners used solar energy in their projects.

YOU ARE WHAT YOU EAT

Carol never skips a meal. She is a number of pounds overweight, but her doctor says that she is undernourished.

Bill eats lots of snacks after school, and his teeth have lots of cavities. Mary also snacks, but she doesn't have any cavities.

Marty's father loves fried foods. But his doctor says that he must cut out these foods or risk having a heart attack.

Sarah's mother puts lots of salt in her food. But all that salt has given Sarah's mother high blood pressure.

All these people, like most people in North America, get enough to eat. But eating enough is not the same as eating wisely.

More and more evidence indicates that what people eat affects their health. Many people eat too much meat, too many dairy products, and too many processed foods. They are taking in too much fat, cholesterol, sugar, and salt—and too many calories. These people are increasing their chances of becoming victims of deadly diseases, including heart disease, stroke, high blood pressure, diabetes, and certain cancers.

▶ WHAT SHOULD I EAT?

Your body needs more than 50 different chemicals to grow and be healthy. These chemicals are called nutrients. They can be put into six basic groups: proteins, carbohydrates, fats, vitamins, minerals, and water.

Each nutrient has specific jobs to do in your body. These jobs cannot be done by any other nutrient. Thus, eating extra vitamin C will not make up for a shortage of vitamin D.

All the nutrients can be found in food. But different foods contain different types and amounts of nutrients. To obtain all the nutrients you need, you must eat a variety of different types of foods.

In 1980 the United States Government issued dietary guidelines. These guidelines tell you what to eat to be healthy:

- Eat a variety of foods every day.
- Maintain ideal weight.
- Avoid too much fat, saturated fat, and cholesterol.
- Eat foods that contain adequate starch and fiber.
- Avoid too much sugar.
- Avoid too much sodium (salt).

Consider the first guideline—eat a variety of foods every day. Your diet should include a selection of the following:

Fruits and vegetables. These give you vitamins A and C, carbohydrates, and fiber, among other things. Fiber is a part of plants, like the stringy part of celery. It is not digestible—that is, it passes through the body without being broken down. Fiber contains very few nutrients, but it is valuable because it helps move food materials and wastes through the digestive system.

Remember, different foods provide differ-

SUGAR IS SWEET BUT NOT SO NEAT!

Sugar causes cavities and tooth decay. As the U.S. Department of Agriculture points out in its 1979 Yearbook, this is a serious problem. One dentist explains the problem like this: If all 100,000 dentists in the United States worked day and night for a year filling cavities, there would still be as many new cavities to fill at the end of the year as when they began.

On the average, each American eats more than 130 pounds (59 kilograms) of sugar and sweeteners a year. Not all this sugar comes from candies, cakes, and other desserts. Many processed foods—including soup, cheese, salad dressing, spaghetti sauce, and even frankfurters—contain sugar.

Eating too much sugar causes other problems besides cavities. Sugar is so highly refined that it gets digested very quickly. It doesn't stay in your stomach very long. That means you may want to keep on eating. What happens then? You suddenly discover you're overweight.

Still another problem with sugar is that it contains "empty calories." It has no vitamins, no minerals, and no protein.

You don't have to stop eating sugar and sugary foods. But it wouldn't hurt to cut down. You'll discover that your desire for sweet things is partly a matter of habit. If you cut down on sugar for several weeks, you'll get used to eating less sugar. And when you go to the dentist, you will probably have fewer cavities.

A meal at your favorite fast-food restaurant can easily add up to a lot of calories. Be sure to eat lightly the rest of the day, or you may gain weight.

"It was one of those fad diets.
For six weeks I ate nothing but spinach."

basketball with the Boston Celtics eat as many as 8,000 to 10,000 calories a day while they are at training camp.

If you eat more calories than your body can use, you will gain weight. This is easy to do, especially if you don't get much exercise. For example, a hamburger-with-everything-on-it from your favorite fast-food restaurant contains about 600 calories. Add a serving of french fries, a soda, and an apple turnover, and you've eaten more than 1,200 calories in one meal. You must eat lightly during the rest of the day, or you will gain weight.

On the other hand, if you eat fewer calories than your body uses, you will lose weight. Many young people find that they have put on too much weight. They decide to go on a diet. But while dieting, a person still needs the same amounts of vitamins and minerals. That's why it's very important that people who want to lose weight choose foods that are low in calories but that provide all the nutrients needed for good health. It's no fun ending up skinny if you get sick at the same time.

▶ SNACKING—GOOD OR BAD?

It's the middle of the afternoon—or late at night—or two hours before lunch. You're feeling hungry. You decide to have a snack, even though you've probably been told a hundred times that you shouldn't eat between meals.

Is snacking really so bad? Not necessarily. The problem isn't snacking. It's what you eat when you snack. Do you choose such foods as milk, fruit, and raw vegetables? Or do you choose ''junk'' foods?

Many snack foods are called junk foods because they have no—or very little—nutritional value. They are filled with ''empty calories.'' This means they contain lots of calories but little else of value. They don't contain vitamins, minerals, and proteins. If you fill up on these foods, you don't have room in your stomach for the foods you need. Or, if you eat the foods you need—plus the junk foods—you will probably end up eating too many calories and too much sugar, fat, and salt.

So the next time you want to snack, pick up an orange or a carrot instead of a cookie or a candy. Have a glass of juice instead of a

ent amounts of each nutrient. Therefore it's important to vary the fruits and vegetables you choose.

Bread and cereal. These foods are rich in some of the B vitamins and in iron. If possible, eat whole grain breads and cereals. They contain fiber and many important minerals that aren't found in refined breads and cereals, even the enriched and fortified ones.

Milk, cheese, and yogurt. These foods give you calcium and several vitamins.

Meat, poultry, fish, eggs, and dried beans and peas. These foods provide protein, iron, zinc, and certain B vitamins.

Then there are foods that provide mainly calories. It would be wise to cut down on these—candy, cookies, pies, french fries, potato chips, and other sweet or fatty foods. Instead, plan to get most of your calories from other foods. By doing this, you will get not only the calories but also the important nutrients that you need.

▶ TURNING CALORIES INTO POUNDS

How many calories do you need in one day? It depends on how active you are. A fairly active 12-year-old needs between 2,200 and 2,800 calories a day. If you are very active you will need more. Some teenagers who participate in sports need more than 4,000 calories a day. Some men who play glass of soda. And if it's almost time for dinner, don't snack. Have a glass of water if you're thirsty, but don't let a snack ruin your appetite for a well-balanced meal.

▶ MAKE YOUR OWN FOODS

Perhaps you're getting the feeling that you should never eat another cookie. Things aren't as bad as that. Just like snacks, there are good cookies and bad cookies. Good cookies are relatively low in sugar. They contain things like oatmeal, raisins, nuts, and dates.

Try making your own cookies. Follow a recipe the first time. The next time, decrease the amount of sugar that the recipe calls for. With many cookie and cake recipes, you'll discover that the amount of sugar can be cut by one-third or even one-half—and you'll still produce delicious treats.

The same is true for the amount of salt that you use in your food. Don't cut salt out. Just use less of it.

Here are some other tips: Make your own salad dressing from oil, vinegar, and herbs.

Use whole wheat flour when you make pancakes. Try a yogurt and fresh fruit shake. When you buy cereal, check the ingredients on the package. Choose a cereal that's low in sugar and salt.

Checking the ingredients of the foods you buy is always a smart thing to do. Was that shake you had yesterday a milk shake, made with milk or ice cream? Or was it a fake shake, made from vegetable oil, nonfat milk solids, emulsifiers, flavorings, and sugar?

Finally, if you want to splurge on a rich, gooey dessert, go ahead. But balance the high sugar by cutting down your sugar intake during the next day or two. If you eat a heavily salted food one day, decrease your salt intake for the next few days. If you eat a fast-food lunch high in fat but low in fruits and vegetables, eat a dinner that supplies the needed nutrients.

Remember, you are what you eat. Eat a well-balanced, nutritious diet, and you will look and feel healthy. It's the best thing you can do for yourself . . . today, tomorrow, and for the rest of your life.

Many snack foods are considered "junk foods" because they contain lots of calories but little else of value.

FUN FOOD FACTS

Here are some facts about foods that may surprise you, your family, and your friends.

BIG EATERS

Babe Ruth once ate 20 hot dogs just before playing a baseball game. But a young woman in Philadelphia ate even more. On July 12, 1977, 21-year-old Linda Kuerth ate 23 frankfurters in 3 minutes 10 seconds. These were regular-sized franks.

It took more than one person to eat the largest sausage ever made. The sausage was made in England in May, 1979. It was 2 miles (3.2 kilometers) long and weighed 2,740 pounds (1,243 kilograms)! The sausage was cooked by Scouts and served at a children's party in London's Hyde Park.

WHAT'S IN A NAME?

Where did foods originally come from? The answer may not be easy to discover. Consider these familiar foods: Italian pasta actually originated in China. French croissants (rolls) were first made in Hungary. The Irish potato is a native of South and Central America. And the good old American hamburger got its start in Germany—in a town called Hamburg.

TOMATO TALES

The fact that we eat and enjoy tomatoes is due, in part, to a man named Colonel Robert G. Johnson. For years many people believed that if you ate a tomato, you would die before morning. Colonel Johnson decided to prove they were wrong.

On September 26, 1820, at noon, Colonel Johnson stood on the courthouse steps in Salem, New Jersey. In front of hundreds of people he ate a whole basketful of tomatoes.

Many people thought Johnson had gone crazy—until, that is, he not only lived but didn't even get sick.

In 1801, Thomas Jefferson became the third president of the United States. But 20 years earlier, Jefferson was one of the first people in the United States to grow tomatoes. But he grew them as a decoration—not for eating.

MILK MACHINES

The average cow produces 62 glasses of milk a day. The record-holder is a cow in Indiana. In 1975 she gave more milk in one day than any other cow ever has—372 glasses. Just imagine how tired that prize-winning cow must have been after her record milk-producing day!

CHICKEN FACTS

There are more chickens in the world today than there are people. And the chicken population is growing faster than the human population. This is because people are eating more and more chickens. Forty years ago, Americans ate about half a pound (0.2 kilograms) of chicken a year. Now they eat an average of about 37 pounds (17 kilograms) of chicken a year.

Not all chickens are raised for their meat. Some are raised to produce eggs. Forty years ago, the average egg-laying hen laid 100 eggs a year. Things have really changed. Today, an average hen lays about 240 eggs a year.

YOU'VE GOT WATER IN YOUR HEAD

Your body is more than half water. Your blood, for instance, is 90 percent water. Your brain is 75 percent water. And there is water in every one of your cells.

You lose about 2½ quarts (2.4 liters) of water a day. Some is lost as urine. Some, as perspiration. Some, when you breathe. But water is usually easy to replace. Every time you eat food, you eat water.

Can you name some foods that contain a lot of water? You probably guessed tomatoes, oranges, and watermelon. But did you know that bread is more than one-third water? Meat is more than half water. And, of course, milk and juice are nearly all water—plus natural flavoring and nutrients.

FOOD FIRSTS

The first public bakery was opened in Rome, Italy, in 171 B.C. Its specialty was a wheat-honey loaf.

Milk chocolate was first made in Vevey, Switzerland, in 1876. Credit goes to Daniel Peter, who believed that adding milk to anything would make it taste better.

Lemonade was first made in Paris, France, in 1603.

The first pizzeria in the United States opened in New York City in 1905.

Apricots were the first fruits planted in California.

FOODS OF THE FUTURE

Imagine that it is 50 years from now. You're hungry. What will you have for dinner? Will you eat the same foods that you ate in the 1980's? Or will you eat such foods as buffalo gourds, tepary beans, square tomatoes, and fat-free beef?

If you don't have time for a regular meal, will you grab a piece of pizza? Or will you grab a "food bar"? The bar looks like a candy bar, tastes like pizza, and contains all the nutrients of a whole meal.

Chances are, the foods you will be eating 50 years from now will differ in a number of ways from the foods of the 1980's.

One difference will be in quality. Most fruits and vegetables will be much larger than they are today. Meats will be more tender and will contain less fat. These changes will result from genetic engineering. Genetic engineering involves changing the reproductive cells of plants and animals so that the plants and animals will produce more—and better—food. For example, scientists are trying to develop plants that put more of their growing energy into the part that we eat, and less into other parts. An ideal lettuce plant would do most of its growing in the leaves. Its roots would stay very small. With beet plants, the roots (the part we eat) would grow big, but the leaves would stay small.

Sometimes genetic engineering is used to produce foods that keep fresh longer or that are easier to pack and ship. Some researchers are trying to develop square tomatoes. These would be much easier to pack than today's round tomatoes.

Growing populations and the need for more foods that are high in protein will lead to the development of food crops unknown to most of us. There are more than 350,000 species of plants on earth. About 80,000 of these species can be eaten. But in the whole course of human history, only about 3,000 plant species have been used for food.

Many scientists think it is a mistake for people to be so dependent on so few foods. They are encouraging people to grow a variety of crops. And they have discovered some plants that may be very important in the future. One is the winged bean. *Every* part of this plant can be eaten. The beans, when dried, contain up to 37 percent protein. The roots provide starch and ten times as much protein as a potato. The leaves taste like spinach. The flowers taste like mushrooms.

Until a few years ago, the winged bean had only been used in Southeast Asia. But now scientists all over the world are studying this plant. And farmers in 70 countries are growing it. It probably won't be long before some part of the winged bean shows up in your diet.

Other plants that may be important parts of the diets of the future are the cocoyam, the buffalo gourd, the marama bean, the tepary bean, and a grainlike crop called quinua.

Another difference between the diets of today and of the future will result from the increasing use of food analogs. These are foods that are like—but still different from—certain other foods. Food analogs are generally made from seeds such as soybeans, peanuts, sunflowers, wheat, corn, and oats. But the finished products do not look or taste at all like the seeds. Analogs may look and taste like carrots, pineapples, cheese, or meat.

Food analogs can be used to make food bars. Some types of food bars are already on the market. Some were used by the astronauts who traveled to the moon. But in the future, manufacturers will be able to make food bars that taste like almost anything the general public wants: pizza, hamburger, ham and eggs, chicken salad, french fries.

There may even be special prescription food bars. If you become sick with the flu, your doctor may prescribe flu bars. If you break a bone, the doctor may prescribe mending bars. These bars won't cure the disease or mend the broken bone, but they will provide the extra nutrients that your body needs while you are ill.

The next time you go to the supermarket, check the inventory. Is the store carrying any foods you never saw before? Are new fruits and vegetables appearing in the produce department? Are food analogs being sold as inexpensive and healthy substitutes for bacon, butter, and whipped cream? You may discover that some of the foods of the future are already here.

KNOW YOUR BODY

What *really* happens to your body when you eat a candy bar? When you don't eat enough iron? When you exercise regularly? When you put on too much weight?

Young people are learning the answers to questions such as these through a program called Know Your Body (KYB). KYB was developed by the American Health Foundation and is being used in a number of schools throughout the United States. An international KYB program is being used in sixteen other countries.

KYB's goal is to teach what *you* can do for your body to keep it healthy. The program begins with a health questionnaire and physical examination, which screen you for "risk factors." Risk factors are health conditions or habits that can lead to disease. Risk factors include cigarette smoking, poor nutritional habits, and inadequate exercise.

During the examination, your height, weight, and blood pressure are measured. Your heart rate is measured before and after you exercise. A sample of your blood is taken. This is sent to a laboratory, which measures the amount of cholesterol and the amount of sugar in the blood. It also determines what percentage of your blood is made up of red blood cells.

The results of all the tests are put on a Health Passport. The passport is yours to keep. You can look at your score for each test and compare it to what is considered the "normal value" for that test.

If your score on one or more of the tests is too high or too low, you are encouraged to try to change the score. Most of these scores can be changed just by improving some of your health habits. For example, let's consider cholesterol. Cholesterol is a fatty substance. Your body uses some cholesterol. But if you eat foods that contain a lot of cholesterol, the extra cholesterol may stick to the walls of blood vessels. Slowly, over the years, the cholesterol builds up until it clogs the vessels. It prevents blood from flowing through the vessels, and this may cause a heart attack or a stroke.

If your cholesterol level is too high, you can lower it by changing your eating habits. What changes do you think you should make? (Hint: red meats, eggs, and ice cream are some foods that are high in cholesterol.)

What you eat, how much you exercise, and cigarette smoking affect your health. They affect your weight, the composition of your blood, the strength of your muscles, your heart rate, and the health of your lungs. If your diet is well balanced, if you exercise regularly, and if you don't smoke, your Health Passport scores will probably be very good. Even more important, you will increase your chances of living a long and healthy life.

As part of the KYB examination, your heart rate is measured both before and after you exercise.

Voyager 1 flew by Saturn in November, 1980, and sent back to Earth incredible photographs.

ENCOUNTER WITH SATURN

Three hundred years ago, the planet Saturn was thought to be at the edge of the solar system. Early astronomers—Copernicus, Kepler, Galileo, Newton—believed there was nothing beyond it but the distant stars. Since their times, three planets even farther away have been discovered. But Saturn has remained unique and beautiful.

Saturn is a large world, only a little smaller than Jupiter. Like Jupiter, it is almost all atmosphere—a huge ball of hydrogen and helium. Saturn is surrounded by numerous moons. But its trademark is its rings. Made up of tiny particles of ice, they form bright, flat bands that stretch outward from Saturn for a distance almost as great as the distance from Earth to its moon.

Until 1979, Saturn could be studied only through telescopes. The Pioneer Saturn spacecraft was the first visitor to Saturn, in September, 1979. As it flew by the planet, it sent back a few closeup pictures, found a new moon, and discovered three new rings (raising the total to six).

Soon the Voyager 1 spacecraft, fresh from its amazing tour of Jupiter in March, 1979, was heading straight for Saturn. It reached the planet on November 12, 1980, ducked under the rings, and passed over Saturn's south pole. Then it flew on at an incredible 56,000 miles (90,000 kilometers) per hour, on a path that would take it out of the solar system.

In those few hectic days in November, more was learned about Saturn than had been learned in centuries of study. Not only did Voyager 1 get a close look at Saturn, but it turned its sharp cameras on the unknown faces of seven of Saturn's moons.

As Voyager 1 approached Saturn, the planet began to reveal features in its atmosphere that had never been seen from Earth. Unlike Jupiter, whose colored belts and spots are in plain sight, Saturn's atmosphere is hidden under a high haze of frozen ammonia crystals. Voyager 1's cameras peered through this haze for the first time. Turbulent streams and belts, stretching east to west like those on Jupiter, appeared. And an oval red spot was seen. It was like Jupiter's but smaller—only about the size of Earth!

▶ SATURN—"LORD OF THE RINGS"

Voyager 1's pictures of Saturn's rings stole the show away from the planet itself and left scientists amazed, baffled, and excited. There were more rings than anyone ever thought possible. As Voyager 1 approached, the seemingly uniform rings were seen to be dozens of distinct, thin ringlets, separated by small gaps. The number of rings rose from 6 to 30 and then to 95. And still more rings were seen. Finally, Voyager 1 flew under the rings, passing only 77,000 miles (124,000 kilometers) from Saturn. The rings hung above the spacecraft like a huge rainbow across the sky. Voyager's cameras saw hundreds of individual ringlets, like the grooves in some cosmic phonograph record. There were rings everywhere. A close view of the Cassini Division, visible as a dark band from Earth, revealed more than 50 rings in what had been thought to be an empty space in the ring system.

Some of the rings were much more complicated than anyone expected. A few rings were not circles but were slightly oval in shape. The thin outer F-ring was made up of several strands of material that seemed to be braided about one another.

Just as baffling were the "spokes," dark lines cutting radially across the rings. Because the ring particles move in circular orbits around Saturn, no one could understand how such cross-cutting structures could form and survive. But the "spokes" changed as Voyager 1 flew past Saturn. They had been dark as the spacecraft approached the planet, but they became bright as Voyager 1 looked back at them while moving away. Fine dust particles change their appearance in just this way. The "spokes" may be clouds of dust, held in place by electrical charges that balance the forces of gravity in the rings themselves.

The Voyager 1 pictures demolished all the theories about how the rings of Saturn work. Before Voyager, the few rings and gaps that were known could be explained by the gravitational actions of some of Saturn's moons on the ring particles. But no theory involving only a few moons could explain the hundreds of rings, the oval rings, the braids, and the "spokes." Nor was it known why such fragile structures had apparently survived for the 4,500,000,000 (billion) years since Saturn and the solar system were formed.

Voyager 1 provided some small examples

This color-enhanced photo of Saturn shows small details in the atmosphere that would not otherwise be visible.

of how the gravity of Saturn's moons does affect the rings. Two small moons were discovered, one on each side of the thin outer F-ring. The moons seem to act as shepherds—their gravity keeps the tiny ring particles from wandering in and out. A third small moon, located just outside Saturn's A-ring, may have a similar stabilizing effect. The problem now is to see what these simple examples can tell us about the entire complex system of more than a dozen moons, hundreds of separate rings, and billions upon billions of tiny, icy ring particles.

▶ SATURN'S MOONS

Three new moons were discovered by Voyager 1, and scientists now believe that Saturn has at least 15 moons. All but two are outside the ring system—the inner moons just beyond, and the others farther out.

Two small moons near the rings are in the same orbit, apparently on course for a collision in early 1982, unless they somehow manage to dodge around each other. Voyager 1 passed close enough to photograph seven of the larger moons—Mimas, Enceladus, Tethys, Dione, Rhea, Titan, and Iapetus. They were unexplored worlds that had previously been seen as tiny bits of light through the telescope.

Even before Voyager 1, we knew that Saturn's moons were very different. In this cold, distant region of the solar system, water does not exist as a liquid. It freezes to a brittle solid. Saturn's moons are literally worlds of ice, huge planetary icebergs. They may have small, rocky cores.

Voyager's cameras revealed a strange combination of landscapes on the moons. There are ancient regions covered with meteorite impact craters. Mimas has a huge crater that makes it look like a staring eyeball. The crater is so big that the impact that formed it almost blasted Mimas into fragments. Dione, Tethys, and Rhea are also heavily cratered. Voyager 1 made an especially close approach to Rhea. The pictures of Rhea show a landscape like the cratered highlands of Earth's moon or the battered surface of Mercury. But Rhea's craters have been sculpted in ice instead of rock.

The surfaces of some moons had clearly been modified by internal forces since the ancient time of tremendous bombardment. Tethys has a huge trench that may be a rift in a spreading crust. Rhea and Dione show strange streaks and swirled structures, side by side with the heavily cratered regions, as though their icy crusts had somehow shifted and deformed after the craters were formed.

Enceladus was a surprise. Its surface was almost completely smooth and crater-free, although it orbits between two heavily cratered moons, Mimas and Dione. Some internal process must have smoothed out the surface. Scientists suggest that the tidal pull of the nearby moon Dione may be strong enough to heat Enceladus. The heating of Enceladus might soften the icy crust so that it flows, removing all earlier features. Perhaps the heating is so strong that icy volcanoes erupt from time to time, and floods of molten ''lava''—liquid water—pour briefly across the surface.

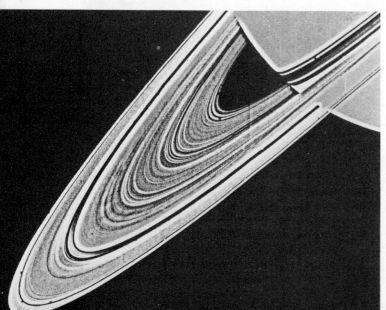

Voyager's pictures of Saturn's rings left scientists amazed and excited. There were rings everywhere —more than anyone had ever believed possible.

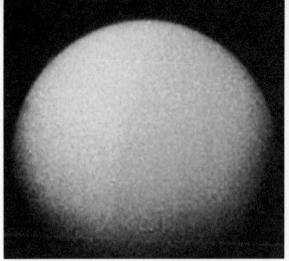

Scientists believe that Saturn has at least 15 moons. Titan (*left*) is the only moon in the solar system known to have an atmosphere. Dione (*right*) is a heavily cratered moon.

Iapetus, seen by Voyager 1 only at a great distance, is even more of a mystery—it is a black-and-white moon. Telescopic studies from Earth revealed that Iapetus has two different sides, one dark and one bright. Voyager's pictures showed the two regions and the sharp boundary between them. But there was still no explanation of the mystery. Voyager 2 will take a closer look at Iapetus in August, 1981.

Titan, the largest moon, is a giant world about the size of the planet Mercury. It is the only moon in the solar system known to have an atmosphere. From Earth, the gas methane had been detected in Titan's atmosphere. Voyager 1 was aimed to take an especially close look at Titan, to probe for its hidden surface and to see what the moon might tell us about other atmospheres and about the origin of life.

Voyager 1 skimmed past Titan only 2,500 miles (4,000 kilometers) above its atmosphere, the closest flyby ever made past any world in the history of space exploration. The spacecraft passed behind Titan, so that its instruments saw a sunset and then, eleven minutes later, a sunrise. The thick yellowish atmosphere blocked off any view of Titan's actual surface, but Voyager 1 probed the atmosphere with a battery of instruments.

Surprisingly, the atmosphere of Titan is not rich in methane. Most of it is nitrogen—the most abundant gas in our own atmosphere. More complex organic molecules, formed by the action of sunlight on the atmosphere, produce a kind of cosmic "smog" not too different from what is found over our own cities.

Titan's atmosphere is very thick, perhaps more than 125 miles (200 kilometers) deep. At Titan's surface, the atmospheric pressure may be two or three times as high as that of Earth, but the temperatures may be as low as −328°F (−200°C). The surface of Titan may be a murky, frozen swamp, with lakes of liquid nitrogen and a rain of organic chemicals (perhaps gasoline?) sleeting down. There may be no life in that incredible cold, but Titan may preserve in its deep-freeze a record of what other primitive atmospheres (including Earth's) were like before they were changed by forces that never affected Titan—volcanoes, oceans, and life.

Voyager 1 will leave the solar system to become the third interstellar space probe (following two earlier Pioneer spacecraft). In ten or twenty years, its voice will fade away. But it may survive in space, drifting between the stars, for billions of years. It may even outlive the Earth from which it came.

But scientists are not through with Saturn. They are just beginning to analyze all the data from Voyager 1, a task that will take years. And Voyager 2 is approaching Saturn, aiming for a close flyby on August 27, 1981. It is following a path that will take it past Saturn to worlds even more distant and strange—Uranus, in 1986, and Neptune, in 1989.

BEVAN M. FRENCH
Discipline Scientist, Planetary Materials
National Aeronautics and Space Administration

THE PROMISE OF GENE SPLICING

In every cell of every living thing there are structures called genes. Genes are the blueprints of living things. Genes are what make a frog a frog and a person a person. Genes shape your toes and stomach and eyes. Genes tell bone marrow how to make red blood cells, teeth how to grow, muscles how to move.

Sometimes there are mistakes in the blueprints. This causes problems. For example, there may be something wrong with the gene that directs the production of red blood cells. Instead of round, healthy red blood cells, the person's bone marrow makes red blood cells that have strange shapes and that cannot work properly. The result is a disease, called sickle-cell anemia, that can be fatal.

Doctors can treat sickle-cell anemia. But they cannot stop the person's bone marrow from making the strange blood cells. They cannot change the blueprints. Imagine if they could! Imagine if faulty genes could be removed and healthy genes put in their place.

Does it sound like science fiction? Well, it may soon be reality. Scientists are working on an exciting new technique called gene splicing. They are combining pieces of genes in new ways. For example, they are causing bacteria to make human insulin.

Bacteria are tiny, one-celled organisms. And they are the most common form of life on the earth.

Insulin is a chemical made by a gland called the pancreas. It controls the amount of sugar in the blood. Scientists took the human gene for making insulin and spliced (put) it into the genetic material of bacteria. They made the human insulin gene part of the bacteria's blueprint. The bacteria began to follow the gene's directions and make in-

HOW BACTERIA ARE USED TO RECOMBINE DNA

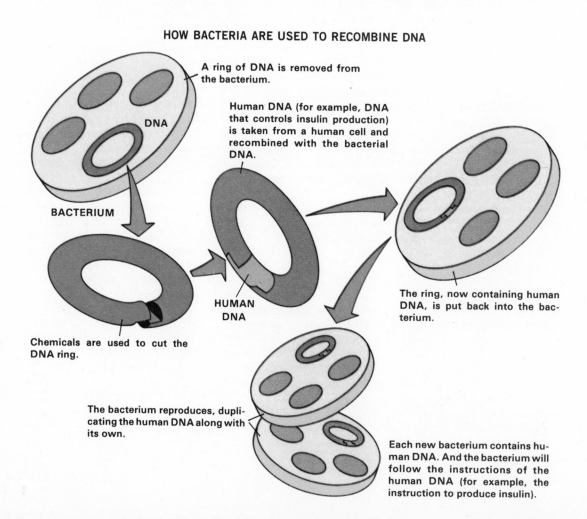

A ring of DNA is removed from the bacterium.

Human DNA (for example, DNA that controls insulin production) is taken from a human cell and recombined with the bacterial DNA.

DNA

BACTERIUM

Chemicals are used to cut the DNA ring.

HUMAN DNA

The ring, now containing human DNA, is put back into the bacterium.

The bacterium reproduces, duplicating the human DNA along with its own.

Each new bacterium contains human DNA. And the bacterium will follow the instructions of the human DNA (for example, the instruction to produce insulin).

As long ago as 1960, a Flash Gordon comic strip showed interferon being used to fight disease—in this case, a strange virus from outer space that was causing an epidemic among the crew of a spaceship.

sulin. The insulin made by the bacteria was exactly like the insulin made by the pancreas of human beings.

Some people cannot make insulin. These people are called diabetics. To stay alive they must use insulin from another source. At the present time, they use insulin made by the pancreases of pigs and cows. This insulin is not the same as human insulin. It is perfect for pigs and cows, but not for humans. Almost 20 percent of the diabetics who take pig or cow insulin get harmful side effects from the drug.

In 1980 scientists began to give diabetics human insulin made by bacteria. The first tests were successful. Soon diabetics everywhere may be receiving human insulin instead of pig or cow insulin.

▶ A REVOLUTIONARY TECHNIQUE

Genes are made of the chemical DNA (deoxyribonucleic acid). In gene splicing, the DNA is recombined, or put together again, in new ways. Thus, gene splicing is also called recombinant DNA. This process involves very advanced technology.

Gene splicing may revolutionize many aspects of our lives. Here are some of the possibilities:

Medicine. In addition to insulin, scientists have been able to get bacteria to produce human growth hormone. This chemical is made by the pituitary gland and controls growth. Some people don't produce enough growth hormone. As a result, they don't grow to normal heights. They are very short and are called dwarfs. Children who don't produce enough growth hormone can be given growth hormone taken from the pituitary glands of people who have died. But this is difficult and expensive. To treat one child for one year requires 50 pituitary glands. Using bacteria to make human growth hormone will make much more of the hormone available. It will also make the hormone less expensive.

Researchers have also spliced the human interferon gene into bacteria. Interferon is a protein made by cells when viruses invade your body. The interferon interferes with (fights) the viruses. Some of the viruses it fights are those that cause colds, flu, German measles, and chicken pox.

Many medical researchers believe that interferon can be used to fight cancer. They believe that interferon prevents the growth and reproduction of viruses that cause cancer. Researchers have begun to test this belief, and some of the results of their experiments are promising. But the researchers have only been able to conduct limited experiments because interferon is very difficult to obtain. It has to be removed from white blood cells. Huge amounts of blood are needed to obtain a tiny amount of interferon. And the interferon obtained in this manner is not pure.

In 1980 researchers announced that they had spliced the human interferon gene into bacteria. The bacteria began to make interferon. Commercial production of human interferon from bacteria promises pure, plentiful, and comparatively cheap supplies. Soon this interferon will be tested on people who have cancer. It will also be tested against the viruses that cause other diseases. Perhaps interferon will be the wonder drug of the coming decades.

Agriculture. Gene splicing may greatly affect agriculture and world food supplies. Researchers have gotten bacteria to produce proline. This chemical forms part of many proteins. Eventually, bacteria-produced proline may be fed to cattle. It will make the cattle grow faster.

Another possible benefit of gene splicing involves certain bacteria, called nitrogen-fixing bacteria, that live on the roots of legumes (plants such as peas and beans). The bacteria take nitrogen from the air and convert it to compounds that the plants need for growth. Other plants don't have this arrangement with the bacteria. They cannot make nitrogen. But they need nitrogen to grow. Farmers have to add nitrogen fertilizers to fields in which they grow corn, wheat, oats, and most other crops. Biologists would like to take the nitrogen-fixing genes from the bacteria and splice them into the genetic matter of corn and other plants. Then these plants could make their own fertilizer.

Industry. Some bacteria naturally break down petroleum into useful products. For example, some bacteria make ethylene oxide. This chemical is a starting material for making plastics. The bacteria only make small amounts of ethylene oxide. If scientists can remove the gene that enables the bacteria to make ethylene oxide and splice it into fast-growing bacteria, the result might be an organism that produces a lot of ethylene

oxide in a short time. This would be cheaper than making ethylene oxide by conventional chemical methods, and less energy would be needed. And unlike the chemical methods, the bacterial method would not pollute the environment.

▶ **NEW FORMS OF LIFE?**

When a cell—or an organism—reproduces, it makes copies of its genetic matter. Each offspring receives a set of the parents' genes. For example, a bacterium reproduces by dividing in two. Each of the two new cells (bacteria) has the same genetic material as the parent cell. If the parent has the human insulin gene, the offspring will also have the human insulin gene.

This raises some interesting questions. Every organism belongs to a certain species. It is like all the other members of that species. What happens when genetic material is taken from members of one species and put into members of another species? If a human gene is put into a bacterium, is that bacterium still like other members of its species? Or has it become a new form of life?

Such questions are being asked not only by scientists but also by business people and lawyers. In 1980 a related issue went before the U.S. Supreme Court. Ananda Chakrabarty, a scientist working for General Electric, developed a bacterium that can eat oil. It could be used to clean up oil spills. Chakrabarty's work did not involve taking genes from one organism and splicing them into another. It involved a different technique. But Chakrabarty and G.E. wanted to patent the new bacterium he had developed. (The owner of a patent has the right to determine who makes, sells, and financially benefits from the invention.) The Supreme Court ruled that because Chakrabarty's bacterium is a new form of life, it could be considered an invention and thus be patented. Because gene splicing may also create new forms of life, it is likely that these new forms could also be patented.

The commercial potential of gene splicing is great. And the potential benefits to people seem endless.

JENNY TESAR
Series Consultant
Wonders of Wildlife

ACID RAIN

Not too many years ago, people who wanted pure water would collect rain in big wooden barrels. But now, the water that collects in a rain barrel is likely to be anything but pure. In fact, it may be very much like vinegar.

Vinegar is an acid. And in more and more parts of the world, the rain and snow that fall from the skies contain acid—acid that kills plants and animals, erodes buildings, and may even harm people.

The problem is caused by power plants and other industries that burn oil and, especially, coal. Cars, buses, and other vehicles that use petroleum-based fuels are also to blame. When coal and oil are burned, sulfur dioxide and nitrogen oxides are produced as wastes. These chemicals enter the atmosphere. They combine with oxygen in the atmosphere to produce sulfuric acid and nitric acid.

Winds may carry the acids thousands of miles from their source. Acids that originate in Ohio may eventually be part of the rain that falls on Quebec. Acids from Ontario may fall on New York. Acids produced in Britain and France may fall on Sweden.

Acid rain seems to cause the greatest damage in lakes and rivers. As these bodies of water become more and more acid, the plants and animals that live there die. Eggs do not hatch. Bacteria that break down dead leaves and other organic matter also die.

People who fished the lakes and rivers of eastern North America were among the first to notice that something strange was happening. Places that used to provide large catches were no longer teeming with fish. People could spend a whole day at their favorite fishing spot and not even get a nibble. When scientists began to study the lakes and rivers, they discovered that the water was too acid to support life. Eventually, they traced the acid back to the industries and cars.

In the Adirondack Mountains of New York, more than 200 lakes have become fishless. In Ontario, 140 lakes are without fish—and the fish in 48,000 other lakes are threatened. In Nova Scotia, 7 rivers that once teemed with salmon now have no fish at all.

Will the situation improve? Not unless some action is taken. More and more sulfur dioxide and nitrogen oxides are being produced. Methods of removing these chemicals from factory smoke and car exhausts are expensive and not always effective. So it seems that there may be increasing amounts of acid in rain.

Many people think acid rain is one of the most serious environmental problems in North America. In 1980, Canada and the United States agreed to work together to control its spread. As one concerned official put it: "What goes up must come down. With acid rain, however, what comes down is much worse than what went up."

"Wonder if acid rain's affected the fishing in this lake?"

SEEING THINGS IN A NEW WAY

The rocklike structures in the photograph below are single salt crystals that have been magnified 150 times. When we look at salt crystals at this magnification and in such great detail, we are looking at a familiar object in a new way. Ordinarily, salt crystals look like smooth, miniature boulders. But in this photograph they look like the remains of some ancient ruin. As you can see, each single, cube-shaped salt crystal is actually made up of many little cube-shaped crystals, packed together to make the larger cube. In some places the little cubes have been broken off, leaving large spaces or gaps in the crystal. By examining the details in magnifications like this one, it is possible to learn a great deal more than can be known by examining an object with the naked eye.

Instruments that can look at objects close up (or magnify them) have been in use for a long time. But they aren't able to look at whole surfaces of objects with the precision and detail that are apparent in the magnification of these salt crystals. There is a tool that has become available in the past twenty years that is able to obtain such detail. This instrument is known as the scanning electron microscope, or SEM.

Microscopes that are most familiar to us use a beam of light to illuminate the object being viewed. Electron microscopes, however, "illuminate" their objects with a

Magnified salt crystals

stream of tiny particles called electrons. These are the same particles that produce electric current as they flow through wires, or create an image as they pass back and forth across a television screen. In the scanning electron microscope, a thin stream of millions of electrons is aimed at an object such as a salt crystal. The stream comes from something called an electron gun. This electron stream is so fine that it can touch only a very tiny spot on the salt crystal. In order to cover the entire surface of the object, the stream is moved back and forth over the surface in a rapid scanning motion. In this way, the tip of the stream is able to touch every wrinkle, bump, and crater on the surface of the salt crystal.

Two things happen as the stream hits the surface of the salt crystal. First, some of the

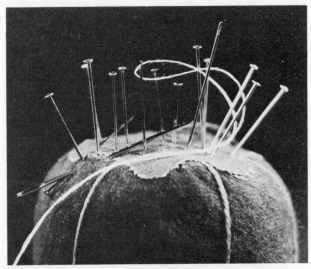

Pins and needles are among the simplest tools made by people. In the micrograph below, the point of the needle appears tapered and not very sharp, and the eye of the needle looks like a huge hole.

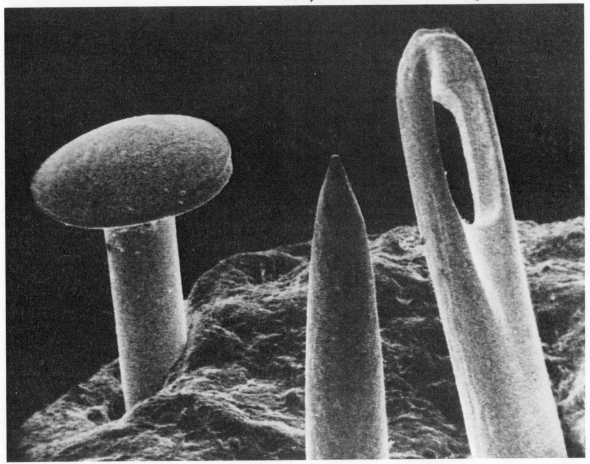

The micrograph above shows what looks like a creature from outer space. It's actually the face of a fruit fly! A fruit fly as you would normally see it is about the size of the head of a pin.

electrons bounce off. Second, electrons present in the salt crystal get knocked out. All these electrons—the ones that bounce off and the ones that get knocked out—are collected by the microscope from each scan of the stream across the salt crystal. The microscope then uses these electrons to form an image on a television screen of what it has just "seen." Gradually, as the scanning action continues, a complete image of the salt crystal is built up on the screen. This picture of the salt crystals is a photograph of what appeared on the television screen. Pictures like this one, taken with a microscope, are called micrographs.

Scientists use the scanning electron microscope to learn about the details, shapes, and

patterns of such things as plant cells, animal cells, viruses, crystals, and even moon rocks. Scientists study the images produced by the SEM to understand why something is the way it is. These images might reveal mysterious, unexpected structures. The surfaces of some familiar objects may look so different that you won't even recognize them. They show us what seems to be a new world, a small world, that exists before our eyes but can best be seen through the scanning electron microscope.

On these pages, you will see pictures of other familiar things both as you know them and as they look greatly magnified.

JOSEPH F. GENNARO, JR., and LISA GRILLONE
Authors, *Small Worlds Close Up*

This micrograph shows the small, boxlike compartments that make up cork. Cork is the thick, light, waxy outer layer of bark of the cork oak tree, and it protects the tree.

SPACE BRIEFS

Does the sun seem smaller lately? Some astronomers think that the sun's diameter may have shrunk by as much as 620 miles (1,000 kilometers) during the last few centuries. Careful measurements of the sun's diameter over only the last few decades suggest a slight shrinkage. More evidence that the sun was once larger comes from studies of the records of solar eclipses that occurred in 1567 and 1715.

But the astronomers aren't too worried. The sun is 864,000 miles (1,390,000 kilometers) in diameter. So the shrinkage is barely noticeable. More exciting is the question of whether there is a connection between the sun's size and Earth's climate. Keeping an eye on the size of the sun may give us a clue to what the climate will be like in the future.

▶ SPACE TOURS—SOVIET STYLE

The Soviet Salyut 6 space station, aloft for more than three years, continued to be a comfortable home for cosmonauts in 1980. Five two-man crews traveled to it and returned in Soyuz spacecraft. The longest residents were Soviet cosmonauts Valery Ryumin and Leonid Popov, who lived in Salyut 6 from April 9 to October 11. Their 185-day stay was 10 days longer than the previous record for continuous living in space, set by a Soviet crew in 1979.

Salyut 6 has also become a kind of international cruise ship of space. Some cosmonauts who visited it in past years, along with Soviet crew members, came from Czechoslovakia, Poland, and East Germany. In 1980, the Soviet Union sent cosmonauts from Hungary, Vietnam, and Cuba on the trip. And on November 28, a new type of Soyuz craft, the Soyuz-T3, docked with the space station. On board was the first three-man crew to be sent aloft by the Soviets since 1971. The crew returned to Earth two weeks later, after having tested and repaired the three-year-old Salyut.

▶ PLUTO—50 YEARS AFTER

Pluto—the distant ninth planet—is growing up. Pluto was only a speck of light in a photograph when it was discovered on February 18, 1930, by a young astronomy student. Now we have learned a lot more about this strange world at the edge of the solar system.

Some scientists have come up with a startling new theory—involving a huge asteroid—about why dinosaurs vanished from our planet.

Pluto seems to be different from the other planets, which are either small rocky worlds like Earth or huge gaseous globes like Jupiter. It seems to be a planetary iceberg made up of rocks and frozen gases. A thin atmosphere of methane gas has been detected, and the surface seems to be covered by methane frost. A small moon (named Charon) has been discovered. Most surprising, Pluto is much smaller than was thought. It is the smallest planet in the solar system, probably not much larger than Earth's moon.

▶ DINOSAURS—WIPED OUT BY AN ASTEROID?

Dinosaurs once ruled Earth. Then, about 65,000,000 years ago, these huge reptiles vanished, along with almost three-fourths of the known species of animals and plants. Why? There have been many theories— changes in the climate, volcanic eruptions, or the appearance of small mammals that ate the dinosaur eggs.

Now several scientists have come up with a new theory. Their idea is that a huge asteroid hit Earth, throwing quantities of dust into the stratosphere. The dust blocked out the sunlight for several years, killing almost all Earth's plant life. The plant-eating dinosaurs and then the meat-eaters died, along with huge numbers of other animals. The idea may seem incredible. But some evidence for it has been found in Italy, in a thin layer of clay that was deposited in the ocean just at the time the dinosaurs vanished. This layer may contain the dust produced by the asteroid impact—it has a high amount of iridium, an element that is rare on Earth but more abundant in meteorites and asteroids.

If the asteroid theory is right, this dust layer should be found all over the world. And scientists are indeed finding it, in places as far apart as Denmark, New Zealand, and Spain.

▶ THE FIVE-WAY QUASAR

Quasars are strange, starlike objects that emit strong radio waves. They are out near the edge of the universe, rushing away from us at tremendous speeds. We don't know how they formed or where their tremendous energy comes from. One quasar is hard enough to explain. How do you handle five, all together?

Soviet cosmonauts Leonid Popov (*left*) and Valery Ryumin set a new record for living in space—185 days.

That was the problem that faced astronomers who used the new multiple-mirror telescope on Mt. Hopkins, in Arizona, to look at an object called PG 1115+08. They saw what seemed to be five separate quasars, all alike. Quintuplets? No, the astronomers think, just five different images of the same single quasar. Einstein's theory of relativity predicts that gravity can bend a beam of light much as a glass lens does. If a large unseen mass (like a dark galaxy or a black hole) were located somewhere between PG 1115+08 and Earth, then the light from the quasar would be bent around it on its way to Earth, producing the multiple images. This explanation reduces the five quasars to one. But scientists still don't know the exact nature of the unseen mass that is bending the quasar's light—or, for that matter, how the single quasar got there in the first place.

BEVAN M. FRENCH
Discipline Scientist, Planetary Materials
National Aeronautics and Space Administration

THE LONG, HOT SUMMER

The summer of 1980 will be remembered for a long time by the people who live in the midwestern and southwestern United States. Day after day, temperatures rose above 100°F (38°C). The Dallas–Fort Worth area of Texas had 33 straight days of temperatures over 100°F. In Wichita Falls, Kansas, the temperature hit 117°F (47°C) one day. In Dallas it reached 113°F (45°C). And in Oklahoma City, 105°F (41°F).

At the same time, the area went without rain. Between June 2 and July 20, Houston, Texas, had 0.6 inches of rain—only 9 percent of the amount that normally falls during this period. Little Rock, Arkansas, had 0.7 inches—only 12 percent of normal.

The cause of the hot, dry weather was a strong high-pressure system. It moved north from the Gulf of Mexico, then stopped over the south-central United States. Usually, there is an alternating pattern of high- and low-pressure systems over an area. But the stalled system was so strong that it kept cloud-carrying low-pressure systems away. Why the system was so strong and why it remained in one place so long are questions that scientists have not yet answered.

The combined heat wave and drought took a tremendous toll. More than 1,260 deaths were blamed on the weather. Most of the victims were elderly and poor people who lived in houses without air conditioning and with poor ventilation.

Thousands of other people had heart attacks, heat strokes, and other illnesses as a result of the weather. In St. Louis, ambulance calls jumped to 350 a day. This was almost twice the normal rate. On July 19 in Houston, 100 children at an outdoor swimming pool had to receive emergency medical treatment for heat exhaustion.

The weather also caused an estimated $12,000,000,000 (billion) worth of damage. Highways buckled and melted. Reservoirs and lakes dried up, killing fish and other organisms. Fires raced through dry forests, burning thousands of acres of trees. Thefts of air-conditioners increased.

Economically, the hardest hit people were the farmers—especially poultry, cattle, and grain farmers. The heat wave killed more than 8,000,000 broiler chickens and some 1,000,000 breeder hens. It greatly cut egg production. A woman in Tennessee gave her

The 1980 heat wave and drought caused many crops to shrivel and die.

130

The blistering weather also caused livestock watering holes to dry up.

chickens ice water three times a day. Nevertheless, 25 of her 88 hens died. And instead of laying 30 dozen eggs a week, the hens laid only 12 dozen eggs a week.

Cattle, which normally gain weight in the summer, lost weight during the 1980 summer. The heat and drought killed the grass on which cattle graze. Rather than feed expensive hay to their cattle, ranchers sold many of the animals. It will take at least a few years to rebuild the herds.

Vast expanses of normally green fields turned brown as plants shriveled up and died. Corn, soybeans, and cotton were among the hardest-hit crops. As with poultry and cattle, consumers as well as farmers will feel the effects. Reduced production means higher prices. Corn, which normally sells for about $2 a bushel, was selling for $3.33 by mid-August. Cotton prices jumped 20 percent. Chicken prices went up 25 percent.

Not everyone suffered from the weather. Air-conditioned shopping centers, ice rinks, and similar facilities enjoyed a jump in business. And some people found at least temporary solutions to the many weather-caused difficulties. A St. Louis bus driver served ice water to his passengers. In southern Texas, ranchers burned the needles off cactus plants so that their cattle could eat the juicy flesh of the plants.

Government groups tried to ease the suffering. Electric fans were delivered to homes without air conditioning. Air-conditioned civic centers were turned into emergency heat-relief centers. Electric utility companies agreed to continue service to elderly people who could not pay their bills. The utilities also agreed to let customers pay their summer bills in installments. (In many places, the high temperatures meant that electric bills were 50 to 60 percent higher than in 1979.)

The heat wave ended by mid-August. And the rains came. But many people worried that the heat and drought would be repeated in 1981. Old-timers in the area remembered the 1930's, when several years of heat and drought turned much of Texas, Oklahoma, Kansas, and Colorado into a giant Dust Bowl. In the 1950's, eight years of low rainfall caused the Great Texas Drought. Did 1980 mark the start of another multi-year drought? No one can answer this question. People will have to see what the next few years will bring. But everyone is hoping that many, many years will pass before there is another long, hot summer.

OUT OF THE PAST

People who study the past learn a great deal from objects that are found in the sea and earth. Such objects are messages out of the past—they tell about civilizations and even forms of life that no longer exist.

▶ SHIPWRECKS FROM A FAMOUS BATTLE

On September 2, 31 B.C.—two thousand years ago—a famous sea battle took place. It was the Battle of Actium, between the two leaders of the Roman Empire. On one side were the forces of Octavian, who ruled the western portion of the Roman world. Opposing him was Mark Antony, who ruled the east.

Actium is located on the northwest coast of Greece. Antony had set up his winter headquarters there. His forces included 120,000 horsemen and 500 large ships. About 60 of the ships belonged to Cleopatra, the queen of Egypt, who was visiting Antony.

A print showing Cleopatra at the Battle of Actium.

Antony's ships were heavily armed. They had *koraxes*—a type of hook that was used to hold onto an enemy ship so that the enemy ship could be boarded and captured.

Octavian's forces were smaller. They included 80,000 infantrymen and 250 light ships. At the front of each ship was an *embolos*—a ramming device.

Octavian moved his forces across the Ionian Sea, from Italy to a position north of Actium, and cut off Antony's supply route. Antony decided to face Octavian's naval fleet. Cleopatra's ships followed Antony's ships into battle. But Antony's ships could not maneuver as well as Octavian's ships, and it became apparent that Antony was losing. His sailors began to surrender. Cleopatra took her ships and sailed for Egypt. Antony followed her, leaving his forces to manage as best they could.

Octavian captured and burned most of Antony's ships. About a week later, Antony's land army surrendered. Because he had won the battle, Octavian was crowned emperor of the entire Roman Empire. He was given the name Emperor Augustus.

As the centuries passed, most of the ships sunk in the Battle of Actium rotted away. But some became buried in mud and sand and did not rot. In 1980, Greek archeologists working in the waters off Actium reported that they had found shipwrecks from the battle. The archeologists hope to raise the wrecks. This would be very exciting because the wrecks are the first Roman warships ever to be found. Studying them would tell us a lot about life in early Roman times.

▶ LIVING THINGS OF LONG AGO

There were living things on our planet for billions of years before Roman times. We know this because we have found fossils (remains of plants and animals that once lived). Some fossils, such as bones, teeth, and shells, are body parts that turned to stone. Other fossils, such as footprints, are impressions in rock.

Fossils are important because they tell us what living things of long ago looked like and when these organisms lived. They also help scientists explain the relationships between different kinds of living things.

In 1980, two important fossil finds were announced. One find was made in the Sahara desert in Egypt. There, scientists found the skeletons of small monkeylike animals. They named the animals *Aegyptopithecus zeuxis* ("connecting ape of Egypt").

The scientists believe that *Aegyptopithecus* was an ancestor of both apes and human beings. That is, they believe that apes and people of today evolved from this animal.

Aegyptopithecus lived about 30,000,000 years ago. It was about the size of a cat. Fossil leg and arm bones indicate that it lived in trees. It probably ran along the tree branches, rather than swinging from limb to limb. Fossil teeth show that it ate fruit. The creature's eye sockets were small, indicating that the eyes were not unusually large. Therefore, the animals were probably active during daylight hours rather than at night.

The second important fossil find took place in northwestern Australia. There, scientists discovered the oldest remains of living things ever found. The fossils are 3,500,000,000 (billion) years old. This means that life has existed on Earth much longer than scientists had believed.

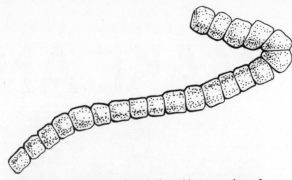

In Australia, scientists found the oldest remains of living things. Each of the tiny ancient organisms consisted of a chain of cells, as in this sketch.

The Australian fossils are very tiny. They can only be seen through a microscope. Each of the ancient organisms consisted of a chain of cells. The organisms looked somewhat like certain bacteria that live today.

The places where both fossil finds were made are hot, dry areas. But long, long ago they were very different. When *Aegyptopithecus* lived, the area that is now the Sahara was covered with grasslands and forests. When the tiny bacterialike creatures lived in northwestern Australia, that area was a warm lake. By studying fossils we learn that living things and the earth were very different millions of years ago than they are today.

In Egypt, scientists found the skeletons of small monkeylike animals (*drawing, below*) that may be the ancestors of both apes and human beings.

MAKE AND DO

With stockings, polyester filling, scraps of material, and some imagination, you can populate your world with pantyhose people.

GLITTERING GLASS

You can make your home sparkle by creating these glittering glass objects—plates, bowls, jars, and bottles. And because you work with waterproof paints, your creations will last and last, even if they are washed over and over again.

Buy inexpensive glass plates and containers. Or use jars, bottles and other glassware that originally held various foods and liquids. A group of empty mayonnaise jars can be turned into a canister set. A wine bottle can become an attractive container for vinegar —or a vase for flowers. Baby food jars can become serving containers for mustard, ketchup, and relish.

The best paints to use are acrylic paints, which are waterproof once they dry. But other types of waterproof paints can also be used. Ask the salespeople in your local craft or art supply store what they recommend. Buy a selection of several colors: red, yellow, green, blue, and perhaps black and white.

It's best to plan your design before you actually begin painting. On a sheet of paper draw the outline of the object you are going to paint. Use colored pencils or felt-tip pens to sketch a design. The complexity of the design depends on your skills as an artist. But you don't have to be a master painter to create attractive objects. Anyone can draw stars or happy faces or funny fish.

Instead of making your own designs, you can also copy interesting designs from books or magazines. The plates shown here are decorated with Pennsylvania hex designs. The designs have special meanings. The star and tulips stand for faith and happiness. The sun and raindrops are for a large, healthy crop.

Any item can be personalized. For example, you might make a set of cereal bowls for your family. In the center of each bowl—or around the side—paint the name of a person in the family.

Once you have your design down on paper, tape it on the inside of the plate. The design should face the outside, or bottom, of the plate. Turn the plate over and simply paint the design, just as you paint within the lines in a coloring book. This method can also be used for bowls, jars, and for bottles with necks wide enough for you to put your hand into. When you cannot use this method, you will have to paint your designs freehand.

One thing is important: Do not put the paint on the side that will touch food. For example, paint the outside of a bottle or jar. Paint the bottom side of a plate or bowl.

Here are some tips:

1. Wash the glassware very well. The glass must be clean or your painted design won't stick to it.

2. Dry the glassware very well.

3. Avoid touching the painting surface. You do not want to leave fingerprints. It is best to handle the glass with tissue paper.

4. Keep a damp piece of tissue paper or a paper towel handy as you paint. If you make a mistake, wipe the paint off immediately, before it has a chance to dry.

5. Let the paint dry thoroughly. If the colors aren't as dark as you would like, apply a second coat.

STRIKE IT RICH!

"Gold!"

It was a magic word. It made people leave their homes, their jobs, their families. They packed a few belongings and set out across a huge continent. They endured desert heat, hunger, disease, and the threat of outlaws. Many of them died. But more kept coming, all driven by the hope of finding gold.

Gold rushes are part of the history of North America. In 1849, 80,000 people poured into California. Most of these "Forty-niners," as they were called, headed into the area around the American River, north and east of Sacramento. Gold had first been found there in January, 1848. The Forty-niners staked their claims and dug, mined, and panned for gold. Few struck it rich, but many of them settled in California and thus helped to open up the Far West. In 1850, California became a state.

In 1858, 25,000 prospectors rushed to the Fraser River in British Columbia after a gold strike there. The next year, the "Fifty-niners" followed the call of gold to Colorado. And beginning in 1897, the Yukon and Alaska became the scenes of the last great gold rushes in North America. Even the severe cold couldn't stop those who dreamed of finding the precious yellow metal.

Most of the prospectors failed. But for some, the dreams of discovery came true. Great fortunes were made. In 1852, $80,000,000 worth of gold was unearthed in California. Even today, almost 130 years later, there are gold prospectors still dreaming of the "big strike"—especially because we are now seeing a tremendous increase in the value of gold.

In the 1850's, gold was worth about $16 an ounce. Over a century later, it was worth about $35 an ounce. In the 1970's, gold prices began to steadily climb, and in 1980 the price of an ounce skyrocketed to over $800. It settled back to about $625, still an enormous sum. Because of the fantastic prices, people are showing a new interest in finding gold. There has been no 1849-style gold rush, but prospectors are once again searching for gold along the banks of the American River, as well as many other streams in North America.

YOU CAN PAN FOR GOLD

Prospecting is not easy. It can take a long time and it offers no guarantee of success. Good luck is often more important than how long or how hard you work. An experienced prospector may find next to nothing in a year of looking for gold; a newcomer may strike pay dirt the first day out. But you won't find anything unless you look, and the panning method is probably the cheapest and simplest way to start prospecting.

As a river or stream flows past a vein of gold, it may break off small bits and flakes of the metal and carry them along in its current. But gold is very heavy—almost twenty times as heavy as water—so the little particles will sink to the stream bed wherever the current slows down.

The best place to pan for gold, then, is a spot where the stream runs slowly. This may be at the inside of a curve in the stream, close to the edge. If you toss a twig or a leaf into the water, you can follow it along to find the spots where the current is losing speed. These would be good locations to start panning.

You'll probably get wet, so it's a good idea to wear waterproof boots. And of course, any water can be dangerous, so always proceed with caution.

THE METHOD

With your shovel, dig as deep as you can into the stream bed. Fill your pan about half full with dirt. Carefully place the pan into the water and shake it a bit. This will move the dirt around and allow the much heavier gold to settle toward the bottom of the pan.

Continue to stir the gravel around in the water, and tip the pan slightly so that the water slowly spills out. Gradually all the light dirt will be washed away, and you will be left with small pebbles and sand—and possibly bits of gold.

You can pick out the pebbles with your fingers and toss them away. Continue dipping the pan in the water and washing away the dirt. Finally you will be left with only fine black sand. If you find no black sand, you will find no gold. Black sand and gold always occur together.

With your tweezers, sift through the black sand that is left. Look for tiny yellow grains

THE EQUIPMENT

If you would like to try panning, you will need the right equipment. The most important implement is the pan. A piepan will do, but it should be made of a heavy metal like tin to keep its shape. Hard plastic pans, made especially for gold hunters, are also suitable.

You should also have a shovel or a small garden spade, tweezers for picking tiny flakes of gold out of the dirt you examine, and a small bottle to put your gold in—if you really strike it rich!

of gold. Don't be fooled by fool's gold. Fool's gold is pyrite, a mineral that is yellow, like real gold, but much harder. Real gold is soft and you can easily press into it or flatten it with your tweezers. Fool's gold will break when you push into it with tweezers or hit it with a hammer.

If you find gold, or something you think is gold, put it into your small bottle and put the cover on tight. Later, if you wish, you can take your gold to an assay office, where it will be tested. The assayer will tell you if you have found real gold.

If you don't find any gold, don't give up your search. There may be some nuggets at the next bend in the stream, or beneath a tree at the water's edge where the current slows to a lazy crawl.

Try prospecting. It's fun, and with a little bit of luck . . .

. . . you may end up with a handful of gold.

STAKING A CLAIM

If luck is with you and you do strike gold, you should immediately stake a claim. A mining claim gives you, and only you, the right to pan for gold at the location of your strike.

First you should put up a sign at your panning site stating that that area is your claim. Then you must find out who owns the property that you are mining on.

If the land is owned by a private individual, you would have to get his or her permission to work the claim. And the owner would probably want some payment in return for allowing you to work the land. If the land is public, you should contact your local, state, provincial, or national government to find out how to make your mining claim.

Good luck!

AUTHOR! AUTHOR!

Ebenezer Scrooge and Bob Cratchit are two characters in *A Christmas Carol,* by Charles Dickens. Bob's son is also a character in this famous story. Do you remember his name? He is one of the 22 characters listed below (in the left column). Match him to Dickens, the author who created him (in the right column). Similarly match the other characters with their creators.

Characters
1. Alice
2. Tom Sawyer
3. Bambi
4. Beth and Jo
5. Brer Rabbit
6. Hans Brinker
7. Hansel and Gretel
8. Heidi
9. Johnny Tremain
10. Kim
11. Long John Silver
12. Madeline
13. Nancy Drew
14. Peter Pan
15. Peter Rabbit
16. Pooh
17. Rip Van Winkle
18. Robinson Crusoe
19. The Cat in the Hat
20. The Ugly Duckling
21. The Yearling
22. Tiny Tim

Authors
a. Louisa May Alcott
b. Hans Christian Andersen
c. Sir James Barrie
d. Ludwig Bemelmans
e. Mark Twain
f. Lewis Carroll
g. Daniel Defoe
h. Charles Dickens
i. Mary Mapes Dodge
j. Esther Forbes
k. Jacob and Wilhelm Grimm
l. Joel Chandler Harris
m. Washington Irving
n. Carolyn Keene
o. Rudyard Kipling
p. A. A. Milne
q. Beatrix Potter
r. Marjorie Kinnan Rawlings
s. Felix Salten
t. Dr. Seuss
u. Johanna Spyri
v. Robert Louis Stevenson

ANSWERS: 1,f; 2,e; 3,s; 4,a; 5,l; 6,i; 7,k; 8,u; 9,j; 10,o; 11,v; 12,d; 13,n; 14,c; 15,q; 16,p; 17,m; 18,g; 19,t; 20,b; 21,r; 22,h

Next, go on a hunt. All 22 characters are hidden in this search-a-word puzzle. Try to find them. To find the names, read forward, backward, up, down, and diagonally. If you wish, cover the puzzle with a sheet of tracing paper. Then you can circle each character's name as you find it. One name has already been circled for you.

A	T	H	E	C	A	T	I	N	T	H	E	H	A	T
L	E	T	E	R	G	D	N	A	L	E	S	N	A	H
O	H	H	W	E	R	D	Y	C	N	A	N	L	E	E
N	A	E	P	L	C	B	A	B	E	R	K	I	T	U
G	N	Y	E	L	E	I	N	A	L	H	D	I	T	G
J	S	E	T	I	G	S	L	N	K	I	O	E	M	L
O	B	A	E	B	E	T	H	A	N	D	J	O	A	Y
H	R	R	R	M	I	T	Y	N	I	T	O	M	P	D
N	I	L	R	T	O	M	S	A	W	Y	E	R	S	U
S	N	I	A	M	E	R	T	Y	N	N	H	O	J	C
I	K	N	B	B	R	E	R	R	A	B	B	I	T	K
L	E	G	B	I	B	M	A	B	V	F	E	R	N	L
V	R	B	I	P	E	T	E	R	P	A	N	Y	L	I
E	I	O	T	M	A	D	E	L	I	N	E	K	B	N
R	O	B	I	N	S	O	N	C	R	U	S	O	E	G

ELEGANT EGGS

Sometimes the most beautiful crafts are the easiest to make. These lovely eggs are a perfect example. They are made of sugar, icing, and bits of jewelry. But the most important ingredient is your imagination. The eggs make wonderful gifts. And they are long-lasting gifts, too. If kept safe and dry, they will last for years.

WHAT TO USE

Sugar
Egg white
Food coloring (optional)
Plastic egg mold
Decorating tube with 10-inch (25-centimeter) bag and small star tip
Confectioners' powdered sugar
Cream of tartar
Bits of broken jewelry, sequins, glitter, gold thread

HOW TO MAKE THE EGG

1. Use about 1 cup of sugar for each egg. Dampen the sugar with the egg white and mix well. The mixture should have the consistency of wet sand. You can make a colored egg by adding a drop or two of food coloring to this mixture.

2. Take the mold for half the egg. Press the damp sugar firmly into the mold.

3. Turn the mold over onto a cookie sheet or a piece of aluminum foil. Gently remove the mold.

4. Repeat steps 2 and 3 using the second half of the mold.

5. Let the sugar dry for about a half hour.

6. Using a teaspoon, scoop out the center of each sugar mold. This must be done very carefully. Hollow out the center until you have a shell that is about ¼ inch (.6 centimeter) thick. (The sugar you remove can be used to make another egg.)

7. Let the egg halves dry overnight.

HOW TO DECORATE THE EGG

1. Prepare the icing. Use about 1 cup of confectioners' sugar for each egg. Add enough water to the sugar to form a smooth paste. Add ¼ teaspoon of cream of tartar to the mixture.

2. Use some of the icing to cement together the two halves of the egg.

3. Let the egg dry for at least three hours. Put the left-over icing in a closed container. Refrigerate the icing until you are ready for step 4.

4. Fill the bag of the decorating tube with icing. Cover the seam where the two egg halves meet with little star-shaped flowers. Also decorate the top of the egg with star-shaped flowers.

5. Finish decorating the egg with pieces of jewelry or other pretty objects. Gently press the pieces into the icing.

6. Let the finished egg dry overnight.

FABULOUS FABERGÉ

The most fabulous eggs ever made were created by Peter Carl Fabergé. Fabergé was a Russian goldsmith and designer who lived from 1846 to 1920. He designed many jeweled items for the rulers of Russia. But he was most famous for his eggs. The eggs were made of enameled metal and were decorated with gold and beautiful jewels. Many of Fabergé's eggs were actually little boxes that could be opened. One of these eggs contained a tiny model of a Russian palace.

STAMP COLLECTING

Famous people and places were featured on stamps from countries around the world in 1980. There were also colorful new stamps displaying the beauties of the natural world. And a new price record was set for a single stamp.

The record was reached with the sale of the only copy of an 1856 magenta 1-cent stamp from British Guiana (now Guyana). This stamp first changed hands in 1873, when a teenage collector who had found it in an attic sold it for about $1.50. In 1980, a collector paid $935,000 for the stamp, now considered the most valuable in the world.

▶ PEOPLE AND PLACES

Many well-known women were portrayed on stamps in 1980. One reason for this was that the year marked the midpoint in the United Nations Decade for Women, a ten-year period that has set as its goal equality between the sexes. The United Nations marked the event with a set of commemorative stamps bearing variations of the same symbol—a dove with the signs for "female" and "equal" woven into the design.

Among the women honored on U.S. stamps were Helen Keller and her teacher, Anne Sullivan. Keller, who was blind and deaf, overcame her disabilities with the help of her teacher and became a symbol of courage. The 15-cent commemorative stamp marked the 100th anniversary of her birth. Brazil also issued a stamp in honor of these two women.

Dolley Madison, the wife of U.S. President James Madison, was shown on a small-size 15-cent stamp. The stamp reflected the grace and style that made her Washington's leading hostess in the early 1800's.

The second stamp in the U.S. Literary Arts series, which began in 1979, depicted Edith Wharton. Wharton's novels of elegant life at the turn of the century won her two Pulitzer prizes. Britain also honored women writers. A block of British stamps showed the 19th-century authors Charlotte and Emily Brontë, George Eliot, and Elizabeth Gaskell. Each stamp featured a portrait of the writer and a scene from one of her novels.

Two of these British stamps were put out as part of the Europa series—the special stamps issued each year by members of the Conference of European Postal and Tele-communications Administrations. The Europa theme for 1980 was famous people. Like Britain, other countries combined the U.N. and Europa themes and depicted famous women. Monaco's stamp, for example, showed the French writer Colette, whose works include the novel *Gigi*. A Greek stamp honored the operatic soprano Maria Callas.

Important men of the past were also honored on 1980 stamps. Ireland's Europa stamps showed two famous writers of the late 1800's and early 1900's—Oscar Wilde and George Bernard Shaw. Wilde was shown in a portrait by the French artist Toulouse-Lautrec; Shaw was presented in a caricature. A Canadian issue showed former prime minister John Diefenbaker. A 15-cent U.S. commemorative in the Black Heritage series portrayed Benjamin Bannecker, an 18th-century mathematician and astronomer. And a 40-cent U.S. airmail stamp honored Philip Mazzei, an Italian who settled in the Virginia colony and became a strong supporter of democracy. His articles, written under the pen name Furioso, helped fuel the revolution. Italy also issued a stamp in his honor, with the same design as the U.S. stamp.

Stamps reflected history in another way in 1980—by portraying landmarks of the issuing countries. China, for example, put out a set of four stamps showing the Great Wall. To mark London 1980, the international exhibition held in May, Britain compressed eight famous London landmarks onto a single 50-pence stamp. Another British issue reproduced watercolors of five landmarks, including Buckingham Palace and Hampton Court. Germany added two new stamps to its series of castles. And Denmark pictured landscapes in northern Jutland, including an ancient Viking burial ground.

In the United States, four stamps continued the Architecture USA series. The buildings portrayed carried the series into the heavy Victorian styles of the 19th century.

146

Letters
Lift Spirits

USA 15c

ÉIRE 12

George Bernard Shaw

CEPT EUROPA

P.S.
Write
Soon

USA 15c

NIPPON

20

DEUTSCHE BUNDESPOST BERLIN

40

12ᴾ

LIVERPOOL AND MANCHESTER RAILWAY 1830

12ᴾ

LIVERPOOL AND MANCHESTER RAILWAY 1830

12ᴾ   12ᴾ

LIVERPOOL AND MANCHESTER RAILWAY 1830   LIVERPOOL AND MANCHESTER R

MONACO

1980 EUROPA 1980

G. COLETTE

1,30

KINGFISHER 10P

USA 15c

HELEN KELLER
ANNE SULLIVAN

17

CANADA

15c

UNITED
NATIONS
DECADE
FOR
WOMEN

UNITED NATIONS

USA Olympics 1980
15c

CÔTE FRANÇAISE
DES SOMALIS
POSTE AERIENNE
40F   RF

**A TOPICAL
COLLECTION OF
UNDERWATER CREATURES**

2¢   KENYA

MARINE LIFE

10¢ POSTAGE   HEALTH 2¢

New Zealand   HEALTH 1979

Coral Reefs USA 15¢
Brain Coral: U.S. Virgin Islands

Coral Reefs USA 15¢
Elkhorn Coral: Florida

Coral Reefs USA 15¢
Chalice Coral: American Samoa

Coral Reefs USA 15¢
Finger Coral: Hawaii

SURINAME

1ct

Liopropoma carmabi

Dactylopterus volitans L.   2D

JUGOSLAVIJA

10
DDR

Spitzschwanz-Guppy

SEA SLUG Robastra arika

10
PAPUA NEW GUINEA

400F

POSTE AERIENNE

REPUBLIQUE DES COMORES

17 postes postage

Canada

Rock Beauty Holacanthus tricolor

½c
British Virgin Islands

CHANNA OBSCURA   50f

République du Burundi

THE NATURAL WORLD

Stamps that draw on the colors and forms of nature for their designs are always among the most beautiful. A 17-cent Canadian commemorative featuring a lush garden is an example. It was issued to mark the international garden and landscape show, Floralies 1980, held in Montreal.

Swaziland, in southern Africa, issued 15 stamps showing just a few of its thousands of flowering plants. Israel portrayed thistles, common in its arid climate, on a set of three stamps. Belgium, Nepal, Andorra, and the Faroe Islands were among other countries that featured flowers and plants on their stamps in 1980.

Some of the loveliest wildlife stamps portrayed birds. Sierra Leone issued a 14-stamp set showing colorful African species. And a set of four British stamps showed water birds, such as the kingfisher, that have been protected in Britain since 1880, under one of the earliest conservation laws.

Endangered species were themes for stamps from many countries. A Canadian stamp showed the prairie chicken, a bird whose natural plains habitat has been largely destroyed by farming. A set of four stamps from the island of Guernsey, in the English Channel, showed golden Guernsey goats. The wild goats were once nearly extinct but are now re-established on the island.

OTHER STAMPS FROM AROUND THE WORLD

The last of the U.S. stamps marking the 1980 Olympic Games came out in February. These were four 15-cent stamps showing sports from the Winter Games. Beginning in 1979, the Postal Service had put out ten stamps, three postal cards, a stamped envelope, and an aerogramme in honor of the Games.

One of the most unusual U.S. issues honored letter writing. These stamps came in sheets that included large and small sizes, in four different designs. Another issue showed windmills, once common throughout the country. The windmill stamps were small and were issued in booklets that contained ten, instead of the usual eight, stamps.

Masks carved by Indians of the Pacific Northwest were featured on the latest addition to the American Folk Art series. Four brightly colored masks, from four different Indian groups, were shown on the 15-cent stamps.

In 1980, the United Nations began a series that will continue for at least ten years. It is devoted to flags of member countries. Sixteen flags were chosen for the first stamps, which bear 15-cent denominations.

Britain honored the 150th anniversary of the first regular passenger-carrying railway, the Liverpool and Manchester, with a set of five commemoratives. Together, the strip of five stamps showed a complete train.

Oriental brushwork was displayed on four stamps from China showing galloping horses. Several Asian countries issued stamps noting the start of the year 4678 of the ancient Chinese calendar—the year of the monkey. Japan's stamp showed a folk toy made up of three clay monkeys, while Taiwan issued two stamps showing monkeys at play.

To mark the year 5741 of its calendar, Israel also released a set of stamps. These showed lamps that are traditionally lighted on the eve of the sabbath.

A TOPICAL COLLECTION

Some of the most beautiful stamps portray the colorful and mysterious world of underwater creatures. Such stamps would make a wonderful topical collection—a collection built around a single theme. You could begin with some of the stamps issued in 1980. Among the most striking were four U.S. stamps that focused on corals and the bright tropical fish that live in coral reefs. Another 1980 issue was a Canadian stamp showing an endangered species—the Atlantic whitefish, a freshwater species that is found only in Nova Scotia.

A topical collection can span all years and all parts of the world. Include a guppy stamp from East Germany, a sea slug stamp from Papua New Guinea, a marine life stamp from Kenya, and stamps with schools of vividly colored tropical fish from the island countries of the Caribbean and the Pacific. Through your topical collection, you'll learn about some of the world's most exotic creatures.

CHARLESS HAHN
Stamp Editor, *Chicago Sun-Times*

A

B

C

READ A ROAD SIGN

How fast can you read? Fast enough to understand a sign that says ROAD CLOSED TO ALL VEHICLES as you whiz past it in a car? What if the sign is in German—or Swahili?

Road signs of many countries solve this problem with pictures. Pictures can be understood instantly, by speakers of any language. And there are other clues. A sign's shape is one. In international signs, a triangle warns of danger, and a circle gives traffic rules. In North America, other shapes are used—a diamond, for instance, means danger. Color is also a clue. North American signs use red for stop and yellow for danger. Most drivers can easily "read" the pictures, shapes, and colors. Can you?

D

E

F

G

Look at these road signs. They come from all over the world. See if you can "read" what they are saying. Each sign has a letter under it. Match each one with its numbered meaning.

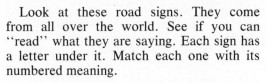

1. WATCH OUT FOR DEER, Virginia
2. WATCH OUT FOR BICYCLISTS, Denmark
3. WATCH OUT FOR TURTLES, Connecticut
4. WATCH OUT FOR CAMELS, Algeria
5. WATCH OUT FOR HIPPOS, Zambia
6. REFRESHMENTS NEARBY, Mexico
7. TRAIN CROSSING, France
8. GAS STATION NEARBY, California
9. WATCH OUT FOR ELEPHANTS, Zambia
10. WATCH OUT FOR THIEVES, Denmark

ANSWERS:
A.3; B.7; C.2; D.8; E.1; F.5; G.6; H.9; I.4; J.10.

H

I

Pas på tyven

J

BOX ART

Here is an easy way to change an ordinary box into one that is pretty—and pretty unusual. The boxes can be used to hold jewelry, paper clips, or any of your favorite small treasures. You can also fill them with candy or small gifts and give them to friends.

Each box will be your own unique creation. You can work with tiny candies, macaroni, dried peas, sunflower seeds, coffee beans—the list of dry foods you can use is long and varied. On a red box, use alphabet pasta to create a message such as "I think you're nice." Paint a box bright blue. Then glue on a snowman made of rice, with peppercorns for the eyes and a red-painted grain of rice for the mouth. Make a tulip using lentils and bay leaves, on a white box.

All you have to do is (1) decide on your design, (2) select the foods you wish to use, (3) choose or paint a box in a complimentary color, (4) arrange the design on the box cover, and (5) glue each piece down.

To prevent the decorations from attracting insects, and to keep the decorations from coming loose, you should seal the surface. Try a water-based sealer or an acrylic spray, both of which are available at art and craft supply stores. Or use clear nail polish. Cover the entire top of the box with the sealer. Be sure to cover the sides and the top of every piece of food. Apply several coats of the sealer. Let each coat dry thoroughly before you apply the next coat.

IT'S A-MAZE-ING!

Hurry up! The volcano is erupting, and you have to get off the mountain-maze.

Place a sheet of tracing paper over the maze. Begin at the arrow on the bottom and try to find your way out (to the arrow at the top). If you come to a blind alley, try using a different-colored pencil and different route.

The solution is on page 381.

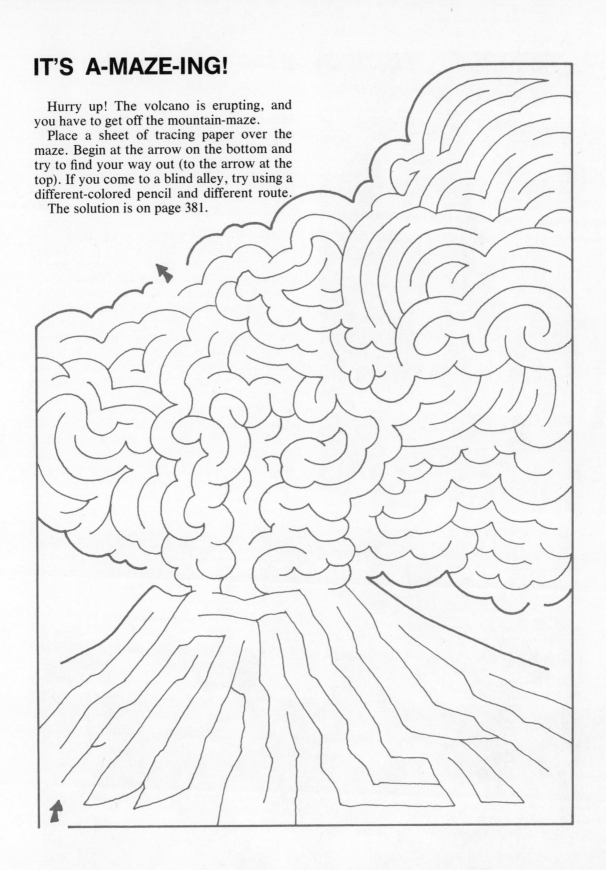

START A COLLECTION

Have you ever come home from an outing to the beach with your pockets bulging with shells? Were they the beginning of a shell collection? Has a stamp ever appealed to you so much that you cut it off an envelope and stuck it in a drawer? Did you soon have a drawerful of stamps?

For many people, collecting is an irresistible passion. People collect bells, whistles, plants, pickle jars, badges, and antique fire-fighting equipment. The items are endless.

The pictures you see on these pages are of collectors and their collections. The hat collector has collected male headgear from all over the world. The comic book collector started his collection by never throwing away comic books when he was a kid. Compassion moved a family to start their Raggedy Ann orphanage. They just can't resist taking home a neglected Raggedy Ann lying all alone in a junk store. The string collector has the largest ball of string in the world. He started it in 1950, and says, "There's solid twine all the way through, though there may be a few acorns inside, since the squirrels like to sit on it." (After all, the squirrels have to keep their acorn collection somewhere!)

ELLEN LAND-WEBER
Author, *The Passionate Collector*

POPULAR CRAFTS

For most people, crafts are more than just rainy day projects. They are a meaningful way to spend leisure time, a way to give special gifts to family and friends, and a way to decorate a home. And even the simplest craft activity gives the satisfaction of having a useful and beautiful item to show for one's labors.

In 1980, a number of new and varied techniques were being used in traditional craft projects. These were some of the most popular craft activities of the year.

▶ ROPE CRAFTS

Macramé is a knot-tying craft, and almost any yarn, rope, or cord can be used. It is basically a free-form craft, because once you have learned a few basic knots, you can experiment and create your own designs.

Knot tying was once a pastime of sailors on many whaling ships. During voyages that lasted two and three years, one of the few leisure activities was knotting. Much of the available rope was used to decorate every possible part of the ship with fancy knot work.

Water was in short supply on the old sailing ships. So the sailors devised a twine covering that could be tied onto any bottle to protect it from breaking. The covering has many names—fender hitching, rib stitch hitching, French hitching. But the key word in all the names is "hitching"—the basic knot is the half hitch used in macramé. The days of the old sailing ships are long gone. But the charming hitched bottle has become an exciting craft project.

▶ DÉCOUPAGE

Découpage needs no expensive equipment and is easy to do, but it does take time and patience to do well. Many people think that

Almost any yarn, rope, or cord can be used in macramé. And once you have learned a few basic knots, you can make baskets, doormats, and charming hitched bottles.

In theorem painting, stencils are used to transfer all the colors of a design onto a piece of material, such as velvet.

In this example of *papier tole* découpage, paper prints have been glued down to form a three-dimensional picture.

découpage is little more than varnish over paper. This is not so. Many découpage techniques use no varnish at all. In its simplest form, découpage is cutout paper prints varnished onto a piece of wood. In a more complex form, called *papier tole*, it is hand-colored paper cutouts glued down in such a way as to create a three-dimensional scene in a shadow box.

Découpage comes from a French word meaning "to cut out." The craft was popular in 18th-century France, where people copied the lacquered Chinese and Japanese furniture that was all the rage in Europe at that time. Découpage was known in early days as "the poor man's lacquer."

If you would like to get started in this most versatile of all craft activities, begin with greeting cards, wrapping papers, scissors, a clear glue, and a wooden cigar box.

▶ THEOREM PAINTING

Theorem painting, first popular in the 1800's, is an attempt to reduce a painting to mathematical precision. In this way, even the beginning painter can be successful. This painting technique was the forerunner of the more recent "paint-by-number" technique.

Velvet is the favorite material to paint on, although paper and cloth ticking can be used, too. Both oil and watercolors are used. But the common denominator for all theorem painting is the stencil.

It is the stencil, used instead of freehand application, that gives theorem paintings their special character. Several stencils are needed to create one painting. A different stencil is used for each color. The number of stencils is determined by the number of colors and by how complex the design is.

To make a theorem painting, you start by drawing a basically simple design, like a bowl of fruit, on a piece of paper. For all the items to be painted red, one stencil is cut. For all the items painted yellow, another stencil is cut, and so on, until all the elements in the picture have been transferred to a stencil.

The next step is to transfer the picture to the velvet, using one stencil at a time. The paint is applied in an up-and-down daubing motion, with the paintbrush nearly bone dry. The bristles on the brush must be stiff enough to stand up to the jabbing brush strokes. Shading is easily achieved by daubing more paint on the dark side of the object and less on the side to be highlighted.

▶ BEADWORK

Decorative beads have played an important part in fashion for centuries. Archeologists have uncovered ancient beadwork from as far back as the time of the pharaohs. Beadwork is still in fashion, and many accessories are simple to make.

Beads come in hundreds of colors, shapes, and sizes—or you can even make your own. Using the basic techniques of threading and knotting, you can string beads to make a necklace, weave with them to make a belt, or embroider with them to make a jewelry box.

"Em-bead-ery," or embroidery with beads,

Em-bead-ery: embroidery with beads instead of stitches.

A "montik" is a style of fabric painting that combines machine-appliquéd fabrics with intricate thread designs, paints and pastels, and other materials.

158

Another type of fabric art combines stockings, polyester filling, and stitchery. The result: these incredibly realistic dolls.

has gained new popularity. Bead embroidery is traditional stitchery with one basic difference—beads are used instead of embroidery threads. The result is a design that is as intricate as any stitchery pattern, but with the added shimmer of beads.

▶ FABRIC ARTS

Hundreds of years ago, quilting was born out of a need for warmth as well as a desire for self-expression. It is popular today, in our energy-conscious society, for the same reasons. Contemporary quilting can be found on everything from pillows to clothing, pocketbooks to wall hangings. Learning how to turn scraps of fabric into a patchwork quilt is only one of the many fabric arts. Fabrics work well with many craft techniques and products—such as hand stitching, appliqué, acrylic paints, felt-tip markers, and glue.

One new style of fabric painting is called "montik." Montiks are paintings that combine machine-appliquéd fabrics with intricate thread designs, paints and pastels, and other materials.

This type of painting begins with a drawing on paper. Using the drawing as a sort of guide, various pieces of patterned cloth are cut out. The pieces are glued onto a sturdy cloth backing and then machine stitched in place.

Shading and details are put on the fabric picture with anything from decorative stitching to felt-tip markers to sequins. This gives the appliqué a feeling of depth and contrast.

Another type of fabric art combines stockings, polyester filling, and stitchery. The result: pantyhose people. And you don't have to be an expert sewer to make these incredibly realistic dolls. The materials that you use are responsible for the results you get. The polyester stuffing makes the body soft and cuddly. The sheer, stretchy, natural-colored stockings provide the dolls with nearly human skin tones and texture.

Making the facial features is like sculpting with needle and thread. You push, pinch, and pull the expression into the face, and then secure each shape with stitches. Just a few stitches define the nose, mouth, eyebrows, and ears. No two faces will be exactly the same, but then no two human faces are exactly the same either.

WENDIE R. BLANCHARD
Managing Editor
Creative Crafts magazine

COIN COLLECTING

New coins from countries around the world marked important events of 1980 and of years gone by. Meanwhile, collectors found the cost of their hobby rising—the price of gold topped $800 an ounce before falling back to around $625; a new price record was set with the sale of nine ancient Greek coins; and the value of collector coins increased in most categories.

▶ COINS FROM AROUND THE WORLD

The 1980 Olympic Games were the subject of special coin issues from several countries. The largest issue was from the Soviet Union, which hosted the Summer Games. It put out 39 silver, gold, and platinum coins, in a program begun in 1977. The Isle of Man issued coins honoring both the Summer Games and the Winter Games, which were held in Lake Placid in the United States. Other countries that issued Olympic coins included China, Cyprus, Equatorial Guinea, Hungary, and San Marino.

Other recent events were marked by coins from a number of countries. Among them was the Netherlands, which issued 1- and 2-guilder coins in honor of the abdication of Queen Juliana in favor of her daughter Beatrix. The coins featured overlapping portraits of the two queens. And Hungary's pure nickel 100-forint coin marked the first space flight of a Hungarian astronaut, in a Soviet space vehicle.

In Egypt, a set of silver and gold "President of Peace" coins was issued to commemorate the peace treaty signed in 1979 by Egyptian President Anwar el-Sadat and Israeli Prime Minister Menahem Begin. Israel, which has been troubled by inflation, issued new currency in 1980. In the new system, agorot and pounds were replaced with new agorot and shekels.

Among the issues marking historical events was a silver 200-kroner coin from Norway. It marked the 35th anniversary of the end of German occupation during World War II. And in Austria, a silver 500-schilling issue was released for the 200th anniversary of the death of Empress Maria Theresa.

▶ NEW GOLD COINS

More and more people are drawn to coin collecting by the gold coin programs offered by various countries. The most popular of these is the South African Krugerrand program, which in 1980 was broadened to appeal to even more people. The one-ounce Krugerrand was joined by versions containing half, one fourth, and one tenth of an ounce of gold.

The U.S. Treasury's American Arts Gold Medallion program was launched in July, offering limited editions of half-ounce and one-ounce pieces. The half-ounce medallion featured singer Marian Anderson, and the one-ounce medallion portrayed artist Grant Wood. They were the first of ten medallions that will be issued through 1984.

Australia released its first gold coin in nearly half a century—a $200 coin showing a

Soviet 1-ruble coin marking the Summer Olympic Games

The Isle of Man's 1-crown coin for the Winter Games

The U.S. Treasury's one-ounce gold medallion

160

Australia's $200 gold coin

The 1980 issue in Canada's $100 gold coin series

lovable koala bear in a eucalyptus tree. Britain issued special proof editions of the first half-sovereign, 2-pound, and 5-pound gold coins since 1937. And Canada continued its $100 gold coin series with a tribute to its far north. The 1980 coin showed an Inuk Indian hunting through ice floes in a kayak. A companion coin in silver showed a polar bear.

▶ U.S. COIN NEWS

New to U.S. coinage for 1980 was a distinctive "P" mintmark on nickels, dimes, quarters, and half dollars struck at the Philadelphia Mint. Marks of the nation's other mints have always been carried on U.S. coins. The Philadelphia Mint has been producing coins since 1793. But only 1979 Anthony dollars and some early 1940's nickels had previously carried a Philadelphia mintmark.

The small-sized Anthony dollar, which was released in 1979 as a money-saver for the government, was not well received by

The Philadelphia mintmark (*circled, at lower left*)

the public. At the end of 1980, more than half the 800,000,000 pieces struck in the first year of production were still in Mint and Federal Reserve vaults. Treasury officials announced that 1981 Anthony dollars would be minted only for inclusion in the year's proof and uncirculated coin sets.

Meanwhile, a design change was being considered for the coin, which some people confuse with a quarter. The coin would retain its portrait of the 19th-century suffragette Susan B. Anthony on the obverse. But the Apollo eagle design on the reverse would be replaced with a large numeral 1 and a laurel sprig. Treasury officials were also considering a copper-aluminum-silicon outer cladding, to give the coin a brassy yellow color and make it easier to identify.

▶ A RECORD PRICE

World coin price records were shattered late in 1980, when a set of ancient Greek dekadrachms was sold for the staggering sum of $4,000,000. One coin in the set, an

The Athens dekadrachm, one of a set of nine ancient Greek coins that sold for a record-breaking price

Athens dekadrachm, carried a price tag of $1,500,000. This easily topped the previous record of $725,000 for a single coin, set in November, 1979, with the sale of a Brasher gold doubloon.

The nine coins formed a complete set of the dekadrachms, which are about the size of quarters. The dekadrachms were the largest silver coins in size and denomination in the ancient Greek monetary system. They were usually issued only to mark great battle victories. The Athens dekadrachm is thought to have been issued to mark the Battle of Marathon in 490 B.C. The coin sold in 1980 is one of the seven known to exist, and it is the only one not in a museum.

CLIFFORD MISHLER
Publisher, *Numismatic News*

161

MANY HANDS COOKING

from India
KAJU (KAH-jew)

Indian cookery varies a great deal from region to region and from cook to cook. But here is one food that is made and enjoyed in the same way by all the people of India: cashew snacks.

Indians roast their own nuts. After preparing the nuts this way, you might mix them in a bowl with raisins. This makes a healthful Indian-style snack.

INGREDIENTS

1½ tablespoons vegetable oil
½   pound (2 cups) raw unsalted cashews
1   teaspoon salt
    dash of cayenne pepper (optional)

EQUIPMENT

measuring spoons   paper towels
large frying pan   mixing bowl
measuring cup   mixing spoon
spatula   serving bowl

HOW TO MAKE

1. Measure the oil and put it in the frying pan over medium heat for half a minute.

2. Add the nuts and sauté them in the oil for three minutes, turning them over and over with the spatula.

3. Remove the nuts and put them to drain on the sheets of paper towel, patting them with the toweling to remove any extra oil.

4. In the bowl, combine the salt and pepper.

5. Put the nuts into the bowl and toss them with the spoon, or your hands, until they are coated with the seasoning.

6. Serve the nuts in an attractive bowl.

   This recipe serves 4 people.

   Note: Almonds, peanuts, pistachio nuts, and other raw nuts can be prepared this way, too. (If you can't find these nuts in the supermarket, try a health-food store.)

from Mexico

GUACAMOLE (gwa-kuh-MO-le)

Mexicans enjoy a very special sort of salad. They serve smooth green guacamole made from avocado. Avocados are sometimes called alligator pears because their green skin is so leathery and tough. Inside that tough skin is soft, delicious pulp with a large hard seed in the center.

For this recipe, the avocado *must* be ripe. To test for ripeness, gently squeeze the avocado between the palms of your hands. The fruit should be soft enough to give slightly.

EQUIPMENT

paring knife
mixing bowl
measuring spoons
fork
mixing spoon

INGREDIENTS

1	large ripe avocado
1½	tablespoons lemon juice
1	small onion
1	small tomato

¾ teaspoon salt
1½ tablespoons mayonnaise
dash of garlic salt
crackers

HOW TO MAKE

1. Cut the avocado in half. Remove the seed.

2. Peel the avocado (or you can scoop the pulp out of the hard skin with a spoon).

3. Put the avocado pulp into the mixing bowl and add the lemon juice.

4. Mash the avocado, mixing the lemon juice into it with the fork.

5. Dice the tomato, and add it with the salt, mayonnaise, and garlic salt to the mashed avocado.

6. Stir until smooth.

7. Peel the onion and chop it into very small pieces.

8. Add the pieces of minced onion to the avocado mixture and stir well.

9. Serve the guacamole with crackers or tortilla chips or as a filling for sandwiches.

This recipe serves 6 people.

Note: You might save the avocado seed and plant it.

SPORTS

The U.S. hockey team rejoices after having beaten Finland, 4–2, for the gold medal at the Olympic Winter Games.

THE 1980 OLYMPIC GAMES

Every Olympics is memorable. Each is like a vast drama, with thousands of athletes acting out their roles against a multicolored background of flags, costumes, and medals. It is a joyful pageant, but never without disappointments as well.

As in previous Olympics, certain events and individuals stood out above all others at the 1980 Olympic Games. The Lake Placid Winter Games had Eric Heiden, who won five gold medals, and the surprising U.S. hockey team. The Moscow Summer Games had two stunning duels between British runners Sebastian Coe and Steve Ovett. But probably the most remembered event of the 1980 Olympics will be the refusal of the United States and other countries to participate in the Moscow Summer Games.

▶ POLITICS AND THE OLYMPICS

In December, 1979, Soviet troops entered Afghanistan and aided in the overthrow of its president. Within weeks, about 90,000 Soviets were in Afghanistan, supporting a new regime and fighting Afghans who resented the Soviets' intrusion into their affairs.

Countries around the world were outraged at the Soviet invasion of Afghanistan. U.S. President Jimmy Carter saw the Soviet move as a military threat, since it put Soviet troops close to the Persian Gulf. The Persian Gulf is considered vital to U.S. interests. Much of the oil bound for the United States comes through that waterway.

The Summer Olympic Games were scheduled to be held in Moscow, the Soviet capital, during July and August. President Carter decided to put pressure on the Soviet Union to withdraw its troops from Afghanistan. In January, he demanded that Soviet troops be out of the country by February 20. Otherwise, he said, the United States would refuse to participate in the Games. And other countries would be asked to join the boycott.

A huge controversy erupted. The Soviet Union reacted by saying that a boycott was ridiculous. It saw its invasion of Afghanistan as being "the correct response to a neigh-

The Winter Games—Lake Placid, New York

bor's call for help." Some U.S. athletes opposed the boycott because they felt it would have little effect on Soviet policies. And the International Olympic Committee (IOC), which runs the Games, said that the Olympics should not be concerned with politics, and that the U.S. boycott was therefore inappropriate.

Nevertheless, the Olympic Games have been affected by politics throughout the century. In 1972, Palestinian terrorists invaded the Olympic Village in West Germany and murdered eleven members of the Israeli team. In 1968, two medal-winning American sprinters gave the black-power salute at their awards ceremony as a protest against racism in the United States. In 1964, South Africa was banned from the Games because of its racial policies. In 1936, the German dictator Adolf Hitler used the Berlin Games as part of his Nazi propaganda effort. In 1944, 1940, and 1916, the Olympic Games were canceled because of the World Wars. So when politics intruded upon the 1980 Games, it was not for the first time.

President Carter's February 20 deadline came and went, and the Soviet troops remained in Afghanistan. Vice-President Walter Mondale strongly stated the U.S. Government's position: "At stake is . . . the future security of the civilized world." And on April 12, the U.S. Olympic Committee voted to support the boycott. No American athletes would go to Moscow.

Two weeks later, the Canadian Olympic Association joined the boycott. Japan, China, and West Germany also said they would not participate, but Australia, Britain, and France decided to compete.

The Summer Games opened on schedule. Over 80 nations competed, but about 50 stayed away, many of them because of the Soviet invasion of Afghanistan. Although many fine athletes did not participate, 36 world records were set. But the fact remained that the part played by the athletes had to a large degree been overshadowed by the part played by politics.

The 1984 Winter Games are scheduled to take place in Sarajevo, Yugoslavia, and the Summer Games in Los Angeles, California. By then, many hope, the athletes will have regained center stage.

The Summer Games—Moscow, U.S.S.R.

THE WINTER GAMES

The Games of the XIII Winter Olympiad were held in Lake Placid, New York, from February 12 to February 24. More than 1,200 competitors from 37 countries sledded, skated, and skied against the backdrop of the scenic Adirondack Mountains.

Athletes from the Soviet Union returned home from the Winter Games with the most gold medals—10. But it was the United States that presented the most spectacular individual performer—speed skater Eric Heiden—and the most astonishing result—a gold medal for its hockey team.

▶ A SPECTACULAR PERFORMER

Heiden and the hockey team accounted for the 6 gold medals won by the United States in the 38 events. Five of them were captured by Heiden. The 21-year-old from Wisconsin won all the men's speed-skating events—500, 1,000, 1,500, 5,000, and 10,000 meters. He established new Olympic records for all five distances. And in his final assault on the clock, he shattered the world record for 10,000 meters.

No other athlete had ever collected as many as 5 gold medals in a single Winter Olympics. From an individual standpoint, Heiden even surpassed the efforts of swimmer Mark Spitz in the 1972 Summer Olympics. Spitz won 7 gold medals, but only 4 in individual events. He earned the others as a member of relay teams.

▶ A SPECTACULAR VICTORY

On their way to the winners' stand, the U.S. hockey players won 6 games and tied 1. Before the Olympics, no one could have guessed that they would do so well. In an exhibition match prior to the Games, the Soviet team had thrashed them by a score of 10–3.

But when the Games began, the Americans showed their talent with a 7–3 upset over a powerful Czech squad. By the time they met the Soviets, the U.S. record had reached 4 wins, 0 losses, and 1 tie. Recent history, however, weighed heavily against the U.S. team. Soviet hockey teams had won four successive Olympic golds since the U.S. triumph at Squaw Valley, California, in 1960.

With millions watching on television, the

Eric Heiden won all five men's speed-skating events, and he set a new world record in the process.

Goalie Jim Craig blocks a shot in the U.S.–Soviet hockey game, which the Americans won, 4–3.

Americans fought a desperate battle on the way to their 4–3 victory. They fell behind, 2–1, and then 3–2. Each time, Mark Johnson hammered the puck into the Soviet net for the goal that tied the score. In the final period, captain Mike Eruzione scored the winning goal.

As the final day of the tournament began, it was still possible for any of four teams— the United States, Finland, Sweden, or the Soviet Union—to win the gold medal. The United States faced Finland. Again the Americans started sluggishly. They trailed 2–1 after two of the three periods. But Phil Verchota, Rob McClanahan, and Johnson scored in the third period for a 4–2 decision. This victory clinched the gold medal for the United States. In the other final-round game the Soviet Union defeated Sweden, 9–2, for the silver medal.

Throughout the tournament, Jim Craig tended goal brilliantly for the Americans. Much credit was also given to Coach Herb Brooks, who trained his enthusiastic players hard and spurred them on to ever-improving performances.

▶ **OTHER WINTER WINNERS**

Alpine skiing is a major part of the Winter Games, and the downhill is the glamour event. Austrians captured both the men's and the women's races. Leonhard Stock and Annemarie Moser-Proell outsped their opponents down a steep Whiteface Mountain course. Ingemar Stenmark of Sweden won gold medals in the men's slalom and giant slalom. Hanni Wenzel of tiny Liechtenstein won golds in the women's slalom and giant slalom. She also picked up a silver medal in the downhill.

The Soviets won 4 of their 10 gold medals in Nordic skiing. Nikolai Zimyatov captured 2 individually, in the 30- and 50-kilometer cross-country events. Then he picked up a third as anchorman on the winning 40-kilometer relay team. Ulrich Wehling of East Germany became the first male athlete to win gold medals in the same individual event in three different Olympic Winter Games. In 1972, 1976, and again in 1980, he took first place in the Nordic combined.

Women's figure skating had been something of a special preserve for Americans. Four Americans had won gold medals in the last six Olympics: Tenley Albright (1956), Carol Heiss (1960), Peggy Fleming (1968), and Dorothy Hamill (1976). But in 1980, the top U.S. competitor, Linda Fratianne, was beaten by East Germany's Anett Poetzsch by the slimmest of margins. The final scoring by the judges was 189.00 points for Poetzsch and 188.30 for Fratianne.

In a dazzling performance, Robin Cousins of Britain won the men's figure skating com-

Figure skater Anett Poetzsch of East Germany skated to the gold medal in the women's singles event.

petition. And the Soviet Union's Irina Rodnina and Alexander Zaitsev repeated their 1976 Olympic triumph in the pairs figure skating. The highly regarded U.S. combination of Tai Babilonia and Randy Gardner, who had won the 1979 world championship, was forced to withdraw because of an injury to Gardner.

Meinhard Nehmer of East Germany won a gold medal in the bobsled competition for the second Olympics in a row. He piloted the four-man sled down the Mount Van Hoevenberg course in record times. Two of the team's four runs were under one minute, the fastest in Olympic history. In the two-man bobsled event, the Swiss team took the gold.

In the luge competition, East Germany dominated the men's events. Bernhard Glass won the singles. The team of Hans Rinn and Norbert Hahn repeated their gold-medal performance of 1976. The women's singles was won by Vera Zozulya of the Soviet Union.

Among the nations that sent their athletes to Lake Placid, the Soviet Union, East Germany, and the United States were the principal collectors of medals. The Russians accumulated the most gold, but the East Germans actually exceeded them in total medals with 23—9 gold, 7 silver, and 7 bronze. The Russians had 22, adding 6 silver and 6 bronze to their 10 gold. The United States totaled 12, with 4 silver and 2 bronze in addition to the 6 gold.

Aside from five-time winner Heiden, silver medalist Fratianne, and the hockey team, the U.S. medalists were: Leah Poulos Mueller, 2 silver, in the women's 500- and 1,000-meter speed skating; Phil Mahre, a silver in the men's slalom; Beth Heiden, a bronze in the women's 3,000-meter speed skating; and Charles Tickner, a bronze in the men's figure skating.

Canadian Olympians won two medals at Lake Placid. Gaetan Boucher of Quebec won a silver in the men's 1,000-meter speed skating. Stephen Podborski of Ontario took the bronze in the men's downhill skiing.

For the United States, the total of 12 medals was the country's best showing at a Winter Olympics since 1952. While this was outstanding, Americans will best remember the 1980 Winter Games for Eric Heiden and the spunky young hockey squad.

Austrian Leonhard Stock outskied all his opponents in the men's downhill.

East Germans Rinn and Hahn won the luge doubles event.

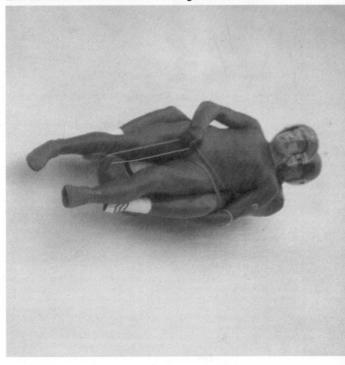

FINAL MEDAL STANDINGS

Winter Games—Lake Placid, New York

Country	Gold	Silver	Bronze	Total
Soviet Union	10	6	6	22
East Germany	9	7	7	23
United States	6	4	2	12
Austria	3	2	2	7
Sweden	3	0	1	4
Liechtenstein	2	2	0	4
Finland	1	5	3	9
Norway	1	3	6	10
Netherlands	1	2	1	4
Switzerland	1	1	3	5
Britain	1	0	0	1
West Germany	0	2	3	5
Italy	0	2	0	2
Canada	0	1	1	2
Hungary	0	1	0	1
Japan	0	1	0	1
Bulgaria	0	0	1	1
Czechoslovakia	0	0	1	1
France	0	0	1	1

ERIC HEIDEN, OLYMPIC HERO

A flashing smile . . . great enthusiasm . . . good humored . . . intense and hard working. These are some of the phrases that have been used to describe Eric Heiden, the Olympic hero of the 1980 Winter Games. The 21-year-old premed student from Madison, Wisconsin, captured the attention and the hearts of the American public when he won all five gold medals for speed skating at Lake Placid, New York. That was the largest number of golds ever attained by one athlete in the Winter Games.

Although Heiden was internationally well known prior to the Olympics, his rise to fame went almost unnoticed by the American public when it began back in 1977. The cause was a lack of interest on the part of Americans in the sport of speed skating—except in the Great Lakes region, Heiden's home base. So when Heiden won the 1977 men's world speed-skating championship at Heerenveen, the Netherlands, not too many Americans paid attention. And they seemed just as unaware when he captured the same title two more times, in 1978 and 1979. The lack of fuss was fine with Heiden, who after becoming an American idol said, "I really liked it best when I was a nobody."

Eric and his younger sister, Beth, an Olympic bronze medalist in speed skating, have never had star complexes. Excellence in sports has always been a natural way of life for them. They were both raised in a down-to-earth, sports-loving home with a gym in the basement. Grandfather Art Thomsen, a former ice hockey coach at the University of Wisconsin, led both Eric and Beth out onto the ice as children. Then he watched over them as they developed into good skaters.

It was Beth who first became interested in speed skating. Then Eric joined her in practice sessions at her speed-skating club. This is where coach Dianne Holum spotted the Heidens and started grooming them for big-time competition. Besides natural talent, both youngsters had two other traits that help make champions. They were very hard workers and had lots of stick-to-itiveness.

That these traits remained with Eric is shown in a story told by Peter Schotting, who coached the U.S. men's speed-skating team at the Lake Placid Olympics. Schotting would sometimes give the team the afternoon off. But he said he always knew there would be one lone figure still working out after the others had gone. That lone figure, always refusing to rest, always striving to keep his body in condition, was Eric Heiden.

As the 1980 speed-skating season was drawing to an end, it appeared that Heiden was thinking of putting his abilities into other sports. He told reporters that he was going to quit competitive skating and turn to bicycle racing and hockey. He also wanted to complete his university studies, specializing in sports medicine.

THE SUMMER GAMES

The Summer Games of the XXII Olympiad were held in Moscow, U.S.S.R., from July 19 to August 3. Nearly 6,000 athletes from 81 countries participated in the program, which included 22 sports. Before the boycott, more than 10,000 athletes had been expected in Moscow. There were mild forms of protest from some of those who appeared. Sixteen nations flew Olympic banners instead of their national flags in the opening parade, and athletes from twelve Western European nations did not march in the parade at all.

Because of the absence of so many competitors, the Soviet team reaped an even larger medal harvest than usual. Soviet athletes won 197 medals, including 80 golds. These totals surpassed the Soviets' previous best Olympic achievements—125 total medals in 1976, and 50 golds in 1972.

East Germany finished second in total medals, 126, and in golds, 47. Bulgaria was third with 40 medals, 8 of which were gold. Among the non-Communist nations at the Games, Britain was the most successful, with 21 medals, including 5 golds.

Track and Field. Track and field, the showcase sport of the Olympics, attracted 100,000 spectators each day at the Lenin Stadium. The competition produced rich hauls of gold for the Soviets and the East Germans, who collected 15 and 11 victories, respectively. But the glamor events were won by athletes from Britain. The British won four golds, led by rival middle-distance stars Steve Ovett and Sebastian Coe. In a tense head-to-head competition, Ovett beat Coe in the 800-meter run. Later in the week, Coe turned the tables on Ovett with a spectacular finish in the 1,500.

The other British victors were Daley Thompson in the two-day, ten-event decathlon, and Allan Wells, a Scot, in the 100-meter dash. Wells was foiled in his bid to win the "sprint double" when Pietro Mennea of Italy nipped him at the tape in the 200-meter race.

Miruts Yifter of Ethiopia won the "distance double"—the 5,000- and the 10,000-meter runs. He ended the reign of Finland's Lasse Viren, who had won both races in each of the two previous Olympics.

World record breakers included East Ger-

Britain's runners were led by rival stars Steve Ovett (279) and Sebastian Coe (254). They each won a gold.

Miruts Yifter (191) of Ethiopia won the "distance double"—the 5,000-meter and 10,000-meter runs.

many's Gerd Wessig in the high jump, Poland's Wladyslaw Kozakiewicz in the pole vault, and Yuri Sedykh of the Soviet Union in the hammer throw. There was also a remarkable effort by long-jump winner Lutz Dombrowski. The East German sailed 28 feet, ¼ inch (8.5 meters), the second best leap in history.

Waldemar Cierpinski of East Germany won his second consecutive Olympic marathon. The only other runner to win two Olympic marathons was Abebe Bikila of Ethiopia, who won in 1960 and 1964.

In the women's competition, Nadyezhda Olizarenko of the Soviet Union took the gold medal in the 800-meter run with a world record time. Her teammate, Tatyana Kazankina, set an Olympic record in winning the 1,500. Kazankina had won both the 800 and the 1,500 at the Montreal Olympics in 1976. Baerbel Eckert Wockel of East Germany bettered her own Olympic record in the 200-meter dash, which she won for the second straight time.

Swimming. The swimming competition, too, produced some excellent performances. Men swimmers of the Soviet Union had failed to win a gold medal in the 1976 Olympics at Montreal, but in their homeland they reached the victor's podium seven times. The absence of the American men may have contributed to the Soviet success. But at least one of the Soviet athletes, Vladimir Salnikov, might very well have been unbeatable even if the Americans had competed.

Salnikov, a 20-year-old student, captured gold medals in the 400-meter and 1,500-meter freestyle events, and as a member of the 800-meter freestyle relay team. In the 1,500, he set a world record of 14:58.27, becoming the first swimmer in history to cover the distance in less than 15 minutes. In the 400-meter, he set an Olympic record.

Duncan Goodhew won Britain's only gold medal in swimming, in the 100-meter breaststroke event.

The East German women were as dominant in the pool as they had been four years

Soviet swimmer Vladimir Salnikov captured gold medals in the 400-meter and 1,500-meter freestyle events, and as a member of the 800-meter freestyle relay team.

174

Soviet gymnast Nelli Kim (right) tied with Nadia Comaneci for the gold medal in the floor exercises.

earlier. In Montreal, they had won gold medals in 11 of the 13 events, and they duplicated that effort in Moscow. Three of the East German women—Rica Reinisch, Barbara Krause, and Caren Metschuck—won three gold medals apiece. Reinisch, a 15-year-old student, shattered world records in winning the 100-meter backstroke and the 200-meter backstroke. She was also a member of the winning medley relay team. Krause captured the 100- and 200-meter freestyle events, and she, too, was on the medley relay team. Metschuck was the 100-meter butterfly victor, and she contributed to two relay triumphs.

Gymnastics. The darling of the 1976 Olympics had been 14-year-old Nadia Comaneci, the Rumanian gymnast. In the 1980 Games, Comaneci tried to repeat her gold-medal victory in the all-around competition. But she had to settle for a silver, as Yelena Davydova of the Soviet Union took the gold. Comaneci did win a gold on the balance beam, and she and Nelli Kim of the Soviet Union tied for the gold in the floor exercises.

In the men's events, Soviet gymnast Alexander Dityatin was the big star. He emerged as the Games' most prolific medal winner: three golds, four silvers, and one bronze.

The Soviet Union won the team titles in both the women's and men's divisions.

Other Events. Boxing, dominated by the United States four years earlier, became almost an all-Cuban show. Of the 11 weight classes, the Cubans won 6 of the gold medals. Cuban heavyweight Teofilo Stevenson repeated his gold medal triumphs of 1972 and 1976. Only one other Olympic boxer, Laszlo Papp of Hungary, has ever won three golds.

In men's basketball, Yugoslavia won the gold medal by defeating Italy. Both teams had beaten the Soviets in early games, and the host team had to settle for the bronze. But in the women's competition, the Soviets took the gold.

In soccer, the Czechs dethroned the defending Olympic champion, East Germany.

Alexander Dityatin, another gymnast from the Soviet Union, won the most medals at the Summer Games: three golds, four silvers, and one bronze.

FINAL MEDAL STANDINGS

Summer Games—Moscow, U.S.S.R.

Country	Gold	Silver	Bronze	Total
U.S.S.R.	80	70	47	197
East Germany	47	36	43	126
Bulgaria	8	16	16	40
Cuba	8	7	5	20
Italy	8	3	4	15
Hungary	7	10	15	32
Rumania	6	6	13	25
France	6	5	3	14
Britain	5	7	9	21
Poland	3	14	14	31
Sweden	3	3	6	12
Finland	3	1	4	8
Yugoslavia	2	3	4	9
Czechoslovakia	2	2	9	13
Australia	2	2	5	9
Denmark	2	1	2	5
Brazil	2	0	2	4
Ethiopia	2	0	2	4
Switzerland	2	0	0	2
Spain	1	3	2	6
Austria	1	3	1	5
Greece	1	0	2	3
Belgium	1	0	0	1
India	1	0	0	1
Venezuela	1	0	0	1
Zimbabwe	1	0	0	1
North Korea	0	3	2	5
Mongolia	0	2	2	4
Tanzania	0	2	0	2
Mexico	0	1	3	4
Netherlands	0	1	3	4
Ireland	0	1	1	2
Uganda	0	1	0	1
Jamaica	0	0	3	3
Guyana	0	0	1	1
Lebanon	0	0	1	1

1980 OLYMPIC GOLD MEDAL WINNERS

WINTER GAMES—LAKE PLACID, NEW YORK

Biathlon
10-km: Frank Ullrich, East Germany
20-km: Anatoly Alabyev, U.S.S.R.
30-km relay: U.S.S.R.

Bobsledding
Two-Man: Switzerland
Four-Man: East Germany

Hockey
Team: United States

Luge
Men's Singles: Bernhard Glass, East Germany
Men's Doubles: East Germany
Women's Singles: Vera Zozulya, U.S.S.R.

Figure Skating
Men's Singles: Robin Cousins, Britain
Women's Singles: Anett Poetzsch, East Germany
Pairs: Irina Rodnina/Alexander Zaitsev, U.S.S.R.
Dance: Natalia Linichuk/Gennadi Karponosov, U.S.S.R.

Speed Skating, Men
500-m: Eric Heiden, U.S.
1,000-m: Eric Heiden, U.S.
1,500-m: Eric Heiden, U.S.
5,000-m: Eric Heiden, U.S.
10,000-m: Eric Heiden, U.S.

Speed Skating, Women
500-m: Karin Enke, East Germany
1,000-m: Natalia Petruseva, U.S.S.R.
1,500-m: Annie Borckink, Netherlands
3,000-m: Bjoerg Eva Jensen, Norway

Alpine Skiing, Men
Downhill: Leonhard Stock, Austria
Giant Slalom: Ingemar Stenmark, Sweden
Special Slalom: Ingemar Stenmark, Sweden

Alpine Skiing, Women
Downhill: Annemarie Moser-Proell, Austria
Giant Slalom: Hanni Wenzel, Liechtenstein
Special Slalom: Hanni Wenzel, Liechtenstein

Nordic Skiing, Men
15-km Cross-Country: Thomas Wassberg, Sweden
30-km Cross-Country: Nikolai Zimyatov, U.S.S.R.
50-km Cross-Country: Nikolai Zimyatov, U.S.S.R.
40-km Cross-Country Relay: U.S.S.R.
70-m Jump: Toni Innauer, Austria
90-m Jump: Jouko Tromanen, Finland
Combined: Ulrich Wehling, East Germany

Nordic Skiing, Women
5-km Cross-Country: Raisa Smetanina, U.S.S.R.
10-km Cross-Country: Barbara Petzold, East Germany
20-km Cross-Country Relay: East Germany

SUMMER GAMES—MOSCOW, U.S.S.R.

Archery
Men: Tomi Poikolainen, Finland
Women: Keto Losaberidze, U.S.S.R.

Basketball
Team, men: Yugoslavia
Team, women: U.S.S.R.

Boxing
Light Flyweight: Shamil Sabyrov, U.S.S.R.
Flyweight: Petar Lessov, Bulgaria
Bantamweight: Juan Hernandez, Cuba
Featherweight: Rudi Fink, East Germany
Lightweight: Angel Herrera, Cuba
Light Welterweight: Patrizio Oliva, Italy
Welterweight: Andres Aldama, Cuba
Light Middleweight: Armando Martinez, Cuba
Middleweight: Jose Gomez, Cuba
Light Heavyweight: Slobodan Kacar, Yugoslavia
Heavyweight: Teofilo Stevenson, Cuba

Canoeing, Men
500-m Kayak Singles: Vladimir Parfenovich, U.S.S.R.
500-m Kayak Doubles: U.S.S.R.
1,000-m Kayak Singles: Rudiger Helm, East Germany
1,000-m Kayak Doubles: U.S.S.R.
1,000-m Kayak Fours: East Germany
500-m Canoe Singles: Sergei Postrekhin, U.S.S.R.
500-m Canoe Doubles: Hungary
1,000-m Canoe Singles: Lubomir Lubenov, Bulgaria
1,000-m Canoe Doubles: Rumania

Canoeing, Women
500-m Kayak Singles: Birgit Fischer, East Germany
500-m Kayak Doubles: East Germany

Cycling
Road Race: Sergei Soukhoroutchenkov, U.S.S.R.
Team Road Race: U.S.S.R.
Pursuit: Robert Dill-Bundi, Switzerland
Team Pursuit: U.S.S.R.

Sprint: Lutz Hesslich, East Germany
1,000-m Time Trial: Lothar Thoms, East Germany

Equestrian
3-Day Event: Federico Euro Roman, Italy
Team 3-Day Event: U.S.S.R.
Dressage: Elisabeth Theurer, Austria
Team Dressage: U.S.S.R.
Jumping: Jan Kowalczyk, Poland
Team Jumping: U.S.S.R.

Fencing, Men
Epee: Johan Harmenberg, Sweden
Team Epee: France
Foil: Vladimir Smirnov, U.S.S.R.
Team Foil: France
Saber: Viktor Krovopuskov, U.S.S.R.
Team Saber: U.S.S.R.

Fencing, Women
Foil: Pascale Trinquet, France
Team Foil: France

Field Hockey
Team, men: India
Team, women: Zimbabwe

Gymnastics, Men
All-Around: Alexander Dityatin, U.S.S.R.
Team: U.S.S.R.
Floor Exercises: Roland Bruckner, East Germany
Horizontal Bar: Stoyan Deltchev, Bulgaria
Long Horse Vault: Nikolai Andrianov, U.S.S.R.
Parallel Bars: Alexander Tkachyov, U.S.S.R.
Rings: Alexander Dityatin, U.S.S.R.
Side Horse: Zoltan Magyar, Hungary

Gymnastics, Women
All-Around: Yelena Davydova, U.S.S.R.
Team: U.S.S.R.
Balance Beam: Nadia Comaneci, Rumania
Floor Exercises: Nelli Kim, U.S.S.R., and Nadia
Comaneci, Rumania
Side Horse Vault: Natalya Shaposhnikova, U.S.S.R.
Uneven Parallel Bars: Maxi Gnauck, East Germany

Handball
Team, men: East Germany
Team, women: U.S.S.R.

Judo
60 kg: Thierry Rey, France
65 kg: Nikolai Solodukhin, U.S.S.R.
71 kg: Ezio Gamba, Italy
78 kg: Shota Khabarell, U.S.S.R.

86 kg: Juerg Roethlisberger, Switzerland
95 kg: Robert Van De Walle, Belgium
Over 95 kg: Angelo Parisi, France
Open: Dietmar Lorenz, East Germany

Modern Pentathlon
Individual: Anatoly Starostin, U.S.S.R.
Team: U.S.S.R.

Rowing, Men
Single Sculls: Pertti Karppinen, Finland
Double Sculls: East Germany
Quadruple Sculls: East Germany
Coxed Pairs: East Germany
Coxless Pairs: East Germany
Coxed Fours: East Germany
Coxless Fours: East Germany
Eights: East Germany

Rowing, Women
Single Sculls: Sanda Toma, Rumania
Double Sculls: U.S.S.R.
Quadruple Sculls: East Germany
Coxless Pairs: East Germany
Coxed Fours: East Germany
Eights: East Germany

Shooting
Free Pistol: Alexander Melentev, U.S.S.R.
Rapid-Fire Pistol: Corneliu Ion, Rumania
Small-Bore Rifle, prone: Karoly Varga, Hungary
Small-Bore Rifle, 3-position: Viktor Vlasov, U.S.S.R.
Rifle, running-game target: Igor Sokolov, U.S.S.R.
Shotgun, trapshooting: Luciano Giovannetti, Italy
Shotgun, skeetshooting: Hans Kjeld Rasmussen, Denmark

Soccer
Team: Czechoslovakia

Swimming and Diving, Men
100-m Backstroke: Bengt Baron, Sweden
200-m Backstroke: Sandor Wladar, Hungary
100-m Breaststroke: Duncan Goodhew, Britain
200-m Breaststroke: Robertas Zulpa, U.S.S.R.
100-m Butterfly: Par Arvidsson, Sweden
200-m Butterfly: Sergei Fesenko, U.S.S.R.
100-m Freestyle: Jorg Woithe, East Germany
200-m Freestyle: Sergei Kopliakov, U.S.S.R.
400-m Freestyle: Vladimir Salnikov, U.S.S.R.
800-m Freestyle Relay: U.S.S.R.
1,500-m Freestyle: Vladimir Salnikov, U.S.S.R.
400-m Medley: Alexander Sidorenko, U.S.S.R.
400-m Medley Relay: Australia
Platform Diving: Falk Hoffmann, East Germany
Springboard Diving: Alexander Portnov, U.S.S.R.

Swimming and Diving, Women
100-m Backstroke: Rica Reinisch, East Germany
200-m Backstroke: Rica Reinisch, East Germany
100-m Breaststroke: Ute Geweniger, East Germany
200-m Breaststroke: Lina Kachushite, U.S.S.R.
100-m Butterfly: Caren Metschuck, East Germany
200-m Butterfly: Ines Geissler, East Germany
100-m Freestyle: Barbara Krause, East Germany
200-m Freestyle: Barbara Krause, East Germany
400-m Freestyle: Ines Diers, East Germany
400-m Freestyle Relay: East Germany
800-m Freestyle: Michelle Ford, Australia
400-m Medley: Petra Schneider, East Germany
400-m Medley Relay: East Germany
Platform Diving: Martina Jaschke, East Germany
Springboard Diving: Irina Kalinina, U.S.S.R.

Track and Field, Men
100-m Dash: Allan Wells, Britain
200-m Dash: Pietro Mennea, Italy
400-m Run: Viktor Markin, U.S.S.R.
400-m Relay: U.S.S.R.
800-m Run: Steve Ovett, Britain
1,500-m Run: Sebastian Coe, Britain
1,600-m Relay: U.S.S.R.
5,000-m Run: Miruts Yifter, Ethiopia
10,000-m Run: Miruts Yifter, Ethiopia
20-km Walk: Maurizio Damilano, Italy
50-km Walk: Hartwig Gauder, East Germany
110-m Hurdles: Thomas Munkelt, East Germany
400-m Hurdles: Volker Beck, East Germany
3,000-m Steeplechase: Bronislaw Malinowski, Poland
Marathon: Waldemar Cierpinski, East Germany
Discus Throw: Viktor Rashchupkin, U.S.S.R.
Hammer Throw: Yuri Sedykh, U.S.S.R.
High Jump: Gerd Wessig, East Germany
Javelin Throw: Dainis Kula, U.S.S.R.
Long Jump: Lutz Dombrowski, East Germany
Pole Vault: Wladyslaw Kozakiewicz, Poland
Shot Put: Vladimir Kiselyov, U.S.S.R.
Triple Jump: Jaak Uudmae, U.S.S.R.
Decathlon: Daley Thompson, Britain

Track and Field, Women
100-m Dash: Lyudmila Kondratyeva, U.S.S.R.
200-m Dash: Baerbel Wockel, East Germany
400-m Run: Marita Koch, East Germany
400-m Relay: East Germany
800-m Run: Nadyezhda Olizarenko, U.S.S.R.
1,500-m Run: Tatyana Kazankina, U.S.S.R.
1,600-m Relay: U.S.S.R.
100-m Hurdles: Vera Komisova, U.S.S.R.
Discus Throw: Evelin Jahl, East Germany
High Jump: Sara Simeoni, Italy
Javelin Throw: Maria Colon, Cuba
Long Jump: Tatyana Kolpakova, U.S.S.R.
Shot Put: Ilona Slupianek, East Germany
Pentathlon: Nadyezhda Tkachenko, U.S.S.R.

Volleyball
Team, men: U.S.S.R.
Team, women: U.S.S.R.

Water Polo
Team: U.S.S.R.

Weight Lifting
Flyweight: Kanibek Osmanoliev, U.S.S.R.
Bantamweight: Daniel Nunez, Cuba
Featherweight: Viktor Mazin, U.S.S.R.
Lightweight: Yanko Roussev, Bulgaria
Middleweight: Assen Zlatev, Bulgaria
Light Heavyweight: Yurik Vardanyan, U.S.S.R.
Middle Heavyweight: Peter Baczako, Hungary
Heavyweight: Ota Zaremba, Czechoslovakia
Second Heavyweight: Leonid Taranenko, U.S.S.R.
Super Heavyweight: Sultan Rakhmanov, U.S.S.R.

Wrestling, Freestyle
Paperweight: Claudio Pollio, Italy
Flyweight: Anatoly Beloglazov, U.S.S.R.
Bantamweight: Sergei Beloglazov, U.S.S.R.
Featherweight: Magomedgasan Abushev, U.S.S.R.
Lightweight: Saipulla Absaidov, U.S.S.R.
Welterweight: Valentin Raitchev, Bulgaria
Middleweight: Ismail Abilov, Bulgaria
Light Heavyweight: Sanasar Oganesyan, U.S.S.R.
Heavyweight: Ilya Mate, U.S.S.R.
Super Heavyweight: Soslan Andiyev, U.S.S.R.

Wrestling, Greco-Roman
Paperweight: Zaksylik Ushkempirov, U.S.S.R.
Flyweight: Vakhtang Blagidze, U.S.S.R.
Bantamweight: Shamil Serikov, U.S.S.R.
Featherweight: Stilianos Migiakis, Greece
Lightweight: Stefan Rusu, Rumania
Welterweight: Ferenc Kocsis, Hungary
Middleweight: Gennady Korban, U.S.S.R.
Light Heavyweight: Norbert Nottny, Hungary
Heavyweight: Gheorghi Raikov, Bulgaria
Super Heavyweight: Alexander Kolchinski, U.S.S.R.

Yachting
Finn: Finland
Flying Dutchman: Spain
470 Class: Brazil
Soling: Denmark
Star: U.S.S.R.
Tornado: Brazil

THE JUNIOR OLYMPICS

Does the idea of competing for an Olympic gold medal in your favorite sport seem far-fetched to you? Would it surprise you to know that each year, in cities and towns across the United States, millions of young people do just that?

These young athletes are competitors in the Junior Olympics, the largest and one of the most important amateur sports programs in the United States. It gives young people the chance to compete in first-class events in sports ranging from basketball and boxing to water polo and wrestling.

The Junior Olympics program is administered by the Amateur Athletic Union (A.A.U.) and sponsored by Sears, Roebuck and Company. The entry requirements are simple. You must be an amateur between the ages of 8 and 18. You don't need to belong to a team or club. If you have competed in a sport at a higher level—for example, in the Pan Am Games or the international Olympic Games—then you cannot compete in that sport in the Junior Olympics. But you can still enter in a different sport.

Your first step in entering a Junior Olympics competition would be to contact the A.A.U. That organization will tell you whom to get in touch with in your area.

When you learn about the events in your area, you would begin to compete at one of more than 2,000 local meets. Winners ad-

Jake Howard, 17, was the long jump winner at the 1980 Junior Olympics. This amateur sports program gives young athletes an opportunity to compete for gold medals in seventeen sports.

The sports competition also offers young people, like 14-year-old gymnast Kimberly Hillner, the opportunity to perfect athletic skills and, perhaps, go on to the international Olympics.

vance to the association (state) level and go on to the regional level. Just 10,000 qualify for the national championships. Medals—gold, silver, and bronze—are awarded to winners from the association level to the national level. There are seventeen sports: basketball, bobsled-luge, boxing, cross-country running, decathlon, diving, gymnastics, judo, pentathlon, swimming, synchronized swimming, track and field, trampoline-tumbling, volleyball, water polo, weight lifting, and wrestling.

The Junior Olympics program was officially inaugurated in 1949 with the permission of the U.S. Olympic Committee. Since then, the impressive performance of former Junior Olympians in the international Olympic Games has been testimony to the success of the program. In the 1976 Montreal Olym-

pic Games, for example, 83 members of the U.S. team were former Junior Olympians. They captured 25 gold and 25 silver medals —three fourths of the gold and silver medals won by the United States.

Some outstanding Junior Olympics alumni in the Montreal Games were long jumper Kathy McMillan; hurdler Mike Shine; swimmers John Naber, Jim Montgomery, John Hencken, and Shirley Babashoff; boxers Sugar Ray Leonard and Leo Randolph; and divers Phil Boggs, Jenni Chandler, and Greg Louganis.

The Junior Olympics program offers an opportunity to perfect your athletic skills, the challenge of keen competition, and the thrill of winning. And you may even acquire the excellence to go on to the international Olympic Games.

BASEBALL

Baseball in 1980 went through a succession of pressure-packed episodes, culminating in a World Series victory for the Philadelphia Phillies over the Kansas City Royals, 4 games to 2. For Philadelphians, that victory represented the end of almost a century of frustration. The Phillies have been part of the National League for 97 years. Since World Series competition began in 1903, the Phillies had participated in only two "fall classics"—1915 and 1950. They won neither.

But this time the Phillies would not be denied. In three of their four wins, they battled from behind to snatch victory away from the Royals. The Phillies won the first two games, 7–6 and 6–4, after trailing by four runs in the opener and by two in the second contest. Kansas City evened the Series by scores of 4–3 (10 innings) and 5–3. In the fifth game, the Phillies again fell behind. But they rallied for two runs in the ninth inning for a 4–3 win. In the sixth game, the Phillies finally took the early lead and went on to clinch the Series with a 4–1 triumph.

Important contributors to the Phillies' success were Mike Schmidt, their third base-

man, and two pitchers, Steve Carlton and relief specialist Tug McGraw. Schmidt was named the Series' most valuable player on the strength of eight hits, including two homers, and seven runs batted in. He was also the National League's MVP for the regular season, after leading the circuit in home runs (48) and runs batted in (121).

"Lefty" Carlton added two World Series triumphs to his season's record of 24 victories, 9 defeats. His masterful pitching during the regular season earned him the Cy Young Award as the league's best hurler. McGraw relieved in four of the six Series games and was credited with one victory and two saves.

The Phillies had to fight every step of the way to get to the Series. They didn't win the division title in the National League East until the final weekend of the season. They had been tied for first place with the Montreal Expos, and the two clubs faced each other in a season-ending, three-game set. The Phillies captured the first two games to clinch the title, the second an 11-inning battle decided by Schmidt's home run.

The Phillies then went through a nerve-wracking five-game pennant playoff against

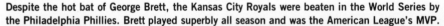

Despite the hot bat of George Brett, the Kansas City Royals were beaten in the World Series by the Philadelphia Phillies. Brett played superbly all season and was the American League's MVP.

Steve Carlton of the Phillies won the Cy Young Award as the best pitcher in the National League.

Phillie Mike Schmidt cracked 48 home runs and was MVP for both National League and World Series play.

the Houston Astros. The Astros had won a one-game playoff for the National League West title against the Los Angeles Dodgers. The Dodgers, down by three games with three to play against Houston, had swept all three to force the extra contest, which the Astros won, 7–1.

Four of the Phillies-Astros games went extra innings. The Phillies won the first game, 3–1. Then the Astros prevailed, 7–4 in 10 innings, and 1–0 in 11 innings. Finally, the Phillies eliminated their stubborn foes, 5–3 and 8–7, as each game went 10 innings.

In the American League, Kansas City coasted to the Western Division crown by a 14-game margin. In the East, the New York Yankees, after gaining a large mid-season lead, were forced to rally in September to hold off a Baltimore challenge. Like the Phillies, Kansas City had failed in its pennant bids after winning division titles in 1976, 1977, and 1978. The Yankees had beaten the Royals each year, but there was a sharp turnabout this time. Kansas City swept to the pennant with three consecutive triumphs, 7–2, 3–2, and 4–2.

George Brett, Kansas City third baseman,

struck the winning blow, a three-run homer in the final game, in keeping with his season-long leadership of the Royals' offense. His .390 batting average for the season was the highest in the major leagues in 39 years, and he also had 118 runs batted in. He was the natural choice as the American League's most valuable player.

Baltimore pitcher Steve Stone was the American League's Cy Young Award winner. He had a 25–7 record and a 3.23 earned run average (ERA). In one stretch during the season, Stone won 14 consecutive victories.

1980 WORLD SERIES RESULTS

		R	H	E	Winning/Losing Pitcher
1	Kansas City	6	9	1	Dennis Leonard
	Philadelphia	7	11	0	Bob Walk
2	Kansas City	4	11	0	Dan Quisenberry
	Philadelphia	6	8	1	Steve Carlton
3	Philadelphia	3	14	0	Tug McGraw
	Kansas City	4	11	0	Dan Quisenberry
4	Philadelphia	3	10	1	Larry Christenson
	Kansas City	5	10	2	Dennis Leonard
5	Philadelphia	4	7	0	Tug McGraw
	Kansas City	3	12	2	Dan Quisenberry
6	Kansas City	1	7	2	Rich Gale
	Philadelphia	4	9	0	Steve Carlton

MAJOR LEAGUE BASEBALL FINAL STANDINGS

AMERICAN LEAGUE

Eastern Division

	W	L	Pct.	GB
New York	103	59	.636	–
Baltimore	100	62	.617	3
Milwaukee	86	76	.531	17
Boston	83	77	.519	19
Detroit	84	78	.519	19
Cleveland	79	81	.494	23
Toronto	67	95	.414	36

Western Division

	W	L	Pct.	GB
*Kansas City	97	65	.599	–
Oakland	83	79	.512	14
Minnesota	77	84	.478	19½
Texas	76	85	.472	20½
Chicago	70	90	.438	26
California	65	95	.406	31
Seattle	59	103	.364	38

NATIONAL LEAGUE

Eastern Division

	W	L	Pct.	GB
*Philadelphia	91	71	.562	–
Montreal	90	72	.556	1
Pittsburgh	83	79	.512	8
St. Louis	74	88	.457	17
New York	67	95	.414	24
Chicago	64	98	.395	27

Western Division

	W	L	Pct.	GB
Houston	93	70	.571	–
Los Angeles	92	71	.568	1
Cincinnati	89	73	.549	3½
Atlanta	81	80	.503	11
San Francisco	75	86	.466	17
San Diego	73	89	.451	19½

*pennant winners

MAJOR LEAGUE LEADERS

AMERICAN LEAGUE

Batting
(top 10 qualifiers)

	AB	H	Pct.
G. Brett, Kansas City	449	175	.390
Cooper, Milwaukee	622	219	.352
Dilone, Cleveland	528	180	.341
Rivers, Texas	630	210	.333
Carew, California	540	179	.331
Bell, Texas	489	161	.329
Wilson, Kansas City	705	230	.326
Stapleton, Boston	449	144	.321
Bumbry, California	641	205	.320
Oliver, Texas	656	209	.319

NATIONAL LEAGUE

Batting
(top 10 qualifiers)

	AB	H	Pct.
Buckner, Chicago	578	187	.324
Hernandez, Saint Louis	595	191	.321
Templeton, Saint Louis	504	161	.319
McBride, Philadelphia	554	171	.309
Cedeno, Houston	499	154	.309
Dawson, Montreal	577	178	.308
Garvey, Los Angeles	658	200	.304
Collins, Cincinnati	551	167	.303
Simmons, Saint Louis	495	150	.303
Hendrick, Saint Louis	572	173	.302

Pitching
(top 5 qualifiers, based on ERA)

	W	L	ERA
May, New York	15	5	2.46
Norris, Oakland	22	9	2.53
Burns, Chicago	15	13	2.84
Keough, Oakland	16	13	2.92
Gura, Kansas City	18	10	2.95

Pitching
(top 5 qualifiers, based on ERA)

	W	L	ERA
Sutton, Los Angeles	13	5	2.20
Carlton, Philadelphia	24	9	2.34
Reuss, Los Angeles	18	6	2.51
Blue, San Francisco	14	10	2.97
Rogers, Montreal	16	11	2.98

Home Runs

	HR
Jackson, New York	41
Oglivie, Milwaukee	41
Thomas, Milwaukee	38
Armas, Oakland	35
Murray, Baltimore	32

Home Runs

	HR
Schmidt, Philadelphia	48
Horner, Atlanta	35
Murphy, Atlanta	33
Carter, Montreal	29
Baker, Los Angeles	29

LITTLE LEAGUE BASEBALL

For the Little League baseball players from Taiwan, the success story is endless. An all-star team from that island in the Far East once again captured the annual World Series, held in Williamsport, Pennsylvania. The 1980 victory marked their fourth successive triumph and their ninth since 1969. Only the final contest was close, a 4–3 win over Tampa, Florida.

On their way to the championship, the Taiwanese rolled up incredible statistics. In the first of their three games at Williamsport, they defeated Curaçao of the Netherlands Antilles, 6–0. Shuh-Shin Li pitched the two-hit shutout and struck out twelve batters. In their semifinal engagement, Taiwan set a Little League tournament record with seven home runs as it overwhelmed Trail, British Columbia, Canada, 23–0. Sheng-Dean Chen, the winning pitcher, hit two home runs—as did Li, who played center field.

The Tampa team was equally impressive in its efforts leading to the clash with Taiwan. Against Pawtucket, Rhode Island, the Floridians stroked 20 hits, for a 20–3 rout. In the semifinal, Tampa again hammered 20 safe blows as it defeated Kirkland, Washington, 16–0.

The finalists thus brought to their meeting spectacular scoring totals: 29–0 for Taiwan and 36–3 for Tampa. But Taiwan prevailed as Li returned to the mound to limit the Florida batters to four hits, while contributing a home run against Tampa hurler Kirk Walker.

The Taiwanese scored two runs in the first inning on a single by Li and a Tampa error. Tyrone Griffin, the Tampa shortstop, cut the margin in half with a homer in the bottom of the first. In the third inning, Li delivered his homer, and Chen followed immediately with an identical drive for a 4–1 advantage. Li and Chen had seven homers between them in the three games.

Tampa tallied in the fourth on Clayton Wilson's double and Walker's single. In the sixth and final inning, Gary Sheffield doubled and reached home on two infield outs, leaving Tampa a run short.

The championship game of the 34th Little League World Series was viewed by a national television audience and a Williamsport crowd of 20,000.

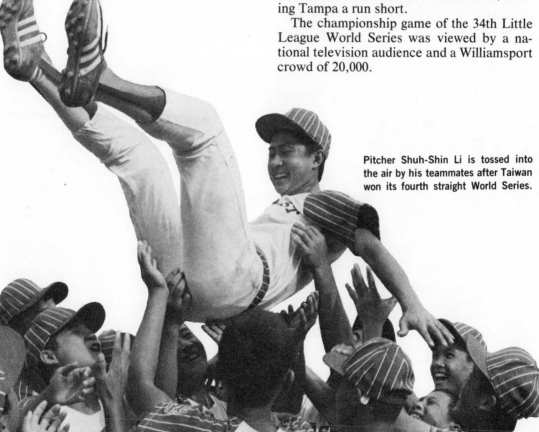

Pitcher Shuh-Shin Li is tossed into the air by his teammates after Taiwan won its fourth straight World Series.

185

BASKETBALL

Kareem Abdul-Jabbar (33) and Earvin (Magic) Johnson (32) led the Los Angeles Lakers to the championship in the NBA final playoffs.

For the eleventh year in a row, professional basketball got a new champion, as the Los Angeles Lakers became the 1980 National Basketball Association (NBA) titlists.

The Lakers defeated the Philadelphia 76ers, 4 games to 2, in the final playoff series. During the first four games, the teams posted alternate victories. Then the Lakers clinched the title with two successive triumphs, the final one in Philadelphia. The 16-point margin in that contest was the largest of the championship series.

The Lakers' success was achieved in a dramatic fashion. They operated with substitute coach Paul Westhead, who had replaced the injured Jack McKinney early in the campaign. And they were led in their final victory by a first-year professional, Earvin (Magic) Johnson. The veteran Kareem Abdul-Jabbar had been the Laker star from the start of the season through the fifth game of the final playoff, during which he sprained an ankle. The rookie Johnson promptly replaced Abdul-Jabbar as the inspirational force behind the team. He scored 42 points in the 123–107 triumph over Philadelphia that gave the Lakers the championship.

During the regular NBA season, the Boston Celtics had finished with the best record, 61–21, two games better than Philadelphia. But for the Eastern Conference crown, the 76ers soundly beat—four games to one—the Boston team, which had won the league title thirteen times in the past. In the Western Conference final, the Lakers dethroned the 1979 champion Seattle SuperSonics by winning four out of five games.

Johnson was named most valuable player (MVP) of the playoff series. For the 20-year-old youngster, who played forward, guard, and center in the playoffs, it was the second MVP award in two years. In 1979, as a Michigan State University sophomore, he had led the Spartans to the top of the National Collegiate Athletic Association (NCAA). For regular-season play, Abdul-Jabbar won a record sixth MVP award. And Boston Celtic forward Larry Bird was chosen rookie of the year.

Collegiate honors for 1980 went to the Uni-

NBA FINAL STANDINGS

EASTERN CONFERENCE

Atlantic Division

	W	L	Pct.
Boston	61	21	.744
Philadelphia	59	23	.720
Washington	39	43	.476
New York	39	43	.476
New Jersey	34	48	.415

Central Division

	W	L	Pct.
Atlanta	50	32	.610
Houston	41	41	.500
San Antonio	41	41	.500
Cleveland	37	45	.451
Indiana	37	45	.451
Detroit	16	66	.195

WESTERN CONFERENCE

Midwest Division

	W	L	Pct.
Milwaukee	49	33	.598
Kansas City	47	35	.573
Chicago	30	52	.366
Denver	30	52	.366
Utah	24	58	.293

Pacific Division

	W	L	Pct.
Los Angeles	60	22	.732
Seattle	56	26	.683
Phoenix	55	27	.671
Portland	38	44	.463
San Diego	35	47	.427
Golden State	24	58	.293

NBA Championship: Los Angeles Lakers

COLLEGE BASKETBALL

Conference	Winner
Atlantic Coast	Maryland (regular season) Duke (tournament)
Big Eight	Missouri (regular season) Kansas State (tournament)
Big Ten	Indiana
Ivy League	Pennsylvania
Mid-American	Toledo
Missouri Valley	Bradley
Pacific Ten	Oregon State
Southeastern	Kentucky (regular season) Louisiana State (tournament)
Southern	Furman
Southwest	Texas A & M
West Coast Athletic	San Francisco/ St. Mary's, Moraga (tied)
Western Athletic	Brigham Young

NCAA: Louisville

National Invitation Tournament: Virginia

The University of Louisville won its first NCAA title by beating ten-time champion UCLA, 59–54.

versity of Louisville, which captured its first NCAA title with a 59–54 triumph over ten-time champion UCLA. Darrell Griffith, who scored 23 points in the final for Louisville, was the MVP.

Among the four semifinalists in the 48-team tournament, Louisville was the only team that had been highly ranked (No. 2) during the regular season. Purdue was No. 20, and UCLA and Iowa were unranked. Surprisingly, UCLA had eliminated top-ranked DePaul in the opening round of the tournament.

Old Dominion University repeated as the champion of the Association for Intercollegiate Athletics for Women (AIAW) by defeating Tennessee, 68–53. Danish-born Inge Nissen led the Lady Monarchs in scoring, with 20 points, and was the tournament MVP. Teammate Nancy Lieberman won her second straight award as player of the year.

FOOTBALL

Among the big news of professional football's 1980 season was what did not happen. The Pittsburgh Steelers, champions of the previous two Super Bowls and four of the past six, failed to make the playoffs for the first time since 1971. Pittsburgh wound up with a season's record of 9–7.

Pro football remained powerful in Pennsylvania, though. The Philadelphia Eagles qualified for the playoffs by winning the National Conference Eastern Division title. Led by such stars as quarterback Ron Jaworski and running back Wilbert Montgomery, the Eagles finished the regular season with a record of 12–4. Eagle wide receiver Harold Carmichael set an NFL record by catching at least one pass in 127 consecutive games. Carmichael's streak, which began in 1972, finally ended in the last game of the regular season.

He sat out most of the game because of an injury, and he caught no passes.

The other division titlists were Minnesota (9–7) and Atlanta (12–4), in the National Conference; and Buffalo (11–5), Cleveland (11–5), and San Diego (11–5), in the American Conference. Other National Conference teams qualifying for the playoffs were Dallas (12–4) and Los Angeles (11–5); other American Conference teams qualifying were Houston (11–5) and Oakland (11–5).

The Dallas Cowboys proved that they could win without quarterback Roger Staubach, who had retired before the 1980 season. Staubach's understudy, Danny White, took over the quarterbacking chores, and the quick-armed passer helped bring the Cowboys into the playoffs. Another "big" help was the return of defensive lineman Ed "Too

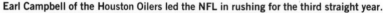

Earl Campbell of the Houston Oilers led the NFL in rushing for the third straight year.

Tall'' Jones, who had taken a year off to pursue a career as a heavyweight boxer.

Houston's Earl Campbell led the NFL in rushing for the third consecutive year. He gained 1,934 yards, the most since O. J. Simpson's single-season record of 2,003 in 1973. Campbell's 203 yards in the last game of the regular season helped Houston clinch its playoff spot. The powerful running back gained 200 or more yards four different times in 1980.

Campbell wasn't the only strong ground-gainer. Rookie Billy Sims of the Detroit Lions ran for 1,303 yards and set a club record of 16 touchdowns. The Lions didn't make the playoffs, but they finished 9–7, their best record since their 10–4 finish in 1970. Sims was nearly everyone's choice as the NFL's top rookie of 1980.

San Diego Charger receivers set a record in 1980. For the first time in history, three players on the same team each had receptions totaling over 1,000 yards. The glue-fingered trio consisted of John Jefferson, Charlie Joiner, and Kellen Winslow. With such enticing targets to aim at, Charger quarterback Dan Fouts had another record-breaking season. He passed for 4,715 yards, breaking his year-old record, and thus becoming the first pro quarterback to gain 4,000 yards in each of two consecutive seasons.

Cleveland Brown quarterback Brian Sipe also reached the 4,000-yard plateau in 1980, the third passer in history (after Fouts and Joe Namath) to do so.

In the Canadian Football League, the Edmonton Eskimos won the Grey Cup championship for the third straight year. The Eskimos whipped the Hamilton Tiger-Cats, 48–10. Tom Scott, formerly of the University of Washington, set a Grey Cup record by catching three touchdown passes. Two came from quarterback Warren Moon, who was named the game's outstanding offensive player.

In college football, fans of the University of Georgia Bulldogs had a lot to cheer about in 1980. Georgia was the only major college team that went undefeated and untied through the regular season, finishing 11–0–0. They were ranked number one in the country by two polls. Georgia met Notre Dame (9–1–1) in the Sugar Bowl.

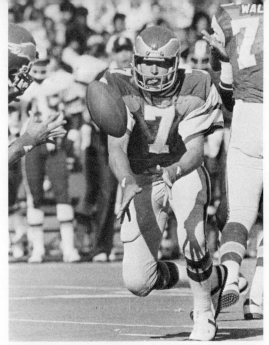

Philadelphia Eagle quarterback Ron Jaworski led his teammates to a 12-4 record.

Georgia's undefeated season was even more remarkable because the Bulldogs had finished only 6–5 in 1979. The main reason for Georgia's new success was freshman running back Herschel Walker. The young tailback set a freshman rushing record by gaining 1,616 yards. Walker was the first freshman to be seriously considered for the Heisman Trophy. He finished third in the balloting.

The winner of the Heisman Trophy, as the nation's outstanding college player, was George Rogers of the University of South Carolina. A senior, Rogers led the nation in rushing with 1,781 yards on 297 carries, an average of an amazing 6.0 yards per carry. During his college career, Rogers gained 100 or more yards in 21 straight games.

Second in the balloting for the Heisman Trophy was Hugh Green, a senior at the University of Pittsburgh. Green, a defensive end, was the top choice as the country's outstanding lineman. Green confronted Heisman winner Rogers when Pitt (10–1–0) played South Carolina (8–3–0) in the Gator Bowl.

Alabama (9–2–0) faced Baylor (10–1–0) in the Cotton Bowl; Michigan (9–2–0) played Washington (9–2–0) in the Rose Bowl; and Florida State (10–1–0) met Oklahoma (9–2–0) in the Orange Bowl.

George Rogers of the University of South Carolina won the Heisman Trophy.

NFL FINAL STANDINGS

AMERICAN CONFERENCE

Eastern Division

	W	L	T	Pct.	PF	PA
Buffalo	11	5	0	.688	320	260
New England	10	6	0	.625	441	325
Miami	8	8	0	.500	266	305
Baltimore	7	9	0	.437	355	387
N.Y. Jets	4	12	0	.250	302	395

Central Division

	W	L	T	Pct.	PF	PA
Cleveland	11	5	0	.688	357	310
Houston	11	5	0	.688	295	251
Pittsburgh	9	7	0	.563	352	313
Cincinnati	6	10	0	.375	244	312

Western Division

	W	L	T	Pct.	PF	PA
San Diego	11	5	0	.688	418	327
*Oakland	11	5	0	.688	364	306
Denver	8	8	0	.500	310	323
Kansas City	8	8	0	.500	319	336
Seattle	4	12	0	.250	291	408

NATIONAL CONFERENCE

Eastern Division

	W	L	T	Pct.	PF	PA
*Philadelphia	12	4	0	.750	384	222
Dallas	12	4	0	.750	454	311
Washington	6	10	0	.375	261	293
St. Louis	5	11	0	.313	299	350
N.Y. Giants	4	12	0	.250	249	425

Central Division

	W	L	T	Pct.	PF	PA
Minnesota	9	7	0	.563	317	308
Detroit	9	7	0	.563	334	272
Chicago	7	9	0	.437	304	264
Tampa Bay	5	10	1	.344	271	341
Green Bay	5	10	1	.344	231	371

Western Division

	W	L	T	Pct.	PF	PA
Atlanta	12	4	0	.750	405	272
Los Angeles	11	5	0	.688	424	289
San Francisco	6	10	0	.375	320	415
New Orleans	1	15	0	.063	291	487

*Conference Champions and Super Bowl Contenders

COLLEGE FOOTBALL

Conference	Winner
Atlantic Coast	North Carolina
Big Eight	Oklahoma
Big Ten	Michigan
Ivy League	Yale
Mid-American	Central Michigan
Pacific Ten	Washington
Southeastern	Georgia
Southern	Furman
Southwest	Baylor
Western Athletic	Brigham Young

Cotton Bowl: Alabama
Gator Bowl: Pittsburgh
Orange Bowl: Oklahoma
Rose Bowl: Michigan
Sugar Bowl: Georgia

Heisman Trophy: George Rogers, South Carolina

Jack Nicklaus blasts out of a sand trap on his way to winning his fourth U.S. Open. In 1980, Nicklaus also captured his fifth PGA championship.

GOLF

PROFESSIONAL		AMATEUR	
	Individual		**Individual**
Masters	Severiano Ballesteros	**U.S. Amateur**	Hal Sutton
U.S. Open	Jack Nicklaus	**U.S. Women's Amateur**	Julie Simpson Inkster
Canadian Open	Bob Gilder	**British Amateur**	David Evans
British Open	Tom Watson	**British Ladies Amateur**	Anne Sander
PGA	Jack Nicklaus	**Canadian Amateur**	Greg Olson
World Series of Golf	Tom Watson	**Canadian Ladies Amateur**	Edwina Kennedy
U.S. Women's Open	Amy Alcott		
Ladies PGA	Sally Little		
	Team		**Team**
World Cup	Canada	**Curtis Cup**	United States

GYMNASTICS

The 1980 American Cup gymnastics meet, held in March in New York City, attracted 40 competitors from 15 countries. But the top two performers were both from the United States. The leading woman gymnast was 13-year-old Californian Tracee Talavera, shown at left on the balance beam. She won the women's all-around title as well as three other events. Florida native Kurt Thomas, 23, shown below on the side horse, won the men's all-around title and four other events, and he tied for first place in a fifth.

HOCKEY

One of the year's most surprising sports accomplishments was the capture of the Stanley Cup by the New York Islanders. Their victory ended the Montreal Canadiens' four-year reign as National Hockey League champions. In the eighth season of their existence, the Islanders became the second expansion team in the league's 63-year history to gain professional hockey's highest honor. The Philadelphia Flyers were the first team to have done so, in 1974 and 1975. To add to the satisfaction of the Islanders, they defeated Philadelphia in the final playoff series, 4 games to 2.

The Islanders gained a strong advantage in the best-of-seven championship series by winning three of the first four games. But the resistance by the Flyers was more stubborn than the final result showed. Two of the Islander victories, in the first and last encounters, were achieved in overtime periods, 4–3 and 5–4.

After New York's success in the opener, Philadelphia evened the series with an easy 8–3 decision. But the 6–2 and 5–2 Islander victories that followed left the Flyers in the weak position of needing three consecutive triumphs to win the title. Still, they battled back and won the fifth game, 6–3. In the sixth game, they recovered from a 4–2 deficit in the third period to tie the score and send the contest into a sudden-death overtime pe-

riod. At 7 minutes, 11 seconds of the extra session, Bob Nystrom's goal won the championship for the Islanders.

It was Nystrom's second goal of the game and his ninth in the 21 playoff engagements. But the honor as most valuable player of the post-season competition went to Islander Bryan Trottier, who was credited with two assists in the last game and a record 29 playoff points.

On the basis of their regular-season performance, the Islanders had been given little chance of winning the cup. They compiled a record of 39 victories, 28 defeats, and 13 ties, for a total of 91 points, which placed them fifth among the league's 21 teams. By contrast, the Flyers had rolled up the circuit's best mark (48–12–20, for 116 points). And the Flyers had been undefeated in a record string of 35 games (25 victories, 10 ties), stretching from October 14 to January 7.

But in post-season competition, the New York team was dominant. En route to the championship series with the Flyers, the Islanders eliminated the Los Angeles Kings, 3 games to 1; the Boston Bruins, 4 games to 1; and the Buffalo Sabres, 4 games to 2.

Montreal's four-year dynasty ended in a quarter-final series with a stunning upset by the Minnesota North Stars, 4 games to 3. Minnesota was subsequently eliminated by Philadelphia, 4 games to 1.

The Islanders and the Flyers battled it out for the Stanley Cup, which New York won, 4 games to 2.

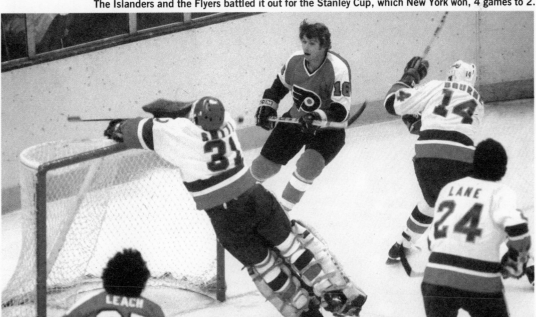

193

Edmonton Oiler Wayne Gretzky took double honors, winning the Hart and Lady Byng trophies.

NHL FINAL STANDINGS

CAMPBELL CONFERENCE

Patrick Division

	W	L	T	Pts.
Philadelphia	48	12	20	116
N.Y. Islanders	39	28	13	91
N.Y. Rangers	38	32	10	86
Atlanta	35	32	13	83
Washington	27	40	13	67

Smythe Division

	W	L	T	Pts.
Chicago	34	27	19	87
St. Louis	34	34	12	80
Vancouver	27	37	16	70
Edmonton	28	39	13	69
Colorado	19	48	13	51
Winnipeg	20	49	11	51

WALES CONFERENCE

Norris Division

	W	L	T	Pts.
Montreal	47	20	13	107
Los Angeles	30	36	14	74
Pittsburgh	30	37	13	73
Hartford	27	34	19	73
Detroit	26	43	11	63

Adams Division

	W	L	T	Pts.
Buffalo	47	17	16	110
Boston	46	21	13	105
Minnestoa	36	28	16	88
Toronto	35	40	5	75
Quebec	25	44	11	61

Stanley Cup: N.Y. Islanders

OUTSTANDING PLAYERS

Calder Trophy (rookie)	Ray Bourque, Boston
Conn Smythe Trophy (Stanley Cup play)	Bryan Trottier, N.Y. Islanders
Hart Trophy (most valuable player)	Wayne Gretzky, Edmonton
Lady Byng Trophy (sportsmanship)	Wayne Gretzky, Edmonton
Norris Trophy (defenseman)	Larry Robinson, Montreal
Ross Trophy (scorer)	Marcel Dionne, Los Angeles
Vezina Trophy (goalies)	Bob Sauve and Don Edwards, Buffalo

Hanni Wenzel of Liechtenstein won the women's World Cup skiing championship. Her brother Andreas won the men's title.

ICE SKATING

FIGURE SKATING

World Championships

Men	Jan Hoffmann, East Germany
Women	Anett Poetzsch, East Germany
Pairs	Marina Chersekova/Sergei Shakrai, U.S.S.R.
Dance	Krisztina Regoeczy/Andras Sallay, Hungary

United States Championships

Men	Charles Tickner
Women	Linda Fratianne
Pairs	Tai Babilonia/Randy Gardner
Dance	Stacey Smith/John Summers

SPEED SKATING

World Championships

Men	Hilbert van der Duim, Netherlands
Women	Natalya Petruseva, U.S.S.R.

SKIING

WORLD CUP CHAMPIONSHIPS

Men	Andreas Wenzel, Liechtenstein
Women	Hanni Wenzel, Liechtenstein

U.S. ALPINE CHAMPIONSHIPS

	Men	Women
Downhill	Dave Irwin	Cindy Nelson
Slalom	Steve Mahre	Christin Cooper
Giant Slalom	Peter Monod	Christin Cooper
Combined	Jim Kirby	Christin Cooper

CANADIAN ALPINE CHAMPIONSHIPS

	Men	Women
Downhill	Ken Read	Laurie Graham
Slalom	Peter Monod	Lynn Lacasse
Giant Slalom	Peter Monod	Ann Blackburn
Combined	Cesare Percini	Ann Blackburn

In Soccer Bowl-80, the New York Cosmos defeated the Fort Lauderdale Strikers, 3–0. Giorgio Chinaglia (*right*) was named MVP of both the NASL playoffs and the championship game.

SOCCER

NORTH AMERICAN SOCCER LEAGUE FINAL STANDINGS

NATIONAL CONFERENCE

Eastern Division

	W	L	GF	GA	Pts.
New York	24	8	87	41	213
Washington	17	15	72	61	159
Toronto	14	18	49	65	128
Rochester	12	20	42	67	109

Central Division

	W	L	GF	GA	Pts.
Dallas	18	14	57	58	157
Minnesota	16	16	66	56	147
Tulsa	15	17	56	62	139
Atlanta	7	25	34	84	74

Western Division

	W	L	GF	GA	Pts.
Seattle	25	7	74	31	207
Los Angeles	20	12	61	52	174
Vancouver	16	16	52	47	139
Portland	15	17	50	53	133

AMERICAN CONFERENCE

Eastern Division

	W	L	GF	GA	Pts.
Tampa Bay	19	13	61	50	168
Ft. Lauderdale	18	14	61	55	163
New England	18	14	54	56	154
Philadelphia	10	22	42	68	98

Central Division

	W	L	GF	GA	Pts.
Chicago	21	11	80	50	187
Houston	14	18	56	69	130
Detroit	14	18	51	52	129
Memphis	14	18	49	57	126

Western Division

	W	L	GF	GA	Pts.
Edmonton	17	15	58	51	149
California	15	17	61	67	144
San Diego	16	16	53	51	140
San Jose	9	23	45	68	95

Soccer Bowl-80: New York Cosmos

U.S. swimmer Bill Barrett set a new world record in the 200-meter individual medley.

SWIMMING

WORLD SWIMMING RECORDS SET IN 1980

EVENT	HOLDER	TIME
	Men	
200-meter freestyle	Rowdy Gaines, U.S.	1:49.16
400-meter freestyle	Peter Szmidt, Canada	3:50.49
1,500-meter freestyle	Vladimir Salnikov, U.S.S.R.	14:58.27
200-meter butterfly	Craig Beardsley, U.S.	1:58.21
100-meter butterfly	Par Arvidsson, Sweden	0:54.15
200-meter individual medley	Bill Barrett, U.S.	2:03.24
	Women	
100-meter freestyle	Barbara Krause, E. Germany	0:54.79
100-meter backstroke	Rica Reinisch, E. Germany	1:00.86
200-meter backstroke	Rica Reinisch, E. Germany	2:11.77
100-meter breaststroke	Ute Geweniger, E. Germany	1:10.11
100-meter butterfly	Mary T. Meagher, U.S.	0:59.26
200-meter butterfly	Mary T. Meagher, U.S.	2:06.37
200-meter individual medley	Petra Schneider, E. Germany	2:13.00
400-meter individual medley	Petra Schneider, E. Germany	4:36.29

Evonne Goolagong Cawley recaptured the Wimbledon crown 9 years after she had first won that tournament.

TENNIS

The 1980 tennis season will be remembered for two electrifying matches—one at Wimbledon, England, and one at Flushing Meadows, New York. Both involved the same players, Bjorn Borg of Sweden and John McEnroe of the United States.

Their first confrontation was on the center court at Wimbledon in July. There, Borg broke his own record for that tournament by winning the men's singles title for the fifth straight time. He defeated McEnroe in a five-set final (1–6, 7–5, 6–3, 6–7, 8–6). The match lasted almost four hours, and in the fourth set they battled through a historic 34-point tie breaker.

Borg and McEnroe were finalists again in September, in the U.S. Open at the National Tennis Center in New York City. This time, in another blistering, four-hour struggle, 21-year-old McEnroe retained the title he had captured in 1979. The scores were 7–6, 6–1, 6–7, 5–7, 6–4. It was the first time in four years that Borg had failed to win a five-set match. And it was another frustrating bid for the U.S. title he has never won. But Borg added to his stature as one of the world's finest players by winning the French Open for the fifth time.

Honors among the women competitors were shared by Evonne Goolagong Cawley of Australia, winner at Wimbledon, and Chris Evert Lloyd, victor in the U.S. Open.

Nine years after she had captured her first Wimbledon crown at age 19, Cawley defeated Lloyd in the final, 6–1, 7–6. The two-year Wimbledon reign of Martina Navratilova ended in a semifinal defeat by Lloyd.

Earlier in the season, Lloyd had won the French and Italian championship tournaments. And she recaptured the U.S. crown, which she had held from 1975 through 1978, by turning back her final foe, Hana Mandlikova of Czechoslovakia (5–7, 6–1, 6–1). The day before, Lloyd had eliminated the defending champion, 17-year-old Tracy Austin (4–6, 6–1, 6–1).

TOURNAMENT TENNIS

	Australian Open	French Open	Wimbledon	U.S. Open
Men's Singles	Guillermo Vilas, Argentina	Bjorn Borg, Sweden	Bjorn Borg, Sweden	John McEnroe, U.S.
Women's Singles	Barbara Jordan, U.S.	Chris Evert Lloyd, U.S.	Evonne Goolagong Cawley, Australia	Chris Evert Lloyd, U.S.
Men's Doubles	Peter McNamara, Australia/ Paul McNamee, Australia	Victor Amaya, U.S./ Hank Pfister, U.S.	Peter McNamara, Australia/ Paul McNamee, Australia	Bob Lutz, U.S./ Stan Smith, U.S.
Women's Doubles	Judy Chaloner, New Zealand/ Dianne Evers, Australia	Kathy Jordan, U.S./ Anne Smith, U.S.	Kathy Jordan, U.S./ Anne Smith, U.S.	Billie Jean King, U.S./ Martina Navratilova, U.S.

Davis Cup Winner: Czechoslovakia

U.S. athlete Mary Decker broke the world record in the 1-mile run.

TRACK AND FIELD

WORLD TRACK AND FIELD RECORDS SET IN 1980

EVENT	HOLDER	TIME, DISTANCE, OR POINTS
	Men	
1,000-meter run	Sebastian Coe, Britain	2:13.40
1,500-meter run	Steve Ovett, Britain	3:31.40
1-mile run	Sebastian Coe, Britain	3:48.80
400-meter hurdles	Edwin Moses, U.S.	0:47.13
High jump	Gerd Wessig, E. Germany	7′ 8¾″
Pole vault	Wladyslaw Kozakiewicz, Poland	18′ 11½″
Javelin throw	Ferenc Paragi, Hungary	317′ 4″
Hammer throw	Yuri Sedykh, U.S.S.R.	268′ 4½″
Decathlon	Guido Kratschmer, W. Germany	8,649 pts.
	Women	
100-meter run	Lyudmila Kondratyeva, U.S.S.R.	0:10.87
800-meter run	Nadyezhda Olizarenko, U.S.S.R.	1:53.50
1,500-meter run	Tatyana Kazankina, U.S.S.R.	3:52.47
1-mile run	Mary Decker, U.S.	4:21.70
100-meter hurdles	Grazyna Rabsztyn, Poland	0:12.36
400-meter hurdles	Karin Rossley, E. Germany	0:54.28
Shot put	Ilona Slupianek, E. Germany	73′ 8″
Discus throw	Maria Vergova, Bulgaria	235′ 7″
Javelin throw	Tatyana Biryulina, U.S.S.R.	229′ 11″
Pentathlon	Nadyezhda Tkachenko, U.S.S.R.	5,083 pts.

SPORTS BRIEFS

Swimmers from the United States were disappointed about not going to the Olympics. But they had their own swim meet—the U.S. Long Course Swimming Championships, in Irvine, California, in August. The meet took place right after the Olympics, so the Americans could compare their times with those of the Olympians. In the 22 Olympic individual events, 10 American times would have been good enough for Olympic gold medals. New Jerseyan Craig Beardsley (*right*) set a world record in the men's 200-meter butterfly event.

The track and field athletes who didn't go to the Olympics had an international competition. More than 25 nations were represented at Philadelphia's Liberty Bell Classic in July. The pentathlon winner was Diane Jones Konihowski of Canada (*below, right*). Konihowski is shown competing with Cornelia Swisk of West Germany in the 100-meter hurdles, one of the five events of the pentathlon.

N RELAYS   PENN RELAYS

It was his first marathon, but Alberto Salazar (*above, right*) is a world-class distance runner. In October's New York Marathon, the 22-year-old from Massachusetts set a new course record for the 26-mile, 385-yard race. The women's winner, Norway's Grete Waitz, broke her own record for women marathoners. Many people believe her to be the finest woman distance runner ever.

The Boston Marathon, the most famous road race of them all, had a familiar winner in April, 1980. Hometown-favorite Bill Rodgers, fighting off exhaustion, took his third straight title and his fourth overall. Proudly wearing the laurel wreath of victory is the women's winner, Jacqueline Gareau of Montreal, Quebec.

Pittsburgh Steeler wide receiver Lynn Swann is known for his graceful, acrobatic catches. His leaping grabs have helped the Steelers win four Super Bowls. Swann credits much of his athletic ability to the ballet training he had when he was young. Ballet training teaches speed, timing, balance, and co-ordination—all qualities of a good wide receiver. Ballet classes helped make Swann a fine football player and also gave him a love for dance. He still practices ballet, and in 1980 he was named to the Board of Trustees of the Pittsburgh Ballet Theater.

It's the longest winning streak in sports, dating back to 1851. In that year, the yacht *America* won a sailing race around the Isle of Wight, England. Since then, yachts from the United States have beaten off all challengers for the America's Cup. The races are now held in the sea off Newport, Rhode Island. In September, 1980, the American yacht *Freedom* (*right*) successfully defended the cup by beating the challenger *Australia,* four races to one. The next America's Cup series is scheduled for 1983.

In 1978, Ben Abruzzo, Larry Newman, and Maxie Anderson became the first people to balloon across the Atlantic. In May, 1980, New Mexican Anderson, 45, was airborne again. This time his partner was his son Kris, 23, and their goal was to balloon non-stop across North America. Their balloon, named the *Kitty Hawk,* took off from Fort Baker, California, and four days later floated down on the Gaspé Peninsula of eastern Canada.

In Montreal on June 20, 1980, two of the world's best prizefighters went at each other for 15 rounds. At stake was the World Boxing Council's welterweight title. When it was over, Roberto Durán (*left*) of Panama had taken the title from Maryland's Sugar Ray Leonard (*right*) by a close, but unanimous, decision. On November 25, they met again, in New Orleans. Durán quit the fight in the eighth round, and a jubilant Leonard reclaimed his title. (Another important match took place on October 2, when Muhammad Ali came out of retirement to fight World Boxing Council champion Larry Holmes for the heavyweight title. Holmes hit Ali pretty much at will for 10 rounds. Ali didn't answer the bell for the 11th round, and the fight was over.)

THE KINETIC SCULPTURE RACE

Some look like insects. Some look like birds. Some look like amusement-park rides. And some look like nothing anyone's ever seen. But they all move, and they all take part in a strange race in Ferndale, California. It's such a strange race that no one even cares who wins. The official name of this event is the Ferndale Kinetic Sculpture Race. ("Kinetic sculpture" is sculpture that can move.)

In one recent race, four young people, whose ages ranged from 3 to 12, piloted a very strange machine. Made mostly of metal pipe, it looked like a red dinosaur skeleton on wheels. They called their vehicle Inch-by-Inch, probably to describe how it progressed down the street. By pushing and pulling at various parts of their contraption, they made it move. Inch-by-Inch won three awards: best artistic design, best mechanical design, and best all-around machine.

Entries in the kinetic sculpture race come in all shapes and sizes. Anything is liable to show up, but no engine-powered devices are allowed. Human energy alone must supply the power, and no driver's feet may touch the ground. One device, the Bubblemobile, was a huge wheel festooned with balloons. Like a hamster on an exercise wheel, the driver ran around the inside of the vehicle, and this motion made the Bubblemobile roll down the street.

The race has taken place every Mother's Day since 1969. And it all began as a joke. In that year, a Ferndale metal sculptor named Hobart Brown took a look at his son's tricycle and decided it was ugly. So he added some decorations and a few more wheels and wound up with a tall, wobbly thing that he called the Pentacycle. ("Penta" means "five." It had five wheels.) This was truly a kinetic sculpture—part art, part vehicle.

As Hobart Brown was working on the Pentacycle, a neighbor said that he could make a better kinetic sculpture. "That's a challenge!" Hobart said. "Build it, and we'll have a race on Mother's Day, right down the center of Main Street, Ferndale!" Soon other people heard about the race and they started fashioning kinetic sculptures, too. Word spread. And on race day, about a dozen kinetic sculptures showed up to race, and thousands of spectators were there to take part in the fun. Hobart Brown's Pentacycle did not win that first race. The grand prizewinner was the Tortoise, a giant turtle made of papier-mâché. It could shoot water and emit steam out of its mouth. And every

Human energy supplies the power to move these kinetic sculptures: Inch-by-Inch . . .

now and then the Tortoise "laid" a polka dot egg that rolled out the back.

After all the excitement, Hobart Brown realized that there would have to be another kinetic sculpture race the following year. And so the Mother's Day tradition began. And year by year, some very strange rigs have turned out for the race. Their names may give some idea of just how strange they are: the Silver Wing Velocipede, Powered Flower, Yellow Submarine, Tyrannosaurus Rust, and the Rickety Chickadee. Few of these machines go very fast. They aren't easy to steer and they often break down. To give an idea of how slow some go, one rule states that to win a prize, a vehicle must finish the three-block race within two hours.

As if a three-block race weren't long enough, a new race was added in 1974—a three-day, 34-mile (55-kilometer) event. It's called the Great Arcata to Ferndale Cross Country Kinetic Sculpture Race. This big race includes a difficult passage over sand dunes and treacherous crossings of Humboldt Bay and the Eel River. The machines in this race not only have to roll, they have to float as well. Among the entries in recent races were such mechanical marvels as the Gossamer Clam, the Double Trouble Mobile, and the Nervous Breakdown. And, just as in the Mother's Day race, no one really cares who wins. It's all done for the fun of it!

. . . and the Bubblemobile.

. . . the Double Trouble Mobile . . .

205

LIVING HISTORY

In 1980, the historic city of Boston celebrated the 350th anniversary of its founding. This Currier & Ives lithograph shows how the city looked in 1848.

A seaborne parade in Boston Harbor was the start of Boston's birthday celebration.

BOSTON—THE CRADLE OF LIBERTY

On a balmy spring day in 1980, a fleet of ships sailed into Boston Harbor. Leading the fleet was the USS *Constitution*—popularly known as Old Ironsides—the oldest commissioned warship in the U.S. Navy. Behind it came some of the greatest sailing ships afloat.

The "tall ships," as these great old sailing vessels are known, led a seaborne parade. There was the *Juan Sebastian de Elcano* from Spain and the Danish Navy training ship *Danmark*. Sails puffed out from varnished masts as sailors scampered like monkeys up the rigging. Fireboats sent up geysers of water in salute, cannon boomed, and 2,000,000 people lined piers and docks or stood on rooftops to watch the spectacle.

The scene brought back memories of Operation Sail in New York City, in 1976—when the United States celebrated the bicentennial of its birth. But this time the birth of one of America's oldest cities was being celebrated—for 1980 was the 350th anniversary of the founding of Boston, Massachusetts.

The parade of ships on May 31 was just the start of a summer-long birthday party that featured parades, outdoor concerts, special exhibits, and a giant picnic in Boston Common, the city's oldest park. "We want the world to know that we are a major world-class city," one city official said.

Indeed, Bostonians take great pride in the role their city has played in American history. They point to the fact that Boston is often referred to as the Cradle of Liberty—the place where the Revolutionary War really began.

Oliver Wendell Holmes, Jr., a Bostonian who became a justice of the U.S. Supreme Court, went even further. He called Boston "the hub of the universe." When Justice Holmes made that statement nearly one hundred years ago, it wasn't much of an exaggeration. Back then, Boston was one of the great trading, cultural, and manufacturing centers of the world.

Since then, Boston has had its ups and downs. In the 1940's and 1950's, the city suffered a decline. But during the last two decades, major city development programs resulted in new buildings and shopping centers. At the same time, many of the city's historic streets and houses were restored. Today, Boston is booming again.

The city of Boston was founded in 1630 by a group of people from England called the Puritans. The Puritans were members of a religious sect who left England because they were being persecuted for their beliefs. Spurred by accounts of New England as a region of great natural wealth—furs, fish, and fertile land—they formed the Massachusetts Bay Company. The company's aim was to explore and settle New England.

On September 20, 1630, a group of Puritans established a settlement on a hilly peninsula overlooking the Charles River. They chose the site because the Charles River flowed into a natural harbor. And they named their settlement Boston because many of them came from an English town called Boston.

The Puritans were a strict people who believed in hard work. They quickly became expert seafarers and shipbuilders, as well as clever traders. By the early 1700's, Boston was the leading seaport in the colonies.

The Puritans also were a hardy and independent breed. They were the first to resist the harsh taxes imposed on the colonies by the British Parliament. When the protests became violent, the British sent troops to Boston to keep order.

The presence of British troops only made matters worse. In March, 1770, British troops fired on a Boston mob during an angry confrontation. Five Bostonians were killed in the incident, which became known as the Boston Massacre.

A few years later, in 1773, a group of Bostonians dressed as Indians boarded British merchant ships and dumped bales of tea into the harbor. They were angry because the British Parliament had put a tax on tea—their favorite drink.

The Boston Tea Party was another in a chain of events that led to the opening battles of the Revolutionary War. In April, 1775, a force of British troops was sent from Boston to nearby Concord to seize weapons and other supplies hidden by American patriots. The Americans were warned by Paul Revere, who rode to spread the alarm.

The next day, April 19, a force of American Minutemen (local militia) fought bloody skirmishes with the British troops at Lexington and Concord. The British retreated to Boston, and soon an army of American rebels laid siege to the city.

In June, the Americans occupied Breed's Hill, near Bunker Hill on Charlestown Peninsula, overlooking the city. On June 17, a force of British troops assaulted the American fortifications on Breed's Hill. During the day-long battle, the British were beaten back twice by a steady and murderous fire from the American militia. Finally, their ammunition exhausted, the Americans were driven from Breed's Hill. But the victory cost the British more than 1,000 casualties. And the battle—which became known as the Battle of Bunker Hill—made clear the determination of the American rebels to go on fighting.

In March, 1776, the American troops, now commanded by General George Washington,

The Boston Massacre (March, 1770), as depicted here by Paul Revere.

In this painting of the Battle of Bunker Hill (June 17, 1775), British redcoats are moving up the heights on Charlestown Peninsula as Charlestown burns from a naval bombardment.

fortified Dorchester Heights and forced the British to abandon the city. The British sailed out of Boston Harbor on March 17—a date still celebrated as a holiday by Bostonians. This was the first major victory of the Revolutionary War.

After the Americans won their independence, Boston flourished as a trading center. By the early 1800's, Boston merchant ships carried rum, tobacco, and fish to the far corners of the globe. They rounded Cape Horn and sailed for ports in distant China. There, they exchanged their cargoes for tea, silk, and other goods.

This was a time of growth and prosperity for Boston. Not only was the city a major center of trade, but it also had manufacturing plants. Boston's factories turned out clothing, shoes, and leather goods.

By the 1850's, Boston had also established itself as a center of cultural life in the United States. Some of America's most famous writers lived in and around Boston. They included Ralph Waldo Emerson, Henry David Thoreau, Nathaniel Hawthorne, and Louisa May Alcott. With all these great literary figures, it is understandable that Boston became a center for the printing and publishing trades.

Long before the Civil War, Bostonians were leaders in the antislavery movement. William Lloyd Garrison published an antislavery newspaper called *The Liberator,* and Harriet Beecher Stowe's famed novel *Uncle Tom's Cabin* was first published in Boston.

During the Civil War, tens of thousands of Bostonians served in the Union Army. One of them, Robert Gould Shaw, organized and commanded the first regiment of black soldiers to be recruited in the North—the 54th Massachusetts Colored Infantry Regiment.

Boston was also a magnet for immigrants. Thousands of Irish people, driven from their homeland by hunger and poverty, settled in Boston. Initially, the Irish immigrants had to take low-paying jobs. Many were house servants or day laborers. But by the early 1900's, the children and grandchildren of these immigrants were starting businesses of their own and entering politics. John F. Fitzgerald, a grandfather of President John F. Kennedy, served two terms as mayor between 1906 and 1914. During his administration, the port of Boston was modernized, local government was revamped, and other civic improvements were made.

Boston has been known throughout its history for its great educational institutions. Public education in the United States began in Boston with the founding of the Boston Public Latin School in 1635. One year later, Harvard College—the first U.S. college—was founded. Some of Boston's other noted colleges and universities include Boston University, Massachusetts Institute of Technology, Radcliffe College for women (which is affiliated with Harvard), and Northeastern University.

Bostonians also take pride in the fact that two natives of their city became presidents of the United States in this century. The first was Calvin Coolidge, who was president from 1923 to 1929. The second was John F. Kennedy, who served from 1961 until his death in 1963. Boston is also the hometown of Edward Brooke, the first black person to be elected to the U.S. Senate.

Visitors to Boston who want to relive some of the city's rich history can start by taking a walk along the Freedom Trail. This is a marked, red-brick pathway that winds its way for 1½ miles (2.4 kilometers) through the downtown and North End sections.

The past becomes the present at Faneuil Hall, a historic colonial meeting place that still exists today.

Along the way, you will pass historic Faneuil Hall, where earlier generations of Bostonians denounced the tyranny of King George III and his government. You can stand in the shadow of Old North Church (Christ Church) from whose belfry a signal was flashed to the patriots, warning that the British were coming. Other sites include the Old Granary Burial Ground, with the graves of Samuel Adams, John Hancock, and other American patriots; Paul Revere's House, the oldest house in Boston; and the Old South Meetinghouse, where the Boston Tea Party was planned. You can also walk the decks of Old Ironsides. The famed U.S. warship, built in 1797, is permanently berthed at the Boston navy yard.

Wherever you may go in Boston, history springs to life. Although Bostonians also look to the future, they are eager to preserve their heritage. Already they are looking forward to the 400th anniversary of their city. As Boston's Mayor Kevin White said: "It's important for each generation to experience this kind of thing at least once, to know who they are and what their city is."

HENRY I. KURTZ
Author, *John and Sebastian Cabot*

By the mid-1800's, Boston was a center of cultural life. And many famous American writers met at the Old Corner Book Store (*below*) to discuss their works.

THE PEARLIES OF LONDON

For most people in London, life is similar to that in any big city. They work or go to school, take care of their homes, and try to get a little rest and relaxation on weekends and holidays. But for one small group of Londoners, weekends and holidays are different. As if touched by a fairy godmother's magic wand, they are transformed into royalty, in clothes that glitter and glow with the sheen of thousands of pearls.

These people are the Pearlies—proud bearers of a tradition that is nearly 100 years old. Their name comes from their costumes, which are covered with mother-of-pearl buttons. And their story begins in the late 1800's, with fruit-and-vegetable venders called costermongers. (A coster is a kind of apple; "monger" means "salesperson.")

The costermongers sold their wares on the streets of London. They were flashy dressers because eye-catching clothes—especially those with a few bright buttons—helped attract attention to their stands. Street selling

wasn't an easy way to make a living, and the costermongers were poor. Still, they tried to help people who were needier than they were. They would often dress up and hold parades to raise money for local hospitals and other charities.

A young man named Henry Croft took part in one of these parades. Henry had grown up in an orphanage, where he had been taught how to sew, and he decided to make a very unusual costume for the parade. He sewed mother-of-pearl buttons all over his clothes.

The costermongers loved Henry's outfit. And Henry became known as the Pearly King. Soon, some of the costermongers were copying Henry's idea. They, too, decorated their clothes with closely sewn buttons.

Henry decided that every district of London should be a Pearly Kingdom and have a Pearly King and Queen. The first kings and queens were elected, and their titles became hereditary—that is, the titles were passed on

to their children. Only when a king and queen had no children was a new royal couple elected.

At one time, there were hundreds of Pearlies in London. But their number has decreased sharply. After World War II, many Pearly families moved out of London to the suburbs. And lifestyles changed. The costermonger stalls were replaced by supermarkets. Mother-of-pearl buttons that once were plentiful and cheap became hard to find and expensive. And younger members of some Pearly families weren't interested in keeping up the tradition. Today there are fewer than 35 Pearlies left.

The Pearlies who remain are members of a Pearly Guild and work hard to uphold their traditions. They put on their glittering costumes for dances, fashion shows, garden parties, and other charitable events in London. The children of the king and queen often take part in these activities. They have costumes, too, and they are called princes and princesses. Even pet dogs sometimes get into the act, wearing pearly collars and cloths as they trot beside the royal family.

Usually each person makes his or her own costume. Suits, dresses, shirts—even ties and hats—are covered with mother-of-pearl buttons. It takes at least 20,000 buttons to decorate a man's suit. One Pearly Queen's dress is covered with 30,000 buttons, and her coat with 60,000 buttons. As you can imagine, it takes months to sew all the buttons on the clothes. And the finished costumes can be very heavy. Some outfits weigh as much as 70 pounds (30 kilograms).

The buttons are sewn on to form flowers, boats, bells, hearts, and other complicated patterns. Each Pearly family has its own design. The Morris family design includes a pattern of doves. The Arrowsmith family is recognized by the butterflies that decorate its costumes. And on the back of each outfit is the name of the Pearly's "kingdom"— an area of London such as Whitechapel, Hampstead, or Lambeth.

As in years gone by, Pearlies don't get paid for their appearances. The money they raise goes to charity. Over the decades the Pearlies have raised many thousands of dollars for sick, needy, and disabled people.

BLOWING IN THE WIND

A wind from the west
Brings weather at its best;
A wind from the east
Brings rain to man and beast.

Will the weather be fair or foul? To learn the latest forecast, you can simply pick up a newspaper or switch on the radio or TV. But 100 years ago, farmers, sailors—in fact, anyone who wanted or needed to know what the next day's weather might be—had to make their own forecasts.

Since ancient times, one of the tools people have used to predict weather has been the weather vane—the familiar rooftop device that shows the direction of the wind. Knowing which way the wind is blowing is helpful in forecasting because certain kinds of weather tend to come along with winds from certain directions. But over the centuries, weather vanes have taken on other uses as well. They have become symbols of power and religion, signs for merchants and tradespeople, and a unique form of folk art.

▶ THE VANES OF THE OLD WORLD

No one knows who made the first weather vane. But one of the most famous vanes of the ancient world was built in Athens, during the 1st century B.C., by the Greek astronomer Andronicus. Andronicus mounted his vane on an eight-sided structure called the Tower of the Winds. The vane itself was a figure of Triton (the half-man, half-fish god of the sea) carrying a wand in one hand. When the wind blew, the figure swung around so that the wand pointed in the direction from which the wind was coming. The Triton vane set the pattern for later vanes in two important ways—it pointed into the wind, and it was decorative as well as useful.

Like the Greeks, the Romans used weather vanes. And through their empire, vanes spread across Europe. Two designs that are still used on weather vanes today—the banner and the cock—developed in Europe during the Middle Ages. Nobles, who by law were the only people allowed to fly banners and pennants, adopted the banner design. Banner vanes showing heraldic de-

The cock is a weather-vane design that developed in Europe during the Middle Ages. It is still popular today.

vices were placed on castle turrets to advertise the owner's rank.

Weather vanes in the form of cocks (roosters), on the other hand, were connected with religion. In the 9th century, the Roman Catholic Church ordered that every church be topped with the figure of a cock, a symbol associated with Saint Peter. Medieval artisans combined the cocks with weather vanes. This design became so widespread that its name, the weathercock, was often used to refer to any weather vane.

Gradually cocks, banners, simple arrows, and more elaborate designs began to be seen on the shops of merchants and homes of common people, as well as on churches and castles. But as a form of folk art, the weather vane reached its peak in North America—especially in the United States—during the 18th and 19th centuries.

▶ THE VANES OF AMERICA

In America, blacksmiths and woodcarvers turned out finely crafted vanes with devices that ranged from cows and horses to mermaids and square-rigger ships. Many of the early vanes were one-of-a-kind designs. A gilded copper grasshopper, for example, was placed on Boston's Faneuil Hall in 1742. It was made by Shem Drowne, who is thought to have been the first American artisan to make a living by designing and building weather vanes.

Other early designs were only slightly less fanciful. Paul Revere topped his coppersmith shop with a wooden codfish. George Washington favored a dove, carrying an olive branch as a sign of peace, for his estate, Mount Vernon. Seafaring designs were seen in coastal towns. Vanes sporting cows, hogs, and sheep were placed on barns that housed these animals. And figures of American Indians were especially popular in western Pennsylvania and New York—perhaps to show that the settlers wanted to be on friendly terms with Indian tribes.

During the 19th century, when patriotic feeling was strong in the United States, eagles and figures of Columbia, the goddess of liberty, topped town halls everywhere. Another popular subject for 19th-century vanes was the horse, which was essential for work and transportation. Vanes patterned after

An unusual weather vane is this copper grasshopper, which has topped Boston's Faneuil Hall since 1742.

As a form of folk art, weather vanes reached their peak in the United States during the 18th and 19th centuries.

Seafaring designs such as mermaids and fish were often seen in coastal towns.

Figures of American Indians were especially popular in Pennsylvania and New York.

workhorses, riding horses, and famous trotting horses raced the wind from the roofs of homes and barns.

In the 19th century, too, vanes became trade signs. A mortar-and-pestle vane might be seen over an apothecary shop, where medicines were made and sold. A figure of a locomotive might mark a railroad station, and a fire-engine vane might swing in the breeze over a firehouse.

The artisans who made these vanes were often traveling carpenters and blacksmiths. They sold their handiwork door-to-door or at taverns along the road. Most of the vanes were flat, carved from wood or shaped from iron or sheet metal. But some were hollow, three-dimensional figures, made by hammering thin sheets of copper into molds for the various parts of the figure. The shaped cop-

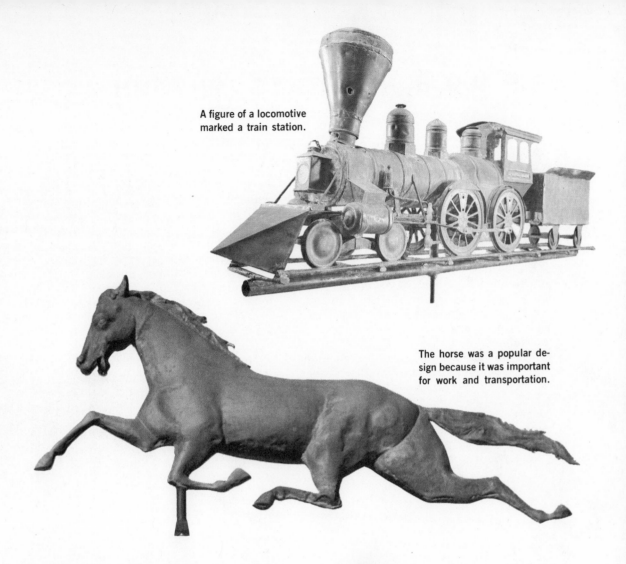

A figure of a locomotive marked a train station.

The horse was a popular design because it was important for work and transportation.

per pieces were then soldered together. Gold leaf or paint was often used to finish the figure.

By the 20th century, factory methods were being used to make most weather vanes. These mass-produced vanes often lacked the originality and fine design of the earlier ones. Vanes remained popular, however. Today a few artisans still make them by hand. And scientists who study weather still use vanes, often in combination with devices that measure and record wind speed.

Some of the old, handcrafted weather vanes can still be seen atop homes, churches, and town halls. But still another use has been found for these vanes—they have become popular collector's items. Today many of the finest ones can be seen in museums of folk art.

Vanes in the design of cows were placed on barns.

THE AUDUBON SOCIETY'S 75th BIRTHDAY

Somewhere in the United States, a group of young people is taking part in an unusual educational program. They are not sitting in a classroom or reading a textbook. They are learning by doing.

This group of students, which includes teenagers from high schools and older college students, is traveling throughout the United States. Their classroom is a bus, and their textbook is the natural environment.

During the nine-month study period, the students will log about 20,000 miles (32,000 kilometers) in travel time. They will camp out under the stars, cook their own meals, and learn about the land, its resources, and its wildlife.

The students are participants in an Audubon Expedition, sponsored by the National Audubon Society's Expedition Institute. Since 1979, the Expedition Institute has been sending out two such nature-study expeditions each academic year.

Those who have been involved in the program agree that it is an exciting experience.

They have explored Martha's Vineyard with geologists and whaling experts. They have canoed through the Florida Everglades with a group of ecologists. They have worked side by side with lobster fishermen in Maine and with farmers in Pennsylvania. And the students have unearthed ancient Pueblo Indian ruins in Arizona.

The unique study program is only one of many educational programs sponsored by the National Audubon Society, whose main goals are to protect wildlife and to provide for a safe and healthy natural environment. In 1980, as the society celebrated its 75th anniversary, it sponsored more than 1,300 film-lecture programs in 200 cities around the United States.

The National Audubon Society was founded in 1905. But the Audubon movement actually began in the 1890's, a period when birds were killed by the hundreds of thousands. Bird lovers estimated that as many as 5,000,000 birds were killed each year in the United States. Their feathers

These young people are on an Audubon Expedition to the Badlands of California.

The National Audubon Society is named after John James Audubon, the naturalist who became famous for his beautiful paintings of birds.

were used to make plumes for women's hats and to decorate dresses.

As hunters' rifles claimed more and more of the feathered creatures, bird lovers became more outraged. And they began to take action to stop the slaughter. In 1896 the first of many Audubon groups—the Massachusetts Audubon Society—was formed. Its purpose was to "discourage the buying and wearing, for ornamental purposes, of the feathers of any wild birds . . . and to otherwise further the protection of native birds."

Audubon societies quickly sprang up in other states. And on January 4, 1905, the Audubon societies of 35 states joined together to form the National Association of Audubon Societies for the Protection of Wild Birds and Animals. (Later the name was shortened to the National Audubon Society.) The organization is named after John James Audubon, the American naturalist who became famous for his beautiful paintings of birds.

Over the years, the Audubon Society has grown tremendously. Today it has over 430 chapters and some 400,000 members. The society manages 73 bird sanctuaries all over the United States. Many are located in the main nesting areas of birds that are rare or are threatened with extinction. The smallest of the sanctuaries is only 9 acres (3.6 hectares) and is located on Long Island, New York. The largest spreads out over 26,000 acres (10,500 hectares) of coastal marshland in Louisiana.

Early Audubon societies were concerned with protecting birds from hunters and with providing sanctuaries where the birds could live undisturbed. The Audubon Society is still concerned with protecting birds, but its activities have expanded.

Today the society is trying to educate people about the importance of protecting all wildlife, as well as forests, plants, and other natural resources. It also

• Encourages research to find better ways to protect the environment.

• Sponsors the creation of nature centers where adults and children can gain a better understanding of the world of nature.

• Works with state and federal government officials to pass laws to protect wildlife and natural resources.

• Encourages research to find new sources of energy that are not harmful to the environment.

After 75 years of conservation activities, the National Audubon Society remains true to its original purpose—the protection of birds and other wildlife—while playing an active role in new areas of concern about the natural environment.

ALBERTA AND SASKATCHEWAN—
A CELEBRATION

The past, it seems, always has a way of catching up with the present. So it was in 1980 for the Canadian provinces of Alberta and Saskatchewan. In September, 1905, the two provinces were created from districts of the Northwest Territories. Seventy-five years later, the more than 2,000,000 people of Alberta and the nearly 1,000,000 people of Saskatchewan celebrated the Diamond Jubilee of their respective provinces. Parades, festivals, concerts, sporting events, theatrical productions, art exhibits, craft fairs, block parties, banquets, and rodeos were all part of the year-long festivities.

The people of both provinces planned their celebrations around three major themes: heritage, celebration, and vision. With these basic concepts as background, the celebrants showed all Canada—and the world—their provinces' past, present, and future.

Above all, the celebration was a time to recall the history of the two provinces. Their story is an important chapter in Canada's westward expansion.

▶ THE PRAIRIE

Alberta and Saskatchewan, with Manitoba to the east, are Canada's Prairie Provinces.

Their broad sweeping plains rise gradually in the west to meet the Rocky Mountains. Some 10,000 years ago, this area was covered by vast glaciers. As the ice slowly melted and drew back toward the North Pole, people came to live on the plains. Long before Europeans explored the area in the 17th and 18th centuries, it was the home of Indians—the Blackfoot, Blood, Plains Cree, and other tribes.

The Europeans came to trade with the Indians. In exchange for metal tools and other items, the Europeans took furs, which were in great demand in their home countries. King Charles II of England granted trading rights in the area to the Hudson's Bay Company in 1670. Agents for this company are thought to have been the first white people to enter the region.

As the fur trade grew, trading posts and small settlements were established. Many of the fur traders made friends with the Indians, lived in their villages, and married Indian women. Their children were called métis—people of Indian and European ancestry.

The Hudson's Bay Company competed with a second company, the North West Company, for the fur trade in the Canadian

Farmers and ranchers were drawn to the broad, sweeping plains of Alberta and Saskatchewan.

Fur traders such as these, shown at a winter shelter, were the first Europeans in the area.

west. Competition was so great that hostilities often broke out between the men who worked for the two companies. But the rivalry ended when the firms merged in 1821 under the name of the Hudson's Bay Company. In 1870, the Canadian Government acquired the land owned by the Hudson's Bay Company, which was known as Rupert's Land. The area that is now Alberta and Saskatchewan thus became part of the newly organized Northwest Territories.

▶ THE SETTLERS

The Canadian Government was eager for people to settle in the new territory. Beginning in 1872, it offered free land to homesteaders who would set up farms on the prairie. But settlement of this new area brought some unique problems. For one thing, traders from the United States were carrying on an illegal liquor trade with the Indians. To stop this trade, the government organized the North West Mounted Police. The "Mounties" established their first major post in 1874 at Fort Macleod, thus becoming the first law enforcement group in the area.

Throughout the 1870's, the Canadian Government signed a series of treaties with the various Indian tribes. The Indians moved to reservations, leaving the land free for settlement. Cattle ranchers from the United States were among the first to come to the wide, open plains. They were followed by homesteaders in covered wagons. Still, there were not many settlers in the new territory.

The situation changed after the building of the transcontinental Canadian Pacific Railway. The railway was begun in the 1870's. It reached Calgary, in what is now Alberta, in 1883, and it was completed two years later. The railway made it easier for settlers to reach the plains. And it provided a way for farmers and ranchers to send their products to distant markets.

The métis and the Indians of the Saskatchewan area were alarmed by the building of the railroad. Most of the métis lived a semi-nomadic life, hunting buffalo, trapping for furs, and fishing in the many lakes and rivers. But their way of life was threatened as more settlers came and as more land was divided up for farms and ranches. In 1885, as the railway neared completion, the métis and the Indians rebelled against the Canadian Government. The rebellion was put down, and its leader, Louis Riel, was hanged. People in Canada were divided in their opinion of the execution and to many, Riel became a symbol of minority rights.

In the 1890's, the government began a huge advertising campaign aimed at drawing people from the eastern provinces and abroad to the plains. The ads promised rich grazing country and fine land for growing wheat, and they were wildly successful. People poured into the prairie from the United States, Britain, Germany, Scandinavia, the Ukraine, and other parts of Europe. Often people who came from the same country or region would settle near one another, and many such communities retained the traditions of the old countries.

The settlers raised cattle and grew wheat, with much of what they produced going for export abroad. At first their homes were crude, perhaps built of blocks of sod cut from the prairie. But by the 20th century, the plains had begun to take on a new look. Ranches, farms, villages, and towns dotted the flat landscape. Churches, newspapers, and schools had been established. And rows of grain elevators rose beside the railway stations, to store abundant crops of wheat.

▶ THE PROVINCES

In 1888, the settlers had gained the right to elect a legislative assembly to represent the Northwest Territories. But the major step toward self-government came in 1905, when the Canadian Government passed an act creating the two provinces. The government kept control of the unsettled lands and the natural resources. In return, it made annual cash payments to the provinces. This arrangement continued until 1930, when control was turned over to the provinces.

The eastern province, Saskatchewan, took its name from the Cree Indian word for "swift-flowing," used to describe the great river that crosses the plains. Regina, which had grown from a railroad stop to the capital of the Northwest Territories, became the provincial capital of Saskatchewan.

Alberta, to the west, was named for a daughter of Britain's Queen Victoria, Louise Caroline Alberta. She was the wife of a for-

This painting by Frederic Remington shows Lac La Biche, a busy settlement in Alberta.

The North West Mounted Police were the first law enforcement group in the plains.

mer governor-general of Canada, the Marquess of Lorne. After some debate, the people of Alberta chose Edmonton as their provincial capital.

Alberta and Saskatchewan have not stopped growing and changing. Agricultural products—especially wheat and cattle—have continued to be Saskatchewan's largest source of income. But mining and industry now also make important contributions to the economy.

In the second half of the 20th century, the development of the oil industry transformed Alberta. A major oil find at Leduc, near Edmonton, touched off the change in 1947. Pipelines now carry Alberta's oil east to Montreal, west to Puget Sound, and south to California. And the development of the oil industry has spurred the growth of other industries in the province as well.

As they celebrated the 75th birthday of their provinces, the people of Alberta and Saskatchewan looked forward to a promising future.

Louis Riel led the métis and Indian rebellion of 1885.

These 12th-century Turkish cards had suits of coins, cups, swords, and clubs.

SUIT YOURSELF

You may be an expert at Crazy Eights, but did you ever notice that the red-suited kings' hair curls in, while the black-suited kings' hair curls out? Do you know which king has no mustache? Which picture cards are one-eyed? Many people enjoy card games, but few ever notice these details.

People have been playing cards for about 1,000 years, although no one knows for sure where the custom originated. Cards found in Turkey date back to the 12th century. The Turkish cards were larger than the ones we use today, and they had suits of coins, cups, swords, and clubs. Similar cards appeared in Italy and Spain almost 200 years after the Turkish cards were made.

Cards then traveled to Germany and France. The invention of printing in Germany meant that cards no longer had to be hand painted. The Germans used suits of bells, leaves, acorns, and hearts. They still use these suits in special games. The French

German suits of bells, leaves, acorns, and hearts are still used today in special games.

were the ones who invented the suits we use today—clubs, diamonds, hearts, and spades. French cards became popular because of the simple shapes, and because the French decided that pictures were not necessary for most cards. The French simply used a stencil for all their numbered cards. This process was less expensive, and soon the French cards took over the market.

The French changed something else. The early European cards had been made only for the royal families, so they generally showed pictures of members of the royal court. But there were no queens in the decks. It seemed that card games were considered to be warlike contests, and women should not be a part of them. It was the French who introduced the queen. But even today, the Italians, Spanish, and Germans use a king and two jacks in some decks.

The French cards crossed the English Channel, and English cards were fashioned after them. Our modern deck looks much like the English cards of 200 years ago, picturing the costumes worn by 15th- and 16th-century English nobility.

There have been only two major changes in cards since about 1850. Before that time, the picture cards had shown the full figures of the members of the court. When the cards were dealt, people tended to turn them so that the heads were right side up. Turning the picture cards could reveal a good hand. The solution was to show only the head, at the top and bottom of the card. Thus cards do not have to be turned around.

The second major change was the corner index. The earlier cards had no corner marks, so a player had to have a hand spread wide to see all the cards. An opponent could easily catch a glimpse of the hand. With the corner index, all the important information about the card—suit and value—is printed in the corner. And a player can hold the hand tightly fanned. It may be that because the corner index shows the essentials of the card, most of us don't notice the details.

So the next time you play, take a closer look at the details. All the queens hold flowers, but one also holds a scepter. Which one?

J. R. BLOCK
Executive Director of Research and
Resource Development, Hofstra University

These modern muppet cards were made in Germany and show Kermit the Frog as king and Miss Piggy as queen.

CARDS AND THE CALENDAR

Here are some interesting comparisons between our modern deck of cards and the calendar:

The 4 suits could represent the 4 seasons.

There are 13 cards in each suit. While we have 12 months, the moon circles the Earth 13 times a year. These periods are called lunar months.

There are 52 cards in the deck and 52 weeks in the year.

If you count all the suit symbols on the face of the cards, in the corners, and beside the heads of the picture cards, there are 348. If you add 4 (for the number of suits) and 13 (for the number of cards in each suit), you get 365—the number of days in a year. You can even add the joker for leap year!

These French full-figure cards date from 1550. It was the French who first introduced the queen into the deck.

THE COUNTING OF AMERICA

Chances are that you and each member of your family went down in history on April 1, 1980—as part of the biggest head count ever undertaken in the United States. The count was the U.S. Government's twentieth census of population and housing. It tried to reach everyone living in the country, more than 220,000,000 people.

Questionnaires were mailed to over 80,000,000 households. Laid end to end, the forms easily would have circled the earth. In all, they asked for some 3,300,000,000 (billion) items of information. What did the government want to know? Beyond mere numbers, the 1980 census was designed to provide a detailed picture of the United States—who its people are, where they're from, and where and how they live and work.

▶ REASONS BEHIND THE CENSUS

The original purpose of the U.S. census was to ensure that everyone is properly represented in the House of Representatives. The Constitution guarantees each state at least one seat in the House. The rest of the 435 seats are divided up among the states on the basis of their populations, using decennial (taken every ten years) census figures.

Every ten years, the seats are reapportioned, or divided up again, to reflect changes in population.

Census figures are also used to draw the boundaries of Congressional voting districts, so that each district will have roughly the same number of people as the next. This helps guarantee that everyone is represented equally in Congress. And state and local governments use the census figures to redraw their own legislative districts.

Other information gotten through the census, along with population figures, helps determine how billions of dollars in federal funds will be used each year. More than 100 federal programs use census information to find out which areas are most in need of funds. These programs range from aid for highway construction to school lunch and reading development programs.

Towns, civic groups, businesses, and individuals use the figures, too. For example, figures showing the number of preschool children in your town could help the town decide if a new school will be needed. And census figures help businesses know where to build new stores for potential shoppers, and new manufacturing plants for potential workers.

► HOW THE CENSUS WAS TAKEN

Most households received a basic questionnaire that took about fifteen minutes to fill out. Some households were asked more detailed questions on a longer form. Most households were instructed to simply mail the form back to a district office of the Census Bureau. But for others, census workers went out to get the forms. Many of these households were in areas where few people live and where mail delivery is sometimes difficult. This meant that the census workers sometimes had to travel up mountain trails or across rough country by jeep or even on horseback.

Census workers also counted people in jails, and hotels, checked in all-night movie theaters and taverns, and went looking for illegal immigrants and others who might have been overlooked when the questionnaires were mailed out. They looked, too, for people who simply hadn't replied to the census.

By law, everyone must answer the census, and the Census Bureau must keep the answers confidential. But some people thought the government's questions were too personal or were afraid the information would be used against them in some way. This problem was greatest in cities and among minority groups. The Census Bureau estimated that in the 1970 census it had undercounted the total population by 2.5 percent but had undercounted blacks by 7.7 percent.

In 1980, the bureau tried to offset the "undercount" by working with minority group leaders. It launched an advertising campaign, with the slogan "We're counting on you." And it developed special programs for schools, in the hope that children would convince their parents to fill out the forms.

► ADDING IT UP

By June, most of the forms had been returned to district offices. Census workers checked them over and then shipped them to one of three processing centers, in Indiana, Louisiana, and California. There, high-speed cameras photographed the forms on microfilm. The microfilm was scanned by an electronic device, and the answers were transmitted with lightning speed to a computer system in Maryland.

The computers whirred around the clock to sort and add the answers. The Census Bureau released some figures in late summer. About 300,000 pages of detailed reports would follow.

The early figures were controversial. Some people said that the results should not be used to apportion seats in Congress because aliens had been counted. And when the figures showed sharp declines in population for many older cities, the cities charged that the census had not been taken carefully. Some cities—and some minority groups—wanted the figures adjusted or recounted. A

More than 80,000,000 households were asked to fill out census questionnaires.

few cities took their cases to court. But census officials said that, even allowing for an undercount, the cities' populations had in fact declined. Some areas seemed certain to lose federal funds and representation in Congress, even if recounts were taken.

▶ HISTORY OF THE CENSUS

The Constitution provided for the first census and for those that followed every ten years. The first census, in 1790, was directed by Thomas Jefferson, who was then secretary of state. He delegated the job to the U.S. marshals, who in turn hired assistants. The census takers fanned out over the thirteen existing states, traveling by foot, horseback, or boat. Travel wasn't easy—roads and bridges were few. It took six days to go from New York to Boston, a trip that takes 40 minutes by jet today.

The census takers asked just six questions: the name of the household head and the numbers of free white males aged 16 or older, free white males under 16, free white females, other free persons, and slaves. No forms were provided, so the census takers jotted the replies on whatever paper was handy. Results, with names, were posted in each town and village. People who hadn't been counted were supposed to add their names to the list. The count showed a population of just under 4,000,000. But many people had avoided the census takers, and others had simply been missed. Jefferson himself had to add his name to the list in Philadelphia.

As the country grew in the 1800's, census takers faced a bigger and bigger job. Printed census forms came into use in 1830. And by 1860, there were six separate questionnaires, with 142 questions. The answers were added by hand, and there were many errors. By 1880, there were 50,000,000 people living in 38 states and 9 territories. Congress set up a census office, which was deluged with data. It was still publishing results in 1887. Then, in time for the 1890 census, a new method of mechanical tabulation was developed. It relied on punch cards, and it revolutionized information processing.

Some of the biggest changes in the census took place in the 20th century. In 1902, the census office became a bureau of the Department of Commerce. The bureau first experimented with mailed forms in 1910, and in 1940 it used scientific sampling for the first time. (Scientific sampling is a way of getting a picture of the whole population by questioning a small number of households.) During World War II, census information was used in hundreds of special surveys of manpower and industrial resources. After the

This 1870 print shows how the census was taken 100 years ago, when workers visited each home.

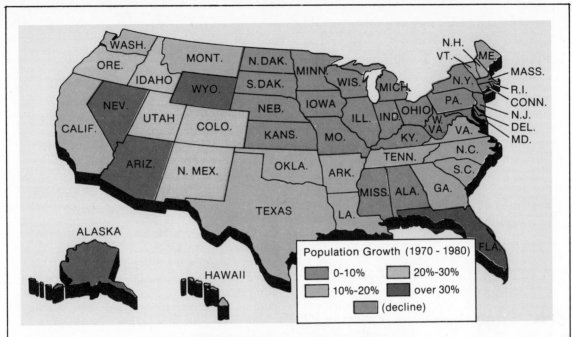

Population Growth (1970 - 1980)

- 0-10%
- 10%-20%
- 20%-30%
- over 30%
- (decline)

LOOKING THROUGH A CRYSTAL BALL

Long before the first questionnaires were mailed out, census officials had been predicting what the 1980 count would show. They were able to do this because each month the Census Bureau surveys about 50,000 households. The results of these surveys give the bureau a sort of crystal ball, through which it can keep abreast of changes in housing and population.

Based on the monthly counts, here are some of the trends that the 1980 census was expected to show:

• People have been leaving the Northeast and moving to southern and western states. This trend would affect seats in the House of Representatives. States that gained population would gain seats—and with them, a stronger voice in the federal government.

• The total U.S. population in 1980 was slightly more than 222,000,000, up about 9 percent from 1970. This would be the smallest percent for any ten-year period since the 1930's. (The actual total turned out to be closer to 226,000,000.)

• The traditional family of mother, father, and one or more children accounted for less than a third of U.S. households, the lowest proportion ever. And the number of households headed by women rose by nearly 50 percent in the ten years since 1970.

• In about half of the husband-wife families, both partners worked—a new high. But family income rose just 4 percent since 1970, compared with a 34-percent increase in the preceding ten years.

• For only the second time in U.S. history, the average age of the population was over 30. (The first time was in 1950, before the "baby boom" that followed World War II began to affect the statistics.) One result of this trend is that people over 65 will soon outnumber teenagers.

war, the bureau offered similar services to government agencies, universities, and research organizations. Computers, introduced in the 1950's, made more information available faster. And in 1960 and 1970, census taking by mail was used extensively.

For nearly two centuries, the growth of the United States and the changes in the life of its people have been chronicled by the U.S. census. Census figures show that if you had been born in the United States in 1850, you probably would have lived on a farm. You probably would not have graduated from high school—only 2 percent of 18-year-olds had done so in 1870. By contrast, if you were born in 1970, you are mostly likely to live in a city or a suburb. And your chances of finishing high school are 80 percent.

WHODUNIT?

People of all ages enjoy mystery stories. Most readers love to guess "whodunit." But how good are readers as detectives? Could they solve a crime if given a chance? In 1980, a transatlantic cruise gave some mystery fans the chance to answer these questions.

Also during the year, a teenage detective named Nancy Drew was making headlines. She was celebrating the 50th anniversary of her first case.

▶ MYSTERIES AT SEA

In April, 1980, the MS *Sagafjord* left Port Everglades, Florida. Its destination was Genoa, Italy. On board were more than 300 passengers—and some very special guests. The guests included a London police officer, a former FBI agent, two private detectives, a mystery book writer, and a "Man of Many Aliases."

The very special guests provided the passengers with some very unusual entertainment. They gave talks on such subjects as "How to Trail a Suspect," "Self Defense Tips for Clumsy People," and "10 Fun Things to Do with Arsenic." They showed passengers how to invent disguises, change one's voice, and create an alibi.

One night there was a Policeman's Ball, and passengers came dressed as their favorite detectives. The person with the best costume won a trench coat, just like those worn by many well-known fictional detectives. The winner appeared as Miss Marple. Miss Marple never wears a trench coat, but she's a famous sleuth in Agatha Christie mysteries.

Perhaps the most fun was provided by the mysteries the passengers were given to solve. The Man of Many Aliases boarded the ship using an alias (a fake name). The passengers were to try to identify him, and they could use a lie detector and fingerprinting equipment. There were also two murders. Of course, these weren't *real* murders, but they seemed like the real thing. There were at least five suspects for each murder and some very important clues.

The first murder took place on the deck of the ship. Bunky Banister was sitting in a deck chair when someone "strangled" him with a pink silk scarf. The second victim was the lovely Hermione Gooddeed. She was "killed" in the ship's swimming pool—in front of five witnesses!

The ship's passengers who tried to solve the mysteries had a rough time of it. The suspects lied and tried to incriminate one another. There were no simple solutions. Prizes were awarded to those passengers

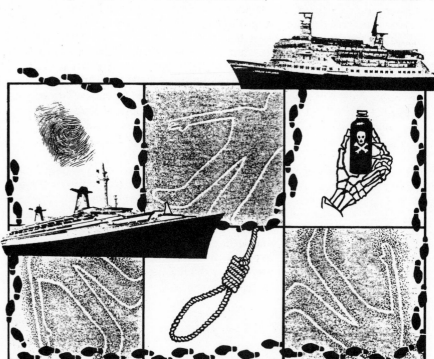

An unusual transatlantic mystery cruise gave passengers a chance to test their skills as detectives.

In 1980 the famous detective Nancy Drew celebrated the 50th anniversary of her first case.

who came up with the most original, the most logical, and the most wicked solutions.

▶ A TEENAGE DETECTIVE

In 1980, Nancy Drew was 18 years old . . . and 50 years old. Nancy is a fictional character who was created in 1930 by Edward Stratemeyer. He wrote three mysteries about the clever and independent girl detective. These first books were rewritten by Stratemeyer's daughter, Harriet Stratemeyer Adams. She went on to write 55 more Nancy Drew mysteries. Adams doesn't publish the books under her own name. She uses the pen name Carolyn Keene.

In the early books, Nancy was 16 years old. Now she is 18. This change was made so that she wouldn't break driving laws in any states. Nancy used to drive a little blue Model-A roadster, which has since been traded in for a modern car. Basically, however, Nancy hasn't changed much through the years.

Adams says, "Nancy is like a daughter who is very close to me. I guess we have grown closer as the years have gone along. Being a fictional daughter, she does exactly what I tell her to, or rather let her, do. She never disagrees, and together we get the job done and the mystery solved."

Many of Nancy's adventures are based on Adams' own experiences and those of her children and grandchildren. "I do on-the-spot research," says Adams. "Then I exaggerate by imagining what might have happened. In Africa, I saw a baboon about to pluck off a woman's wig, and I yelled to stop him. I incorporated this into a story in which I let the baboon succeed in order to embarrass an annoying young woman."

The Nancy Drew mysteries are read all over the world. The books have been translated into over a dozen languages, including French, Dutch, Japanese, and Icelandic.

People often ask Adams how to write a good mystery. "It's simple," she says. "Catch interest on the first page and never let it wane."

And so, before you have turned very many pages in a Nancy Drew mystery book, you will find her involved in two or even three plots. Sometimes Nancy gets into trouble and must be rescued by her friends. But everything ends happily—except for the person who committed the crime. Nancy always learns "whodunit"!

THE OLD RHINEBECK AERODROME

The rattling sound of machine guns mixes with the growling roar of rotary engines. A bright red German Fokker triplane streaks across the sky, its twin machine guns belching fire. Up ahead, a British Sopwith Pup twists and turns nervously as it tries to evade the pursuing enemy plane.

For a moment, it seems as if the British fighter plane will surely be blown out of the air. But with a sudden burst of speed, the Sopwith banks sharply and does a complete turnaround. The maneuver works. And now it's the Fokker that's in trouble. The British pilot aims his squat biplane straight at the German fighter's tail and opens up with his machine gun.

The Fokker's engine sputters and coughs. Black smoke spurts from its fuselage. And then the German fighter plunges earthward, disappearing behind a low hill.

The dreaded Black Baron of Rhinebeck has been shot down—once again.

On the ground below, spectators applaud and cheer. For the air battle between the vintage World War I fighter planes is strictly entertainment. The bullets are duds and the black smoke is charcoal dust. It's all part of an air show held every Sunday—from May through October—at the Old Rhinebeck Aerodrome in New York.

The air show is part of a unique, living-history museum that features aircraft from the early 1900's to the late 1930's. At the aerodrome's museum and in the hangars that surround the tiny runway, visitors can see the fragile, pioneer aircraft that first allowed people to conquer the sky.

A few of the antique planes are originals. These include a 1918 Curtiss JN4H, popularly called the Jenny. This was the first U.S. military training plane, and it was also used as a mail carrier. There is also an original Blériot XI, a primitive French monoplane (single-wing). Its designer was Louis Blériot, the French aviator who in 1909 made the first successful airplane flight across the English Channel.

Most of the planes—like the Fokker DR-1 triplane flown by the Black Baron and the Sopwith Pup—are extremely accurate reproductions. Many were built from scratch by the antique plane buffs and part-time pilots who work at the aerodrome. Among the reproductions are a mothlike 1910 Hanriot (an early French plane) and a 1916 Avro 504 K (a British fighter plane).

The Old Rhinebeck Aerodrome was founded about 20 years ago by Cole Palen, who built or rebuilt many of the planes now on exhibit. In the late 1950's, Palen bought an abandoned farm in New York's Hudson River valley, carved out a runway, and began giving occasional air shows.

During the early years, only a few people turned out for the shows. Now all of that has changed, and the aerodrome has become a popular tourist attraction, with as many as 4,000 people jamming the open stands for the

Most of the planes at the Old Rhinebeck Aerodrome—like the bright red Fokker DR-1 in the foreground—are extremely accurate reproductions of antique airplanes.

For those who want to share in the flying adventures at Old Rhinebeck, there are short rides in a 1929 Pitcairn Mail Wing.

weekend flying shows. Two different shows are given during the summer months. The Saturday show features planes from the Lindbergh era—the late 1920's and early 1930's. Audiences can watch them perform various aerial maneuvers.

But the Sunday World War I show is the spectacular one. It features a cast of heroes and villains that could be found in a comedy-thriller, pitting the evil Black Baron of Rhinebeck against the noble Sir Percy Goodfellow and the lovely Trudy Trulove. Against this backdrop of slapstick comedy routines, the audience is given a chance to learn about the early days of flying.

British planes swoop down to bomb and strafe the Black Baron's forces in a mockup of a German village on one side of the airstrip. On the ground, a German armored car battles it out with an authentic French Whippet tank. A German officer in a spiked helmet careens around the field on a motorcycle. He tries to shoot down the British fighter planes with a machine gun mounted on a sidecar.

As planes take off and land, an announcer informs the audience about how the slow but maneuverable biplanes (two-wingers) were operated. "Those old planes had no brakes and no throttle," he says. "So the only way a pilot could control the speed was to push a button and 'blip' off his engine, then push the button again and hope it went back on. Otherwise, it meant a quick nose dive to the ground."

In the big finale, a large Avro 504K bombs the German village, angering the Black Baron. So the villain leaps into his Fokker DR-1 triplane and takes off after the Avro. (The Fokker triplane is a replica of the one flown by German air ace Baron von Richthofen—the famous Red Baron of World War I.)

Soon a third plane joins the fray. A Sopwith Pup is wheeled onto the field. The ground crew snaps the propeller until the engine sputters on. Then wing-walkers guide the plane along the runway until it is ready to zoom skyward.

In a few minutes, the planes are fighting it out in an aerial gun duel. The Avro goes down and for a while it looks like the Black Baron will triumph. But the Sopwith Pup finally gets the upper hand and the Black Baron bites the dust—to the cheers of all.

For those who want to share in the adventure, there are fifteen-minute rides in a 1929 Pitcairn Mail Wing. Passengers are outfitted with the same soft leather helmets and goggles worn by the pilot. Then they fly off over the woodlands and farms of the area.

It's all part of the fun and thrills at Old Rhinebeck Aerodrome. There, old planes made of wood, linen, and bailing wire fly again, piloted by daring men in leather riding boots and silk scarves. Just like it was back in the days of the Red Baron and Charles Lindbergh.

HENRY I. KURTZ
Author, *John and Sebastian Cabot*

YOUTH

For kids only: a playground where you can "swim" through an ocean of brightly colored plastic balls, at San Diego's Sea World.

New Beginning, by Shelly Stoft, 17, Reseda, California

YOUNG PHOTOGRAPHERS

On these pages, ghostly flowers sprout from a weathered house. A tiger changes its stripes. Fire-red berries are locked in ice and a tree is transformed by geometry. These images, like the others shown here, share one striking quality—all were planned and photographed with painstaking care.

The photographs have something else in common, too. They were winners in the 1980 Scholastic/Kodak Photo Awards program, which was open to junior and senior high school students in the United States and Canada. What advice do the winning young photographers have for others? Make your photographs interesting. Be patient when you take them. And practice until you can take a perfect picture.

Diamond Shapes,
by Bill Wood, 16, South Bend, Indiana

Teardrops from Heaven, by Devin Lushbaugh, 15, High Point, North Carolina

Colorful Tiger, by Joni Dwyer, 18, Aurora, Colorado

Our Gang, by Jeff Sedlik, 17, Reseda, California

Desert Inn,
by Perry Kuklin, 17, Reseda, California

Untitled, by Kathy Kovacs, 17, Aurora, Colorado

YOUNG HEADLINERS

Desirée Ruhstrat began playing the violin when she was 3 years old. She made her debut with the Chicago Symphony Orchestra at the age of 6. And in 1980, at 11, she was a featured soloist with the Denver Symphony and was planning a concert tour of Europe. Desirée, who lives in Colorado, is a sixth-grade honor student who enjoys swimming, soccer, and basketball. She practices the violin at least six hours a day. Her goal is to enter the famous Tchaikovsky Competition in Moscow in a few years.

In 1980, 13-year-old Billy Hsieh became the youngest person to earn the rank of life master—the highest rank in contract bridge. It is awarded only to players who accumulate more than 300 points in tournaments, a feat that usually takes eight to ten years. Billy, a high school sophomore who lives in New York City, went over the limit after just four years of play. He learned contract bridge by looking on as his father taught his older brother the game.

Prince Hiro of Japan came of age in 1980, and the royal family marked the event with a ceremony almost 1,300 years old. On his 20th birthday, in February, Hiro was crowned with a black silk coronet. A horse-drawn carriage took him to the shrines of the Imperial Palace in Tokyo, where he declared his coming of age to the spirits of his ancestors. Finally, he was awarded the Grand Cordon of the Supreme Order of the Chrysanthemum. Hiro, a student at Gakushuin University, is the grandson of Emperor Hirohito and will come to the throne after his father, Crown Prince Akihito. The position is now largely symbolic. But the ceremony reflects the importance of the age-old traditions.

Michael Morris, an eighth-grader from New York City, scooped the news media in 1980—by obtaining the first exclusive interview with former president Richard M. Nixon in more than a year. Michael did the interview as part of a social studies assignment. He bicycled to Nixon's New York home and handed a note requesting the interview to a Secret Service agent. A few days later, Nixon telephoned him. Michael visited with Nixon for about half an hour, talking about politics and basketball.

Twelve-year-old Tracey Wainman of Toronto, Canada, skated her way to a record in 1980—as the youngest person ever to compete in the World Figure Skating championships, held in West Germany. Tracey is now shooting for a gold medal at the 1984 Winter Olympics. Her training schedule includes skating each morning at 6:30 A.M., before school, and then again for three hours when classes are over. In her spare time, Tracey enjoys reading, watching television, and playing baseball.

You may think that a stockholder meeting would be a dull affair, full of people in drab suits who mutter about financial matters. But meetings can get pretty lively at Irwin Toys, Ltd., Canada's largest toy manufacturer—because almost 15 percent of the stockholders are under 18. At a June meeting of the Junior Shareholders Club, in Toronto, hamburgers and ice cream were on the menu, and hundreds of product samples were handed out. But the young stockholders aren't interested only in having fun. They take an active interest in the business, and they ask company officials tough questions about sales and overhead.

TRACEE TALAVERA— A TERRIFIC TUMBLER

Tracee Talavera, a young American gymnast, is a rising star. And she has talent and courage that no amount of disappointment seems to shake.

This tiny athlete (about 5 feet, or 150 centimeters, tall) first entered the sports spotlight at the American Cup gymnastics competition held in New York in March, 1979. In that meet Tracee surprised everyone by winning the events on the balance beam and the uneven parallel bars and by placing third in the all-around. She was so good that her coach wanted her to enter the world championships in December. She made the American team but was kept out of the meet because she was 12 years old—one year too young to qualify.

Tracee was disappointed, but she kept on training and competing. And in March, 1980, she entered the American Cup for the second time. This time she placed first in the all-around competition, beating some of the world's best gymnasts. Tracee was exceptionally good in the uneven parallel bars; the balance beam competition, in which she did sprightly tumbling along a 4-inch (10-centimeter) wide beam; and the floor exercise, in which she combined energetic tumbling with a whimsical pantomime to the song "Whistle While You Work."

But even as Tracee trained for the American Cup, she saw that her hope of entering the 1980 Summer Olympics in Moscow was flickering out. And in April, the United States announced its decision to boycott the Summer Games. No American athlete went to Moscow, and once again Tracee suffered a big disappointment.

In December, 1981, the pixyish gymnast will finally be old enough to enter the world championships. She was expected to perform there with her usual energy and grace —perhaps even adding to her roster of wins with a top score in this major world competition that is held every other year.

Tracee first thought about being a champion gymnast back in 1972, when she and her older sister Coral watched the Soviet gymnast Olga Korbut perform amazing feats in

that year's Olympics, broadcast on television. Tracee was only 5 at the time, but both girls rushed out into the yard to see how well they could imitate Olga. Soon both girls began to go to regular gymnastics classes. When Tracee was 9, the family decided that the girls should live at a gymnastics training academy in Eugene, Oregon—a nine-hour drive from the Talavera home in Walnut Creek, California. The schedule at the academy was tough, and after six months Coral quit and turned to ballet. But Tracee stayed on at the academy, working hard and seeing her family only on visits and holidays.

Tracee loves gymnastics, and her deep interest is what makes her perform better and better every year. Watch for her at the 1984 Olympics. You may just see Tracee tumble her way to a gold medal.

SCOUTING

In May, 1980, Girl Scouts from the United States studied wildlife at sea and ashore in a special program called Wildlife and Windjammers. The Cadette and Senior Scouts spent two weeks aboard the sail training ship *Young America*. They stood watch, handled the ship's sails, and shared galley duty. The sailing adventure was one of a series of programs called Wider Opportunities.

The Boy Scouts of Canada also sponsored a number of special trips and events during the year. Among them was a whitewater canoe trip down rushing rivers in northern Saskatchewan.

New uniforms were developed for Boy Scouts in the United States by fashion designer Oscar de la Renta. The uniforms, for Scouts and Scout leaders, come in colors of tan and olive green for Boy Scouts and navy blue for Cub Scouts. They reflect the traditional look of Scouting. But they're made of easy-care fabrics and are designed to stand up to strenuous activities.

U.S. Girl Scouts also got new uniforms in 1980. Here, Girl Scouts and Brownies from Washington, D.C., model their new mix-and-match wardrobes at the White House. New badges and a new top award—the Girl Scout Gold Award—were also unveiled at the event, which was hosted by Rosalynn Carter.

High Adventure Bases offer U.S. Boy Scouts who are 14 and older a chance to explore wilderness areas while backpacking, snorkling, canoeing—and sailing. The bases are used by more than 6,000 people each year.

For the second year in a row, a pack from Sandy, Utah, won the Cub Scout Physical Fitness Contest. The three-member team from Pack 353 topped more than 100,000 youngsters who competed at local, regional, and national levels. They scored a total of 1,991 points—a record—in the five events in the contest: push-ups, sit-ups, standing long jump, softball distance throw, and 50-yard dash.

Girl Guides of Canada marked their 70th anniversary in 1980. Here, Guides, Pathfinders, Rangers, Cadets, and adult volunteers celebrate at an open house at the Guides' Toronto headquarters. "Seventy years of involvement"—in service to the community—was the underlying theme of the celebration.

John Gelinas of Scarsdale, New York, made Scouting history in 1980 by becoming one of the few Scouts ever to earn all possible merit badges. The 18-year-old Eagle Scout earned his 121st and final badge in water-skiing. But the toughest badges, he says, were in beekeeping and rabbit raising.

HAPPY BIRTHDAY, DISNEYLAND

The year 1980 marked 25 years of dreams-come-true for Disneyland—"the happiest place on earth." The celebrations held during the Magic Kingdom's 25th year made up one of the longest, biggest, and brightest birthday parties ever seen.

When Disneyland opened on July 17, 1955, in Anaheim, California, guests quickly recognized that it was like no other place on earth. Through the years, Walt Disney's Magic Kingdom has become a symbol of happiness to the world. Nearly 200,000,000 people of all ages, including kings, queens, and presidents, have shared in the special magic and fun that is Disneyland.

The Magic Kingdom was a twenty-year dream-come-true for Walt Disney. Walt was known as both the "showman of the world" and Disneyland's chief "imagineer." He was also the "father" of such lovable characters as Mickey Mouse, Donald Duck, and Goofy.

Walt began to dream about his new idea in family entertainment during the 1930's. "Disneyland really began," Walt said, "when my two daughters were very young. Saturday was always 'Daddy's Day,' and I would take them to a merry-go-round, and

sit on a bench eating peanuts while they rode. And sitting there, alone, I felt that there should be something built, some kind of a family park where parents and children could have fun together."

The place Walt dreamed of, and began planning to create, was not to be just another amusement park. It was to be something both marvelous and unique. "I don't want the public to see the world they live in while they are in Disneyland," Walt said. "I want them to feel they are in another world." And that is just what he achieved.

▶ **THE SEVEN LANDS**

Disneyland is an entertainment world made up of seven "lands." Each land is a realm of yesterday or tomorrow, fantasy or adventure. (1) **Main Street, U.S.A.,** recaptures the friendly way of life in smalltown America at the turn of the century. (2) In **Fantasyland,** storybook dreams and Disney film classics come to life for both the young and young at heart. (3) **Adventureland** is a wonderland of nature's own design, where adventure lurks around every bend. (4) In **Frontierland,** the pioneer backwoods of

Davy Crockett, Mark Twain's riverboat country, and the Wild West can be explored. Highlighting the many Frontierland adventures is Big Thunder Mountain Railroad, which you can board for a headlong race through an avalanche. (5) The future is now in **Tomorrowland,** where the stout-hearted can be launched on a twisting, turning rocket journey through Space Mountain. (6) **New Orleans Square** is the home of the rowdy Pirates of the Caribbean, and also of the 999 happy ghosts, ghouls, and goblins who are just ''dying'' to meet you in the Haunted Mansion. (7) **Bear Country,** Disneyland's newest land, is the setting for the rip-roaring-est show in the woods—the Country Bear Jamboree. This foot-stompin', hillbilly hoe-down features a zany den of singin' and fiddle-playin' bears.

▶ THE BIRTHDAY CELEBRATION

Disneyland's 25th birthday party was a spectacular, year-long celebration, featuring a special parade presented daily. Led by Mickey Mouse and the Disneyland Band, the colorful pageant saluted each of the seven lands with fanfare, music, and fun. From Main Street, U.S.A.'s comical Keystone Kops and the Royal Street Bachelors of New Orleans Square—to Adventureland's Tahitian Terrace Dancers and Cinderella's Crystal Coach from Fantasyland—the parade was memory-filled with Disney delights.

The year 1980 was a time to celebrate

Walt Disney, the creator of Disneyland.

some of the many special moments that helped make Disneyland ''the happiest place on earth'' during its first 25 years. But any day is a special day in Disneyland, perfect for enjoying its world of adventure and fantasy, yesterday and tomorrow.

One of the most beautiful highlights of the birthday parade was Cinderella's Crystal Coach.

A MUSEUM FOR YOU

Would you like to climb down a manhole? Report today's news on television? Explore an attic in an old Victorian house? Work on an assembly line? You can do all these things in a day—at the Children's Museum in Boston, Massachusetts.

The museum opened in 1913, but it recently moved into a large 19th-century warehouse on Boston's waterfront. As you approach the brick and timber building, the object that first catches your eye is a giant milk bottle. The bottle is three stories tall and serves as a dairy stand where people can buy ice cream and frozen yogurt. It is also a reminder of the containers in which milk used to be packaged.

The museum takes up three floors in the building and has many exciting "hands-on" exhibits designed especially for children. These are some of the more unusual exhibits.

The Giant's Desktop is twelve times as big as a normal desktop. So is everything on it—telephone, pencil, paper clips, blotter, coffee cup, and ruler. You can walk on the desktop, jump up and down on the telephone's push-buttons, and even try to write with the huge pencil.

City Slice is a cross section of a city street. There's a traffic light you can operate. You can climb into a manhole and a sewer catch basin. From the outside, the brick-and-mortar catch basins look like large beehives. This kind of construction is no longer used. But such structures are still seen in older cities such as Boston. Also in City Slice are a car and a house that have been "sliced" open so that you can see how they have been put together.

Grandparents' House is a three-story model of a Victorian home. In the attic you can sew on an antique sewing machine. There are also trunks filled with old clothes for you to try on. Downstairs is a cozy parlor where you can read an old book or play a big old radio. In the kitchen you can discover how people cooked and washed dishes in days gone by. In grandfather's cellar you can use old tools.

The Japanese House is an authentic artisan's house and shop from Kyoto, Japan. It's a two-story structure that was built about 150 years ago. The house was taken apart, shipped to Boston, and rebuilt at the museum. It contains six rooms plus a bathroom, kitchen, and entry. There's a small garden complete with plants and statues. Special programs and exhibits held in the house teach visitors about life in Kyoto. For example, rotating exhibits explain how to make noodles, tatami (mats), shoji (paper screens), and pots. A colorful Children's Day festival includes folk dancing, kite making, martial arts demonstrations, and calligraphy.

What If You Couldn't? shows visitors what it's like to have a disability. You can get an idea of the problems faced by people who are unable to walk, who cannot see or hear, or who have learning problems or mental handicaps. For example, you can sit in a wheelchair and try to maneuver it over different kinds of surfaces. You can wear masks that decrease or completely block out your ability to see.

Factory lets visitors work at a company that makes spinning tops. First you punch in on a time clock. Then you join an assembly line. Your job may be to stamp discs out of cardboard. Or you may put a wooden peg through the center hole in each disc. Or you may be responsible for quality control. This means that you must check each top to make sure it's made correctly. Or perhaps you'll work for a while in the shipping department or the payroll office.

Work also lets you explore the world of jobs. You can work in a grocery store called the Congress Street Superette. Or you can work in the Health Care Clinic.

The Computer Center has twelve computer terminals. Visitors can play such games as tic-tac-toe, Hunt the Wampus, and Inchworm. ''How's It Work?'' is a program that explains how computers function. There is also an electronic ''turtle'' that navigates by computer commands.

Step on the pushbuttons of a huge telephone on the Giant's Desktop.

Explore City Slice and see how a house is put together.

Visit Grandparents' House and try on old clothes in grandmother's attic . . .

. . . read a book in the old-fashioned parlor . . .

. . . and use old tools in grandfather's cellar.

Wander through the Japanese House and see how the same room can be used for different purposes.

We're Still Here looks at the lives of New England's American Indians. It compares the way they lived centuries ago, when Europeans first came to New England, with the way they live today. Featured in the exhibit are a wigwam and a modern home.

At other exhibits in the Children's Museum, you can animate your own movies or use such tools as drills and lathes. WKID-TV is a news studio, where you can pretend you're a famous newscaster reporting a big story. Or you can operate a camera in the closed-circuit system. There are exhibits of dollhouses and toys. In a natural history corner you can watch common city animals such as mice, ants, worms, and cockroaches.

In addition to exhibits, the museum has a resource center where people can borrow books, games, audiovisual materials, and educational kits. Workshops are also held there. In one workshop, children dyed cloth using techniques developed in Nigeria. In another workshop they learned how to build a bird nest. In still another workshop they learned about Eskimo life. They examined fur clothing and hunting and fishing gear from the museum's collection. They learned how Eskimo people use dogsleds and snowmobiles. And they learned about the importance of storytelling in Eskimo societies.

The museum also encourages visitors to recycle materials in creative ways. Museum workers collect things that factories throw away—wood, foam, paper, and plastic parts. These odds and ends serve as raw materials for arts, crafts, and science projects.

In a place like the Boston Children's Museum, people have lots of fun and learn many exciting and useful things. It's a wonderful place to spend a day.

Walk into the recycling room, where all kinds of throwaway items are collected and reused.

YOUNG ARTISTS

These pictures toured the world in 1980, in the Tenth Annual International Children's Art Exhibition. There were several hundred drawings and paintings in the exhibit, chosen from more than 12,000 works of art by children 5 to 15 years old. A panel of Japanese art teachers selected the winners.

The pictures came from 48 countries. But the panel judged the entries on qualities that are found in children's art everywhere—among them originality, imagination, and a sense of joy.

To find out how to enter a future competition, write to:
International Children's Art Exhibition
2715 Columbia Street
Torrance, California 90503

Center Piece,
by Mac Thomas, Jr., 10, United States

Construction, by Derek Manning, 10, Canada

The Japanese Harvesters, by Pau Ortiz, 11, Spain

The School Mistress, by Eman Farouk Hasson, 10, Egypt

CREATIVITY

Two Hummingbirds and Two Varieties of Orchids *(1882–1884), by Martin Johnson Heade. Throughout history, artists have captured the magic and beauty of flowers, giving pleasure to people everywhere.*

IN CELEBRATION OF PICASSO

"When I was a child, my mother said to me, 'If you become a soldier you'll be a general. If you become a monk you'll end up as a Pope.' Instead I became a painter and wound up as Picasso."

Pablo Picasso wound up as the most famous and most important artist of the 20th century. In 1981, the world celebrates the 100th anniversary of his birth—on October 25, 1881, in Málaga, Spain. Actually, the celebration began in 1980, with two major events.

The first event was an exhibition at the Museum of Modern Art, in New York City. Almost 1,000 works by Picasso were exhibited. Included were drawings the artist did when he was only 13 years old and paintings done when he was 90 years old. There were also wood and metal sculptures, pottery, and dolls. It was the largest exhibit of Picasso's work ever held.

The second important event of 1980 involved Picasso's political masterpiece, *Guernica*. Picasso painted this large mural in 1937, after civil war broke out in Spain. German bombers, fighting on the side of Francisco Franco, destroyed Guernica, a town in northern Spain. The mural expresses Picasso's horror at the pain and death caused by the bombing.

Picasso lent the mural to the Museum of Modern Art. He indicated that it was to be given to Spain when democracy returned to that country. Franco ruled Spain as a dictator until his death in 1975, two years after Picasso himself had died. Then a new government instituted democratic reforms, including free elections. And so, in 1980, *Guernica* went to Spain.

▶ TAKING RISKS

Picasso began drawing when he was very young. His mother said he began to draw before he began to talk. His extraordinary talent soon became obvious, even to one of his severest critics—his father, who was also an artist. By the time he was 13, the son was a better artist than his father. Picasso's father gave his brushes and paints to his son and said he would never paint again.

Picasso's first paintings were in the academic, or traditional, style. He could have made a career by painting in this realistic style. But Picasso wanted to take risks, to experiment, to do new things.

In 1900, Picasso moved to Paris. Many of his paintings in the next few years pictured poor and lonely people. And many were painted almost completely in tones of blue. In 1904 he began to move from this blue period into a rose period. His paintings were brighter and warmer. The rose paintings were followed by paintings done mostly in beiges and grays.

Another, more dramatic change also took place—Picasso moved away from showing things as they looked from one side. Instead, he tried to show how things looked from all sides at once. He was concerned with the structure of things rather than with the appearance of things as we see them. This type of painting became known as cubist painting.

Guernica, 1937

The Old Guitarist, 1903

Picasso and his friend Georges Braque were the first cubist painters.

There is great variety in Picasso's cubist paintings. Some are in a style called analytical cubism. In these paintings, geometric structure is the only important factor. Objects are painted as cubes, circles, cones, and triangles. Color and surface design are almost nonexistent. Later, Picasso created paintings in a style called synthetic cubist. The jazzy *Three Musicians* is a famous example of a synthetic cubist painting. Geometric patterns are very much a part of these paintings. But they are painted in bright colors that help make the objects in the paintings seem three-dimensional.

Picasso was the first modern artist to do collages. Collages are works of art that include bits of the "real world"—such as pieces of paper, string, tacks, silver foil. In 1912, Picasso produced a collage called *Still Life with Chair Caning.* It is a cubist painting that includes a piece of oilcloth, which is printed to look like chair caning. His *Bottle of Suze* is a collage that includes newspaper clippings and pieces of wallpaper.

Picasso's sculptures, like his paintings, were cubist—they explored the structure of objects. Many of them were built rather than carved or molded. Picasso's first "construction," in 1912, was a guitar made from metal and wire.

Three Musicians, 1921

Still Life with Chair Caning, 1912

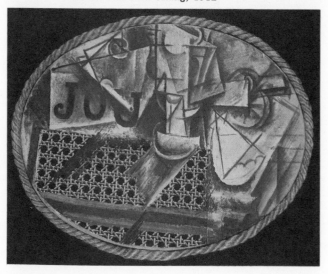

Someone once asked Picasso, "What is art?" "What isn't?" he replied. To prove his point, he made some of his sculptures out of discarded objects. For example, he joined two colanders, some springs, and pieces of metal. The result: *Head of a Woman*.

Throughout his career, Picasso was influenced by other styles and periods. Many of his paintings, for instance, seem to reflect African art. In others, he used an impressionist technique, pointillism, in which the canvas is painted entirely with tiny dots of color. In the 1920's, he returned to realism in many of his paintings, often portraying large, bulky women. Other paintings have the delicate beauty of Renaissance masterpieces.

Picasso was also influenced by the work of

other artists. In the 1930's he was influenced by the surrealists—artists who tried to portray what is seen by the subconscious mind. Picasso's *Girl Before a Mirror,* painted in 1932, is an example. The reflection in the mirror is not physically identical to the girl. Rather, it suggests her inner being.

Women were Picasso's favorite subject. He showed them reading, sleeping, crying, screaming, on the beach, in bed, seated in chairs, looking in mirrors. Picasso also liked to paint children. Some of his loveliest paintings are portraits of his son Paolo. The bullring and the circus are also frequent themes of his work.

In 1949 a friend brought Picasso a white dove. Picasso painted the bird. The painting was used on a poster for a world peace conference and was reproduced again and again.

Head of a Woman, 1930–31

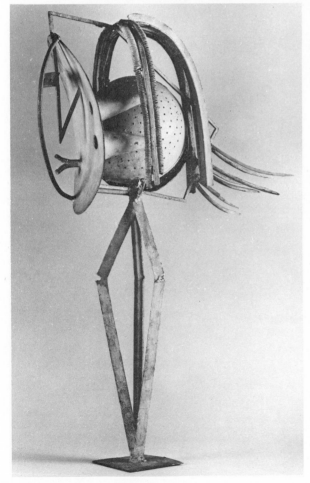

The Peasants' Repast, after Le Nain, 1917–18

Picasso's white dove "flew" around the world, into the hearts of people everywhere.

▶ NEVER TIRING, NEVER GROWING OLD

Until the 1950's, Picasso spent most of his time in Paris. Then he moved to the south of France. He spent a lot of his time there doing ceramics and sculptures, but he continued to produce hundreds of paintings. His output was astonishing. In 1969, when he was 88, he produced at least 165 paintings and 45 drawings. "Painting is my hobby," he said. "When I am finished painting, I paint again for relaxation."

Perhaps Picasso was so energetic because he refused to accept the fact that he was getting old. When he was almost 90 he said, "Everyone is the age he has decided on, and I have decided to remain 30."

Through his paintings and other works of art, this wonderful artist who refused to grow old will always live.

Dustin Hoffman (best actor) and Meryl Streep (best supporting actress) in *Kramer vs. Kramer* (best motion picture).

1980 ACADEMY AWARDS

CATEGORY	WINNER
Motion Picture	*Kramer vs. Kramer*
Actor	Dustin Hoffman (*Kramer vs. Kramer*)
Actress	Sally Field (*Norma Rae*)
Supporting Actor	Melvyn Douglas (*Being There*)
Supporting Actress	Meryl Streep (*Kramer vs. Kramer*)
Director	Robert Benton (*Kramer vs. Kramer*)
Foreign Language Film	*The Tin Drum* (West Germany)
Song	"It Goes Like It Goes" (*Norma Rae*)
Documentary Feature	*Best Boy*
Documentary Short	*Paul Robeson: Tribute to an Artist*
Cinematography	Vittorio Storaro (*Apocalypse Now*)

Sally Field (best actress) in *Norma Rae.*

Melvyn Douglas (best supporting actor) in *Being There.*

PARK OF MONSTERS

Imagine that you're walking through a rocky, wooded glen. Tired, you clamber onto a mossy boulder and sit down. Suddenly, with a shock, you realize that this is no simple rock—you're sitting on the knee of a stone monster!

In Italy, north of Rome, there is a garden filled with these strange stone beings. Called the Park of Monsters, it was designed in the 1500's by an Italian prince, Vicino Orsini. Over the years, trees, vines, and bushes covered the huge figures, and the garden was forgotten. Then, about 30 years ago, the trees were pruned back and the garden was opened to visitors.

About a dozen truly monstrous figures loom up from behind trees or around bends in the paths. There are also other fanciful statues, a tilted room, and a miniature temple.

Most of the figures are carved from natural rock outcroppings. Some—like one of a woman balancing a bowl of greenery on her head—seem to mock the graceful lines of classical sculpture. Others look like giants or trolls that have stepped out of a fairy tale and suddenly turned to stone. But all the figures are harmless. If you visit the garden, you may touch, climb, and in some cases even walk inside the monsters.

NETSUKE—MINIATURE SCULPTURES

The carvings you see on these pages are called netsuke (NET-skay). Most of them are small enough to fit into the palm of your hand. They were made in Japan by master carvers, mostly in the 18th and 19th centuries. Some netsuke have very intricate designs, and so it is not surprising that a carver sometimes needed two or three months to make a single netsuke.

Today many netsuke are recognized as fine works of art. But they weren't originally made as works of art. They had an ordinary, everyday function—much as jewelry and furniture have everyday functions.

Nowadays most Japanese people wear the same kinds of clothes worn by people in North America. But this has not always been true. The traditional Japanese outfit was a loose robe called a kimono. Around the waist of the kimono was a sash called an obi. The kimono had no pockets. How, then, could Japanese people carry small objects such as money and pipe tobacco?

This problem was solved by putting the objects into small containers. A cord was threaded through small holes in the container, and a netsuke was attached to the free end of the cord. The netsuke rested on the upper edge of the obi, serving as a counterweight for the container, which hung down below the obi. Both netsuke and container enhanced the beauty of the kimono.

No one is certain when netsuke were first used. The earliest ones were quite simple in design, and there was not much demand for them. But by the late 1700's, so many people wanted these small objects that hundreds of carvers did nothing but carve netsuke.

Most netsuke are made of ivory or wood. But other materials have also been used, including bone, horn, shell, amber, stone, metal, and porcelain. Although each netsuke is unique, all netsuke do have some characteristics in common. They are smooth. There are no sharp edges that could tear the kimono. Each netsuke has two small holes through which the cord can pass. These holes are often cleverly worked into the design, so that they are difficult to see.

Among the most popular subjects for netsuke are animals. Some of the animals are easily recognized—monkeys, horses, rats, dogs, tigers, snakes, fish, even insects and snails. Other animals derive from mythology or legend, such as the shishi, the shokuin, and the kappa. The shishi is a curly-haired cross between a dog and a lion. It is a symbol of strength and courage. Male shishis are often shown with open mouths. Female shishis usually have closed mouths.

This netsuke illustrates the legend of Chōkwarō.

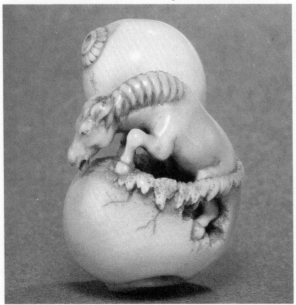

Plum blossoms are popular netsuke subjects.

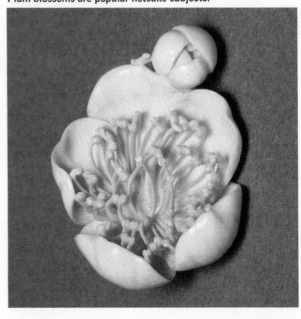

The shokuin is a dragonlike beast. It has the head of a man and the body of a snake. It is believed to control the changing of the seasons.

The kappa was an imaginary creature that lived in rivers. He is usually shown having the head of a monkey, the body of a tortoise, and webbed feet. Japanese children were often warned to watch out for the kappa. Sometimes children who didn't know how to swim would go into rivers and drown. Their deaths were blamed on the kappa. Many netsuke show the kappa sitting on a turtle, one of his companions in the river. Others show him wearing a turtle shell. Another netsuke shows a kappa clutching a large cucumber. The kappa was believed to love cucumbers, and Japanese people sometimes left cucumbers beside river banks. They hoped these offerings would please the kappa, so that the kappa wouldn't bother them.

One beautiful ivory netsuke shows a horse coming out of a gourd. It refers to the legend of Chōkwarō, a Chinese religious figure who was believed to have lived around the end of the 7th century. According to legend, he had a white horse that could carry him thousands of miles in a single day. When his trip was finished, Chōkwarō would put the horse in a small gourd. When he wanted to ride the horse again, all he had to do was wet the gourd and the horse would come out.

Another netsuke subject is Ono no Koma-

This dragonlike creature is a shokuin.

chi, a famous poet who lived in the 9th century. Some netsuke show Komachi when she was young and beautiful. Others show her when she was old and no longer attractive. They make us think of some of her poetry:

> The cherry blossoms
> Have passed away, their color lost,
> While to no avail
> Age takes my beauty as it falls
> In the long rain of my regret.

The delicate flowers of cherry, plum, and other plants are also popular subjects of netsuke carvers. So is the chrysanthemum, which is one of the favorite flowers of the Japanese people.

Today netsuke are collected by people all over the world. Many are worth more than their weight in gold. A netsuke of good quality costs from several hundred dollars to more than $20,000. And the value keeps going up.

Master carvers in Japan are still making netsuke. People seldom wear kimonos, but they still buy netsuke because the tiny sculptures are so very beautiful to look at.

Reviewed by MARY GARDNER NEILL
Curator of Oriental Art
Yale University Art Gallery

The kappa was an imaginary river creature.

THE MUSIC SCENE

Variety was the name of the music game in the first year of the 1980's. Hit groups and popular recording stars did not seem to fall into any particular category. "We have three different audiences," said a spokesperson for the musical group Ambrosia. "One audience hears us from *Life Beyond L.A.*, the progressive side. Another audience comes from the soul-flavored ballads like our current hit, 'You're the Only Woman,' the smooth side, the soft side. Still another audience comes because they think we're a rock 'n' roll band, which we are. We're all three."

Ambrosia, like many other top musical talents of the year, put out albums that contained a bit of every type of music. And just like the performers they admire, the audiences and record-buying public also refused to be categorized. They were not into "rock" or "middle-of-the-road" or "country." They were into everything.

▶ WHAT'S OUT? WHAT'S IN?

Disco music, once a strong favorite with listeners and dancers alike, continued to lose some of its popularity. Several artists, however, refused to abandon the disco sound. Blondie's "Call Me" was a smash. And, after five hitless years, the Spinners were back with a best-selling disco album and hit single—"Working My Way Back to You" from *Dancin' and Lovin'!*

While there was some debate about whether heavy metal rock was in or out, music lovers bought record numbers of Led Zeppelin's *In Through the Out Door* and Rush's *Permanent Waves*. Both albums had

Variety was the name of the music game in 1980. Ambrosia, like many other top performers, put out albums that contained a bit of every type of music.

Styx's "Babe" from *Cornerstone* contributed to the melodic pop rock sound.

lots of the heavy, insistent drum beat and the metallic guitar sounds of heavy metal rock.

The new-wave sounds of Elvis Costello and the Police did not appear to take hold during the year, but Devo attracted a wide audience with "Whip It" from their album *Freedom of Choice.* Subtler new wave was heard in Tom Petty and the Heartbreakers' "Don't Do Me Like That" from *Damn the Torpedoes;* ZZ Top's "I Thank You" from their album *Deguello;* Pink Floyd's *The Wall;* Queen's "Another One Bites the Dust"; and the Knack's "Good Girls Don't." These artists tried to recapture the vitality and high energy of early rock 'n' roll. Linda Ronstadt, the queen of country-pop, also displayed the new-wave sound in *Mad Love,* an album in which grating guitars and a doubling-time bass accompanied a raucous vocal.

The trend toward melodic pop rock was strong with a number of recording artists. The Eagles' "I Can't Tell You Why" from *The Long Run,* Supertramp's "Take the Long Way Home" from *Breakfast in America,* Styx's "Babe" from *Cornerstone,* and

Barbra Streisand's "Woman in Love" from *Guilty* contributed to the new melodic sound.

Meanwhile, the middle-of-the-road category kept its popularity with Barry Manilow's "When I Wanted You" from his *One Voice* album, Rupert Holmes's "Him" and "Escape" (The Piña Colada Song), Andy Gibb's "Desire" from *After Dark,* Dan Fogelberg's "Longer" from *Phoenix,* and the Captain & Tennille's smash single "Do That to Me One More Time" from *Make Your Move.* And the peaking popularity of Kenny Rogers, whose "Lady" followed "You Decorated My Life" and "She Believes in Me," brought him to the top of the charts. Many fans applauded the reappearance of ballads as a welcome relief to the thumping beat of disco and heavy metal rock.

▶ OLD NAMES, NEW SONGS

Of the well-established groups, the Rolling Stones continued their amazing fifteen-year hold on the public's ear. Adding punk pungency to their hard-rock style, they bounded to number one on album and single charts with *Emotional Rescue.* Diana Ross used her

269

Michael Jackson had two big singles during the year: "Don't Stop 'Til You Get Enough" and "Off the Wall," both from his *Off the Wall* album.

breathless singing style to send "Upside Down" to the top of the charts. Ross had another big hit with "It's My Turn," from the film of the same name. And British super-guitarist Eric Clapton, veteran of such top groups as the Yardbirds and Cream, produced a gold album with *Just One Night*.

For three long-time popular groups, 1980 was a banner year. In "What a Fool Believes" and "Minute by Minute," the soulful Doobie Brothers achieved Top Ten singles that netted them four major Grammy awards. Kool & the Gang found an eager public waiting for "Too Hot" and "Ladies Night," both from their hit *Ladies Night* album. And Australia's favorite musical export, the Little River Band, continued their string of hits with *Backstage Pass*.

Very few artists have achieved the remarkable growth shown by Stevie Wonder. As a teenager in 1963, he scored a number-one hit with "Fingertips." Since then, he has recorded countless best-selling records and received many awards. His latest accomplishment was *Journey Through the Secret Life of Plants,* a score that he wrote for a film of the same title. Playing virtually all the instruments, scoring his own music, and serving as his own producer, Stevie Wonder created music that was not only eclectic in its range, but symphonically elegant.

Michael Jackson, who began his career as a pre-teenager with the Jackson 5, added two smash singles to his array of hits: "Don't Stop 'Til You Get Enough" and "Off the Wall," both from his *Off the Wall* album.

John Lennon returned to the studio after a long absence and produced the hit single "Starting Over," from *Double Fantasy*. It was his last recording. On December 8, Lennon was shot and killed in New York City. Fans around the world mourned the death of the ex-member of the Beatles, the group that so strongly influenced popular music.

▶ SOMETHING DIFFERENT

Some of the year's new singing artists had actually been around for a while, but doing things in other areas of the music industry. Bernie Taupin, who used to spend much of his time collaborating with Elton John, re-corded *He Who Rides the Tiger*. Songwriter Kim Carnes teamed up with Kenny Rogers, and the result was "Don't Fall in Love with a Dreamer." This disc propelled her into the ranks of star performers. Jazz/blues guitarist George Benson was also no stranger to the music industry. His instrumental *Breezin'* had been the first jazz LP to go platinum. But with "Give Me the Night," Benson stepped up to the microphone and sang the song onto the Top Ten chart.

Stephanie Mills, who played Dorothy in *The Wiz* on Broadway for a number of years, left the stage and entered the recording studio, hitting it big with her album *Sweet Sensation*. Melissa Manchester and Emmylou Harris, both of whom were not new to the business, finally hit the big time with a wallop. Melissa recorded *Melissa*, and Emmylou made the charts with the award-winning *Roses in the Snow*.

In recent years, Canada's contributions to the music world have included superstars Anne Murray and Gordon Lightfoot. Bruce Cockburn was the newest Canadian name to hit the best seller list. His jazz rhythms and ringing guitar tone were heard in his new album, *Dancing in the Dragon's Jaws*.

The major comeback of the year was the return of Frank Sinatra. Although he had been active in the recording studio, none of his recent musical efforts had proved to be big hits. But in 1980, Sinatra recorded "New York, New York" and a remarkable album titled *Trilogy*. In this three-record album, Sinatra explored his musical past, present, and future, singing great standards from each era of his life. The album was well-received by the public.

Just as Frank Sinatra once hit the charts with a duet ("Something Stupid") with his daughter Nancy, Neil Sedaka found his way onto the best seller list with the help of his daughter, Dara. Their "Should Have Never Let You Go," an original ballad that had proved to be a flop for Sedaka as a solo disc, brought instant fame to the new father-daughter duo.

▶ MUSIC AND FILM

In 1980, the road from records to films became a busy and crowded highway. John

Jazz/blues guitarist George Benson stepped up to the microphone and sang "Give Me the Night" onto the Top Ten chart. And Emmylou Harris made the charts with the award-winning *Roses in the Snow*.

Belushi and Dan Aykroyd—former stars of the television show "Saturday Night Live" —wrote and starred in the film *The Blues Brothers*. The co-stars included top soul singers James Brown, Ray Charles, and Aretha Franklin.

Willie Nelson, the maverick of Nashville, starred in *Honeysuckle Rose,* a film loosely based on his life. Nelson also wrote the original songs for the film score.

Paul Simon, the Simon of Simon and Garfunkel, wrote the script and composed the music for, and starred in, *One-Trick Pony.* One of the cuts from the soundtrack, "Late in the Evening," a Salsa-inflected uptempo number, made the Top Ten charts.

Other musical names who lent their talents to film were Kenny Loggins, formerly of Loggins and Messina, who composed the original score for *Caddyshack,* and Meat Loaf, who starred in *Roadies,* a cinematic tribute to the people behind the microphones, lights, amplifiers, and recording gadgets.

Two popular films made celebrities of three musical personalities. *Fame,* a film that dealt with life at New York City's High School of Performing Arts, led Irene Cara on her way to fame and fortune. Her recording of the title song almost became a permanent resident on the Top Ten list. *Urban Cowboy,* which starred John Travolta, yielded a hit for Johnny Lee in "Looking for Love." A newcomer to the recording scene, Lee sang for many years at Gilley's, the gathering place for would-be cowboys in Houston, Texas, where *Urban Cowboy* was filmed.

Bette Midler gave an outstanding performance in the film *The Rose,* which earned her an Academy Award nomination as Best Actress.

272

1980 GRAMMY AWARDS

Record of the Year	"What a Fool Believes"	The Doobie Brothers, artists
Album of the Year	52nd Street	Billy Joel, artist
Song of the Year	"What a Fool Believes"	Kenny Loggins, Michael McDonald, songwriters
New Artist of the Year		Rickie Lee Jones, artist
Pop Vocal Performance—female	"I'll Never Love This Way Again"	Dionne Warwick, artist
Pop Vocal Performance—male	52nd Street	Billy Joel, artist
Pop Vocal Performance—group	Minute by Minute	The Doobie Brothers, artists
Rhythm and Blues Vocal Performance—female	"Deja Vu"	Dionne Warwick, artist
Rhythm and Blues Vocal Performance—male	"Don't Stop 'Til You Get Enough"	Michael Jackson, artist
Country Vocal Performance—female	Blue Kentucky Girl	Emmylou Harris, artist
Country Vocal Performance—male	"The Gambler"	Kenny Rogers, artist
Original Score for a Motion Picture	Superman	John Williams, composer
Score from an Original Cast Show	Sweeney Todd	Stephen Sondheim, composer/lyricist
Classical Album	Brahms: Symphonies Complete	Sir Georg Solti conducting the Chicago Symphony
Recording for Children	The Muppet Movie	Jim Henson, creator

One of the most outstanding performances by a musical star was given by Bette Midler in *The Rose*. Her performance earned her an Academy Award nomination as Best Actress. And Bette's rendition of the title song, "The Rose," went straight to the top of the charts. She continued her movie career with *Divine Madness,* a film about her highly successful concert tour.

Two musical films in 1980 were box office disappointments. But they met with some success at the record counters. The soundtracks of *Xanadu* (which starred Olivia Newton-John) and *Can't Stop the Music* (which featured the Village People) drew larger audiences than the films did.

▶ **AND THE FUTURE?**

If you listen to Willie Nelson, Barry Manilow, Diana Ross, Natalie Cole, Carole King, and Kenny Rogers, you may detect new developments and new sounds in popular music. In their hit recordings, these artists, and many others, may be signaling the approach of a softer, more melodic and nostalgic period.

Carole King, who had made a musical career for herself in the 1970's by recording original songs such as "You've Got a Friend," turned back the clock. In her new album, *Pearls,* Carole sang songs she wrote with her former husband, Gerry Goffin, in the 1960's. Willie Nelson, whose *Stardust* album of pop ballads of the 1930's and 1940's was a two-million seller, said that he was planning to cut an album featuring standard ballads such as "Over the Rainbow" and "Mona Lisa."

And singers were not the only ones to suggest that changes were taking place. Just listen to the music behind the singers. After all the years of guitar domination, the piano was returning as the most important accompanying instrument. "Still," one of the Commodores' biggest hits, is a good example of the new sound in popular music. A solo voice and the stark sound of the piano dominate the first chorus of the song. The piano can still be vividly heard even after the musical ensemble enters.

After so many years, the dense "wall of sound" seems to be giving way to something simpler.

ARNOLD SHAW
Author, *The Rock Revolution* and
52nd St.: The Street of Jazz

PEOPLE IN THE ARTS

Once typecast as a cute comic, 33-year-old **Sally Field** won the Academy Award for best actress in 1980. "There was never a time when I didn't want to be an actress," Field says. She took part in high school plays and enrolled in an acting workshop after graduation. She was still in her teens when she appeared on television as a coy teenager named Gidget. Later, she became Sister Bertrille in the TV series "The Flying Nun." But her most successful part—and the one that earned the Oscar—was a serious role in the movie *Norma Rae,* as a union activist in a Southern textile mill. Field is still studying and learning. She still enjoys doing comedy. But she is also making important contributions as a serious actress.

Phil Donahue has the hottest talk show on television. Every morning millions of people watch his one-hour program. They tune in because Donahue covers a great variety of timely and interesting subjects with wit and charm. His guests usually have controversial viewpoints. Often, people in the audience ask questions or share their experiences. Off camera, Donahue spends time with his wife, actress Marlo Thomas, and with his five children from his first marriage. In 1980, Donahue published a book, *Donahue,* which describes his life and his show. The book quickly became as popular as the television show.

Czeslaw Milosz is considered one of the greatest poets of this century. But until he received the 1980 Nobel prize for literature, many people did not know of him. Born in 1911, he grew up in Poland. During World War II, he was a freedom fighter in Warsaw. The horrors of war became part of him forever. "The real tragedy of events pushed imaginary tragedies into the shade," he later wrote. In 1960, after ten years in France, he moved to the United States. He teaches at the University of California at Berkeley. He has published many books of poetry. His poems express sorrow and anger, but they express hope, too. Life, they say, goes on.

Luciano Pavarotti, shown here as Nemorino in Donizetti's *L'Elisir d'Amore,* is a superstar of the opera world. His tenor voice is one of the most beautiful the world has ever heard, and his records and television appearances have brought it to people everywhere. Pavarotti was born in 1935 in Modena, Italy, and he began singing opera as a young child. He made his professional debut in Italy in 1961. When not performing, he spends his time with his wife and three daughters. He is known as a warm, friendly man, whose size is evidence of one of his favorite pastimes—cooking. Other pleasures include painting and playing tennis.

FLORALIES 1980

Flowers from all over the world bloomed in Montreal, Canada, in 1980, as part of an international floral exhibition. The show filled an indoor stadium with colorful blooms and created a vast outdoor floral park on an island in the St. Lawrence River.

The exhibition, called Floralies 1980, had a long tradition behind it. The concept goes back to the early 1800's, when large indoor flower shows were held in Belgium. In recent years, Floralies have been regular events in Europe. But Floralies 1980 was the first show in North America.

During May, 21 countries and the host province of Quebec exhibited in the stadium. There were cut and potted flowers, cactuses, orchids, dried flowers, and all sorts of floral displays. When the indoor show closed, the outdoor show opened on the Ile Notre Dame. There, a dozen countries and four Canadian provinces created gardens reflecting the best of their landscape design. And when Floralies ended in September, the plantings remained to form a permanent park.

The Corn Poppies, **by Claude Monet**

FLOWERS IN ART

A field of poppies and other wildflowers brings a sigh of pleasure from almost anyone who views it. So does a rosebush in full bloom or a vase filled with fragrant, freshly cut daffodils.

Paintings of flowers also give people great pleasure. In almost every culture and at almost every point in history, artists have captured the beauty and the magic of flowers. Their paintings have enriched the lives of people all over the world.

▶ PAINTINGS THAT MIRROR NATURE

People haven't always portrayed plants exactly as they are in nature. The ancient Greeks made naturalistic, or true-to-life, drawings of plants. They took this style to Asia Minor, where it continued. But the naturalistic style did not survive in Europe. It wasn't until late in the Middle Ages, in the 14th century, that Europeans began to observe plants closely.

Some of the earliest European works with accurate plant paintings were herbals. Herbals are books that describe plants. Most of the plants described in early herbals were thought to have medicinal value. For example, French lavender was recommended as a remedy for headaches, chest diseases, and "falling sickness." Filbert nuts were recommended for fevers. The roots of dandelions were used to make a drink that was said to be a good "stomach cleanser." And marsh marigolds, with their bright yellow flowers, were thought to cure toothaches.

People reading such a book might want to gather some marsh marigolds or dandelions. But they wouldn't know how to recognize the plants unless the book contained good, lifelike illustrations.

Above: *Red Clover*, by an artist of the school of Jean Bourdichon. Left: *Iris trojana*, by Albrecht Dürer.

279

Among the best-known illustrators of herbals were Jean Bourdichon and Albrecht Dürer. Bourdichon, a Frenchman, lived from about 1458 until about 1520. One of his most famous works was *Hours of Anne of Brittany*. This was a prayer book. It contained paintings of almost 350 plants, each labeled with its French and Latin names. Each plant had some medical, food, or other value.

Dürer, a German, lived about the same time as Bourdichon. His paintings of plants are among the most naturalistic ever made. Dürer's painting of an iris is an excellent example. It accurately portrays the structure of the stems, leaves, and delicate flowers. It also perfectly expresses the plant's habit—the way it grows. As you look at the Dürer painting, you see what almost seems to be a living iris plant.

Paintings of flowers were not only popular as illustrations for herbals. Consider, for example, Jan Brueghel. He was a Flemish painter who lived from 1568 to 1625. People called him Jan the Elder or Flower Brueghel, to distinguish him from other artists in the Breughel family. His lush paintings showed his great love for flowers. They also made him rich and famous. Because his paintings were so well liked by Archduke Albert, Brueghel didn't have to pay taxes. He was also given the right to study the rare plants that grew in the archduke's palace.

The bouquet of flowers in a Brueghel painting cannot be appreciated at a quick glance. There is just too much to see. The first flowers you notice are large—peonies, tulips, lilies, or perhaps irises. But as you look closer, you see that the background consists of a wealth of smaller flowers, each as beautifully painted as the larger blossoms.

Brueghel's paintings prove that he knew a great deal about the structure of flowers. He had obviously studied them closely, so that he could paint them from every angle and at every stage of their life. Roses are seen from above, in profile, and from underneath. Tulips are shown in bud as well as in full bloom. Lilies display their stigma and stamens. Even the leaves and stems are botanically correct.

Flowers in a Vase, by Jan Brueghel

Hibiscus, by Tani Buncho

At the same time that naturalistic painting was developing in Europe, people were beginning to explore the Americas. Naturalistic painters who journeyed to the New World made an important contribution to Europeans' knowledge of the far-off lands. The artists brought back detailed illustrations of tobacco, corn, and other plants that were unknown in Europe. At first, most of the artists concentrated on plants that had economic value. But by the 17th century, many were interested in discovering and portraying plants simply to increase scientific knowledge and understanding of the plant world.

Even today, artists who can correctly portray plants are needed. The link that developed between artists and botanists continues to be important. Natural history museums, for example, hire artists to travel on expeditions to remote places. People who publish plant books hire artists to make drawings that will help the reader identify plants in nature.

▶ **FLOWERS WITH LIGHT, LIFE, AND MEANING**

Not all flower painters have been interested in accurately copying the structure of plants. Some have been more interested in expressing feelings of life and movement. They have tried to express their emotions and bring out similar emotions in people who look at their paintings. For these artists, simplicity is important. Exact details are not.

Chinese and Japanese artists are masters of this type of painting. Some of their flower paintings are detailed, true-to-life studies. But most are very different from naturalistic paintings. Yet they are just as impressive—and just as "real." With only a few strokes of a brush, these artists can portray a bamboo stem or a lush hibiscus.

The impressionist artists of 19th- and 20th-century Europe also ignored exact details. They were interested in the way different light conditions changed the appearance of a subject. The characteristics of light depend on the time of day and on the weather. By showing an object as it appears in certain

281

light, an impressionist painting portrays a fleeting moment.

Some of the best examples of this style are the paintings of water lilies by the French artist Claude Monet (1840–1926). Monet built a beautiful garden at his home in Giverny, west of Paris. In the garden he made a pond, in which he planted water lilies. He painted these flowers over and over again, under every condition. The flowers are almost without form. But a viewer has no difficulty recognizing them and understanding the joy and love that Monet expressed.

Some flower paintings are simply meant to be decorative. In Pennsylvania during the 18th and 19th centuries, artists made watercolors called fracturs. These were documents, such as birth or marriage certificates, with decorative writing and pictures. Most fracturs included colorful flowers. Some of the flowers—tulips in particular—were drawn realistically enough to be recognizable. Other flowers were generalized forms that could not be identified as specific plants.

Throughout history many people have believed that plants have symbolic meanings.

The lily, for example, has long been considered a symbol of purity. The dandelion, a bitter-tasting plant, is a symbol of grief. The violet is a symbol of humility. A red rose may symbolize the shedding of blood. In the Roman Catholic religion, roses also symbolize love, and they are frequently associated with the Virgin Mary.

In Europe, painters of religious subjects often included flowers in their works. Some German paintings of the crucifixion of Jesus Christ include dandelions. Italian paintings of the Virgin Mary often show her holding a rose. And a painting of St. Francis of Assisi shows roses sprouting where drops of his blood fell to earth.

Why do artists paint flowers? As you see, there is no simple answer to this question. Rather, there are many reasons—reasons that depend on where and when the artists lived and on how they viewed the world.

As you look at the paintings of flowers on these pages, try to imagine what their creators were like. What do you think the artists were trying to say in their paintings? What would you want to say in a flower painting?

A fractur birth certificate

282

MONET'S GARDENS AT GIVERNY

Claude-Oscar Monet, a master of impressionist painting, spent the last years of his life in the little village of Giverny, on the banks of the Seine River in France. There he lived in quiet isolation, in a farmhouse enclosed by high walls. Paris, the center of the art world, seemed far away.

It was during his years at Giverny—1883 through 1926—that Monet painted some of his most widely praised works. For subject matter, he drew on the spectacular gardens that surrounded his home.

▶ **THE GARDENS THEN AND NOW**

Monet's eyes were ever alert to the beauty of masses of brilliant colors. At Giverny, with the help of several gardeners, the artist produced an untamed array of colorful blossoms, bunched informally in long borders. Rose trellises, flower-decked arches, and flowering trees graced the landscape.

Monet expanded the original garden by purchasing a neighboring strip of land. At the center of this new garden he created a pond, fed by a stream that ran through the property. Over the water arched a Japanese-style bridge hung with wisteria. A thicket of delicately leafed bamboo grew nearby. And the surface of the pond bore the exotic blooms of water lilies. A barge was moored in the pond, and Monet, who believed in painting outdoors, used it as a studio.

After his death in 1926, Monet's cherished gardens fell victim to weeds, termites, rats, and nettles. Fifty years later, the French Academy of Fine Arts began work to restore the gardens. The restorers pored over old photographs and many of Monet's paintings in an effort to duplicate the original colorful masses of blooms. On June 1, 1980, the gardens were officially opened, making a spectacular scene available to the public.

Today people traveling to Giverny may see the pond, the richly colored blossoms, and all the earlier beauty of the gardens. Poppies, pansies, roses, and many other brightly hued flowers adorn the restoration. And water lilies, of course, bloom in the pond, flanked by banks of irises, rhododendrons, and azaleas. In this setting, you can almost see the heavyset, bearded artist at work, clad in a ruffled shirt, baggy trousers buttoned at the ankles, and coarse boots.

▶ **"ONLY WHAT I SEE"**

Monet was born in Paris, in 1840, but grew up in Le Havre. He showed artistic talent early—as a boy, he drew caricatures of his teachers. As a young man, he decided to become a landscape painter. His parents were horrified. Nonetheless, Monet took his paints and brushes to Paris. He spent two years in Algeria as a soldier in the French Army, and the light and colors of Africa fascinated him. By 1863 he was back in Paris, where he studied at the studio of Charles Gleyre. There were other influences on his painting style—the landscapes of the English painters J. M. W. Turner and John Constable, for example, which he saw on a visit to London. Then, when visiting Amsterdam, he discovered Japanese prints. A tray of these brightly colored pictures in a shop introduced him to the orderly, flat design of Oriental art.

Monet was determined to paint in his own way. "I paint only what I see," he said. He became one of the leaders of a group of painters called impressionists. In fact, one of his early paintings, *Impression: Sunrise*, gave this name to the group. From the 1860's through the 1880's, these artists experimented with new techniques that broke all the established rules of painting. In 1874 they exhibited their works in Paris. One critic, while viewing the *Sunrise* painting at the exhibit, scornfully dubbed the group of artists "Impressionists."

The term stuck, largely because it was a good way to describe what the painters were trying to do. Rather than painting their subjects in realistic detail, they tried to give an overall impression of what the subject looked like at a given point in time. They were interested in the way light was reflected from their subjects, and they used small dabs of unmixed color to help portray its effects. Monet in particular would paint the same subject over and over again, producing a series of paintings that showed how the subject

This 1926 photograph of Giverny shows what the pond actually looked like.

looked at different times of the day and in different types of weather.

Monet's determination to paint things as he saw them often meant there would be no money in his pocket and no food on the table. Like the other impressionist painters, he struggled along. The task of getting art dealers and art lovers to like his work seemed impossible.

By 1872 there had been rewards. He had met Paul Durand-Ruel, a dealer with an eye for new trends in art. And he had found a home for his wife, Camille (the subject of many of his works), and their son Jean at Argenteuil. But Camille's death in 1879 plunged him into grief, and he was temporarily unable to paint.

Comfort came after Monet settled in Giverny, amid the flowers and trees he loved to paint, and married Alice Hoschede. At Giverny he reached the peak of his artistic powers. And he discovered in the pond—adorned with water lilies and surrounded by leafy greenery—a source of artistic subject matter to last him the rest of his life.

▶ THE WATER LILIES

The water lilies were the subject of Monet's last magnificent series, *Les Nymphéas* ("The Water Lilies"). Although his eyesight began to fail toward the end of his life, the mural-sized paintings in this series capture an almost endless variety of light effects.

This painting, *Pool of Water Lilies* (1900), shows the pond as Monet "saw" it.

In an early work in the series, *Pool of Water Lilies,* you can see how the artist used thick paint, applied in broad, skillful strokes. Color shows how the sunlight falls on the pond. Where the water lilies are in full sun, they shimmer with white and a rainbow of tints. But where the Japanese bridge casts its shadow, they reflect the soft blue-green of the water. A photograph of the same scene, taken in 1926, the year of Monet's death, shows what the pond actually looked like. But on canvas, Monet captured what *he* saw at the time—the play of sunlight and shadow on the water, the softness of the blossoms, and the shadowy branches of trees along the banks.

Monet outlived the other artists in the impressionist group. Because he did, he was the only one of the group to see this startling way of painting come into acceptance. During Monet's years at Giverny, people began to clamor for his works. After his death, the water-lilies series was presented to the French Government.

The great French artist Paul Cézanne once said of Monet: "He is nothing more than an eye—but what an eye!" Monet's paintings reflect his life-long determination to paint only what he saw. And like the restored gardens at Giverny, they are memorials to a great artist with an independent spirit.

LOUISE D. MORRISON
The Harpeth Hall School
(Nashville, Tennessee)

Much of the cast of *Star Wars* hopped on board for *The Empire Strikes Back*. From left: Chewbacca, See-Threepio, Princess Leia, and Han Solo.

THE EMPIRE STRIKES BACK

Do the names Han Solo, Luke Skywalker, Princess Leia, and Darth Vader sound familiar? They all played a large part in a very popular film that was released in 1977. The movie was *Star Wars,* and it turned out to be one of the most successful films of all time.

It seems, however, that *Star Wars* was only the beginning of a space-age adventure series. George Lucas, who created and directed *Star Wars,* decided that that important film would be just one chapter in a nine-part story. The second chapter is *The Empire Strikes Back.* And it appears that this new story of brave rebels fighting the cruel forces of a galactic empire will break all the box-office records set by *Star Wars.*

When we last saw the rebel heroes—Luke Skywalker, Han Solo, and Princess Leia—they had just destroyed the Empire's Death Star and were honored with medals for their brave deed. As *The Empire Strikes Back* opens, the villainous Empire commander Darth Vader returns to torment the heroes. He sends the Imperial forces to destroy the rebels' new headquarters on the planet Hoth.

Han, Leia, the apelike Wookiee Chewbacca, and the friendly robot See-Threepio just manage to escape in Han's spaceship. After a dangerous flight through an asteroid field and a short, unexpected visit inside a huge monster, the heroes land in Bespin, a city that hovers in the clouds of a distant planet. Bespin is ruled by Lando Calrissian, an old friend of Han Solo, and the space travelers think they have found a safe haven. But the evil Darth Vader has outwitted them again. The unspeakable horrors he has in store for Han Solo will have to remain just that—unspeakable.

Meanwhile, Luke Skywalker and his tiny robot companion, Artoo-Deetoo, are on a journey of their own. After their escape from Hoth, they make their way to the jungle planet Dagobah in search of Yoda, the grand master of the Jedi Knights—the forces of good. Luke finds Yoda—or rather, Yoda finds Luke. Yoda tries to teach Luke the ways of the Jedi and the uses of the Force, an unexplainable power that guides and protects all good people. Yoda tells him that the Force provides wisdom and knowledge to all who are on the side of good. But, he cautions, it takes more than desire to use the Force. Luke must have absolute faith in it. If his belief is strong enough, Luke can accomplish the impossible.

Provided with this knowledge, Luke is determined to carry the Force with him. But when his studies with Yoda are only partly complete, Luke learns that Han Solo and Princess Leia are in grave danger in Bespin. Armed with the Force, he takes off to rescue them. But once he arrives in the cloud city, he knows he will need more than the Force to fight Darth Vader. He will need trust and belief in himself. Can he overcome the opposition? Will truth, belief, and wisdom prevail? You'll have to see *The Empire Strikes Back* to find out the answers.

▶ OLD FACES, NEW FACES

One of the most important parts of making a film is assembling a cast. But that wasn't a problem for the makers of *The Empire Strikes Back*. Many of the cast members who were in *Star Wars* hopped on board once again. Mark Hamill returned to play Luke Skywalker, and Harrison Ford came back as Han Solo. Carrie Fisher re-created her role of Princess Leia. And the actors who played Darth Vader, See-Threepio, Artoo-Deetoo, and Chewbacca also returned.

But two important new cast members were added to *The Empire Strikes Back*. They were Billy Dee Williams and Frank Oz—the same Frank Oz who helped create the famous Muppet characters. Billy Dee Williams played Lando Calrissian, the boss of the cloud city Bespin. The most surprising new character was Yoda, the Jedi master. Yoda is part elf and part wizard, a gnome who has been teaching Jedi Knights for 800 years. The fact that he is only 26 inches (66 centi-

meters) tall does not disturb him. Yoda is operated by Frank Oz, who also supplies the master's voice.

▶ VERY SPECIAL EFFECTS

The actors aren't the only stars of *The Empire Strikes Back*. The most thrilling parts of the film are the hundreds of extraordinary special visual and sound effects. The jungle-and-swamp planet Dagobah, the ice planet Hoth, ice monsters (half dinosaur, half llama), robots, space-age weapons, and interplanetary vehicles all help make this movie memorable.

The three new planets in *The Empire Strikes Back* are technical works of wonder. The scenes that take place out-of-doors on Hoth were shot on a large glacier in Finse, Norway. But the scenes at the rebel headquarters on Hoth and in the jungle and swamps of Dagobah were filmed in huge studios near London, England.

Many of the unusual sound effects had never before been produced for a film. Wind and surf noises were combined to form the sounds heard on Hoth. The strange noises that created eeriness on Dagobah were actually slowed-down recordings of gull, tern, sea lion, and dolphin sounds. But the most unusual sound may be the voice of Chewbacca. It was put together from the noises of bears growling, a walrus grunting, a seal barking, a tiger roaring, and a lizard hissing.

The Empire Strikes Back was cheered by audiences as a worthy follow-up to *Star Wars*. Keep a lookout for the next chapter in this continuing space saga.

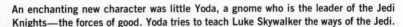

An enchanting new character was little Yoda, a gnome who is the leader of the Jedi Knights—the forces of good. Yoda tries to teach Luke Skywalker the ways of the Jedi.

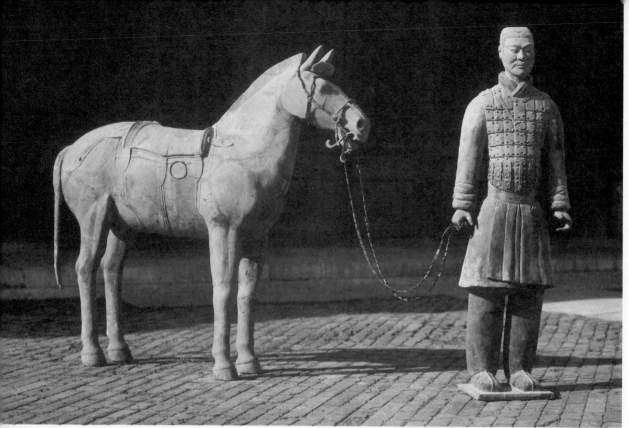

Thousands of life-sized soldiers and horses were found in the tomb of the first emperor of China.

TREASURES OF ANCIENT CHINA

When the first emperor of China, Shi Huang Di (Shih Huang Ti), died in about 210 B.C., he did not go alone into the afterworld. He was escorted by more than 7,000 soldiers and horses.

The soldiers and horses were not real. They were made of clay. But they looked real. They were life-sized, and each was individually modeled and painted in vivid colors. Great attention was given to the soldiers' facial features, hairstyle, clothing, armor, even the soles of their shoes. The horses were also very accurately portrayed.

These magnificent figures were hidden in the emperor's tomb for more than 2,000 years. Their discovery, in 1974, was one of the most amazing archeological finds ever made. Nothing like the statues had been seen before.

Now people outside China have a chance to see some of the figures. An exhibit traveling through the United States in 1980–81 includes six soldiers and two horses, as well as many bronze and jade objects. The exhibit, which is called "The Great Bronze Age of China," includes works from five major periods in Chinese history—the Xia (Hsia), Shang, Zhou (Chou), Qin (Ch'in), and Han dynasties. (Shi Huang Di, the first emperor, unified China and founded the Qin dynasty.) These periods span China's Bronze Age, which lasted from about 1700 to 100 B.C.

In most Bronze Age cultures, bronze was first used mainly for tools and weapons. But in China the metal was used chiefly for containers that held food or wine. It was used only by rulers and nobles because it was too precious to be used by ordinary people.

The containers were used in religious rituals, to hold offerings that were made to a person's ancestors. Each ancestor required different offerings, at different times of the year. And when kings or other important people died, their vessels were used in the funeral ceremonies and left in the tomb.

Some of the bronze objects are very sim-

The intricate vessel (*left*) and fierce-looking rhino (*above*) were made during the Zhou dynasty.

The elaborate elephant (*above*) and ceremonial ax (*below*) were made during the Shang dynasty.

ple. Others are extremely elaborate, their surfaces completely covered with designs. Animals are often part of the designs. Some of the animals are abstract; you have to look closely to see them. Other animals are portrayed much more realistically—it is easy to recognize tigers, elephants, and birds, as well as imaginary beasts such as dragons.

One particularly wonderful container is shaped like a rhinoceros. Its surface is decorated with an intricate scroll design that was originally inlaid with gold. Another container is shaped like a small elephant with a long trunk that curves up in the shape of a dragon. Its body is decorated with abstract patterns and animal forms.

Some of the vessels have inscriptions that record events in Chinese history. These are among the earliest written records of what happened in China long ago.

The exhibit also includes some jade objects made during the same time period. Jade was the most highly valued stone in ancient China. It was used for knives and ornaments.

All these Bronze Age objects have greatly increased our understanding and appreciation of the cultures of ancient China.

HANDS-ON ART

This art exhibit turned the tables on museum visitors and made them part of the show. The exhibit, at the San Francisco Museum of Modern Art in 1980, was called Project Hands-On. It featured a group of paintings done on metal, by California artist Jananne Lassetter—all of them incomplete.

Hanging on the walls were realistic landscapes, abstracts of colored stripes or squares, and plain white canvases. Nearby were magnetized cutouts of everything from insects to hot-air balloons, as well as colorful geometric shapes. Visitors were invited to step up and finish the paintings by sticking on the cutouts. A striped abstract might become a seascape or a desert scene. A landscape might be peopled with geometric forms or animals. Or a visitor might just have fun experimenting with the cutout shapes on a white canvas.

Lassetter's idea was to let people learn firsthand how artists use shape, color, space, and scale to create pictures. And she liked what the visitors did. "Maybe I've found a quick way to discover genius," she said.

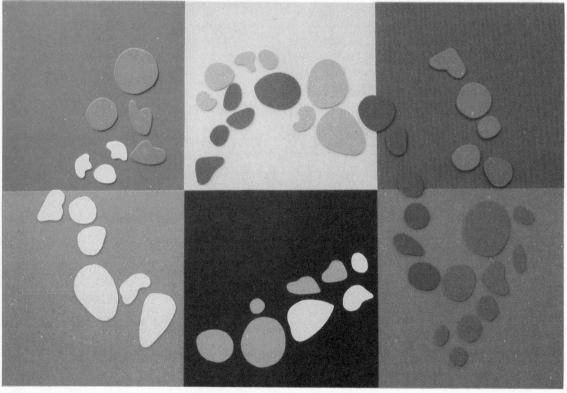

Journey to the Bright Kingdom, written by Elizabeth Winthrop, is an enchanting story based on an old Japanese folktale.

A Spy for the Union

Women have served as spies throughout history. They have played a role in every war that the United States has fought. But it was in the Civil War that women spies truly came to the fore. As one historian put it: "The ladies were terrific . . . and never since have the nation's women taken such an active part as spies. . . . They connived endlessly, they took great risks, and they pushed through to success in ways impossible to simple males."

Both the North and the South used women as spies. The Confederacy had the colorful Belle Boyd and the clever Rose O'Neal Greenhow, who operated a Southern spy network in the shadow of the White House. Among the women who served the Union as spies, one stood above all the rest: Elizabeth Van Lew.

Elizabeth Van Lew was a born and bred Southerner. Her father, a descendant of a Dutch family that settled in New York in colonial times, had been a prominent businessman in Richmond, Virginia. The Van Lews lived in a stately mansion in the heart of Richmond, which became the capital city of the Confederacy in the early months of the Civil War.

Because of her Southern birth and upbringing, one might have expected Elizabeth Van Lew to be a loyal supporter of the Confederacy. But Van Lew was a strong-willed woman with a mind of her own. She was a staunch Unionist who believed that her first loyalty was to her country and not to her state. And she hated the institution of slavery with a passion. Long before the war, she had written: "Slave power crushes freedom of speech and of opinion. Slave power degrades labor. Slave power . . . is cruel, is despotic, not only over the slave but over the community, the state."

Van Lew did more than just speak out against slavery. She practiced what she preached. Her family owned several slaves who were used as house servants. Van Lew freed them and then offered them jobs with pay. When she learned that relatives of her former slaves were going to be sold by their masters, she bought them so she could free them, too.

Elizabeth Van Lew was deeply saddened when Virginia seceded from the Union in 1861. She immediately wrote to Union officials in Washington offering to provide information. During the four long and bitter years of war that followed, Van Lew did many things to aid the Union cause—often at great personal risk. She comforted Union prisoners of war held in Richmond, and helped those who escaped to make their way back to the North. Most important of all, she organized—with the help of her mother and other Union sympathizers—one of the most effective spy rings of the Civil War. By the final months of the war, her spy system was so good that secret messages—along with fresh-cut flowers from the Van Lew family garden—arrived at General Ulysses Grant's Union Army headquarters promptly at breakfast every morning.

According to General George Sharpe, chief of the Union intelligence service, most of the important military information passed on to Grant's army in the final year of the war "we owed to the intelligence and devotion of Miss E. L. Van Lew . . . For a long, long time, she represented all that was left of the power of the United States government in the city of Richmond."

What follows is a dramatized account of some of the activities and exploits of this brave woman who served her country in wartime as well as any soldier.

The woman had an odd look about her as she strolled past a group of Confederate soldiers lounging in front of the red brick warehouse that now served as a prison for captured Union officers. She walked with a nervous gait, her head bobbing back and forth like that of a person who is a little crazy. And she seemed to be mumbling, the sound of her words carried away by the sharp wind that blew in from the James River.

The soldiers eyed her suspiciously. Her clothes were those of a woman born to wealth, although the brocaded silk dress was frayed and worn, and the expensive-looking velvet coat was spattered with mud. Her dark blond ringlets dangled from under a battered bonnet that seemed too large for her head. And her sharp blue eyes, though lively, seemed to dart about aimlessly. She carried a large basket filled with items of clothing and books.

A strange sight indeed, the soldiers thought as the short and slender woman ambled by them. They watched as she approached the main entrance to the warehouse. Over the large door a faded sign announced "William Libby & Son, Ship's Chandlers"—although the Libby family no longer did business there. Now the four-story building was known as Libby Prison.

The woman turned sharply as if intending to enter the building. One of the soldiers brought his long-barreled Enfield rifle to port arms and moved quickly to block her way.

"Just a minute, Miss," the soldier said curtly. "Don't you know this is a military prison? You can't enter without a pass."

The woman drew back momentarily, then thrust her head forward and replied in a loud voice, "I know full well what this horrid place is used for. I have permission to enter as I please. You must be new here or you would know that."

She drew a rumpled paper and dangled it before the face of the startled soldier, close enough so that he could read the handwriting. "The bearer of this pass, Miss Elizabeth Van Lew, is hereby authorized to freely enter all Confederate military prisons in Richmond for the purpose of caring for captured Federal soldiers." It was signed "Brigadier General John Winder, Provost Marshall."

The soldier lowered his rifle and moved back. Just then a corporal stepped out of the doorway. "Pay no mind to her," he called out to the soldier who had blocked the woman's path. "That's only Crazy Bet. She comes here all the time."

The group of soldiers broke into laughter. Van Lew did not acknowledge the remark or the laughter. She gave a haughty toss of her head and swept by the guards at the entrance.

The soldiers' laughter trailed after her as she walked up a flight of stairs and into one of the large rooms where the prisoners were held. The air, as always, was oppressive. Narrow streams of light filtered through the barred windows, illuminating the grim faces of some of the hundreds of men who were crowded into the dirty, vermin-infested warehouse.

Captured Union soldiers lounged about, some chatting in small

groups. Others were stretched out on the heavy oak plank floor.
There were no real beds in Libby, and the prisoners used army
blankets, rags, and whatever they could scrounge up as makeshift
bedding. Over 1,000 men were packed into the old warehouse.
Many were seriously ill or suffering from hunger. On this gray
winter day in 1864, as on days before, some of them would die.

Van Lew could not help to save them all. But she could try to
ease the misery of a few by giving them the fresh vegetables and
warm clothing she had brought. As she made her way through
the throng of prisoners, many of the Northern soldiers touched
their caps in salute or offered warm words of greeting. "Good
day, ma'am" . . . "Thank you for coming again, Miss Van
Lew" . . . "You can't know how grateful we are for what
you're doing."

Van Lew nodded back to each greeting, saying little. She did
not want to attract the attention of the guards by having long
conversations with the prisoners. For there were some Confederate officials who suspected her of being a Union spy, and the
guards had been told to watch her carefully. Outside the prison,
Confederate secret service agents constantly followed her.

That was why she had started wearing shabby clothes and acting a bit strange. The "Crazy Bet" routine was a clever act to
throw the hounds off the scent. Now, as she paused to hand a
warm shirt, a bit of food, or a book to a prisoner, she looked for
some quiet signal indicating that the prisoner had some information to pass on to her.

As Van Lew passed one bearded man, who wore the yellow
shoulder straps of a cavalry officer, she caught such a sign.

"Good afternoon, Captain Sloan. How are you feeling today?"
she asked the officer.

"A bit better, ma'am, thank you. The doctor gave me something for the dysentery and it seems to be helping. Perhaps you have a good book to help me pass the hours."

She handed the Union officer a volume of short stories by Washington Irving. "I hope this may provide you with a few pleasant hours," Van Lew said, then hurried on.

Continuing her rounds, she spotted another prisoner coughing and moaning while several of his friends tried to comfort him. When she asked what was wrong with the ailing man, one of the officers replied: "We think he's got pneumonia, ma'am. Been coughing this way for nigh on a week."

Van Lew bristled. "Why that's outrageous! This poor man must be taken to a hospital."

She waved at one of the guards and beckoned him over. "I insist that you remove this man to a military hospital at once."

The guard turned sullen. "Now listen, you crazy old maid," the rebel soldier snarled. "You may have permission to come into this prison, but you ain't got no right giving any orders. I don't see why you're so concerned about these Yankees anyway. Why, if you were a decent Southern woman, you'd be doing things to comfort our own brave lads. There's barely enough food and medicine for our soldiers who are suffering in the trenches as bad as these damn Yankees."

Van Lew fixed her eyes coldly on the guard. "If I report your insolent manner to General Winder, perhaps he will transfer you to General Lee's army so you can see for yourself just how our 'brave lads' are suffering."

Faced with this threat, the guard backed down. Everyone in Libby knew that old General Winder, who was both Provost Marshall and Inspector General of Military Prison, was an old friend of the Van Lews. And they also knew how Elizabeth Van Lew had won favor with the vain general by making flattering comments about his good looks. For despite the fact that she was in her forties, Van Lew was still an attractive woman. And like all Southern belles of her day, she knew how to charm a man.

There was a hasty conference among the guards. A Confederate doctor was summoned, and after examining the sick Union officer the doctor ordered him transferred to a military hospital.

Having won her victory, Van Lew finished distributing food and clothes and started to leave the warehouse. On her way out, she passed Captain Sloan again. He motioned for her to stop and handed back the book she had given him.

"Beg pardon, Miss Van Lew, but I recollect now that I have read this book," he said.

Van Lew took the book and smiled knowingly at the captain. "I shall bring you another one tomorrow," she said, then walked out the door.

Once outside the prison, she hurried to where she had left her buggy in the care of one of her black servants. As the black man helped her mount the wagon, he whispered, "Best be careful,

Miss Elizabeth, there's a man been watching you since we came here." The servant nodded in the direction of a group of army tents in front of the prison.

Van Lew pretended to adjust her dress, turning slightly so she could catch a glimpse of the spy. She spotted a man in a bowler hat and dark suit. He had heavy sidewhiskers and harsh features. She recognized him at once as one of the Confederate detectives who had been trailing her for weeks.

"Thank you, James," she said to the servant. "Now let's go home."

The buggy made its way through the streets of Richmond to the large mansion on Church Hill where the Van Lew family had lived for nearly half a century. The house, with its magnificent columns and portico, was located just opposite the old church in which Patrick Henry had made his immortal cry, "Give me liberty or give me death."

While James took the horse and buggy around to the stable, Van Lew went quickly inside. She passed through the spacious parlor, with its large crystal chandeliers, and into the library. For a brief moment she recalled more pleasant days before the war when the Van Lews had entertained many prominent people. Jenny Lind, the great singer, had visited them, and one night Edgar Allen Poe had recited some of his poems in this very room.

Her mother was waiting for her in the library. "Mr. Haley has been in touch again," she said quietly. "He will be expecting you tonight at the usual place. Oh yes, and the seamstress is here as you requested."

"Good. I will see her shortly. And I shall not disappoint Mr. Haley."

Mrs. Van Lew, a small and gentle woman, looked concerned. "Frankly, Elizabeth, I think you are taking too many risks. The rebels have spies everywhere."

Elizabeth gently placed her hand on her mother's shoulder. "We must be willing to take risks, Mother, if we are to bring this awful war to an end. Come now, let's see what information our friend Captain Sloan has given us."

The two women sat down at a small table. Van Lew turned up a kerosene lamp and took out the volume of short stories the Union officer had returned to her. Months earlier, Van Lew and the captain had worked out a code system for getting out information. The captain would make tiny pinpricks over the letters of different words in a chapter of a book she brought him. He would tear a tiny corner from the first page of the chapter to indicate which it was.

By using a magnifying glass to spot the tiny pin marks, Van Lew and her mother pieced together letters to form words, and words to form sentences: "Rumor that Federal prisoners in Richmond to be sent to Georgia . . . New forts being built on Danville Road . . . Pickett's division now in Petersburg . . . Three regiments of rebel cavalry disbanded by Lee for want of horses."

When they were finished, Van Lew announced, "This is important information. I must see that Mr. Haley has it."

Van Lew carefully printed the information on small slips of paper. Then she called in the seamstress and ordered her to sew the slips of paper inside the folds of the dress she was planning to wear for her nighttime excursion.

When all was in readiness, Van Lew slipped into the dress. Then she put on leather leggings, a belted canvas coat, and a large bonnet so that she would look like a farm woman. That done, she ordered the stable boy to hitch the buggy and bring it around to a side entrance.

Shortly before ten o'clock Van Lew drove off in the direction of the family summer house and farm, just south of the city. The night sky was overcast, with only an occasional glimmer of a faint star and a sliver of hazy moon. By the time Van Lew had passed through the outskirts of the city, a soft rain had begun to fall.

Van Lew preferred to travel alone on these nighttime excursions. But tonight she had an eerie feeling that she was not completely alone. Some sense told her that unfriendly eyes were watching her, that she was being followed. Now and then she would glance nervously over her shoulder. She could see no one.

About two miles outside the city, Van Lew spotted a small campfire. She could see the shadowy forms of men huddled around the fire as she drew closer. A Confederate patrol, she thought to herself. There was no going around them, so she rode boldly forward.

A sentry stepped forward to challenge her. "Halt and identify yourself," the soldier ordered.

"I am Elizabeth Van Lew from Richmond," she replied. "I have a pass signed by General Winder permitting me to travel in and out of the city."

Some of the other soldiers now gathered around the wagon. They were a mixture of young boys and older men, for the Confederacy was now using whatever manpower was left. Their gray and butternut uniforms were badly worn and patched. A few wore captured Union army coats and trousers and several had no shoes. Although she opposed the Southern cause, Van Lew could not help feeling pity for these men who continued to fight on despite great odds.

The sentry finished inspecting the pass. He was about to wave her on when the sound of a horse coming up the road distracted him. Van Lew looked over her shoulder and saw a man with sidewhiskers and a bowler hat dismount and hurry forward. It was the same man who had been spying on her that afternoon.

"Hold that woman. Don't let her go through," the man shouted.

The sentry protested, "But she has a pass signed by General Winder."

The newcomer's lips curled in a sneer. "Never mind her damn pass. I am H. L. Rusk of the secret service, and I, too, have a

paper. Mine is signed by James Seddon, secretary of war, and it gives me the right to arrest spies.''

Rusk pointed a finger menacingly at Van Lew. ''This woman is a Union spy.'' Then he reached up, grabbed her arm roughly, and forced her to dismount.

Van Lew wrenched her arm free, her face flushing in anger. ''How dare you put your hands on me,'' she cried. ''I demand that you let me go.''

The Confederate agent did not budge. ''Don't put on uppity airs with me, Miss Van Lew. I know you are carrying dispatches for your Yankee friends and I aim to prove it.''

Rusk pushed her against the wagon. There was a cruel look in his eyes. Van Lew tried to squirm loose, but the man was too strong for her.

A few of the soldiers protested his handling of the woman, but Rusk waved them off. Suddenly, a voice of authority sounded from across the road. ''Take your hands off that woman, sir.''

Van Lew looked to her right and saw a Confederate officer approaching them. He was a tall man, with a neatly trimmed beard and the three bars of a captain on the collar of his uniform.

''A gentleman does not treat a woman in such a manner,'' the captain declared. Then, turning to Van Lew, he bowed and said, ''My apologies, ma'am, for this man's rude behavior.''

The Confederate agent was livid. "Dammit, Captain, this woman is a spy and she carries secret messages under her clothes. I'm certain of it." The Confederate officer looked over at Van Lew. He asked her to identify herself and to tell him why she was out so late at night. For the next few minutes, Van Lew calmly explained that it was her custom to go to her family's summer house and farm at night to bring back vegetables.

"Fresh vegetables are hard to come by in Richmond, as you probably know, Captain," she concluded.

The Confederate officer nodded his understanding. "Then I have but one other question for you, madam," he said. "Are you carrying any secret papers under your—if you'll pardon my bluntness—your dress?"

Van Lew looked the captain straight in the eye. "I give you my word, sir, that I carry no messages under my clothes. Of course, if you insist, I will remove my dress . . ."

The captain blushed. "That won't be necessary, ma'am. You may proceed at once." Casting a glance in Rusk's direction, he snapped coldly, "And if this man tries to interfere with you, I shall have him sent back to Richmond under arrest."

A few moments later, Van Lew was on her way. Behind her, she could hear Rusk still arguing with the rebel captain. A half hour later, Van Lew arrived at her family's small farm. Mr. Haley, one of the many Union sympathizers she used to carry messages through the lines, was waiting for her. Van Lew used a small knife to slit open the folds of her dress where the dispatches were hidden. She could not resist a quiet laugh as she removed the papers. She was glad she hadn't had to lie to the Confederate officer who rescued her. The secret papers were not hidden *under* her dress. They were concealed *inside* the dress.

As soon as Haley had mounted his horse and sped off, Van Lew filled the buggy with vegetables and fruit and hurried back. She was home in two hours, her mission a success.

In the months that followed, Van Lew performed many other acts of espionage. Information she supplied about the condition of Union prisoners in Richmond prompted Union authorities to launch a cavalry raid to save them. The rescue mission failed, but the raid threw a big scare into the Confederate capital.

A few weeks later, more than 100 Union officers tunneled out of Libby Prison in the most daring escape of the Civil War. Van Lew was out on another errand when word of the escape reached her. She hurried home, got her buggy, and went out looking for escaped prisoners.

By going to the homes of several Union sympathizers, she located three of the Union officers. Hiding the men under stacks of peach saplings in the back of her wagon, she took them to her own house. There they stayed in a hidden room at the back of the mansion until it was safe to smuggle them out of the city.

All the while, Van Lew continued to build up her network of spies. By the summer of 1864, as General Ulysses S. Grant hammered his way through the wilderness and moved closer to Richmond, Van Lew was supplying the Union commander with daily reports about Confederate troop movements. Learning that Confederate President Jefferson Davis needed another house servant, Van Lew planted one of her own former slaves in the Confederate White House. Twice each week, the young black woman and Van Lew met after dark to exchange information.

Confederate spies, including the dogged Rusk, continued to follow her. But she was always too clever for them and eluded their traps. Van Lew also continued to make visits to Libby Prison. In addition to the pinpricks-in-the-book trick, she also used a large serving dish with a double bottom to carry messages. Once a suspicious guard demanded that she hand over the dish. But Van Lew had been warned that the guard was on to her. She had filled the dish, which she held cradled in her shawl, with boiling hot water. When the guard took the dish from her, it scalded his hands and he dropped it with a howl.

Summer gave way to autumn, and the Confederacy continued to lose ground. General William Sherman captured Atlanta and set out on his "March to the Sea." Phil Sheridan swept Confederate forces out of the Shenandoah Valley, and Admiral David Farragut took the city of Mobile, Alabama. Meanwhile, Grant's army had laid siege to Petersburg, just 20 miles from Richmond. It was only a matter of time before the Confederacy collapsed.

But Elizabeth Van Lew still went on with her work as a spy. One evening, she sent her servant James out with an important message hidden in the sole of one of his brogans. James had hardly been gone half an hour when he came dashing back with troublesome news. Confederate troops were seizing all remaining horses in the area for use by the army.

"They'll get Alexander for sure," James said, referring to the family's remaining horse.

"No, they won't!" Van Lew said firmly. "Come on, James, we'll find a nice safe hiding place for him."

By the time the Confederate soliders arrived at the Van Lew mansion, Alexander was nowhere to be seen. The Southern troops searched the stable and the smokehouse in back of the house, but they could find no trace of the animal.

One of the soldiers demanded to know where the horse was hidden. "We know that you have a horse, Miss Van Lew," the soldier said. "You might as well tell us where he's been put."

Van Lew shrugged. "Why, if you mean our old carriage horse Alexander, he's been dead for over a month."

The soldiers prowled about the grounds for over an hour. But they couldn't find the animal. Finally, they gave up and left. After the troops had trotted off, Elizabeth's mother asked her daughter, "Whatever did you do with Alexander?"

"Come, Mother, I'll show you."

The two women walked up the stairs to the library. With a flourish, Elizabeth threw open the door. There, standing quietly

amid some straw that James had put down, was the big stallion.

"Such a good horse, not even a whinny," Elizabeth said proudly.

"Yes, but look, he's chewed up some of our books," her mother noted.

Elizabeth walked over to where the remains of one leather-bound volume were strewn about. "Our Alexander is a horse with good taste, Mother," she said with a laugh. "He has devoured an entire volume of plays by Mr. Shakespeare."

The final months of the war passed without much excitement for the Van Lews. Gradually, Lee's lines at Petersburg buckled. Finally, on April 2, 1865, word was flashed that Lee's army had been forced out of Petersburg. Confederate authorities had ordered Richmond evacuated. The following day, the last Confederate troops marched out of the Confederate capital. As they left, they set fire to some of the public buildings so that Confederate records would not fall into Union hands. Looters set fire to other buildings, and soon much of the city was blazing.

Amid the confusion, Van Lew set herself one last task. She walked to the Capitol building to look amid the rubble for any unburned secret papers that she could turn over to the Union Army.

As she rummaged through the smoldering ruins, she was startled by the familiar figure of a man in a bowler hat. His clothes were disheveled and his face was drawn. But there was no mistaking the cruel features. It was Confederate Detective H. L. Rusk.

Van Lew recoiled as she saw him approaching. She felt a sudden chill of fear.

"I thought I might find you here, Miss Van Lew," Rusk sneered. "I've caught you red-handed, you damn Yankee spy. Well, you won't escape this time."

He moved closer, drawing a Colt revolver from his belt. "I'd like to see you hang like a spy should. But we've no time for that. A bullet will have to do."

Rusk cocked the pistol and raised it, his lips spread in a vicious grin. Although she was trembling with fright, Van Lew managed to blurt out, "You're a fool. Union troops will be here soon and when they find out what you've done, you'll be the one who is hanged."

Rusk paid no attention to her words. He continued to come toward her. Suddenly, Van Lew heard the clatter of horses' hooves and the jangle of sabers. Rusk heard it, too, and whirled in time to see a detail of Union cavalry galloping toward them. The rebel agent dropped his pistol and raced off. But not fast enough. Union troopers ran him down and brusquely dragged him back.

A Union officer dismounted and rushed over to Van Lew. "Are you all right, Miss?" he asked.

Van Lew's heart was pounding furiously, but she nodded.

"Would you be Elizabeth Van Lew?" asked the Union officer.

She was barely able to say "Yes."

"Well then, I'm certainly glad we found you," the officer said, smiling broadly. "General Grant sent us to offer you and your family protection. When we went to your house, your mother told us you had come here. I'm glad we arrived in time."

He pointed at Rusk. "Who is this man?"

"A rebel detective," Van Lew told him. "He has been hounding me for months."

The Union officer put a comforting hand on her shoulder. "You need not fear this man," he told her. "The Union Army now occupies Richmond, and you and your family will be well guarded."

Elizabeth Van Lew slept soundly that night, no longer troubled by thoughts of war or fears of rebel agents. In the morning, when she went to the window, she could see the Stars and Stripes fluttering from the partly burned Capitol.

Later that day, as Van Lew and her mother were having tea, they heard the tramp of marching troops and a bugle sounding flourishes. Rushing to the front door, they saw Union troops cheering and tossing their hats in the air as a group of mounted officers approached the house.

Near the entrance to the mansion, the party halted and several officers dismounted. One of them was a short man, with a thick beard and the stub of a cigar in his mouth. He carried no sword and wore a plain uniform jacket with only the three stars of a lieutenant general on his shoulder straps to mark his rank.

Van Lew knew immediately who he was. As the general came up the steps, she stepped forward and greeted him. "General Grant, I am delighted to meet you. I am Elizabeth Van Lew."

The Union commander removed his hat, clasped her hand warmly, and replied, "Miss Van Lew, I am truly honored to have this opportunity to thank you for what you have done for our cause. The United States Government owes you a great debt."

Van Lew smiled. "My mother and I would be truly pleased if you would join us for tea."

"With pleasure, Miss Van Lew," said the general.

Van Lew took General Grant's arm and escorted him into the house. Outside, a fife and drum corps struck up "John Brown's Body."

HENRY I. KURTZ
Author, *John and Sebastian Cabot*

304

The Better Mousetrap

It was a bad day for business in Elmdale. Jim and Jan, the Wickham twins, had set up their lemonade stand soon after lunch. Now it was nearly three o'clock, and they had sold only one glass of lemonade.

"I can't understand why nobody is thirsty," groaned Jim. "It's a blistering hot day, at least ninety in the shade."

"At this rate, we'll lose money instead of making it," Jan sighed.

The twins might not have been so concerned if the money they had invested in the lemonade had been their own. But the money belonged to Jim's Scout troop. On the last meeting before summer recess, Mr. Martin, the Scoutmaster, had given each of his Scouts two dollars. "Invest these dollars wisely, and they will grow for you," he had told them. "It will be an experience for you all to learn how to make money grow. In the fall we'll see which one of you made his dollars grow the most. Then we'll use all the profits on a long overnight trip."

At the time, Jim had been very excited about the project. When he told Jan about it she promised to help him. But now that their first financial venture seemed doomed, they were beginning to lose their enthusiasm.

Jim flopped down on the lawn and wiped his hot, sticky forehead. "We ought to ride down to the pool on our tandem, instead of boiling here in the hot sun," he grumbled.

Jan poured herself some lemonade and considered Jim's suggestion. Riding the old two-seater bike that their father had fixed up for them was great fun. The trip to the pool would be so cool and airy, and the water would feel even cooler. It was really a strong temptation to close up shop.

"I think we'd better stick it out awhile longer," Jan said at last. "We have fifty cents of your two dollars invested in lemonade. Let's see if we can at least break even this afternoon."

Just then their neighbor, Mr. Cunningham, came strolling along. He was carrying his salesman's briefcase and fanning himself with his hat.

"Lemonade, sir?" called Jim. "Only ten cents a glass."

"Well, I've had three glasses already this afternoon," Mr. Cunningham replied. "But one can get mighty warm on a day like this. I guess I could drink another glass."

Jan handed him a glass of the cool, tangy beverage. "Ah," said Mr. Cunningham, smacking his lips, "that's the best I've had today."

"Where did you buy your other glasses of lemonade?" asked Jim.

"Why, there are stands set up all over town," he replied.

"No wonder business has been so bad!" cried Jim. "I bet every guy in our Scout troop had the same idea today." Then he told Mr. Cunningham about their investment project.

Mr. Cunningham thought for a moment. "You know," he said, "you kids ought to build a better mousetrap."

"What do you mean by that?" asked Jan.

"There's an old saying by a very wise philosopher named Emerson," he explained. "It goes something like this: 'Build a better mousetrap, and the world will beat a path to your door.' "

"Oh! I think I know what it means," said Jan. "It means that people who have new and unusual ideas are apt to be the most successful."

"Exactly!" Mr. Cunningham replied. "Build that better mousetrap, and Jim's bound to go back to his Scout troop with his pockets full."

"But how else can we earn money?" asked Jim. "It wouldn't be fair to earn it by mowing lawns, or anything like that. Mr. Martin said the money we bring back in the fall must have been earned by investing our dollars and making them grow."

"Just put on your thinking caps," Mr. Cunningham told them. "You're sure to come up with an idea soon."

After their neighbor had left, the twins began wondering what they could do, or sell, that would be new and different. But they could not come up with one original idea between them.

"It's really too hot to think on a day like this," muttered Jim.

"Have another glass of lemonade then," suggested Jan.

"I'm sick of that old lemonade!" Jim growled. "I wish I had a nice icy popsicle to eat."

Suddenly Jan began to grin. She jumped to her feet and shouted, "Yippee! You just gave me a great idea for a better mousetrap. We'll sell homemade popsicles—the kind we make in our ice-cube trays."

"You're a genius!" crowed Jim. "We'll start working first thing tomorrow."

Early the next morning, the twins launched their new business. First they received permission from their mother to use one corner of her big chest freezer. Then Jan went to borrow extra ice-cube trays from friends and relatives. Jim went to the store and bought supplies with the investment money.

When they got back home they mixed up several packages of sweetened, flavored ade. Then they poured the mixtures into some of the ice-cube trays. They filled the rest of the trays with plain water, then set all of them in the freezer. After the mix started to freeze, they put a stick into each cube.

"We've been making these little popsicles for years," said Jan. "Too bad we didn't think of selling them sooner."

"Let's just hope that they do sell," said Jim. "Every last cent of the money is gone. If we fail this time, I'll have to go back to Mr. Martin completely empty-handed."

While they waited for the popsicles to freeze, the twins took a ride on their tandem. It was Jim's turn to ride on the front seat. They rolled out of the drive, Jan doing her share of the pedaling from her seat in the back. Their collie dog, Gyp, caught up with them at the corner. He followed them, yapping ten yips to the second. Barking at the tandem was Gyp's favorite pastime.

As the lively trio wheeled around the block, neighbors waved to them and laughed. They liked to watch the Wickham twins ride their tandem. It reminded them of days gone by, when a bicycle-built-for-two was a very common sight on the roads.

After a while Jim and Jan put their tandem into the garage and went inside for lunch. As soon as they had eaten, they brought a big red picnic cooler up from the basement. They filled the cooler with the plain water ice cubes. They carefully removed the small popsicles from the trays and set them on long cookie sheets. They laid the cookie sheets on top of the ice cubes, then carried the cooler out to the front yard. Jan put up a sign that said: POPSICLES FOR SALE. ONLY 2¢ EACH.

Soon their neighbors, Susie Carter and Nancy Lee, came by. "Popsicles!" squealed Susie. "I'll buy three!"

"Me too!" cried Nancy. "I'm tired of that lemonade everyone's been selling lately."

Jim waited on the girls. Then they ran to tell their friends that the Wickham twins were selling popsicles.

A few minutes later five more children came running over to buy popsicles. Soon customers were coming from all over the neighborhood. By two-thirty the popsicles were about one-third gone. Then business came to a standstill. A half hour passed, but not a single customer showed up.

"Do you suppose they didn't like our popsicles?" Jim fretted.

"No, I think business here is over for the day," Jan said. "The neighbors probably have spent all they can afford."

"Well, we sure have a lot left," sighed Jim. "If we don't sell them soon, every bit of our profits will melt away."

Sitting in the hot summer sun, they waited for a new batch of customers to appear. But though some of the children came back to see how they were making out, no one bought more popsicles.

"Hah!" scoffed Jan. "Build a better mousetrap, and the world will beat a path to your door! I don't see anybody crowding *our* path!"

Jim propped his elbows on his knees and began to think. "If we were real popsicle sellers like the ones we see in the city, there wouldn't be any problem," he said. "All we'd have to do is drive our popsicles around in one of those white motor scooters and ring a bell. We'd have customers all over town then."

Jan's eyes began to gleam. "We don't need a motor scooter," she shouted. "We have the tandem!"

"With a bell on it!" cried Jim, scrambling to his feet. "And we have noisy old Gyp, who's a better advertisement than any bell."

Quickly the twins rushed to the garage for their tandem. They rolled it across the lawn to the cooler.

"We forgot about the cooler," groaned Jan. "Those white motor scooters have built-in freezers. How are we going to carry that bulky cooler around on our tandem?"

"We ought to have a little trailer," said Jim. "How about our old red cart?"

Back they bounded to the garage. Jim dusted the cart and hunted for a length of rope, while Jan painted a new sign. Soon they rode the tandem out of the yard. Tied to the back fender, the little cart came trundling along behind them. On the cart was the cooler with Jan's new sign pasted on it: JIM AND JAN, YOUR POPSICLE TWINS.

Gyp, his voice in fine pitch, came prancing along after them. Jim merrily jingled the tandem bell. All in all it was a very jolly, eye-catching procession.

Slowly Jim and Jan pedaled their bike up and down the streets of Elmdale. Parents and children came hurrying out of their homes to see what all the barking and jingling was about. They laughed when they spied the two young popsicle sellers on their old-fashioned tandem.

The twins stopped at every corner to sell popsicles. All the

children wanted them, of course, and so did many of the parents. "What nice little popsicles," some of the mothers remarked. "They are so inexpensive, and small enough so that they won't spoil any appetites for dinner."

"Will you be back again tomorrow?" many children asked.

"Jim and Jan, your popsicle twins, will be around every day this summer," Jan happily assured them.

An hour or so later, the tired but happy procession wended its way home. "Hey, Jim," Jan called from the back seat, "I've been doing some mental arithmetic. We've cleared about two dollars in two hours!"

"Think what our profits will be by fall!" crowed Jim. "I'll have to carry the money to Mr. Martin in big potato sacks. I could never have done it without you, Jan. I'm going to tell Mr. Martin how much you helped."

As they pulled into their drive, they met Mr. Cunningham coming home for dinner. "Well, I declare!" he cried, eyeing Jan's sign on the cooler. "What have we here?"

"Popsicles for sale. It's our better mousetrap," Jim explained. "Only the world didn't beat a path to our door. So we put our mousetrap on wheels and *we* beat a path to the *world's* door instead."

Mr. Cunningham began to laugh. "As pupils of Mr. Emerson, you surely do him credit," he chuckled. "Yes sirree! By the way, do you have any popsicles left?"

"No," grinned Jan, "but we'll save you some tomorrow. I think we may make a double batch!"

POETRY

SCARBOROUGH FAIR

Are you going to Scarborough Fair?
Parsley, Sage, Rosemary and Thyme,
Remember me to one who lives there,
For once she was a true love of mine.

Tell her to make me a cambric shirt—
Parsley, Sage, Rosemary and Thyme,
Without any seam or needlework
She shall be a true love of mine.

Tell her to wash it in yonder dry well
Parsley, Sage, Rosemary and Thyme,
Where water ne'er sprung nor drop of
     rain fell
She shall be a true love of mine.

Well, will you find me an acre of land
Parsley, Sage, Rosemary and Thyme,
Between the sea foam and the sea sand?
You shall be a true love of mine.

And will you plow it with a lamb's horn
Parsley, Sage, Rosemary and Thyme,
And sow it all over with one peppercorn?
And you shall be a true love of mine.

And will you reap it with a sickle of leather
Parsley, Sage, Rosemary and Thyme,
And tie it up with a peacock's feather?
And you shall be a true love of mine.

And when you're done and finished your
     work
Parsley, Sage, Rosemary and Thyme,
Then come back to me for your cambric
     shirt
And you shall be a true love of mine.

TRADITIONAL BALLAD

SPELLBOUND

The night is darkening round me,
The wild winds coldly blow;
But a tyrant spell has bound me
And I cannot, cannot go.

The giant trees are bending
Their bare boughs weighed with snow.
And the storm is fast descending,
And yet I cannot go.

Clouds beyond clouds above me,
Wastes beyond wastes below;
But nothing drear can move me;
I will not, cannot go.

EMILY BRONTË (1818–1848)

THE MELANCHOLY PIG

There was a Pig that sat alone,
     Beside a ruined Pump.
By day and night he made his moan:
     It would have stirred a heart of stone
To see him wring his hoofs and groan,
     Because he could not jump.

LEWIS CARROLL (1832–1898)

UNSATISFIED YEARNING

Down in the silent hallway
    Scampers the dog about,
And whines, and barks, and scratches,
    In order to get out.

Once in the glittering starlight,
    He straightway doth begin
To set up a doleful howling
    In order to get in.

                R. K. MUNKITTRICK (1853–1911)

VELVET SHOES

Let us walk in the white snow
In a soundless space;
With footsteps quiet and slow,
At a tranquil pace,
Under veils of white lace.

I shall go shod in silk,
And you in wool,
White as a white cow's milk,
More beautiful
Than the breast of a gull.

We shall walk through the still town
In a windless peace;
We shall step upon white down,
Upon silver fleece
Upon softer than these.

We shall walk in velvet shoes:
Wherever we go
Silence will fall like dews
On white silence below.
We shall walk in the snow.

                ELINOR WYLIE (1885–1928)

UNTITLED

Because river-fog
Hiding the mountain-base
Has risen,
The autumn mountain looks as though it
    hung in the sky.

        KIYOWARA FUKUYABU (c. 900–930)

SONG

The feathers of the willow
Are half of them grown yellow
    Above the swelling stream;
And ragged are the bushes,
And rusty now the rushes,
    And wild the clouded gleam.

The thistle now is older,
His stalk begins to moulder,
    His head is white as snow;
The branches all are barer,
The linnet's song is rarer,
    The robin pipeth now.

RICHARD WATSON DIXON (1833–1900)

DEEP REFLECTION

Patiently fishing in the lake, the crane's
Long red legs have shortened since the rains.
                        BASHÔ (1644–1695)

SPRING

Spring is a beautiful time of year.
Spring tells that roses are all too near.
It's a time to play on tennis courts.
It's a time to go outside in shorts.
It's a time to swim in a pool.
It's a time to feel cool.
It's a time for you to love.
It's a time to feel the sun from above.
And sometimes, it's time to drop a tear.
Spring is a beautiful time of year.

JOE DISTEL
age 11
Philadelphia, Pennsylvania

WHAT IS YELLOW?

Yellow is the bright sunlight,
Shining through my window pane.
Yellow is a rainbow stripe,
Arching through the summer's rain.

Yellow is a lemon tree,
Proudly showing off its fruit.
Yellow is a bumble bee,
Dressed up in his Sunday suit.

Yellow is a field of wheat,
Reaching for the sky.
Yellow is the corn so sweet,
Stacked up on a platter high.

Yellow is a daffodil,
Swaying on a lonely hill.

MARISA MCDANIEL
age 10
West Lafayette, Indiana

PERFECT ORDER

Everything neat. No chaos or bustle.
The grown-ups just sit.
They don't move a muscle.
"Keep quiet," they say.
"Go play with the cat."
"Mind your manners."
"Go read."
"Go do something."
"Now, scat!"
"Go outside."
"I'm busy," or
"I'm on the phone."
It doesn't seem to matter that this is
        your home.
Adults—they're the rulers, the kings,
        and the queens.
They don't seem to know what "Hey,
        Mom," really means.
To them they are words that are used by
        a pest.
Those words, they've determined, will
        give them no rest.
Although they think that you're in the
        way,
Grown-ups, I think, are really OK.

KAREN WEAVER
age 13
Barbourville, Kentucky

MISTY MOUNTAIN

Up in the misty mountain with snow-
        capped peak
Nothing is gray, nothing is bleak.
For up in the misty mountain love,
        peace, and joy abide;
And if you listen closely the melody will
        be your guide.
Go visit the misty mountain and as you
        climb the side—
Listen very closely, to the melody, your
        guide.

HEATHER ANNE BAILEY
age 12
Tilbury, Ontario, Canada

SILENCE

In the library,
Silence comes in,
And sits down,
And listens.

LAUREL D. OSBORNE
age 7
Excelsior, Minnesota

TUMBLEWEEDS

Tumbleweeds march across
the fields like soldiers
at their drills.

Tumbleweeds are like little
children playing leapfrog
at recess.

Tumbleweeds are like little
boys at playtime in school,
wrestling each other.

Tumbleweeds play chase in
the wind. They chase
each other down the hillsides.

Tumbleweeds like to snuggle up
in the corners of
the fences near the houses.

Tumbleweeds are as cute as babies
when they are just sprouting
out of the ground.

CHANEY CALDWELL
age 8
Lancaster, California

FIRE

The fire is hot;
the fire is spitting sparks.
The fire is burning brightly;
the fire is cosy.
All the kids like it.

JAMES FORRER
age 12
St. Gallen, Switzerland

ME

They say I have my father's toes,
My mother's nose,
But don't they know?
I'm really me inside?

They say I have my granny's hair,
My granpa's flair,
But they should learn;
I'm no one else but me!

They say I draw like Uncle Sam,
But I am only what I am,
They say I write like Great-Aunt Dot,
But I'm entitled to my thought.

I guess they don't know who I'm like,
But I can tell them off!
I AM EXACTLY LIKE MYSELF!
(Applause, ho-hum, cough, cough!)

HEIDI ARDIZZONE
age 11
Worcester, Massachusetts

MY GRANDMOTHER'S DOG

''What are you doing, great black dog,
Staring down the shadowed stair;
Thumping the ground with your great black
    tail
And looking wistful?''

Sitting, with a grand air,
And then he leaps down the stairs
In joyful glee,
Smothering me with licks.

Then he forgets me
And turning, he hits me with his great black
    tail
As though I had never been there.

EMMA SPEED
age 11
Cobham, Surrey, England

The Christmas Bear

Long ago in Finnmark, which is in northern Norway, there lived a man whose name was Lars. His father's name had been Lars Larsson, or Son of Lars.

One day Lars went out hunting and trapped a large white polar bear. He gave her the name of Freya.

About this time the King of Denmark sent out heralds to announce: "The man who brings His Majesty a tame polar bear for Christmas can ask for anything and the King will grant his wish!"

This was music to the ears of Lars. He put a collar around Freya's neck and fastened a chain to it, and they started off for Denmark.

As they journeyed southward, the man and the bear lost track of time. Yet they sensed that Christmas was near, for the days were short and dark.

Soon they reached the Dovre Mountains, which are the home of trolls of every shape and size. The trolls would hide in the dark mountain caves and come out only at night. Then they would prowl and frighten folk with their fiendish pranks.

When Lars and Freya came through the mountain passes of Dovre, they were cold and hungry. They longed for fire and food and shelter. As they passed between high cliffs, they saw below them a cottage of polished brown logs. Blue smoke rose from the chimney. "Let us hope that is the home of decent folk," said Lars to the bear. "There we'll ask for food and shelter."

"I like my ice cave better," grumbled the bear.

When they had come down the hill and knocked at the door, a woodsman with sad blue eyes opened it to them.

"We're on the way to the King of Denmark," began Lars. "He wants a tame white bear for Christmas, and my bear, Freya, is really tame!"

"You're rather late for Christmas in Denmark," muttered the man, whose name was Halvor. "It's Christmas Eve tomorrow."

"Can we get food and shelter here?" asked Lars.

"We're not safe here ourselves," mumbled the man half to himself. "And I am not used to having bears in my house."

"But you have the shelter of a roof," said Lars. "I vow that Freya is as gentle as a cat." Halvor ignored this last remark.

"Tomorrow this home will become the lair of trolls," said the host. "Every Christmas Eve they come rolling down the mountains and take possession of our house. Here they hold their Christmas feast. Yet we can do nothing against them. They are far too strong." The man's eyes looked dark and troubled.

To cheer him, Lars replied, "There is an old Norse saying that when strangers enter a home, they bring good luck. There's no harm in letting us try."

"No one can keep the trolls away," said Halvor grimly. "But do come in to warm yourselves."

Lars and the white bear stepped into the house. Beside the open hearth sat a handsome dark-eyed woman, spinning. She looked about the same age as Halvor and she wore a bright red jacket with full sleeves, a white blouse, and a long blue skirt embroidered in brilliant colors.

Opposite her sat a young woman with the same kind of blue eyes as her father, except that hers were not sad but were flashing and bright. Her blond hair peeped out from beneath a white embroidered cap, and she wore a costume similar to her mother's.

"This is my wife, Helga, and my daughter, Elsa," said Halvor as he showed Lars into the house.

Lars's heart skipped as he saw the lovely young woman. And he thought to himself: If I can rid this house of trolls, maybe it won't be so long before I can woo her for my bride.

He greeted the two women with a deep bow, and the two strangers were asked to move closer to the fire. Soon they were comfortably settled, and Lars was served a warm spiced drink and small sweet-smelling cakes, while Freya was given a huge sausage. Lars felt he had just arrived in heaven.

"Do tell me about the trolls," he said as his eyes took in the brightly painted furniture, the shining copper bowls along the shelves, and the handmade tapestries on the walls.

"As far back as we can remember," said Halvor, "trolls troop down from the mountain caves each Christmas Eve to find a place where they can hold their feast. No matter what we do, on holy days the trolls bring wrack and ruin with them. They infest our home! If you can free us from this evil, whatever you ask for in our house is yours."

After much talk it was agreed that the woodsman and his family would leave the house on the morning of Christmas Eve. Then Lars and his white bear would move in and try to rid the house of the trolls.

The next day, with a sinking heart, Lars watched Halvor and his wife and pretty daughter take off on their skis down the snowy

slopes toward the neighboring village where they were to spend the night.

"If I ever see them again, my life and fortune are made," Lars said aloud. "If not, then heaven help us!"

"Oh, never fear! We will not only see them, but they will thank us," answered Freya calmly.

The holy day passed under a soft, silent snowfall. The mountains were dazzling white, and the fields looked blue with deep purple shadows under pine and spruce.

Dark came early, but inside the house was firelight and warmth. Out-of-doors a sharp wind cried like a lost creature. The pines and the spruces moaned softly in the stillness. Stars seemed to twinkle and dance on the distant ice of a lake. All appeared peaceful and holy over the valley and the mountain slopes.

"This is a strange Christmas Eve," said Lars to Freya. "We should be home dancing around a tree and bringing in the Christ-

mas logs. We should be drinking the good wine and feasting on the Christmas boar. Instead we're waiting in a strange valley to face trolls in a strange house far from home.''

"This is because we are traveling to the King of Denmark," grumbled Freya. Soon she was asleep with her nose in the warm ashes of the fireplace.

Lars went to a wall bunk and pulled aside the handwoven curtain and climbed into bed. He pulled a reindeer-skin cover over himself, and soon he was asleep in the dark, still house.

Suddenly Lars awakened and sat up in bed. He heard yelping, yelling, and shouting, as if a pack of wild animals were tumbling down the mountain slope toward the house.

Lars peered out from the tiny window near his bunk. Against the moonlit snow, a throng of dark forms was rushing toward him.

Lars leaped out of bed and shouted, "Wake up, Freya. Here come the trolls!"

The bear did not waken but slept on. The yelling and yelping came ever closer.

Lars was trembling. "Wake up, Freya!" he shouted. "The trolls are here!" He shook the bear. She opened her eyes and gazed at him calmly.

"Why fear trolls? Don't you know that a polar bear has the strength of twelve and the wit of more?" Freya got on her hind legs and stretched herself. She seemed to fill the whole room with her creamy white pelt.

"No matter how strong or clever you are," Lars raced on, "trolls are trolls! They are less than human, and theirs is the strength of evil!"

Freya merely grunted and lay down again. This time she placed her huge body under the long table at the far end of the cottage. On the slope, the uproar grew louder and wilder. Now the trolls were banging at the door. Lars leaped back into the bunk and pulled the curtain.

At that moment the troll pack tore open the door and flooded in like a torrent of demons.

Lars peered out and saw that the trolls were wild creatures, half man and half beast. Some were gigantic; some, as small as dogs. Some were humpbacked; some, knock-kneed. Some had noses as long as spades; others, noses as round as hams. All had small, evil eyes, burning like live coals.

The ugliest troll shouted: "Witch, bring in the feast!" An old witch with the face of a wolf rushed through the door, followed by others even more dreadful. Presently they came back with sacks of troll food: dragon tails garnished with seaweed, wolf hearts stewed in blood, and more, far too horrible to describe.

In one corner an old wizard wearing elk horns sat down and began to beat a troll drum marked with magic signs.

When the feast had been set upon the long table, the troll pack gathered round, rubbing their paws, smacking their jaws, and patting their huge potbellies.

They began to gorge themselves. Their tearing and gulping of food and drink became bloodcurdling to hear.

The troll drum was beating louder and faster. The trolls began to chant, but their chanting seemed the screaming of eagles and the howling of wolves.

The troll feast went on and on. Lars trembled in his bunk. To him the feast seemed to last a year and a day.

Suddenly one young troll picked up a bone and, waving it in the air, cried, "Where's the house pet to gnaw this bone?" With that he ducked his head under the table and came up squealing. He had discovered Freya lying underneath.

"Look at my big white cat!" the troll-youngster shrieked. "It's the biggest cat in all of Dovre! Can I take you home to my cave?"

With that he tickled Freya's nose with the bone. The great bear shook herself and, with one movement of her immense body, got to her feet. The table under which she had slept was lifted and knocked over in one swoop. The bear stood erect on her hind legs and looked about with calm eyes. The house was hushed and not a creature moved. The trolls gaped at this towering beast.

Then Freya began to roar. Her voice was the sound of Arctic waves lashing against cliffs of ice. It echoed beyond the house as if there were no barrier to her thunder.

Freya stretched her heavy white arms to crush the trolls in a death-hug. At once the demons vanished out of the house into the night as if blown away by a gale. They rushed across the snowy fields, whisked up the slopes, and vanished into their mountain caves.

"So?" asked Freya, as she lay down again to warm her nose in the ashes. "What did I tell you?"

Lars said nothing but crept from his bunk and began to put the house in order.

"Didn't I tell you that it is good luck to take in a stranger on Christmas Eve?" asked Lars when the woodsman's family had returned the next day to find peace and quiet reigning in the house.

"Since you've freed our home from trolls, stay and celebrate with us," Halvor cried with a great show of warmth.

So Lars stayed. And not long after, he wooed and wed the pretty daughter.

No trolls were ever seen again in the valley where this adventure took place. It is clear that Freya really scared them out of their wits.

As for Freya, she went back to Finnmark. If you ever travel far up into the North Sea, you may find some of her children's children riding on the ice floes.

a Norwegian story from *Scandinavian Stories*
by MARGARET SPERRY

OX-CART MAN

This book describes the life of a 19th-century New England family. In October the family fills a cart with things they have made or grown during the year. The father hitches his ox to the cart and heads for Portsmouth Market. There he sells the goods, and even his beloved ox. With the money he receives he buys things needed by the family. In the following months, new items are made and new crops and animals are raised. The book, written by Donald Hall and illustrated by Barbara Cooney, won the 1980 Caldecott Medal for excellence in illustration.

A GATHERING OF DAYS

Many children keep diaries in which they describe their thoughts and what they have seen and done. This novel is in the form of a diary, written by a girl named Catherine. Catherine lived on a farm near Meredith, New Hampshire, in the early 1800's. As the diary begins, she is 13 years old. She lives with her widowed father and her younger sister. When her father remarries, Catherine gets a new mother and a stepbrother. In the diary, Catherine writes about her family, her best friend, and the things that happen at school. She describes such pastimes as making quilts and stenciling. The practice of slavery in parts of the country bothers Catherine. And when she meets a runaway slave, she gives him a quilt to keep him warm. This book, by Joan W. Blos, was awarded the 1980 John Newbery Medal for "the most distinguished contribution to American children's literature."

JOURNEY TO THE BRIGHT KINGDOM

This book, written by Elizabeth Winthrop and illustrated by Charles Mikolaycak, tells an ancient Japanese folktale about a young woman who is blind. Her greatest sorrow is that she cannot see her daughter, Kiyo. The woman tells Kiyo about a magic land ruled by mice, where there is no sadness and no blindness. Kiyo finds the mice, who bring her and her mother to their magical kingdom. And for a few hours, the blind woman is able to see her daughter's face.

The Twelve Dancing Princesses

One night, in a place far, far away, a farm boy falls asleep in the forest. In his dreams a rosebush speaks to him: "Travel west along the rainbow, west and west again, and if you are steadfast and true you will find your heart's desire." The boy meets an old woman, who tells him of a land with a golden palace, twelve beautiful princesses, and a very sad king. The boy travels to the land, where he solves the mystery that has made the king sad. This makes the king very happy and he gives the boy a wonderful reward. The book, an old legend retold by Janet Lunn and illustrated by Laszlo Gal, was awarded a Children's Literature Prize by the Canada Council.

The Mystery of the Grecian Vase

Janelle Russell flung the yellow sweatshirt with "Callaway" on it in big letters over her shoulder and hurried after her cousin, who threatened to disappear in the sidewalk crowds.

"Gary, slow down! It's too hot to rush," she called, squinting against the early afternoon glare. "Neal gave us a lift downtown. We've plenty of time."

"OK." The boy stopped and waited for her. "If Neal hadn't been late for work at the missile plant, he'd have taken us all the way."

"Your brother's job is interesting, isn't it?" Janelle asked as she fell into step. "Does he draw plans for the big Navy experimental rocket?"

"No. That's top secret. Almost nobody has security clearance for it. They're afraid of spies or something."

Janelle's brown eyes twinkled. "In Middleburg? Gary Brooks! That's silly. Oh, look! There's some of the volleyball team up ahead. I hope Sue Lacy's well enough to play today. Our girls' team needs her."

Gary glanced back. "There are more players behind us."

"Yes. Anybody can tell something's going on at Callaway Park to—oof!" Her words disappeared into the brown suit coat of the burly figure that suddenly zigzagged into her.

"Pardon me, little lady. Are you all right?" Concern enveloped the stranger's face.

Janelle gasped, then swallowed. "I think so."

"Good! Are you kids headed for Callaway Park, too?"

Gary answered. "Yes, today's the big volleyball tournament with the kids from Blountstown."

"Say, could you do me a favor and deliver a gift?" He jerked his thumb toward a paper-wrapped package hugged against his body. "It's on your way. My friend lives across from the park."

"I don't know—" Janelle hesitated.

"I was on my way but was delayed, and I'm afraid that I'll miss my plane if I go." He tilted his head upward, narrowing his pale eyes as if to scan the sky for his plane. Then, despite the heat, he shoved his cocoa-colored straw hat farther down toward his bushy brows and looked at Janelle.

"I suppose we could," Gary said doubtfully.

"I'd sure appreciate it. My friend lives on Cedar Drive, directly across from the park. I don't know the number, but his house is the only one on the block with a big bed of moss roses blooming in the yard. I went by there earlier this morning."

"Moss roses? What are they?" Janelle asked.

"Oh, small flowers, all colors . . . red, yellow, orange, and pink. You can't miss the place." He held out the box. "It's a

Grecian vase for my friend's birthday. I know you'll take good care of it.''

The man spoke rapidly, and all the while his oddly colorless eyes searched the faces of passersby. He fished a dollar bill from his pocket and, glancing around once more, hurriedly shoved the money and package at Gary.

"Hey, we don't want any pay!" The boy held out the dollar, but the man was gone. Gary whistled. "What an oddball."

"Poor man. He was really worried about missing his plane." The girl started off. "Come on. Let's get rid of the box before the games begin."

They soon reached the block across from the park. Janelle checked the street sign. "Cedar Drive—it should be nearby."

"Yep."

"Those look like flower beds," Janelle said a few minutes later, pointing to the spacious grounds of a dark green, three-story house. It was decorated with faded, painted wood gingerbread and had a veranda that curved from front to rear.

Gary looked dubious. "Maybe. But those plants have a sort of red stem and green top. They're not all colors like the flowers he described."

"Well, no," Janelle admitted.

They moved along in the sultry heat, past overgrown vacant lots and neat yards, scanning each one.

"Here's the last house." Gary stopped at the corner. "Not one has flowers."

Janelle gnawed her lip. "He said he saw them this morning. Could someone have cut them down?"

"Don't ask me. We might as well give up. Besides, there's Sue across the street calling us. It's almost time for the games."

"I guess we'll have to worry about it later. Put the box on the picnic table and cover it with our sweatshirts so it'll be safe." '

Much later Gary sat on the picnic bench tying his shoelace. "What a tournament! We were lucky—both our teams won."

"Boy, did they!" Janelle ducked into her sweatshirt. She looked around the park and at the long ribbons of shadow unfurled across the grass. "We're the last ones here. Hurry up."

"Yeah, it's getting late. But what about the package?"

"I talked to Sue Lacy while you were playing. Her mother gardens. We figured out what happened to the flowers. I even know the right house."

"Yeah? Clue me."

"It's the one with the gingerbread."

"Then let's get rid of this pronto." He grabbed the package from the table and swung it around.

"Gary, don't! You might—" The box hit the ground. "Oh, Gary! Suppose you broke that vase."

"Aw, it's probably well packed."

"Maybe. Open it and see if it's OK."

Gary scratched his head. "I don't know, Jan. Something tells me that guy wouldn't want us opening his gift."

"But we have to check. What if it *is* broken?"

Gary shrugged and laid the parcel on the table. Carefully, he unknotted the heavy cord and untaped the outer wrapping.

"Here, let me." Janelle lifted off the top. "It sure is well packed." She removed wad after wad of crumpled, pale green tissue paper, piling it on the table. At last she reached the object within.

Gary edged closer. "Is it OK?"

Silently, she shoved the box toward the boy. Gary stared at it. Dull pieces of red clay pottery lay jumbled like a child's jigsaw puzzle.

"Gosh, I didn't mean to drop it. Can't we glue it together?"

Janelle shook her head. "Not a chance. We'll have to tell the man that we broke it. We can offer to pay for it."

Suddenly Gary said, "Jan, if that was a Grecian vase, I'll eat my shoelaces."

"But the man said—"

"I know. But look for yourself. This was a cheap dime-store vase. We can get another and easily switch it. The man'll never know the difference."

Janelle shook her head again. "No. We have to tell him and offer to pay for it. He'll understand. Help me put the packing back."

"We missed this." Gary scooped a ball of green tissue paper from the ground.

"Too late now. I've already tied up the package. Stick it in the trash can."

"There's none around." He put it in his pocket. "Let's get going."

They crossed the park toward the gingerbread house.

"You're sure that this is the place, Jan?"

"Positive. I'll explain later."

They hurried up the broken walk. The dark old house wore a faintly sinister air like a shadowy mantle that could not be brightened even by the rosy gold of the setting sun. The brass bell pealed loudly at Gary's twist. They listened.

"Nobody's home. Let's go." Gary turned.

"What'll we do with the package? Wait. I'll ring the bell again."

"Aw, come on. There's no one home."

The sudden creak of hinges startled them.

"Yes?" A broomstick figure of a man loomed in the doorway.

"Er—hello," Janelle stammered. "A friend of yours asked us to deliver this package."

The man's beady eyes sized them up. "How nice of you," he said softly. Reaching out, he took the box. "Come in. I'm Mr. Treemert."

"Oh, no thanks," Gary declined hastily. "We have to get home."

"I'm afraid we had a little accident with the vase, Mr. Treemert, but we'll be glad to get you another," Janelle said.

"Accident?" A shrewd look crossed his face.

"Gary dropped the box and—"

"Your friend said that he was giving you a Grecian vase," Gary interrupted. "But it's just a common old flowerpot."

The man's eyes widened with something like alarm. "You opened it?"

"Yes," Janelle began.

"I dropped the box, so we checked to see if the vase was broken," Gary explained.

"It's odd that your friend said it was a Grecian vase when it was an old clay pot packed in that funny green paper. Do you suppose they tried to pawn it off—"

"How should I know?" the man growled, interrupting Janelle. Then his voice softened. "We must discuss it further. Please come in." He smiled invitingly.

"Thanks, Mr. Treemert, but—" Janelle stared, hypnotized by the metallic glint of the ugly, snub-nosed revolver pointed at her.

It can't be real, Janelle thought; it looks like the toy guns Gary used to play with. But one look at the man's face, and she knew. He wasn't playing games.

"I expected you much earlier," he was saying.

"But I don't understand," Janelle said.

The brief smile on the thin lips began and ended there. "My friend phoned from the airport." He motioned with the gun, and Gary followed his cousin into the dim hallway. The man nodded toward the worn stairway. "Up there."

Janelle started up the steps. Gary followed. Their captor was close behind them.

"Why are you holding us?" Gary demanded, stopping suddenly on the stairway.

"None of your business, kid. Get on up there like I say if you don't want to get hurt."

"Come on, Gary," Janelle urged.

For a long second the boy stood unmoving. Slowly he resumed his climb. Janelle let out her breath. The only noise was the protesting of creaking treads.

On the second floor, the tall figure pointed to the next flight. "Keep going. If you know what's good for you, you won't waste your breath hollering for help. I'll tie and gag you if you do. Anyway, the neighbors are on vacation."

He herded them into a dusty, empty room near the head of the stairs. Janelle looked around, straining her eyes in the fading twilight that filtered through the slit of a window. The lock clicked in the stout oak door. The sound of clumping footsteps receded.

"Ugh!" Janelle shuddered, trying to wipe off a cobweb.

Gary stood in the middle of the floor, his head almost touching the low beams. "Old Beanpole's crazy! Locking us up for breaking a cheap vase. What do you suppose is behind all this, Jan?"

"I don't know," Jan whispered. "Do you realize nobody knows where we are?" Her eyes widened.

Gary nodded absentmindedly. "The man in the brown suit acted awfully odd. He kept looking over his shoulder as if somebody were on his trail. Then, when he gave us the box—pfft! He went up in smoke."

Janelle took a deep breath. "The vase must be the key to this whole mystery. But it was only an old flowerpot, and there wasn't a letter or note."

"Well, let's worry about it later. The big question now is how do we get out?" Gary crossed to the narrow window.

Janelle tiptoed after him. All she could see was a jumble of gables and a steep roof. "After Beanpole's warning, we'd better not yell."

"He was pretty sure nobody would hear us. But we could write a message and throw it out."

The girl nodded. "It's worth a try. Somebody might find it in the morning. What can we write on?"

Gary's eyes searched the bare room. He shook his head. "Wait! Here's that extra piece of packing paper. We can use it." He handed her the crumpled green wad and a pencil stub.

Kneeling, Janelle smoothed the paper against the floorboards. Suddenly she cried, "Gary, look!" She held the paper toward the light from the window. "There are sketches on this. What do you suppose they are?"

Gary squinted. "They look like plans to me. Do you think they could be for the secret Navy rocket? Jan, I'll bet these men are spies!"

"So that's why Beanpole kidnapped us. Gary, we've got to get out of here and warn the police."

"Yeah! Get busy! Write that SOS."

As Gary peered over her shoulder, Janelle printed, "HELP! CALL POLICE! LOCKED IN BIG GREEN HOUSE WITH 'GINGERBREAD.' Janelle Russell, Gary Brooks."

Quickly wrapping the paper around his pocketknife, the boy fastened it with a rubber band and handed it to her. "Hold it while I open the window." He placed the heels of both hands under the top of the sash frame and strained to lift it.

"Maybe it's locked."

"No, stuck. Give me a hand." He moved to one side. "One, two, push!"

Creaking slightly, the window moved a few inches, then suddenly shot upward, shattering the stillness. They froze, listening. Then, hurriedly, Gary heaved the knife through the opening.

Hardly daring to breathe, they listened for the footsteps that must surely come. A faint noise like the slamming of a door

floated upward through the window. Then all was quiet. They slid to the floor and waited.

"He didn't hear it," Gary said in a low voice about twenty minutes later. "I'm going to climb down."

"Gary, you can't! We're miles high. And what if he comes back?" She glanced toward the locked door as if expecting it to burst open.

"I know it's scary, but we can't wait. My rubber soles will help keep me from sliding." He strained his eyes to see through the semidarkness. "Look, I'll drop onto that roof below, and maybe there'll be a chimney or ventpipe or something."

"Please be careful," Janelle whispered.

"Sure. And I'll be back with help before you even know I'm gone." He swung one leg over the sill, dropped to the sloping roof, and disappeared.

Time seemed suspended. After a while, Janelle stirred. She rubbed her cramped legs. It seemed years since Gary had gone. Had he reached the ground safely? Surely she would have heard him if he had fallen. She thought of her parents. By now they would be looking for her and Gary.

Suddenly she tensed. Faint sounds broke the stillness. Gary? No. The noise came from inside the house. As she listened, it grew louder. Her heart thumped. Using the wall as a guide, she felt her way to the door. She put her ear against it.

Footsteps! He was climbing the stairs! What would he do when he found Gary gone? A board creaked in the hallway.

Hurriedly she backed away from the door. If only there were someplace to hide. Maybe she could pretend to be asleep. She dropped to the floor and lay still, eyes closed.

A key clicked. She heard the door open, then footsteps. A light found her face. She lay tense.

"Get up!" Treemert's voice commanded.

Blinking, she shielded her eyes. Her mind whirled. If only she could think of some way to outwit him. Slowly, she sat up. He grabbed her hand and jerked her upright.

"Downstairs. Get a move on."

She wrenched her hand free. "OK."

On rubbery legs she stumbled toward the sickly hall light, then down the stairs. Why hadn't he asked where Gary was? A sinking feeling flooded her.

"To your right, to the kitchen." The man nudged her as she reached the last step. Janelle moved forward into the bright light, blinking. Inside the doorway she gasped, "Oh, no!"

Bound and gagged, Gary sat on a straight chair. She ran and knelt beside him. "Are you hurt?"

He shook his head.

"He's tied. Do you have to gag him, too?" Janelle demanded.

"You were warned. Untie his feet. We're leaving."

Oh, no, Janelle thought as she fumbled with the rope around Gary's ankles. If they left the old house now, no one would ever find them, at least not in time.

Out of the corner of her eye she saw Treemert hastily stuffing papers from a cabinet into a satchel. His gun lay on the counter at his elbow.

The old doorbell pealed urgently through the big house. Janelle's heart leaped. Was it help?

Treemert froze. He turned his head, listening.

Janelle dashed toward him and shoved the gun from the counter. It clattered across the tiled floor, coming to a stop against the wall under a small table.

"You little—!" He darted after the gun.

Janelle raced from the room. How could she get out? She spied a heavy bolted door. Fumbling, she slid the bolt and yanked. Uniformed figures burst past her. The police!

"In there!" she gasped, pointing. "He's got a gun."

"Come out hands up, Treemert! You're covered on all sides."

Everything happened fast then. Minutes later the little group on the sidewalk watched as the scowling, handcuffed Treemert was whisked away in a patrol car.

"Hop in, kids. Officer Nelson will take you down to headquarters to get your story, and then we'll take you home." A broad-shouldered plainclothesman pointed to a police car.

Speechless, Janelle obeyed.

"Were we glad to see you, officer," Gary said as they sped away. "How'd you find us?"

The policeman grinned. "It took real teamwork, Gary. For weeks we've been working with the FBI on this case. We suspected the man in the brown suit, and we hoped he would lead us to his partner."

"And he did," Janelle said.

"Well, indirectly. He got wise, eluded the FBI man trailing him, and slipped the package to you."

"Hoping we'd deliver it," Gary interrupted.

"Correct. Then he tried to skip the country, but we picked him up at the airport."

"But how did you find us?" Janelle asked.

"Your folks were worried when you didn't come home, and called Sue Lacy. She remembered the package, and your parents phoned us. We put the pieces together and came running."

"I was never so glad to see anybody in my life," Janelle said. "I'd forgotten about Sue."

"By the way, Jan. How'd you and Sue figure the right house?" Gary asked.

"Well, Sue told me that there are some flowers, like four-o'clocks, that close up at certain hours, perhaps because of the heat and bright sunlight."

"So you decided that the moss roses might have closed," Gary said.

Janelle nodded. "Yes, and they had. Do you remember that we saw the green flower beds at the gingerbread house?"

"Yeah. And those men really were spies, Officer Nelson?"

"Absolutely, Gary. They were only amateurs, but they had the most important parts of the Navy rocket plans."

Janelle giggled. "One piece was missing." She told him about the paper on which they'd written their note.

"We'll get it." He radioed the policemen at the Treemert home.

"You know," Gary said to no one in particular, "just today, certain folks were laughing at the idea of spies in Middleburg."

Janelle laughed. "OK. I apologize. And if there are any more spies around, you can have them."

"Not me," Gary said. "One spy adventure is enough!"

Janelle agreed.

THE NEW BOOK OF KNOWLEDGE
1981

The following articles are from the 1981 edition of *The New Book of Knowledge*. They are included here to help you keep your encyclopedia up-to-date.

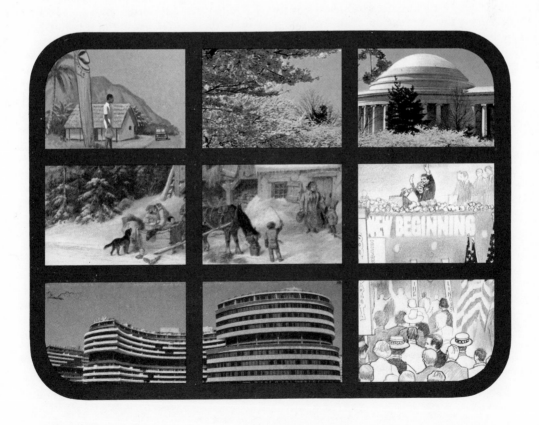

RONALD WILSON REAGAN (1911–   )
40TH PRESIDENT OF THE UNITED STATES

REAGAN, RONALD WILSON. The life of Ronald Wilson Reagan is a story of unlikely successes. Reagan was born of poor parents in a small town in Illinois. He graduated from college during the Depression of the 1930's. Yet he became a successful actor in motion pictures and on television. When his entertainment career began to decline, he began a new career—in politics. In 1966 he ran for governor of California as a Republican. He won, despite the fact that most California voters were Democrats.

In 1968 and again in 1976, Reagan sought the Republican nomination for president. He lost both times. After that, many people thought that Reagan's age—then 65—would prevent his party from nominating him. But he worked hard for the nomination in 1980 and demonstrated to the voters' satisfaction that he could stand up to the stress of a job that may be the most difficult in the world.

▶ EARLY YEARS

The 40th President of the United States was born in Tampico, Illinois, on February 6, 1911. His father, John Edward Reagan, was an Irish-American shoe salesman. His mother, Nelle Wilson Reagan, was of English and Scottish ancestry. Neither parent had more than an elementary school educa-

tion. Ronald had one brother, Neil, who was two years older. Neil picked up the nickname Moon, and Ronald was called Dutch.

Reagan's father often moved the family around the state in search of a better-paying job. But life in the small towns of Illinois was pleasant. "My existence turned into one of those rare Huck Finn–Tom Sawyer idylls," Reagan recalled in his autobiography, *Where's the Rest of Me?* "Those were the days when I learned the riches of rags."

Dixon, a small town to which the family moved when he was 9, was the place where Reagan got most of his schooling. He was not an outstanding student. But his interests in drama, sports, and politics began early. His mother gave dramatic readings before clubs and in prisons and hospitals, and he got his first exposure to acting before he started school. He began to play football— one of the great loves of his life—before he was 10, in impromptu neighborhood games.

"There was no field; no lines, no goal. Simply grass, the ball, and a mob of excited youngsters," he later wrote. "Those were the happiest times of my life." Reagan graduated from that kind of football to action as a guard and end on the Dixon High School team. He also participated in basketball and track, acted in school plays, and was president of the student body. During most of his high school and college summers, he worked as a lifeguard.

After his high school graduation in 1928, Reagan enrolled at Eureka College, a small school in Eureka, Illinois. He majored in economics; joined his school's football, track, and swimming teams; and acted in school plays. He washed dishes at his fraternity house and saved money from summer jobs to help pay his expenses. His grades were not exceptional, but he earned acceptable marks through "quick studies" before tests. He served a year as president of the student body.

As a freshman, Reagan took part in a student strike that resulted in the resignation of the college president, who had proposed cutting back the curriculum and the teaching staff because of a shortage of funds. Reagan made the main speech at a rally that won support for the strike from nearly all the students. He later said that he learned then what it was like to succeed with an audience. His skill with audiences was to be a major factor in his successes in later life.

▶ HIS ACTING CAREER

Reagan earned a B.A. degree from Eureka in 1932, at a time when the Depression had left many people without jobs. He spent one last summer as a lifeguard. Then he set out to obtain a job as a radio announcer. He won a tryout for a job announcing football games at WOC in Davenport, Iowa, not far from Dixon. His tryout consisted of making up a play-by-play broadcast for an imaginary football game. He did well enough, and he was signed on. That job led to work at WOC's larger affiliate, WHO in Des Moines. By the time he was 25, he was one of the top sports broadcasters in the Middle West.

In 1937, Reagan traveled with the Chicago Cubs to their spring training camp near Los Angeles, California. While there he managed to obtain a screen test from Warner Brothers, and he was offered an acting contract. He quickly accepted. Reagan's movie career spanned more than 20 years and over 50 movies. His most successful roles were in *Knute Rockne—All American* in 1940 and in *King's Row* in 1941. In *Knute Rockne,* Reagan played star halfback George Gipp, who died imploring his coach to have his teammates "win one for the Gipper."

In 1942, during World War II, Reagan entered the Army as a second lieutenant. He was disqualified for combat duty because of poor eyesight, and he spent the next four years making military training films. He then returned to the motion picture industry. Until this time, Reagan had been a Democrat and had supported many liberal causes. But after the war his views became more conser-

Ronald Reagan when he was a young child (*right foreground*), with his parents and his older brother, Neil.

In the movie *Knute Rockne—All American*, Reagan drew on his love of football to play star halfback George Gipp.

As governor of California in 1967, Ronald Reagan signs a bill into law. Members of the state legislature look on.

children—Patricia (Patti), born in 1952, and Ronald, born in 1958.

▶ GOVERNOR OF CALIFORNIA

Reagan's entry into politics was hastened by a speech he gave in October, 1964, on behalf of the Republican presidential candidate, Senator Barry Goldwater of Arizona. The nationally televised speech, ''A Time for Choosing,'' won Reagan a national following. It was credited with drawing more political contributions than any other speech in the nation's history. The speech also brought Reagan to the attention of powerful figures in the Republican Party. They urged him to seek the governorship of California.

Reagan announced his candidacy early in January, 1966. He easily won the Republican primary. In the election, he faced Edmund G. (Pat) Brown, who had been a popular Democratic governor for eight years. Reagan was critical of government spending and welfare payments that he believed were too high. He won by nearly 1,000,000 votes. Four years later, Reagan easily defeated California State Assembly speaker Jesse Unruh for a second term. He served as governor through 1974.

As governor, Reagan tried to keep government spending down. But his efforts were not always successful. Early in his first term, he was forced to seek a large income tax increase. But later, he was able to sponsor large rebates in property taxes. California's spending increased considerably during Reagan's two terms. But it was generally thought that he kept costs below what they might have been.

Reagan fought with the state legislature through much of his first term, but he learned to deal with it effectively. He regarded as his biggest accomplishment as governor the passage of welfare reform legislation. This legislation cut down the number of people

vative. This change was caused in part, he later said, by government inefficiency he had witnessed in the Army.

Reagan served as president of the Screen Actors Guild, the labor union for actors and actresses, from 1947 to 1952. And he became a strong opponent of Communism. In 1947 he went to Washington, D.C., to testify before the House Committee on Un-American Activities about Communist influence in Hollywood.

By 1954, Reagan was less in demand for leading-man roles in films. He accepted a job with the General Electric Company, as the leading personality on the firm's television show, ''General Electric Theater.'' Between shows, he traveled around the nation for the company, making speeches about the dangers of big government and the blessings of free enterprise. When ''General Electric Theater'' went off the air in 1962, Reagan became host of another show, ''Death Valley Days.'' Meanwhile, the high salaries he earned in movies and on television, together with real estate investments, had made him wealthy. He had married Jane Wyman, an actress, in 1940. They had two children—a daughter, Maureen, born in 1941, and a son, Michael, who was adopted as an infant in 1945. The marriage ended in divorce in 1948. Four years later, Reagan married another actress, Nancy Davis. They had two

IMPORTANT DATES IN THE LIFE OF RONALD WILSON REAGAN	
1911	Born in Tampico, Illinois, February 6.
1932	Graduated from Eureka College, Eureka, Illinois.
1937	Acted in his first film, *Love Is on the Air*.
1942–1946	Served in the United States Army.
1947–1952	Served as president of the Screen Actors Guild.
1966–1974	Served as governor of California.
1980	Elected president of the United States.

getting welfare benefits in the state, while increasing payments to those considered truly needy. The law meant substantial savings for California taxpayers. Reagan also increased the budget of California's state college and university system. But he strongly opposed the student demonstrations of the late 1960's.

► CAMPAIGNING FOR THE PRESIDENCY

Reagan first sought the Republican presidential nomination in 1968. He presented himself as a spokesman for conservative elements in the party. But his effort was too little and too late. Richard M. Nixon was nominated and eventually won the office. In 1976, Reagan waged a strong campaign for the nomination. But he lost narrowly to Gerald R. Ford, who had become president when Nixon resigned in 1973. The Democratic candidate, Jimmy Carter, won the 1976 election.

Reagan started the 1980 campaign not long after his 1976 fight had been lost. He called on his skills as a speaker to win support. And his views seemed to reflect growing conservatism in the country. His hard work and that of his staff paid off when he won the nomination in an overwhelming victory. His nearest opponent was George Bush, a former ambassador to the United Nations and for-

mer director of the Central Intelligence Agency. He was chosen as Reagan's vice-presidential running mate. Another contender for the Republican nomination, Representative John B. Anderson of Illinois, ran against both Reagan and Carter as an independent candidate.

In the campaign, Reagan took solidly conservative positions. He favored reducing total government spending while increasing the amount spent on national defense. He also supported large tax cuts and state or local control of programs such as welfare. And he felt that the United States should take firmer stands against Communism and in support of friendly governments.

Reagan was sometimes criticized for making general statements instead of offering specific solutions to the country's problems. Some of his critics said that his call for a stronger foreign policy might be seen as warlike by other countries. But Reagan campaigned hard. He presented himself well in a televised debate against Carter. And he found widespread support for his positions. He won the election with 489 electoral votes, to 49 for Carter, and his share of the popular vote exceeded Carter's by 10 percent.

JAMES O. BELL
Assistant National Editor
The *Los Angeles Times*

The Reagans wave to supporters at the 1980 Republican convention. From left: son Ronald; Patti; Nancy and Ronald Reagan; Michael with his wife, Colleen, and son, Cameron; and Maureen.

In *The Habitant Farm* (1856), Cornelius Krieghoff painted a picture of life on a Quebec farm.

NATIONAL GALLERY OF CANADA

The National Gallery of Canada, in Ottawa, is a public museum, owned by the people of Canada. It houses the world's largest single collection of Canadian art, but works of art from Europe and Asia are also represented there.

The early history of the National Gallery is linked with the founding of the Royal Canadian Academy of Arts in 1880. The Royal Canadian Academy was begun with the help of the Marquis of Lorne, the governor-general of Canada, and his wife, Princess Louise, a daughter of Queen Victoria. The academy, in turn, established the gallery.

In spite of a snowstorm, a large group of people arrived by sleigh to see the gallery's first exhibition. It was made up of seventeen works of art donated by artists who were members of the Royal Canadian Academy.

In 1913, an act of Parliament recognized the National Gallery and stated that its purpose was to encourage public interest in art and to promote Canadian art. The National Gallery was declared one of the National Museums of Canada in 1968.

▶ THE COLLECTIONS

Over the years, the collections of the National Gallery have grown steadily. They now include more than 30,000 works of art —paintings, sculpture, prints, drawings, decorative art objects, and photographs. More than one half of them are by Canadian artists.

In developing the Canadian collection, the curators look for works of art that will help explain the growth and history of art in Canada. The collection includes works by such well-known 19th- and 20th-century artists as Antoine Sébastien Plamondon, Cornelius Krieghoff, Emily Carr, Paul Émile Borduas, Alex Colville, and Tom Thomson and the group of Toronto painters known as the Group of Seven. The best and most imaginative works by Canadian artists of today are also represented.

Works from other countries, especially countries from which Canadians have come, help Canadians trace the traditions of their own art. The curators of the European collection have chosen works that show how art

Above: *Portrait of Soeur Saint-Alphonse* (1841), by Antoine Sébastien Plamondon. Right: *The Jack Pine* (1916–17), by Tom Thomson, a painter of Canada's rugged north.

has developed from the Middle Ages to the present. Works by masters such as Bernini, Rembrandt, Jordaens, Turner, and Cézanne are included. Other collections include art from Asian countries, fine-art photographs, and examples of the decorative arts such as silver objects and fine furniture.

Some works of art are purchased by the National Gallery, but many others are donated. Two important donations are the Douglas Duncan collection of Canadian prints and drawings and the Henry Birks collection of Canadian silver. The Heeramaneck collection of South Asian art is another notable gift. It includes stone and wood sculpture and miniature paintings from India.

Parts of the National Gallery's collection are always on exhibit. About 20 special exhibitions are prepared each year. Many of them are sent on tour across Canada. Some are also shown in other countries, including Britain, France, Italy, and the United States.

▶ SPECIAL SERVICES

Because many works of art become fragile as they get older and can be easily damaged, the National Gallery has established a special laboratory, the Restoration and Conservation Laboratory. The experts in this laboratory, who are called conservators, perform scientific tests on each piece of art to determine the best kind of care and treatment. The conservators also offer advice to other museums and galleries on handling their collections. And they provide private owners with information on caring for their works of art.

The Reference Library of the National Gallery maintains records of all publications on Canadian art. These records are a valuable tool for researchers and art historians. In its Documentation Centre, the library also keeps up-to-date records of the life and work of Canadian artists.

The Education Department of the National Gallery helps visitors understand and appreciate what they see. Each year thousands of people are given conducted tours. Many others attend lectures and gallery talks. The Education Department also has special films and programs for children.

LORNA JOHNSON
Education Services
National Gallery of Canada

The Capitol dominates Washington's skyline. Beyond are the buildings of the Supreme Court (*far left*), the Library of Congress, and the offices of the House of Representatives.

WASHINGTON, D.C.

Washington, D.C.—with its long, tree-lined avenues, white marble buildings, and many parks—looks more spacious and handsome than many United States cities. One reason for this is that Washington was designed from the beginning to be a capital city.

In 1790, the U.S. Congress decided that the new federal government should have its capital in a federal district—a place that is not part of any state. George Washington selected the site, and the name "District of Columbia" was chosen in honor of Christopher Columbus. The district occupies an area of 174 square kilometers (67 square miles) on the northeastern shore of the Potomac River, between the states of Maryland and Virginia.

As the capital and political center of the United States, Washington today is one of the country's most important cities. It is the city where the national legislators meet to make laws, where the president executes (carries out) the laws, and where the country's highest court meets to judge questions about the laws.

▶ GOVERNMENT CITY

Washington's most important buildings are those of the federal government. They are big buildings, but most are not more than seven or eight stories tall. Congress decided in the early 1900's that there would be no skyscrapers in Washington.

The impressive Capitol building dominates the skyline of Washington. Standing on a hill, it looks out over the length and breadth of the city. The Capitol divides the city into four sections—Northeast, Northwest, Southeast, and Southwest. Wide avenues radiate from the Capitol like spokes of a great wheel. The streets that run north and south are numbered. Those that run east and west are lettered. Many of the avenues that run diagonally across the city are named after states. Among them is Pennsylvania Avenue, where the White House is situated.

On Capitol Hill

The U.S. Congress meets in the Capitol to write laws and to decide how to gather and spend federal taxes. George Washington laid the cornerstone for the building in 1793. The House of Representatives and the Senate first met in two small buildings separated by a passageway. These two buildings were rebuilt in 1814 after British troops burned the Capitol in the War of 1812. A rotunda with a wooden dome replaced the passageway.

The old House and Senate chambers are now in the middle of a much bigger building, completed, more or less, in 1865. Congress needed more and more space as new states were created after the Revolutionary War and these states elected senators and representatives. Marble wings were added on the north and the south sides of the building in the 1850's. The Senate now meets in the chamber on the north side, and the House in the larger chamber on the south.

At the same time, Congress decided to replace the small wooden dome of the old Capitol with the present enormous cast-iron dome, designed by the architect Thomas U. Walter. The dome rises to a height of nearly 88 meters (288 feet). It is capped by a statue of Freedom, by the sculptor Thomas Crawford, which was set in place in 1862. Around the base of the dome are 36 columns—one for each state in the Union at the time the dome was completed. Beneath the dome, on the walls of the great rotunda, are paintings of eight episodes in American history. Above these paintings are other historic scenes. Nearby, visitors can see the National Statuary Hall, which has some 40 statues of such famous Americans as Daniel Webster, Robert E. Lee, and Sam Houston. One can also visit the old Senate, House, and Supreme Court chambers, as well as the houses of Congress when they are in session.

Members of Congress have offices in white marble buildings to the north and south of the Capitol grounds. They can ride a special subway train between their offices and the Capitol. They also have restaurants, barber shops, and their own post office.

In 1874, Congress asked Frederick Law Olmsted to design the U.S. Capitol grounds. He planned the East Plaza, where many presidents have been inaugurated, and the great lawn framed by trees on the slope of the hill below the Capitol. He also suggested the terrace structure around the west side of the building, which was built in the 1890's. This terrace gives a sweeping view of the whole city. In 1961 a new east front was added to the center of the building.

The Supreme Court began to meet in the Capitol in 1801, in a crypt in the basement. Later it moved to a separate wing and, in 1935, to its own building on the east side of the Capitol. Cass Gilbert designed the building. It was constructed of white marble, with a portico of Corinthian columns.

For over 70 years, the Library of Congress was also housed in the Capitol, in a room in the west front. In 1897 it moved to a huge gray stone building with a low copper dome, across the Capitol grounds to the east. A second building, the Jefferson Building, was built in 1939, and a third, the Madison Building, opened in 1980.

The Library of Congress is a research library for Congress, the federal government, and the American people. Founded in 1800, it is the largest library in the United States, with more than 75,000,000 books, newspapers, manuscripts, prints, photographs, musical compositions, and other items. Because it administers the copyright laws, it receives copies of all works that are to be copyrighted. It has one of the world's best rare book rooms, with especially valuable Chinese, Russian, and Japanese books. There, one can see one of three known perfect copies of the Gutenberg Bible; an original copy of the Bill of Rights; the first two drafts of the Gettysburg Address, in Lincoln's handwriting; and Jefferson's rough draft of the Declaration of Independence.

Along the Mall

The National Mall (or simply the Mall) is a strip of open parkland stretching from the Capitol westward to the Lincoln Memorial. Many of the most interesting and important government buildings—including the National Archives, the Bureau of Engraving and Printing, and the Federal Bureau of Investigation—are located near the Mall.

The White House, begun in 1792, was the first of Washington's public buildings to be completed. Every president except George

Washington has lived there. The building also houses the president's offices and rooms where guests are entertained. An article on the White House appears in Volume WXYZ.

The Smithsonian Institution began in 1829 as a small collection of scientific specimens, costumes, books, paintings, machinery, and other items housed in a little brownstone castle on the Mall. Since then, the collection has grown to include millions of items, most of them housed in buildings lining both sides of the Mall from the Capitol to the Washington Monument. An article on the Smithsonian Institution appears in Volume S.

The Smithsonian Castle's first neighbor on the Mall was the Washington Monument. The cornerstone was laid on July 4, 1848. But it took 40 years to build the monument to its full height of about 170 meters (560 feet). Work was halted in 1855 when the monument was far from complete. Congress authorized more money in 1876, and construction was finished in 1884. The monument is a hollow shaft of marble and granite. More than 1,000,000 visitors a year ride in the elevator in the monument or climb the 898 steps inside the monument to enjoy a sweeping view of Washington from the top.

The Lincoln Memorial, on the shore of the Potomac River, was dedicated in 1922. Henry Bacon designed it as a Greek temple of white marble. A statue of Lincoln seated, by Daniel Chester French, is inside. The statue looks out over a long reflecting pool to the Washington Monument and the Capitol beyond. French captured Lincoln's thoughtful sadness and strong, lined face. The memorial is particularly beautiful at night.

The Jefferson Memorial, designed by John Russell Pope, is a circular marble building

The Washington Monument. It honors George Washington, the first president of the United States.

similar in style to buildings that Jefferson designed himself. It was dedicated in 1943. Inside is a huge bronze statue of Jefferson standing. Behind the statue are four stone panels carved with excerpts from Jefferson's most famous writings. They include the Declaration of Independence.

Other Places of Interest

Across the Potomac River from the Lincoln Memorial lies Arlington National Cemetery, with the graves of many soldiers and sailors and their leaders. A memorial in Arlington Cemetery contains the graves of President John F. Kennedy and his brother Robert F. Kennedy. Nearby are a memorial amphitheater and the Tomb of the Unknown Soldier, which honors three nameless U.S. servicemen. (The article UNKNOWN SOLDIER appears in Volume UV.) Overlooking Arlington National Cemetery is Arlington House (long known as the Custis-Lee Mansion). The Civil War general Robert E. Lee lived there until he became commander in chief of the Confederate Army in 1861.

More than 140 nations now have permanent representatives in the capital. The embassies are housed mainly in great mansions along Massachusetts Avenue, from Dupont

The Supreme Court Building, completed in 1935. Over the entrance are the words "Equal Justice Under Law."

Circle to Wisconsin Avenue. The embassies are remarkably elegant and often provide examples of the arts, crafts, and traditions of the nations they represent. One of the largest is the British embassy. Washington is also the headquarters of the World Bank, the International Monetary Fund, and the Organization of American States.

▶ EDUCATION AND CULTURE

Washington has six universities and several colleges. Georgetown University, founded in 1789 by a Jesuit order, is the oldest Catholic college in the United States. Howard University was founded by the federal government shortly after the Civil War as a school of higher learning for freed slaves. Now it is a university with an international enrollment. George Washington University was founded in 1821, Catholic University in 1887, and the American University in 1893. The University of the District of Columbia was formed by the merger in 1975 of the Washington Technical Institute, Federal City College, and Miner College. Gallaudet College, the world's first college for the deaf, was founded in 1857.

Some of the country's leading scholarly research and scientific institutions are in Washington. The city is also the headquarters of the National Geographic Society, the National Education Association, and the American Red Cross. The Folger Shakespeare Library, with its Elizabethan theater, has one of the world's finest collections of Shakespearean material. Dumbarton Oaks is Harvard University's center for Byzantine, Pre-Columbian, and early Christian culture.

In 1971, the John F. Kennedy Center for the Performing Arts was completed, just upstream from the Lincoln Memorial. The center provides Washington with a theater, concert hall, and opera house under one roof. It also houses the American Film Institute.

Many other theaters can be found in the Washington area. Among the most important are the Arena Stage and the Kreeger Theater, which opened in the 1960's in Southwest Washington. One of the oldest theaters is the National Theater. Ford's Theater, which closed after Lincoln was shot there in 1865, reopened in 1965. There are also many summer theaters near Washington, including Wolf Trap Farm Park for the Performing Arts near Vienna, Virginia.

Washington has many fine galleries and museums, including the National Gallery of Art, the Museum of African Art, and the Renwick, Freer, Corcoran, and Phillips galleries. An article on the National Gallery of Art appears in Volume N.

▶ THE PEOPLE AND WAY OF LIFE

Washington is the center of a metropolitan area with a population of about 3,000,000. One third of the workers who live in or around Washington are employed by the federal government—helping the Congress, the Supreme Court, or the president and the many federal departments, agencies, and commissions to do their work. Many live in the city's residential neighborhoods—Capitol Hill, Georgetown, Woodley Park, Dupont Circle, Kalorama, Shaw, Foggy Bottom, and Cleveland Park. Many commute to the city from suburbs in Maryland and Virginia. And some travel out from the city—to agencies such as the National Institutes of Health in Bethesda, Maryland, and the Pentagon in Arlington, Virginia—because the activities

The statue in the Lincoln Memorial. The sculptor Daniel Chester French captured Lincoln's thoughtful sadness.

The Jefferson Memorial. In the spring, cherry blossoms frame the Tidal Basin, next to the memorial.

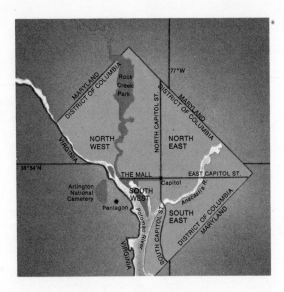

of the capital have spread into the neighboring states.

A number of people work for business organizations, labor unions, law firms, and professional, cultural, and scientific organizations that have offices in Washington. Many others work in hotels, restaurants, and stores that serve the millions of visitors who come every year to tour Washington or to deal with the federal government. Still others work in real estate and construction. But compared to other cities, Washington has fewer people who work in factories.

Like many large cities, Washington is a home for people of different nationalities and races. Today about 70 percent of the people are black. Blacks have always played an important role in the life of the city. Black slaves had a part in the building of the U.S. Capitol. Benjamin Banneker, a self-taught black mathematician and astronomer, was an assistant surveyor who helped to lay out the streets of Washington. Slaves were sold in Lafayette Square across from the White House until 1850. Their masters in the surrounding areas allowed them to be hired out. Often they could save the money they earned to buy their freedom. In 1840 there were twice as many free blacks as slaves living in the city. They were seamstresses, gardeners, and construction workers. Some went from being cooks to running restaurants.

After the Civil War, many freed slaves went to Washington. Some of them found

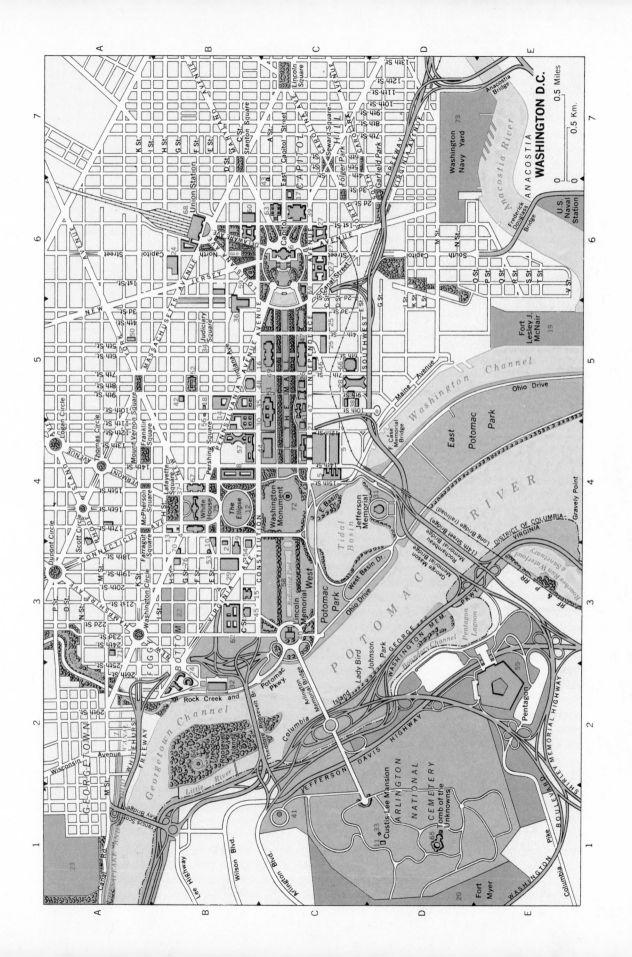

WASHINGTON D.C.

homes in new neighborhoods, such as Anacostia. For almost 20 years after the war, they had freedom to get an education, participate in government, and become successful business people, lawyers, doctors, and architects. But from 1890 to the 1950's, segregation laws denied equal opportunity to the district's black residents. Despite these handicaps, Dunbar High School, the Howard Theater, and Howard University gave some blacks opportunities to be successful. Ralph Bunche, a graduate of Dunbar High School, won the 1950 Nobel peace prize for his work as a deputy secretary-general to the United Nations. Entertainers such as Ella Fitzgerald and Pearl Bailey were discovered as major talents in Washington. The poet Paul Lawrence Dunbar lived near Howard University.

Other groups have had an important part in the city's life as well. The Chinese first came in the 1880's. They settled at first along Pennsylvania Avenue, between the White House and the Capitol. In the 1930's they moved to H Street between 6th and 8th streets, Northwest. This part of town, called Chinatown, has many small Chinese restaurants, grocery stores, and specialty shops.

In the late 1960's and 1970's other groups became important in Washington life. Among them were the Hispanics and the Vietnamese, who settled in Washington as well as in its suburbs.

Transportation and Communication

Washington's impressive Union Station is a terminal for Amtrak trains. It is also a visitors' center, where tourists can get information about the city. The city is served by three airports—Dulles International Airport, Washington National Airport, and the Baltimore-Washington International Airport. After it opened in 1976, the Metro subway system, with its impressive stations and quiet trains, became a tourist attraction. It supplements the Metro bus system and several other bus lines that come into the city.

Washington has two daily newspapers, the *Washington Post* and the *Washington Star*. It also has several television stations, including public television, and more than a dozen radio stations. One of the largest publishers in the world has its home in Washington. This is the Government Printing Office. One of its most important jobs is the day-to-day printing of the Congressional Record, the account of the proceedings of Congress.

Recreation

Washington and its surrounding suburbs are fortunate in having many parks. Plans for the Mall, Rock Creek Park, and the parklands along the Anacostia and the Potomac rivers were set forth by the Senate Park Commission in 1901. Much of the land for the park around the Lincoln and Jefferson memorials was reclaimed from the Potomac River in the early 20th century. Washington's famous cherry trees were a gift from the city of Tokyo, Japan. They bloom in April around the Tidal Basin, near the Jefferson Memorial.

Rock Creek Park is a wide band of woodland that meanders through Northwest Washington. The National Zoological Park, part of the Smithsonian Institution, is in Rock Creek Park. Landscaped parkways along the Potomac River lead south to George Washington's home, Mount Vernon, and north to the Great Falls of the Potomac. Theodore Roosevelt Island, a wooded sanctuary in the Potomac River, has been set aside as a national memorial.

Sports are also a part of the city's life. The Washington Redskins of the National Football League play home games at Robert F. Kennedy Stadium, east of the Capitol. There are also professional basketball and hockey teams in the Washington metropolitan area.

▶ HISTORY AND GOVERNMENT

The city of Washington was established in 1791 on land donated by Maryland and Virginia. The site was a swampy tract, in a bowl formed by low hills to the north and south. But it was near two port cities—Alexandria, Virginia, and Georgetown, which merged with Washington in 1895. Virginia grew impatient with the slow growth of the capital city, and its land was returned in 1846.

George Washington, who chose the site, also chose the designer of the new city— Major Pierre Charles L'Enfant (1754–1825). He was a brilliant French engineer and architect who had fought in the Revolutionary War under General Lafayette.

L'Enfant's plans for the capital were dar-

Elegant row houses, carefully restored, are found in Georgetown, a residential area in Northwest Washington.

The Watergate Complex, near the Potomac River, is among the most striking of the city's newer buildings.

ing, imaginative, and difficult for even Washington and Jefferson to understand fully. For the first time in history, a brand new capital city was being planned on an empty site. L'Enfant wanted the city spread out over a large area. It would be connected by both a checkerboard pattern of streets and a radiating pattern of avenues, such as could be found in Paris or Rome. He wanted to create a capital magnificent enough to grace a great nation. Jefferson had earlier thought that the city should be laid out in square blocks, as were many later American cities. L'Enfant quarreled with Washington and Jefferson, and he was dismissed. Major Andrew Ellicott, with Benjamin Banneker, carried out a simplified version of L'Enfant's plan.

The development of the city was uneven. L'Enfant's plan seemed lost as a red brick city arose out of the swamp in the 1800's. Hot, humid summers and nearby swamps brought disease—malaria and yellow fever. For the first 100 years, Washington grew very slowly.

Congress set aside Washington's elected form of government in 1871 because it considered the earlier forms of government corrupt and inefficient. This meant that the people of Washington, not being citizens of any state, did not have the right to vote in any election. Government officials were appointed by the president.

Alexander Robey Shepherd, who was appointed governor of the District of Columbia in the 1870's, managed to get the streets paved, shade trees planted, and sewer pipes laid. But he bankrupted the city. Congress assumed the debts and then took over the government of the city for the next 100 years.

The Senate Park Commission, in 1901, revived the spirit of L'Enfant's concept and planned for most of the monumental buildings and memorials in Washington today. After World War I and World War II, the city grew tremendously. In the 1930's most of the huge buildings along the south side of Pennsylvania Avenue between the Capitol and the White House were built, forming what is now called the Federal Triangle. Since then, a new business district has been built in the area of L'Enfant Plaza to the south of the Mall.

The Twenty-third Amendment to the Constitution, ratified in 1961, gave residents of the District of Columbia the right to vote for president and vice-president. The district was allotted three electoral votes. In 1970, the district gained the right to elect a nonvoting delegate to the House of Representatives. Four years later, Congress gave district residents the right to elect a mayor and a 13-member city council. But Congress retained control of the budget and the right to set aside council action.

Thanks to air conditioning and improved transportation, Washington has overcome some of its disadvantages as a site for a capital. It is now an international city, and it has developed cultural as well as governmental and private institutions to match its ever-expanding role.

CHARLES CAPEN McLAUGHLIN
American University

347

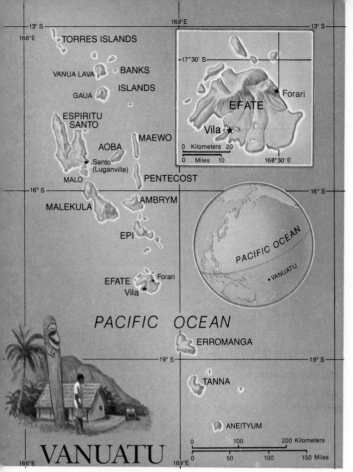

cessed for export. Meat and fish processing, tourism, banking, and the manufacture of building materials and soft drinks are other industries. Manganese is mined on Efate.

▶ **THE LAND**

Vanuatu is a Y-shaped chain of coral and volcanic islands. It includes twelve large islands, where most of the people live, and about 60 smaller ones. Most of the islands are heavily forested. Temperatures range from 16 to 32°C (60 to 90°F). Annual rainfall averages 2,310 millimeters (91 inches).

▶ **HISTORY AND GOVERNMENT**

A short-lived Spanish settlement was founded on Espiritu Santo in 1606. French and British explorers visited the islands in the late 1700's, and French and British settlers soon followed. Joint French and British rule of the islands was formally established in 1906. Separate schools, hospitals, and churches were set up for speakers of English and French. The islands were a major Allied base during World War II. The area was the setting of James Michener's book *Tales of the South Pacific*.

Vanuatu became independent on July 30, 1980. Shortly before independence, rebels on Espiritu Santo and Tanna tried unsuccessfully to break away from the other islands.

HAROLD M. ROSS
St. Norbert College

VANUATU

Vanuatu, long known as New Hebrides, is an island nation in the Pacific Ocean, east of Australia. It became independent in 1980, after years of rule by Britain and France.

▶ **THE PEOPLE AND THE ECONOMY**

Most of the people of Vanuatu are descendants of the original inhabitants of the area, who are known as Melanesians. English and French are the official languages. Bislama is the simplified local language spoken by almost everyone. Many people are Christians. Some belong to various cults.

Education is not compulsory, but most children attend primary school. There are few secondary schools. Malapoa College, in Vila, offers teacher-training courses.

Most of the people live along the coasts. For food, they grow yams, taro, manioc, sweet potatoes, and breadfruit. They also raise cattle and pigs and catch fish. Coconuts, cacao, and coffee are grown and pro-

---

FACTS AND FIGURES

REPUBLIC OF VANUATU is the official name of the country.

CAPITAL: Vila.

LOCATION: Southwest Pacific Ocean. **Latitude**—15° 15′ S to 20° 12′ S. **Longitude**—166° 55′ E to 199° 46′ E.

AREA: 14,800 km² (5,750 sq mi).

POPULATION: 113,000 (estimate).

LANGUAGE: English, French, Bislama.

GOVERNMENT: Republic. **Head of state**—president. **Head of government**—prime minister. **International co-operation**—Commonwealth of Nations.

ECONOMY: Agricultural products—coconuts, yams, taro, manioc, sweet potatoes, breadfruit, cacao, coffee. **Industries and products**—copra, processed meat, fishing and fish processing, tourism, banking, building materials, soft drinks, handicrafts. **Chief minerals**—manganese. **Chief exports**—copra, fish, processed meat, cocoa, coffee. **Chief imports**—food and beverages, metal products, oil, machinery, ships, vehicles. **Monetary unit**—New Hebrides franc.

INTERNATIONAL STATISTICAL SUPPLEMENT

Independent Nations of the World

The United States

Senate

House of Representatives

Cabinet

Supreme Court

Governors

Canada

INDEPENDENT NATIONS OF THE WORLD

NATION	CAPITAL	AREA (in sq mi)	POPULATION (estimate)	GOVERNMENT
Afghanistan	Kabul	250,000	15,500,000	Babrak Karmal—president
Albania	Tirana	11,100	2,700,000	Enver Hoxha—communist party secretary Mehmet Shehu—premier
Algeria	Algiers	919,593	19,200,000	Benjedid Chadli—president
Angola	Luanda	481,351	6,900,000	José Eduardo dos Santos—president
Argentina	Buenos Aires	1,068,297	27,100,000	Jorge Rafael Videla—president
Australia	Canberra	2,967,895	14,400,000	Malcolm Fraser—prime minister
Austria	Vienna	32,374	7,500,000	Rudolf Kirchschläger—president Bruno Kreisky—chancellor
Bahamas	Nassau	5,380	230,000	Lynden O. Pindling—prime minister
Bahrain	Manama	240	360,000	Isa ibn Sulman al-Khalifa—head of government
Bangladesh	Dacca	55,598	88,000,000	Ziaur Rahman—president
Barbados	Bridgetown	168	250,000	J. M. G. Adams—prime minister
Belgium	Brussels	11,781	9,900,000	Baudouin I—king Wilfried Martens—premier
Benin (Dahomey)	Porto-Novo	43,483	3,600,000	Mathieu Kerekou—president
Bhutan	Thimbu	18,147	1,300,000	Jigme Singye Wangchuk—king
Bolivia	La Paz Sucre	424,163	5,400,000	Luis García Meza—president
Botswana	Gaborone	231,804	800,000	Quett Masire—president
Brazil	Brasília	3,286,478	119,000,000	João Figueiredo—president
Bulgaria	Sofia	42,823	8,900,000	Todor Zhivkov—communist party secretary Stanko Todorov—premier
Burma	Rangoon	261,217	33,000,000	U Ne Win—president U Maung Maung Kha—prime minister
Burundi	Bujumbura	10,747	4,300,000	Jean-Baptiste Bagaza—president
Cambodia (Kampuchea)	Pnompenh	69,898	5,000,000	Heng Samrin—president
Cameroon	Yaoundé	183,569	8,200,000	Ahmadou Ahidjo—president
Canada	Ottawa	3,851,809	23,900,000	Pierre Elliott Trudeau—prime minister
Cape Verde	Praia	1,557	320,000	Aristides Pereira—president
Central African Republic	Bangui	240,535	2,400,000	David Dacko—president
Chad	N'Djemena	495,754	4,400,000	Goukouni Oueddei—president

NATION	CAPITAL	AREA (in sq mi)	POPULATION (estimate)	GOVERNMENT
Chile	Santiago	292,257	11,100,000	Augusto Pinochet Ugarte—president
China	Peking	3,705,390	975,000,000	Hua Guofeng—communist party chairman Zhao Ziyang—premier
Colombia	Bogotá	439,736	27,200,000	Julio César Turbay Ayala—president
Comoros	Moroni	838	400,000	Ahmed Abdallah—president
Congo	Brazzaville	132,047	1,500,000	Denis Sassou-Nguessou—president
Costa Rica	San José	19,575	2,200,000	Rodrigo Carazo Odio—president
Cuba	Havana	44,218	9,800,000	Fidel Castro—president
Cyprus	Nicosia	3,572	620,000	Spyros Kyprianou—president
Czechoslovakia	Prague	49,370	15,200,000	Gustáv Husák—communist party secretary and president Lubomir Štrougal—premier
Denmark	Copenhagen	16,629	5,100,000	Margrethe II—queen Anker Jorgensen—premier
Djibouti	Djibouti	8,494	120,000	Hassan Gouled—president
Dominica	Roseau	290	81,000	Mary Eugenia Charles—prime minister
Dominican Republic	Santo Domingo	18,816	5,400,000	Antonio Guzmán—president
Ecuador	Quito	109,483	8,100,000	Jaime Roldós Aguilera—president
Egypt	Cairo	386,660	41,000,000	Anwar el-Sadat—president
El Salvador	San Salvador	8,124	4,500,000	J. Napoleón Duarte—president
Equatorial Guinea	Malabo	10,831	360,000	Teodoro Obiang Nguema—president
Ethiopia	Addis Ababa	471,777	30,400,000	Mengistu Haile Mariam—head of state
Fiji	Suva	7,055	620,000	Ratu Sir Kamisese Mara—prime minister
Finland	Helsinki	130,120	4,800,000	Urho K. Kekkonen—president Mauno Koivisto—premier
France	Paris	211,207	53,500,000	Valéry Giscard d'Estaing—president Raymond Barre—premier
Gabon	Libreville	103,346	540,000	Albert B. Bongo—president
Gambia	Banjul	4,361	600,000	Sir Dauda K. Jawara—president
Germany (East)	East Berlin	41,768	16,800,000	Erich Honecker—communist party secretary Willi Stoph—premier
Germany (West)	Bonn	95,976	61,500,000	Karl Carstens—president Helmut Schmidt—chancellor
Ghana	Accra	92,099	11,500,000	Hilla Limann—president
Greece	Athens	50,944	9,400,000	Constantine Caramanlis—president George John Rallis—premier
Grenada	St. George's	133	110,000	Maurice Bishop—prime minister

NATION	CAPITAL	AREA (in sq mi)	POPULATION (estimate)	GOVERNMENT
Guatemala	Guatemala City	42,042	7,000,000	Romeo Lucas García—president
Guinea	Conakry	94,926	4,900,000	Sékou Touré—president
Guinea-Bissau	Bissau	13,948	780,000	Joâo Bernardo Vieira—head of government
Guyana	Georgetown	83,000	870,000	Forbes Burnham—president
Haiti	Port-au-Prince	10,714	4,900,000	Jean-Claude Duvalier—president
Honduras	Tegucigalpa	43,277	3,700,000	Policarpo Paz García—head of state
Hungary	Budapest	35,919	10,700,000	János Kádár—communist party secretary György Lazar—premier
Iceland	Reykjavik	39,768	230,000	Vigdis Finnbogadottir—president Gunnar Thoroddsen—prime minister
India	New Delhi	1,269,340	651,000,000	Neelam Sanjiva Reddy—president Indira Gandhi—prime minister
Indonesia	Jakarta	735,269	143,000,000	Suharto—president
Iran	Teheran	636,294	37,000,000	Ruhollah Khomeini—religious leader Abolhassan Bani-Sadr—president Mohammed Ali Rajai—prime minister
Iraq	Baghdad	167,925	12,800,000	Saddam Hussein—president
Ireland	Dublin	27,136	3,400,000	Patrick Hillery—president Charles J. Haughey—prime minister
Israel	Jerusalem	8,019	3,900,000	Yitzhak Navon—president Menahem Begin—prime minister
Italy	Rome	116,303	57,000,000	Alessandro Pertini—president Arnaldo Forlani—premier
Ivory Coast	Abidjan	124,503	7,900,000	Félix Houphouët-Boigny—president
Jamaica	Kingston	4,244	2,200,000	Edward P. G. Seaga—prime minister
Japan	Tokyo	143,737	116,000,000	Hirohito—emperor Zenko Suzuki—premier
Jordan	Amman	37,738	3,100,000	Hussein I—king Mudar Badran—premier
Kenya	Nairobi	224,959	15,300,000	Daniel Arap Moi—president
Kiribati	Tarawa	264	58,000	Ieremia Tabai—president
Korea (North)	Pyongyang	46,540	17,500,000	Kim Il Sung—president Li Jong-ok—premier
Korea (South)	Seoul	38,025	37,600,000	Chun Doo Hwan—president Nam Duck Woo—premier
Kuwait	Kuwait	6,880	1,300,000	Jaber al-Ahmed al-Sabah—head of state
Laos	Vientiane	91,429	3,600,000	Souphanouvong—president Kaysone Phomvihan—premier
Lebanon	Beirut	4,015	3,100,000	Elias Sarkis—president Shafiq al-Wazan—premier

NATION	CAPITAL	AREA (in sq mi)	POPULATION (estimate)	GOVERNMENT
Lesotho	Maseru	11,720	1,300,000	Moshoeshoe II—king Leabua Jonathan—prime minister
Liberia	Monrovia	43,000	1,800,000	Samuel K. Doe—president
Libya	Tripoli	679,360	2,900,000	Muammar el-Qaddafi—president
Liechtenstein	Vaduz	61	26,000	Francis Joseph II—prince
Luxembourg	Luxembourg	999	360,000	Jean—grand duke Pierre Werner—premier
Madagascar	Antananarivo	226,657	8,500,000	Didier Ratsiraka—president
Malawi	Lilongwe	45,747	5,800,000	H. Kamuzu Banda—president
Malaysia	Kuala Lumpur	127,316	13,300,000	Sultan Ahmad Shah—paramount ruler Hussein Onn—prime minister
Maldives	Male	115	145,000	Maumoon Abdul Gayoom—president
Mali	Bamako	478,765	6,500,000	Moussa Traoré—president
Malta	Valletta	122	350,000	Sir Anthony Mamo—president Dom Mintoff—prime minister
Mauritania	Nouakchott	397,954	1,600,000	Mohammed Khouna Ould Haidalla—president
Mauritius	Port Louis	790	940,000	Sir Seewoosagur Ramgoolam—prime minister
Mexico	Mexico City	761,602	67,400,000	José López Portillo—president
Monaco	Monaco-Ville	0.6	25,000	Rainier III—prince
Mongolia	Ulan Bator	604,248	1,600,000	Yumzhagiyn Tsedenbal—communist party secretary
Morocco	Rabat	172,413	19,500,000	Hassan II—king Maati Bouabid—premier
Mozambique	Maputo	309,494	10,200,000	Samora Machel—president
Nauru	—	8	8,000	Hammer DeRoburt—president
Nepal	Katmandu	54,362	13,700,000	Birendra Bir Bikram Shah Deva—king Kirtinidhi Bista—prime minister
Netherlands	Amsterdam	15,770	14,100,000	Beatrix—queen Andreas A. M. van Agt—premier
New Zealand	Wellington	103,736	3,100,000	Robert D. Muldoon—prime minister
Nicaragua	Managua	50,193	2,500,000	Sergio Ramírez Mercado—head of junta
Niger	Niamey	489,190	5,200,000	Seyni Kountche—head of government
Nigeria	Lagos	356,668	75,000,000	Shehu Shagari—president
Norway	Oslo	125,181	4,100,000	Olav V—king Odvar Nordli—prime minister
Oman	Muscat	82,030	860,000	Qabus ibn Said—sultan

NATION	CAPITAL	AREA (in sq mi)	POPULATION (estimate)	GOVERNMENT
Pakistan	Islamabad	310,403	80,000,000	Mohammed Zia ul-Haq—president
Panama	Panama City	29,761	1,900,000	Aristides Royo—president
Papua New Guinea	Port Moresby	178,260	3,100,000	Julius Chan—prime minister
Paraguay	Asunción	157,047	3,000,000	Alfredo Stroessner—president
Peru	Lima	496,223	17,300,000	Fernando Belaúnde Terry—president
Philippines	Manila	115,830	46,600,000	Ferdinand E. Marcos—president
Poland	Warsaw	120,724	35,600,000	Stanislaw Kania—communist party secretary Jozef Pinkowski—premier
Portugal	Lisbon	35,553	9,900,000	António Ramalho Eanes—president Pinto Balsemão—premier
Qatar	Doha	4,247	210,000	Khalifa ibn Hamad al-Thani—head of government
Rumania	Bucharest	91,700	22,000,000	Nicolae Ceauşescu—communist party secretary Ilie Verdet—premier
Rwanda	Kigali	10,169	4,800,000	Juvénal Habyalimana—president
St. Lucia	Castries	238	113,000	Allan Louisy—prime minister
St. Vincent and the Grenadines	Kingstown	150	100,000	Milton Cato—prime minister
São Tomé and Príncipe	São Tomé	372	84,000	Manuel Pinto da Costa—president
Saudi Arabia	Riyadh	829,997	8,100,000	Khalid ibn Abdul-Aziz—king
Senegal	Dakar	75,750	5,500,000	Léopold Senghor—president
Seychelles	Victoria	107	63,000	France Albert René—president
Sierra Leone	Freetown	27,700	3,500,000	Siaka P. Stevens—president
Singapore	Singapore	224	2,400,000	Benjamin H. Sheares—president Lee Kuan Yew—prime minister
Solomon Islands	Honiara	10,983	220,000	Peter Kenilorea—prime minister
Somalia	Mogadishu	246,200	3,500,000	Mohammed Siad Barre—head of government
South Africa	Pretoria Cape Town	471,444	28,500,000	Marais Viljoen—president Pieter W. Botha—prime minister
Spain	Madrid	194,897	37,500,000	Juan Carlos I—king Adolfo Suárez González—premier
Sri Lanka (Ceylon)	Colombo	25,332	14,700,000	Junius R. Jayewardene—president Ranasinghe Premadasa—prime minister
Sudan	Khartoum	967,497	17,900,000	Gaafar al-Numeiry—president
Surinam	Paramaribo	63,037	380,000	Henk Chin a-Sen—president
Swaziland	Mbabane	6,704	530,000	Sobhuza II—king
Sweden	Stockholm	173,731	8,300,000	Carl XVI Gustaf—king Thorbjörn Fälldin—prime minister

NATION	CAPITAL	AREA (in sq mi)	POPULATION (estimate)	GOVERNMENT
Switzerland	Bern	15,941	6,300,000	Kurt Furgler—president
Syria	Damascus	71,498	8,300,000	Hafez al-Assad—president Abdel Raouf al-Kassem—premier
Taiwan	Taipei	13,885	17,500,000	Chiang Ching-kuo—president Sun Yun-suan—premier
Tanzania	Dar es Salaam	364,898	18,000,000	Julius K. Nyerere—president
Thailand	Bangkok	198,456	46,100,000	Bhumibol Adulyadej—king Prem Tinsulanonda—premier
Togo	Lomé	21,622	2,500,000	Gnassingbe Eyadema—president
Tonga	Nuku'alofa	270	95,000	Taufa'ahau Tupou IV—king Prince Tu'ipelehake—prime minister
Trinidad & Tobago	Port of Spain	1,980	1,100,000	Sir Ellis Clarke—president Eric Williams—prime minister
Tunisia	Tunis	63,170	6,400,000	Habib Bourguiba—president
Turkey	Ankara	301,381	45,000,000	Kenan Evren—head of state Bulent Ulusu—prime minister
Tuvalu	Funafuti	10	8,000	Toalipi Lauti—prime minister
Uganda	Kampala	91,134	13,200,000	Milton Obote—president
U.S.S.R.	Moscow	8,649,512	262,500,000	Leonid I. Brezhnev—communist party secretary and president Nikolai A. Tikhonov—premier
United Arab Emirates	Abu Dhabi	32,278	860,000	Zayd ibn Sultan—president
United Kingdom	London	94,226	55,900,000	Elizabeth II—queen Margaret Thatcher—prime minister
United States	Washington, D.C.	3,618,467	226,000,000	Ronald W. Reagan—president-elect George H. Bush—vice-president-elect
Upper Volta	Ouagadougou	105,869	6,700,000	Saye Zerbo—head of government
Uruguay	Montevideo	68,037	2,900,000	Aparicio Méndez—president
Vanuatu	Vila	5,700	100,000	Walter Lini—prime minister
Venezuela	Caracas	352,143	13,500,000	Luis Herrera Campíns—president
Vietnam	Hanoi	127,202	52,700,000	Le Duan—communist party secretary Pham Van Dong—premier
Western Samoa	Apia	1,097	156,000	Malietoa Tanumafili II—head of state
Yemen (Aden)	Madinat al-Shaab	128,559	1,800,000	Ali Nasser Mohammed—president
Yemen (Sana)	Sana	75,290	5,700,000	Ali Abdullah Saleh—president
Yugoslavia	Belgrade	98,766	22,200,000	Lazar Mojsov—president Veselin Djuranovic—premier
Zaïre	Kinshasa	905,565	28,000,000	Mobutu Sese Seko—president
Zambia	Lusaka	290,585	5,600,000	Kenneth D. Kaunda—president
Zimbabwe	Salisbury	150,333	7,100,000	Canaan Banana—president Robert Mugabe—prime minister

THE CONGRESS OF THE UNITED STATES

UNITED STATES SENATE

(53 Republicans, 46 Democrats, 1 Independent)

Alabama
Howell T. Heflin (D)
Jeremiah Denton (R)*

Alaska
Ted Stevens (R)
Frank H. Murkowski (R)*

Arizona
Barry Goldwater (R)
Dennis DeConcini (D)

Arkansas
Dale Bumpers (D)
David H. Pryor (D)

California
Alan Cranston (D)
S. I. Hayakawa (R)

Colorado
Gary W. Hart (D)
William L. Armstrong (R)

Connecticut
Lowell P. Weicker, Jr. (R)
Christopher J. Dodd (D)*

Delaware
William V. Roth, Jr. (R)
Joseph R. Biden, Jr. (D)

Florida
Lawton Chiles (D)
Paula Hawkins (R)*

Georgia
Sam Nunn (D)
Mack Mattingly (R)*

Hawaii
Daniel K. Inouye (D)
Spark M. Matsunaga (D)

Idaho
James A. McClure (R)
Steven D. Symms (R)*

Illinois
Charles H. Percy (R)
Alan J. Dixon (D)*

Indiana
Richard G. Lugar (R)
Dan Quayle (R)*

Iowa
Roger W. Jepsen (R)
Charles E. Grassley (R)*

Kansas
Robert J. Dole (R)
Nancy Landon Kassebaum (R)

Kentucky
Walter Huddleston (D)
Wendell H. Ford (D)

Louisiana
Russell B. Long (D)
J. Bennett Johnston (D)

Maine
William S. Cohen (R)
George J. Mitchell (D)**

Maryland
Charles M. Mathias, Jr. (R)
Paul S. Sarbanes (D)

Massachusetts
Edward M. Kennedy (D)
Paul E. Tsongas (D)

Michigan
Donald W. Riegle, Jr. (D)
Carl Levin (D)

Minnesota
David F. Durenberger (R)
Rudy Boschwitz (R)

Mississippi
John C. Stennis (D)
Thad Cochran (R)

Missouri
Thomas F. Eagleton (D)
John C. Danforth (R)

Montana
John Melcher (D)
Max Baucus (D)

Nebraska
Edward Zorinsky (D)
J. James Exon (D)

Nevada
Howard W. Cannon (D)
Paul Laxalt (R)

New Hampshire
Gordon J. Humphrey (R)
Warren Rudman (R)*

New Jersey
Harrison A. Williams, Jr. (D)
Bill Bradley (D)

New Mexico
Pete V. Domenici (R)
Harrison H. Schmitt (R)

New York
Daniel P. Moynihan (D)
Alfonse M. D'Amato (R)*

North Carolina
Jesse Helms (R)
John P. East (R)*

North Dakota
Quentin N. Burdick (D)
Mark Andrews (R)*

Ohio
John H. Glenn, Jr. (D)
Howard M. Metzenbaum (D)

Oklahoma
David L. Boren (D)
Don Nickles (R)*

Oregon
Mark O. Hatfield (R)
Bob Packwood (R)

Pennsylvania
H. John Heinz III (R)
Arlen Specter (R)*

Rhode Island
Claiborne Pell (D)
John H. Chafee (R)

South Carolina
Strom Thurmond (R)
Ernest F. Hollings (D)

South Dakota
Larry Pressler (R)
James Abdnor (R)*

Tennessee
Howard H. Baker, Jr. (R)
James R. Sasser (D)

Texas
John G. Tower (R)
Lloyd M. Bentsen (D)

Utah
E. J. (Jake) Garn (R)
Orrin G. Hatch (R)

Vermont
Robert T. Stafford (R)
Patrick J. Leahy (D)

Virginia
Harry F. Byrd, Jr. (I)
John W. Warner (R)

Washington
Henry M. Jackson (D)
Slade Gorton (R)*

West Virginia
Jennings Randolph (D)
Robert C. Byrd (D)

Wisconsin
William Proxmire (D)
Robert W. Kasten, Jr. (R)*

Wyoming
Malcolm Wallop (R)
Alan K. Simpson (R)

(R) Republican
(D) Democrat
(I) Independent

* elected in 1980
** was named to replace Edmund S. Muskie

UNITED STATES HOUSE OF REPRESENTATIVES

(242 Democrats, 192 Republicans, 1 Independent)

Alabama
1. J. Edwards (R)
2. W. L. Dickinson (R)
3. W. Nichols (D)
4. T. Bevill (D)
5. R. Flippo (D)
6. A. Smith (R)*
7. R. Shelby (D)

Alaska
D. Young (R)

Arizona
1. J. J. Rhodes (R)
2. M. K. Udall (D)
3. B. Stump (D)
4. E. Rudd (R)

Arkansas
1. W. V. Alexander, Jr. (D)
2. E. Bethune, Jr. (R)
3. J. P. Hammerschmidt (R)
4. B. Anthony, Jr. (D)

California
1. E. Chappie (R)*
2. D. H. Clausen (R)
3. R. Matsui (D)
4. V. Fazio (D)
5. J. L. Burton (D)
6. P. Burton (D)
7. G. Miller (D)
8. R. V. Dellums (D)
9. F. H. Stark, Jr. (D)
10. D. Edwards (D)
11. T. Lantos (D)*
12. P. N. McCloskey, Jr. (R)
13. N. Y. Mineta (D)
14. N. Shumway (R)
15. T. Coelho (D)
16. L. E. Panetta (D)
17. C. Pashayan (R)
18. W. Thomas (R)
19. R. J. Lagomarsino (R)
20. B. M. Goldwater, Jr. (R)
21. B. Fiedler (R)*
22. C. J. Moorhead (R)
23. A. C. Beilenson (D)
24. H. A. Waxman (D)
25. E. R. Roybal (D)
26. J. H. Rousselot (R)
27. R. K. Dornan (R)
28. J. Dixon (D)
29. A. F. Hawkins (D)
30. G. E. Danielson (D)
31. M. Dymally (D)*
32. G. M. Anderson (D)
33. W. Grisham (R)
34. D. Lungren (R)
35. D. Dreier (R)*
36. G. E. Brown, Jr. (D)
37. J. Lewis (R)
38. J. M. Patterson (D)
39. W. Dannemeyer (R)
40. R. E. Badham (R)
41. B. Lowery (R)*
42. D. Hunter (R)*
43. C. W. Burgener (R)

Colorado
1. P. Schroeder (D)
2. T. E. Wirth (D)
3. R. Kogovsek (D)
4. H. Brown (R)*
5. K. Kramer (R)

Connecticut
1. W. R. Cotter (D)
2. S. Gejdenson (D)*
3. L. DeNardis (R)*
4. S. B. McKinney (R)
5. W. Ratchford (D)
6. T. Moffett (D)

Delaware
T. B. Evans, Jr. (R)

Florida
1. E. Hutto (D)
2. D. Fuqua (D)
3. C. E. Bennett (D)
4. W. V. Chappell, Jr. (D)
5. B. McCollum (R)*
6. C. W. Young (R)
7. S. M. Gibbons (D)
8. A. P. Ireland (D)
9. B. Nelson (D)
10. L. A. Bafalis (R)
11. D. Mica (D)
12. C. Shaw (R)*
13. W. Lehman (D)
14. C. D. Pepper (D)
15. D. B. Fascell (D)

Georgia
1. R. B. Ginn (D)
2. C. Hatcher (D)*
3. J. Brinkley (D)
4. E. H. Levitas (D)
5. W. F. Fowler, Jr. (D)
6. N. Gingrich (R)
7. L. P. McDonald (D)
8. B. L. Evans (D)
9. E. L. Jenkins (D)
10. D. D. Barnard, Jr. (D)

Hawaii
1. C. Heftel (D)
2. D. K. Akaka (D)

Idaho
1. L. Craig (R)*
2. G. V. Hansen (R)

Illinois
1. H. Washington (D)*
2. G. Savage (D)*
3. M. A. Russo (D)
4. E. J. Derwinski (R)
5. J. G. Fary (D)
6. H. J. Hyde (R)
7. C. Collins (D)
8. D. Rostenkowski (D)
9. S. R. Yates (D)
10. J. Porter (R)*
11. F. Annunzio (D)
12. P. M. Crane (R)
13. R. McClory (R)
14. J. N. Erlenborn (R)
15. T. J. Corcoran (R)
16. L. Martin (R)*
17. G. M. O'Brien (R)
18. R. H. Michel (R)
19. T. Railsback (R)
20. P. Findley (R)
21. E. R. Madigan (R)
22. D. Crane (R)
23. C. M. Price (D)
24. P. Simon (D)

Indiana
1. A. Benjamin, Jr. (D)
2. F. J. Fithian (D)
3. J. Hiler (R)*
4. D. Coats (R)*
5. E. H. Hillis (R)
6. D. W. Evans (D)
7. J. T. Myers (R)
8. H. Deckard (R)
9. L. H. Hamilton (D)
10. P. R. Sharp (D)
11. A. Jacobs, Jr. (D)

Iowa
1. J. A. S. Leach (R)
2. T. Tauke (R)
3. C. Evans (R)*
4. N. Smith (D)
5. T. R. Harkin (D)
6. B. W. Bedell (D)

Kansas
1. P. Roberts (R)*
2. J. Jeffries (R)
3. L. Winn, Jr. (R)
4. D. Glickman (D)
5. R. Whittaker (R)

Kentucky
1. C. Hubbard, Jr. (D)
2. W. H. Natcher (D)
3. R. L. Mazzoli (D)
4. G. Snyder (R)
5. H. Rogers (R)*
6. L. Hopkins (R)
7. C. D. Perkins (D)

Louisiana
1. R. L. Livingston, Jr. (R)
2. C. C. Boggs (D)
3. W. J. Tauzin (D)*
4. C. Roemer (D)*
5. J. Huckaby (D)
6. W. H. Moore (R)
7. J. B. Breaux (D)
8. G. W. Long (D)

Maine
1. D. F. Emery (R)
2. O. Snowe (R)

Maryland
1. R. Dyson (D)*
2. C. D. Long (D)
3. B. A. Mikulski (D)
4. M. S. Holt (R)
5. G. N. Spellman (D)
6. B. Byron (D)
7. P. J. Mitchell (D)
8. M. Barnes (D)

Massachusetts
1. S. O. Conte (R)
2. E. P. Boland (D)
3. J. D. Early (D)
4. B. Frank (D)*
5. J. Shannon (D)
6. N. Mavroules (D)
7. E. J. Markey (D)
8. T. P. O'Neill, Jr. (D)
9. J. J. Moakley (D)
10. M. M. Heckler (R)
11. B. Donnelly (D)
12. G. E. Studds (D)

Michigan
1. J. Conyers, Jr. (D)
2. C. D. Pursell (R)
3. H. Wolpe (D)
4. D. A. Stockman (R)
5. H. S. Sawyer (R)
6. J. Dunn (R)*
7. D. E. Kildee (D)
8. B. Traxler (D)
9. G. A. Vander Jagt (R)
10. D. Albosta (D)
11. R. Davis (R)
12. D. E. Bonior (D)
13. G. Crockett, Jr. (D)*
14. D. Hertel (D)*
15. W. D. Ford (D)
16. J. D. Dingell (D)
17. W. M. Brodhead (D)
18. J. J. Blanchard (D)
19. W. S. Broomfield (R)

Minnesota
1. A. Erdahl (R)
2. T. M. Hagedorn (R)
3. B. Frenzel (R)
4. B. F. Vento (D)
5. M. Sabo (D)
6. V. Weber (R)*
7. A. Strangeland (R)
8. J. L. Oberstar (D)

Mississippi
1. J. L. Whitten (D)
2. D. R. Bowen (D)
3. G. V. Montgomery (D)
4. J. Hinson (R)
5. T. Lott (R)

Missouri
1. W. L. Clay (D)
2. R. A. Young (D)
3. R. A. Gephardt (D)
4. I. Skelton (D)

5. R. Bolling (D)
6. E. T. Coleman (R)
7. G. Taylor (R)
8. W. Bailey (R)*
9. H. L. Volkmer (D)
10. B. Emerson (R)*

Montana
1. P. Williams (D)
2. R. Marlenee (R)

Nebraska
1. D. Bereuter (R)
2. H. Daub (R)*
3. V. Smith (R)

Nevada
J. D. Santini (D)

New Hampshire
1. N. E. D'Amours (D)
2. J. Gregg (R)*

New Jersey
1. J. J. Florio (D)
2. W. J. Hughes (D)
3. J. J. Howard (D)
4. C. Smith (R)*
5. M. Fenwick (R)
6. E. B. Forsythe (R)
7. M. Roukema (R)*
8. R. A. Roe (D)
9. H. C. Hollenbeck (R)
10. P. W. Rodino, Jr. (D)
11. J. G. Minish (D)
12. M. J. Rinaldo (R)
13. J. Courter (R)
14. F. Guarini (D)
15. B. Dwyer (D)*

New Mexico
1. M. Lujan, Jr. (R)
2. J. Skeen (R)*

New York
1. W. Carney (R)
2. T. J. Downey (D)
3. G. Carman (R)*
4. N. F. Lent (R)
5. R. McGrath (R)*
6. J. LeBoutillier (R)*
7. J. P. Addabbo (D)
8. B. S. Rosenthal (D)
9. G. Ferraro (D)
10. M. Biaggi (D)
11. J. H. Scheuer (D)
12. S. A. Chisholm (D)
13. S. J. Solarz (D)
14. F. W. Richmond (D)
15. L. C. Zeferetti (D)
16. C. Schumer (D)*
17. G. Molinari (R)*
18. S. W. Green (R)
19. C. B. Rangel (D)
20. T. Weiss (D)
21. R. Garcia (D)
22. J. B. Bingham (D)
23. P. Peyser (D)
24. R. L. Ottinger (D)
25. H. Fish, Jr. (R)
26. B. A. Gilman (R)

27. M. F. McHugh (D)
28. S. S. Stratton (D)
29. G. Solomon (R)
30. D. Martin (R)*
31. D. J. Mitchell (R)
32. G. Wortley (R)*
33. G. Lee (R)
34. F. Horton (R)
35. B. B. Conable, Jr. (R)
36. J. J. LaFalce (D)
37. H. J. Nowak (D)
38. J. Kemp (R)
39. S. N. Lundine (D)

North Carolina
1. W. B. Jones (D)
2. L. H. Fountain (D)
3. C. O. Whitley, Sr. (D)
4. I. F. Andrews (D)
5. S. L. Neal (D)
6. E. Johnston (R)*
7. C. Rose (D)
8. W. G. Hefner (D)
9. J. G. Martin (R)
10. J. T. Broyhill (R)
11. B. Hendon (R)*

North Dakota
B. Dorgan (D)*

Ohio
1. W. D. Gradison, Jr. (R)
2. T. A. Luken (D)
3. T. Hall (D)
4. T. Guyer (R)
5. D. L. Latta (R)
6. B. McEwen (R)*
7. C. J. Brown (R)
8. T. N. Kindness (R)
9. E. Weber (R)*
10. C. E. Miller (R)
11. J. W. Stanton (R)
12. B. Shamansky (D)*
13. D. J. Pease (D)
14. J. F. Seiberling (D)
15. C. P. Wylie (R)
16. R. Regula (R)
17. J. M. Ashbrook (R)
18. D. Applegate (D)
19. L. Williams (R)
20. M. R. Oakar (D)
21. L. Stokes (D)
22. D. Eckart (D)*
23. R. M. Mottl (D)

Oklahoma
1. J. R. Jones (D)
2. M. Synar (D)
3. W. W. Watkins (D)
4. D. McCurdy (D)*
5. M. Edwards (R)
6. G. English (D)

Oregon
1. L. AuCoin (D)
2. D. Smith (R)*
3. R. Wyden (D)*
4. J. Weaver (D)

Pennsylvania
1. T. Foglietta (I)*
2. W. Gray (D)

3. R. F. Lederer (D)
4. C. Dougherty (R)
5. R. T. Schulze (R)
6. G. Yatron (D)
7. R. W. Edgar (D)
8. J. Coyne (R)*
9. B. Shuster (R)
10. J. M. McDade (R)
11. J. Nelligan (R)*
12. J. P. Murtha (D)
13. L. Coughlin (R)
14. W. Coyne (D)*
15. D. Ritter (R)
16. R. S. Walker (R)
17. A. E. Ertel (D)
18. D. Walgren (D)
19. W. F. Goodling (R)
20. J. M. Gaydos (D)
21. D. Bailey (D)
22. A. J. Murphy (D)
23. W. Clinger, Jr. (R)
24. M. L. Marks (R)
25. E. Atkinson (D)

Rhode Island
1. F. J. St. Germain (D)
2. C. Schneider (R)*

South Carolina
1. T. Hartnett (R)*
2. F. D. Spence (R)
3. B. C. Derrick, Jr. (D)
4. C. Campbell, Jr. (R)
5. K. Holland (D)
6. J. Napier (R)*

South Dakota
1. T. A. Daschle (D)
2. C. Roberts (R)*

Tennessee
1. J. H. Quillen (R)
2. J. J. Duncan (R)
3. M. L. Bouquard (D)
4. A. Gore, Jr. (D)
5. W. H. Boner (D)
6. R. L. Beard, Jr. (R)
7. E. Jones (D)
8. H. Ford (D)

Texas
1. S. B. Hall, Jr. (D)
2. C. Wilson (D)
3. J. M. Collins (R)
4. R. Hall (D)*
5. J. A. Mattox (D)
6. P. Gramm (D)
7. B. Archer (R)
8. J. Fields (R)*
9. J. Brooks (D)
10. J. J. Pickle (D)
11. J. M. Leath (D)
12. J. C. Wright, Jr. (D)
13. J. E. Hightower (D)
14. W. Patman (D)*
15. E. de la Garza (D)
16. R. C. White (D)
17. C. Stenholm (D)
18. M. Leland (D)
19. K. Hance (D)
20. H. B. Gonzalez (D)
21. T. Loeffler (R)
22. R. Paul (R)

23. A. Kazen, Jr. (D)
24. M. Frost (D)

Utah
1. J. Hansen (R)*
2. D. D. Marriott (R)

Vermont
J. M. Jeffords (R)

Virginia
1. P. S. Trible, Jr. (R)
2. G. W. Whitehurst (R)
3. T. Bliley, Jr. (R)*
4. R. W. Daniel, Jr. (R)
5. D. Daniel (D)
6. M. C. Butler (R)
7. J. K. Robinson (R)
8. S. Parris (R)*
9. W. C. Wampler (R)
10. F. Wolf (R)*

Washington
1. J. M. Pritchard (R)
2. A. Swift (D)
3. D. L. Bonker (D)
4. S. Morrison (R)*
5. T. S. Foley (D)
6. N. D. Dicks (D)
7. M. Lowry (D)

West Virginia
1. R. H. Mollohan (D)
2. C. Benedict (R)*
3. M. Staton (R)*
4. N. J. Rahall (D)

Wisconsin
1. L. Aspin (D)
2. R. W. Kastenmeier (D)
3. S. Gunderson (R)*
4. C. J. Zablocki (D)
5. H. S. Reuss (D)
6. T. E. Petri (R)
7. D. R. Obey (D)
8. T. Roth (R)
9. F. J. Sensenbrenner, Jr. (R)

Wyoming
R. Cheney (R)

(R) Republican
(D) Democrat
(I) Independent

*elected in 1980

Chief Justice Warren E. Burger

UNITED STATES SUPREME COURT

Chief Justice: Warren E. Burger (1969)

Associate Justices:
William J. Brennan, Jr. (1956)
Potter Stewart (1958)
Byron R. White (1962)
Thurgood Marshall (1967)
Harry A. Blackmun (1970)
Lewis F. Powell, Jr. (1971)
William H. Rehnquist (1971)
John Paul Stevens (1975)

UNITED STATES CABINET

Secretary of Agriculture: Bob S. Bergland
Attorney General: Benjamin R. Civiletti
Secretary of Commerce: Philip M. Klutznick
Secretary of Defense: Harold Brown
Secretary of Education: Shirley Mount Hufstedler
Secretary of Energy: Charles W. Duncan, Jr.
Secretary of Health and Human Services:
Patricia Roberts Harris
Secretary of Housing and Urban Development:
Moon Landrieu
Secretary of the Interior: Cecil D. Andrus
Secretary of Labor: F. Ray Marshall
Secretary of State: Edmund S. Muskie
Secretary of Transportation: Neil E. Goldschmidt
Secretary of the Treasury: G. William Miller

GOVERNORS OF THE UNITED STATES

Alabama	Forrest H. James, Jr. (D)	Montana	Ted Schwinden (D)*
Alaska	Jay S. Hammond (R)	Nebraska	Charles Thone (R)
Arizona	Bruce E. Babbitt (D)	Nevada	Robert List (R)
Arkansas	Frank D. White (R)*	New Hampshire	Hugh J. Gallen (D)
California	Edmund G. Brown, Jr. (D)	New Jersey	Brendan T. Byrne (D)
Colorado	Richard D. Lamm (D)	New Mexico	Bruce King (D)
Connecticut	Ella T. Grasso (D)**	New York	Hugh L. Carey (D)
Delaware	Pierre S. du Pont IV (R)	North Carolina	James B. Hunt, Jr. (D)
Florida	Robert Graham (D)	North Dakota	Allen I. Olson (R)*
Georgia	George Busbee (D)	Ohio	James A. Rhodes (R)
Hawaii	George R. Ariyoshi (D)	Oklahoma	George Nigh (D)
Idaho	John V. Evans (D)	Oregon	Victor Atiyeh (R)
Illinois	James R. Thompson (R)	Pennsylvania	Richard L. Thornburgh (R)
Indiana	Robert D. Orr (R)*	Rhode Island	J. Joseph Garrahy (D)
Iowa	Robert D. Ray (R)	South Carolina	Richard W. Riley (D)
Kansas	John Carlin (D)	South Dakota	William J. Janklow (R)
Kentucky	Julian M. Carroll (D)	Tennessee	Lamar Alexander (R)
Louisiana	David C. Treen (R)	Texas	William P. Clements (R)
Maine	Joseph R. Brennan (D)	Utah	Scott M. Matheson (D)
Maryland	Harry Hughes (D)	Vermont	Richard A. Snelling (R)
Massachusetts	Edward J. King (D)	Virginia	John N. Dalton (R)
Michigan	William G. Milliken (R)	Washington	John Spellman (R)*
Minnesota	Albert Quie (R)	West Virginia	John D. Rockefeller IV (D)
Mississippi	Cliff Finch (D)	Wisconsin	Lee S. Dreyfus (R)
Missouri	Christopher S. Bond (R)*	Wyoming	Ed Herschler (D)

*elected in 1980; **William A. O'Neill to take office Jan. 1, 1981

CANADA

Capital: Ottawa
Head of State: Queen Elizabeth II
Governor General: Edward Richard Schreyer
Prime Minister: Pierre Elliott Trudeau (Liberal)
Leader of the Opposition: Joe Clark (Progressive Conservative)
Population: 23,900,000
Area: 3,851,809 sq mi (9,976,139 km²)

PROVINCES AND TERRITORIES OF CANADA

Alberta
Capital: Edmonton
Lieutenant Governor: Frank Lynch-Staunton
Premier: Peter Lougheed (Progressive Conservative)
Leader of the Opposition: Rod Sykes (Social Credit)
Entered Confederation: Sept. 1, 1905
Population: 2,000,000
Area: 255,285 sq mi (661,188 km²)

British Columbia
Capital: Victoria
Lieutenant Governor: Henry P. Bell-Irving
Premier: William R. Bennett (Social Credit)
Leader of the Opposition: David Barrett (New Democratic Party)
Entered Confederation: July 20, 1871
Population: 2,400,000
Area: 366,255 sq mi (948,600 km²)

Manitoba
Capital: Winnipeg
Lieutenant Governor: Francis L. Jobin
Premier: Sterling P. Lyon (Progressive Conservative)
Leader of the Opposition: Howard Pawley (New Democratic Party)
Entered Confederation: July 15, 1870
Population: 1,022,000
Area: 251,000 sq mi (650,090 km²)

New Brunswick
Capital: Fredericton
Lieutenant Governor: Hédard Robichaud
Premier: Richard B. Hatfield (Progressive Conservative)
Leader of the Opposition: Joseph Z. Daigle (Liberal)
Entered Confederation: July 1, 1867
Population: 678,000
Area: 28,354 sq mi (73,436 km²)

Newfoundland
Capital: St. John's
Lieutenant Governor: Gordon A. Winter
Premier: A. Brian Peckford (Progressive Conservative)
Leader of the Opposition: Len Sterling (Liberal)
Entered Confederation: March 31, 1949
Population: 620,000
Area: 156,185 sq mi (404,517 km²)

Nova Scotia
Capital: Halifax
Lieutenant Governor: John Elvin Shaffner
Premier: John M. Buchanan (Progressive Conservative)
Leader of the Opposition: A. M. (Sandy) Cameron (Liberal)
Entered Confederation: July 1, 1867
Population: 828,600
Area: 21,425 sq mi (55,491 km²)

Ontario
Capital: Toronto
Lieutenant Governor: John Aird
Premier: William G. Davis (Progressive Conservative)
Leader of the Opposition: Stuart Smith (Liberal)
Entered Confederation: July 1, 1867
Population: 8,571,000
Area: 412,582 sq mi (1,068,582 km²)

Prince Edward Island
Capital: Charlottetown
Lieutenant Governor: J. A. Doiron
Premier: J. Angus MacLean (Progressive Conservative)
Leader of the Opposition: W. Bennett Campbell (Liberal)
Entered Confederation: July 1, 1873
Population: 123,000
Area: 2,184 sq mi (5,657 km²)

Quebec

Capital: Quebec City
Lieutenant Governor: Jean-Pierre Côté
Premier: René Lévesque (Parti Québécois)
Leader of the Opposition: Claude Ryan (Liberal)
Entered Confederation: July 1, 1867
Population: 6,235,000
Area: 594,860 sq mi (1,540,700 km²)

Saskatchewan

Capital: Regina
Lieutenant Governor: Irwin McIntosh
Premier: Allan E. Blakeney (New Democratic Party)
Leader of the Opposition: Eric Berntson (Progressive Conservative)
Entered Confederation: Sept. 1, 1905
Population: 970,000
Area: 251,700 sq mi (651,900 km²)

Northwest Territories

Capital: Yellowknife
Commissioner: John H. Parker
Reconstituted as a territory: September 1, 1905
Population: 43,000
Area: 1,304,896 sq mi (3,379,684 km²)

Yukon Territory

Capital: Whitehorse
Administrator: Douglas Bell
Government Leader: Christopher Pearson
Organized as a territory: June 13, 1898
Population: 25,000
Area: 186,299 sq mi (482,515 km²)

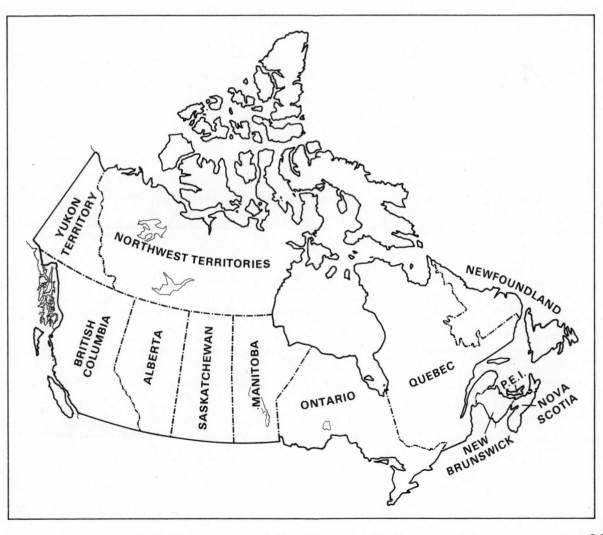

INDEX

D

G

H

T

U

V

Z

ILLUSTRATION CREDITS AND ACKNOWLEDGMENTS

The following list credits or acknowledges, by page, the source of illustrations and text excerpts used in THE NEW BOOK OF KNOWLEDGE ANNUAL. Illustration credits are listed illustration by illustration—left to right, top to bottom. When two or more illustrations appear on one page, their credits are separated by semicolons. When both the photographer or artist and an agency or other source are given for an illustration, they are usually separated by a dash. Excerpts from previously published works are listed by inclusive page numbers.

10– Michael Evans—Sygma
11
14– UPI
15
16 UPI
17 Gamma/Liaison
18 Alain Mingam—Gamma/Liaison
19 UPI
20 Bruce Hoertel—Camera 5
21 Peer Pedersen—Photoreporters
22– Wide World
23
24 Sygma
25 *Montreal Gazette*
26 Pictorial Parade
27 Philippe Gault—Sygma
28 UPI
29 Don Wright—*The Miami News*/NYT Special Features
30 Canadian Press
31 Henri Bureau—Sygma
32 Wide World
34 © 1968 Mirisch Corporation
35 Piramallo—Gamma/Liaison
37 © David McGough—Retna; © Fred Ward—Black Star
38 © 1980 Roger Sandler—Black Star
39 Steve Liss—Gamma/Liaison
40 UPI
42 Henri Bureau—Sygma
43 Christine Spengler—Sygma
44 David Rubinger—Black Star
45 Wide World
46 Bernard Gotfryd—*Newsweek*
47 Sipa Press—Black Star
48 UPI
49 Sipa Press—Black Star
50 Wide World
51 Louise Gubb—Gamma/Liaison
52 Michael Evans—Gamma/Liaison
53 Canadian Press
55 Shostal Associates
56 Mario Ruiz
57 Frank Lodge—*The New York Times*
58 Jim Cummins—*The New York Times*
59 © 1980 Dennis Brack—Black Star
60 A. DeJean—Sygma
61 Marc Bulka—Gamma/Liaison
62 © 1980 Gianfranco Gorgoni—Contact
63 © 1980 Bob Schalwijk—Black Star
64 Apesteguy-Mingam-Simtn—Gamma/Liaison; © Dirck Halstead—Contact
65 Michel Artault—Gamma/Liaison; Tass from Sovfoto
66– Dan Guravich
67
68 Joe B. Blossom—Photo Researchers
69 Alpha; Russ Kinne—Photo Researchers
70 Anthony Mercieca—Photo Researchers; Gary R. Jones—Bruce Coleman
71 Bob Barrett—The Image Bank; Leonard Lee Rue III

72 Schmidecker—FPG; © 1979 John Serrano—Photo Researchers
73 L. W. Walker—National Audubon Society
74– San Francisco SPCA Hearing Dog Program
75
76 © Silvester—Rapho/Photo Researchers; Tom Myers—Photo Researchers
77 © Jack Fields—Photo Researchers
78 © E. Hanumantha Rao—Photo Researchers; © Tom McHugh—Photo Researchers
79 William H. Amos—Bruce Coleman; © J. H. Robinson—Photo Researchers; Keith Gunnar—Bruce Coleman
82 Barry E. Parker—Bruce Coleman; © 1977 John C. Deitz—Photo Researchers; © Chesher—Photo Researchers
83 Jane Burton—Bruce Coleman; Soames Summerhays—Photo Reserachers
84– Peter D. Capen—Terra Mar Productions
85
86 © 1980 Richard Schoer; Tass from Sovfoto
87 © 1980 National Geographic Society; UPI
88 © Joan Lebold Cohen—Photo Researchers
89 Allan Power—Bruce Coleman
90 © Joseph Van Wormer—Bruce Coleman
91 Jeff Foott—Bruce Coleman
92 © Soames Summerhays—Photo Researchers
93 © Robert C. Hermes—Photo Researchers
94 © Kjell B. Sandved—Photo Researchers
95 © drawing by Sam Gross, reprinted from *Audubon* © 1980; © 1973 Norman R. Lightfoot—Photo Researchers
96– James Mason—Black Star
97
98 © 1980 David Olson—Black Star
99 © 1980 Douglas Kirkland—Contact; Ralph Perry—Black Star
100 Courtesy General Motors; Courtesy Ford Motor Company
101 Oliphant © 1980 *Washington Star*
102 Wide World
103 Courtesy Gulf & Western
104 Library of Congress
105 Courtesy Sharp Electronics Corporation; Courtesy Rose Associates, Inc.
106– National Energy Foundation
107
108 Michèle McLean/Pamela Carley Petersen
109 Mike Mazzaschi—Stock Boston
110 Reprinted from *Cosmopolitan* © 1980 Randy Glasbergen
111 William Hubbell
112– *What's to Eat and Other Questions Kids Ask*
113 *About Food*, United States Department of Agriculture
115 Peter Knock—American Health Foundation
116– NASA—JPL
117
118 UPI
119 NASA—JPL
120 Frank Senyk
121 © 1960 King Features Syndicate, Inc.

123 Ed Uluschak
124– Adapted from *Small Worlds Close Up* by Lisa
127 Grillone & Joseph Gennaro. Copyright © 1978 by Lisa Grillone & Joseph Gennaro. By permission of Crown Publishers, Inc.
126 Fruitfly photo (actual size): Lisa Grillone & Joseph Gennaro
128 American Museum of Natural History
129 Tass from Sovfoto
130 Connally—Gamma/Liaison
131 UPI
132 Culver Pictures
133 Wide World; Sketch by Steven Kimbrough
134– Rob Lewine
135
136– Michèle McLean
137
138 The Granger Collection
140 Michèle McLean
141 Gamma/Liaison; P. Tatiner—Gamma/Liaison
144 Michèle McLean
145 Michèle McLean; H. Peter Curran—The Forbes Magazine Collection
150 Barry Tenin; © Porterfield-Chickering—Photo Researchers; Danish Ministry of Foreign Affairs; Phil & Loretta Hermann; Virginia Department of Highways and Transportation
151 Tom Stack & Associates; © Porterfield-Chickering—Photo Researchers; Tom Stack & Associates; © Mario Fantin—Photo Researchers; © Dr. Georg Gerster—Photo Researchers
152 Michèle McLean
153 Jacques Chazaud
154– Ellen Land-Weber from *The Passionate*
155 *Collector*

156 Tom Crabb—Courtesy *Creative Crafts* magazine
157 Marian Rubinstein—Courtesy *Creative Crafts* magazine; Ronald Pilling—Courtesy *Creative Crafts* magazine
158 Ellen Appel—Courtesy *Creative Crafts* magazine; Jeff Smith—Courtesy *Creative Crafts* magazine
159 Ellen Appel—Courtesy *Creative Crafts* magazine
160–161 Courtesy Krause Publications, Inc.
162–163 From *Many Hands Cooking: An International Cookbook for Girls and Boys,* written by Terry Touff Cooper and Marilyn Ratner, illustrated by Tony Chen. Text © 1974 by Terry Touff Cooper and Marilyn Ratner. Illustrations © 1974 by Tony Chen. By permission of Thomas Y. Crowell, Publishers
164–165 Dave Houser—Tom Stack & Associates
166 J. Zimmerman—FPG
167 Bevilacqua—Sygma
168 Thomas Zimmermann—FPG
169 Focus on Sports
170 Paul J. Sutton—Duomo
171 Steven E. Sutton—Duomo; Gale Constable—Duomo
172 UPI
173 Hans Paul—Lehtikuva/Photoreporters; Lehtikuva/Photoreporters
174 Tony Duffy—Duomo
175–176 Don Morley—Duomo
180 © Lorraine Rorke—AAU/USA Junior Olympics
181 Ellen Findlay—AAU/USA Junior Olympics
182 Focus on Sports
183 Focus on Sports; Wide World
185 Vannucci Foto Services
186 Mitchell B. Reibel—Focus on Sports
187 UPI
188–190 UPI
191 Wide World
192 Barton Silverman—*The New York Times;* Sara Krulwich—*The New York Times*
193 Mitchell B. Reibel—Focus on Sports
194 UPI
195 UPI
196 Chuck Solomon—Focus on Sports
197 © 1980 Gale Constable—Duomo
198 Fred Mullane—Focus on Sports
199 © 1980 Steven E. Sutton
200 Steven E. Sutton—Duomo; Keith Meyers—*The New York Times*
201 Wide World; Steven E. Sutton—Duomo; © 1980 Rick Friedman—Black Star
202 Gustavo Lago; UPI
203 Michael Heller—Black Star; UPI
204 Vince Streano
205 Vince Streano; Vince Streano; Christopher Casler—Camera 5
206–207 The Bettmann Archive
208 Owen Franken—Stock Boston
209 The Granger Collection
210 Garbisch Collection; The National Gallery of Art, Washington D.C.
211 Paul De Paola—FPG; The Bettmann Archive
212–213 Jenny Tesar
214 Sid Bernstein—Photo Researchers

215 Philip Jon Bailey—The Picture Cube
216 The Shelburne Museum, Shelburne, Vermont; The Shelburne Museum, Shelburne, Vermont; Abby Aldrich Rockefeller Folk Art Center, Williamsburg, Virginia
217 Abby Aldrich Rockefeller Folk Art Center, Williamsburg, Virginia; © Guy Gillette—Photo Researchers; Charles H. Phillips
218 Courtesy Expedition Institute
219 National Audubon Society
220 Shostal Associates
221 The Bettmann Archive
222 Culver Pictures
223
224–225 Dr. J. R. Block
226 Courtesy Advertising Council, Inc.
227 Courtesy U.S. Census Bureau
228 The Bettmann Archive
230 Graphic by *Newsday*
231 Courtesy Wanderer Books
232–233 Henry Kurtz
234–235 © Jim Howard—Alpha
236–239 Courtesy of Scholastic Photography Awards, conducted by Scholastic Magazines, Inc. and sponsored by Eastman Kodak Company
240 Rona Talcott—*People Weekly* © 1980 Time Inc.; Barry Staver—*People Weekly* © 1980 Time Inc.
241 UPI; © 1980 Allen Urkowitz
242 Frank Prazak; *The New York Times*
243 UPI
244 Courtesy Girl Scouts of the USA; Courtesy Boy Scouts of Canada
245 Courtesy Boy Scouts of America; Courtesy Girl Scouts of the U.S.A.
246 Courtesy Boy Scouts of America
247 Courtesy Girl Guides of Canada; Mario Ruiz
248 © 1980 Walt Disney Productions
249 © 1979 Walt Disney Productions; © 1980 Walt Disney Productions
250 Steve Rosenthal
251 Steve Rosenthal; Boston Children's Museum
252–253 Steve Rosenthal
254–255 Courtesy Pentel of America, Ltd.
256–257 © Sotheby Parke-Bernet—EPA
258 *Paris Match*—Pictorial Parade
259 On extended loan to the Museum of Modern Art, New York, from the estate of the artist; Courtesy Art Institute of Chicago
260 Philadelphia Museum of Art, Galletin Collection; Musée Picasso—Cliché des Musées Nationaux Paris
261 Musée Picasso—Cliché des Musées Nationaux Paris
262 © 1979 Columbia Pictures
263 Movie Star News—© 1979 Twentieth Century Fox; Movie Star News—© 1979 United Artists
264–265 © 1978 William Hubbell
266–267 Joseph Szaszfai—Collection of Joseph and Edith Kurstin
268 © Chris Walter—Retna
269 Arthur D'Amario III—Retna
270 Barry Schultz—Retna
271 Michael Putland—Retna; © David Redfern—Retna

272 Peter Sorel—Gamma/Liaison
274 UPI
275 © 1980 Thomas Victor; Courtesy Metropolitan Opera
276 © Mial et Klaus—Valan
277 Malak
278 Scala—EPA
279 Kunsthalle, Bremen; British Library, London
280 EPA
281 The British Museum, London
282 Abby Aldrich Rockefeller Folk Art Center, Williamsburg, Virginia
284 Prakapas Gallery—International Museum of Photography
285 Courtesy Art Institute of Chicago
286–287 © 1980 Lucasfilm, Ltd. All rights reserved
288–289 The People's Republic of China
290–291 Courtesy Jananne Lassetter
292–293 Holiday House
296 Judith Cheng
300 Judith Cheng
303 Judith Cheng
305–309 Text by Frances B. Watts, from *Easy Economic Stories,* © 1977 by the Saturday Evening Post Company, Indianapolis, Indiana. Reprinted by permission of the publisher; Artist, Ralph Pereida
310–313 Reprinted by permission from *The Christian Science Monitor* © 1978; 1979. The Christian Science Publishing Society. All rights reserved
314–319 Adapted from *Scandinavian Stories,* by Margaret Sperry. Illustrations by Jenny Williams. Illustrations © 1971 by Franklin Watts, Inc. Used by permission
320 From *The Ox-Cart Man* by Donald Hall. Copyright (illustrations) © 1979 by Barbara Cooney. Reprinted by permission of Viking Penguin, Inc.
321 From *A Gathering of Days* by Joan W. Bloss, Charles Scribner's Sons. Jacket design by Honi Werner
322 Illustration by Charles Mikolaycak for *Journey to the Bright Kingdom* © 1979 by Charles Mikolaycak. Reprinted by permission of Holiday House, Inc.
323 Methuen Publishing © 1980 *The Twelve Dancing Princesses* by Janet Lunn, illustrated by Laszlo Gal
324–332 Text by Carroll S. Karch from *Child Life* magazine © 1966 by Review Publishing Company, Indianapolis, Indiana. Reprinted by permission of the publisher; Artist, Michèle A. McLean
334 George Sottung
335 Reagan-Bush Committee
336 Wide World
337 UPI
338 The National Gallery of Canada, Ottawa. Gift of the estate of the Honorable W. C. Edwards, Ottawa, 1928
339 National Gallery of Canada
340 James Pickerell Associates
342 G. Tames—Globe; K.B. Roche—Monkmeyer
343 Sidney Bernstein—Photo Researchers; Tom Hollyman—Photo Researchers
347 Dennis Brack—Black Star; The Image Bank
348 George Buctel
359 UPI

Put The World At Your Fingertips . . .
ORDER THIS EXQUISITELY DETAILED LENOX GLOBE!

The world's never looked better! Why? Because this Lenox Globe — the most popular raised-relief model made by Replogle — is as stunning to look at as the living planet it represents.

Handsomely crafted and easy-to-use, the Lenox is the latest word in the state of the mapmaker's art — an ingenious marriage of classic, antique styling with clean, modern readability.

The Lenox is a giant 12-inch globe, beautifully inscribed with eye-catching "cartouches" and colorful compass "roses" . . . solidly-mounted on an elegantly sturdy, 18-inch Fruitwood stand . . . and covered with three dimensional "mountain ranges" children love to touch!

Five pounds light, the Lenox comes complete with a 32-page **STORY OF THE GLOBE** — a richly-illustrated, full-color handbook you and your whole family will refer to over and over again.

TO ORDER, simply send us your name and address, along with a check or money order for $29.95* to:

Grolier Yearbook, Inc.
Lenox Globe
Sherman Turnpike
Danbury, Connecticut 06816

*Please note: New York and Connecticut residents must add state sales tax.

THE LENOX GLOBE . . . by Replogle. Make it yours *today.*